*Primordiality, Science
and Value*

Truth and Denotation
The Notion of Analytic Truth
Toward a Systematic Pragmatics
Intension and Decision
Belief, Existence, and Meaning
Logic, Language, and Metaphysics
Whitehead's Categoreal Scheme and Other Papers
Events, Reference, and Logical Form
Semiotics and Linguistic Structure
Peirce's Logic of Relations and Other Studies
Pragmatics, Truth, and Language

Primordiality, Science, and Value

R. M. MARTIN

State University of New York Press

ALBANY

Published by
State University of New York Press, Albany
© 1980 State University of New York
All rights reserved
Printed in the United States of America
No part of this book may be used or reproduced
in any manner whatsoever without written permission
except in the case of brief quotations embodied in
critical articles and reviews.
For information, address State University of New York
Press, State University Plaza, Albany, N.Y., 12246

Typesetting by Rocky Mountain Type
Twin Falls, Idaho 83301

Library of Congress Cataloging in Publication Data
Martin, Richard Milton.
    Primordiality, science, and value.
    Bibliography: p.
    Includes index.
    1.   Philosophy——Addresses, essays, lectures.
2.   God——Addresses, essays, lectures.   3.   Science——
Philosophy——Addresses, essays, lectures.   4.   Values——
Addresses, essays, lectures.   5.   Logic, Modern——
Addresses, essays, lectures.   I.   Title.
B29.M3678   110   80-14724
ISBN 0-87395-443-2
ISBN 0-87395-444-0 (pbk.)

iv

For
M. v.W. M.

nostri pectoris consortio iugi fideli simplici concordia iuuans maritum

Contents

Preface

The various papers of this volume comprise collectively perhaps the most extensive attempt yet made to study some problems in metaphysics and theology in the light of the methods of modern logic and systematic semiotics (syntax, semantics, and pragmatics). The notion of God, for example, is probably the loftiest theological and metaphysical construct we have, and every effort should be made to try to characterize it in the most adequate way possible and in the clearest terms. We should spare no effort to seek these terms and should not rest content until we feel we have found them, or at least approximations to them. The methods of modern logic, including semiotics, have been extraordinarily successful in helping to gain clarity in mathematics and the sciences, not only as regards the forms of the sentences needed in these subjects but as regards the assumptions needed as well. It has been long thought by many philosophers and methodologists that these methods should be applicable to metaphysics and theology as well. Very little really serious work, however, has been made to establish such a claim, especially in theology, and such work as has been done in this direction can be counted on the fingers of one hand.

That traditional methods do not suffice was pointed out years back by Jan Salamucha in his pioneering work on the *ex motu* argument of St. Thomas, in *The New Scholasticism* XXXII (1958) but first published in 1934. Although modern logic is a comparatively young science, he noted, it provides us "with many new and subtle tools for exact thinking. To reject them is to adopt the attitude of one who stubbornly insists on travelling by stage-coach, though having at his disposal a train or airplane. . . . The great philosophers of the past did not rely exclusively on those weak logical tools left to them by their predecessors. The very problems themselves and their own scientific genius forced them to build rational reconstructions that went far beyond those of their own time."

As goes fundamental theology, so goes metaphysics, both systematic and historical. The great historical views need continually to be refashioned and restated in contemporary terms and in the light of advances in the sciences and in methodology. Not only should specific texts be examined and their vocabulary clarified, some attempt at an overall rational reconstruction however difficult should be made. Some such attempts are undertaken in this book in dealing with some aspects of Thomism, with the cosmological scheme of Plotinus, with absolute idealism, and with some problems in process metaphysics. Every rational metaphysics has its own logic, its own *logica utens,* so to speak, even if it is very difficult to eke out just what it is in any particular case. And, as has often been said, the great enduring metaphysical views should not be allowed to languish in terms merely of the original texts, but should continually be brought up to date in the light of new knowledge and more exact techniques of formulation.

Modern logic and semiotics are themselves under continual development and scrutiny. Some discussion, both critical and constructive, of alternative formulations is therefore in order. Also logico-semantical techniques have recently been showing themselves useful in aesthetics and the theory of value, to which attention should be called. Such areas of application might be dubbed 'humanistics', in which a very considerable development may be expected in the years to come.

The main topics of this book are the primordial God, the nature of science (including mathematics and logic itself), and the search for value. They are intimately fused here not only in being discussed in various alternative ways by means of a common methodology; they are also intimately interwoven in attempted analyses of "the real internal constitution" of the nature of God, to use Whitehead's provocative phrase. The complexity and true fullness of that nature cannot be understood, it is contended, short of a deep probing of the precise way in which both fundamental scientific law and the grounds of value are comprehended in it.

The papers in this volume are, more specifically, as follows. In I the role of modern logic in philosophy is discussed in general terms, and a plea is made for a more self-conscious use of it. Although most of the points made here have been made elsewhere, these *reminders* will be useful by way of introduction to the subsequent papers. There is also discussion of important recent work along similar lines by Huston Smith, George Schlesinger, Father Bocheński, and E. E. Harris. In II a new characterization of *God's nature* is put forward which, although based somewhat on that of Whitehead, goes far beyond it in fundamental respects. In III essentially this same material is discussed from a more *Thomistic* point of view. These two papers together might be subtitled "From Whitehead to St. Thomas," the journey, however, being an arduous one. In IV there is discussion of *God's permission of evil,* in which the material of II and III is connected with some of the work of Jacques Maritain.

In V the attempt is made to give a logical reconstruction of some features of *absolute idealism* and to harmonize that view with modern science. The great cosmological vision of *Plotinus* is treated in similar vein in VI with particular emphasis on the logic of the AllSoul or *Psyché*. In VII an idealist theory of *individuals* is suggested, along somewhat Plotinic lines, in which individuals are construed, not as separate beings, but wholly in terms of the "forms" in which they participate.

In VII there is a dialogue on *philosophical ecumenism* with a follower of John Findlay, concerning in particular his critical views on logic. And in IX there are some musings on *Hartshorne's methodological maxims.* Both of these papers are in part discussions of papers by Findlay and Hartshorne, respectively, presented at the 1977 and 1978 meetings of the International Society for Metaphysics.

X is devoted to a defense of the views put forward in II (and to some extent in III) against some recent criticism of them by *Bowman Clarke.* In XI there is a critical but sympathetic discussion of *Henry Veatch's* view that two logics, not just one, are needed for metaphysics and humanistics generally. And in XII there is a critical discussion of *Jaako Hintikka's* approach to philosophical analysis via the theory of possible-worlds semantics. In XIII some especially simple theories for *semantics and systematic pragmatics* are put forward. Although extremely sparse as to ontic commitment and involvement, as well as axiomatic assumption, these theories are still powerful enough for some important metaphysical and linguistic purposes.

In XIV an attempt is made to characterize the *language of music theory* in terms of the kind of logical underpinning used throughout. XV is devoted to a discussion of some points raised in Nelson Goodman's recent *Ways of Worldmaking,* and to an examination of the logic of some fundamental *aesthetic relations.*

In XVI some comments concerning the *second antinomy* of Kant are put forward and a purported "solution" to it is suggested. In XVII some steps toward a *constructive idealism* are outlined, differing from those of V in some basic respects. XVIII and XIX are concerned with

C. S. Peirce, in particular with his analysis of the notion of an *event* and with his so-called *Hegelism.* Finally, in XX, there is a critical discussion of some views of *Moritz Schlick,* that great arch-enemy of metaphysics, but with some constructive suggestions arising out of it.

That essentially the same methods are applicable to such diverse topics as are covered in this book is thought to be a positive merit. It is easy enough to keep to one topic, as Whitehead frequently noted, and then turn to another with an ostensibly different vocabulary and mode of procedure, and make no attempt to interrelate the two. Not to do this latter, however, is to suggest a dichotomy *in dicto* where in fact there may be none *in re.* The cosmos and all of our experience in it is a unified whole in a most fundamental way, it is thought, and our ways of talking about it should reflect this circumstance. Thus the unified mode here of treating subjects seemingly so diverse as theology, metaphysics, semantics, the foundations of aesthetics and of humanistics generally -- and even the philosophy of mathematics, which is touched upon in passing -- is thought to be of especial interest.

It has been contended by an eminent logician that "in formalizing philosophical concepts a high degree of rigor should be expected," even though rarely achieved, and if so usually only with great difficulty. Perhaps we should say rather that high rigor is not to be expected equally on all topics at their present stages of development. Greater rigor can be attained more readily in subjects that have been much discussed from a logical point of view than in those that have not. Many of the papers in this book contain first attempts to deal with their subject-matter in a rigorous way, and no doubt better, more adequate, more elegant, more "smooth-running" formulations will be forthcoming in the future. Also, on each topic there are always interesting alternatives to be considered. But even so, as Alexander Pope said of his translation of Homer, "with whatever judgment or study a man may proceed, . . . he must hope to please but a few; those only who have at once a taste of poetry, and competent learning." So here, the reader should have a liking of metaphysical and theological notions, and a desire to see them handled in modern logical terms. "For to satisfy such as want either, is not in the nature of this undertaking; since [unfortunately] a more modern wit can like nothing that is not modern" -- and a more conventional one, nothing that is not well-rehearsed in terms of the vagaries of the original texts or is otherwise too new or technical for ease of comprehension. And if the qualified reader should be displeased with the material here or find it wanting in this respect or that, the hope is that he will at least find it useful in his own attempts to do better.

The various papers here may be read independently of each other, although there is considerable overlap in spirit and general intent, as well as in some technical details. Even so, each has its own little song to sing, and not always in the same key or tempo. Some of them were written in response to special invitations, and it has seemed best here to allow them to retain some of their occasional character, and even to present them in a more or less chronological order. I and V are papers delivered at meetings of the International Society for Metaphysics in 1978 and 1977, respectively. II and III constitute the substance of a paper presented to the American Theological Society in 1976. IV was presented before the American Maritain Association in 1978, and VI before the International Society for Neo-Platonic Studies in 1977. Some of the material of XIV was presented as part of the program for composers at the Berkshire Music Center, Tanglewood, in 1978, and later at the New England Conservatory of Music and at Wheaton College. XVI was delivered at the University of Rochester at a conference in honor of Lewis Beck in 1979. XVIII was presented at the Institute for Philosophy and Religion at Boston University in 1979, and XIV, at a meeting of the Charles S. Peirce Society, also in 1979. Some of the other papers have appeared previously, and thanks are herewith expressed to the editors of the *Review of Metaphysics,* the *Notre Dame Journal of Formal Logic,* D. Reidel Publishing Company, the *Southern Journal of Philosophy,* and the *Journal of Aesthetics and Art Criticism* for kind permission to use them here.

The author wishes also to thank Northwestern University and the Boston University Center for the Philosophy and History of Science for support during the writing of these papers.

CHAPTER I

Truth, Justification,
and Metaphysical Method

Saepe creat molles aspera spina rosas.

So far as their constructive progress and development are concerned, metaphysics and theology are becoming increasingly difficult
fields of study in these closing decades of the twentieth century. The
simplistic views and formulations that satisfied philosophers in previous centuries have been tried and found wanting, even though they
may be based on insights of permanent value. These subjects, in their
growth to maturity, are now becoming "hard" ones, akin to the "hard
sciences," leaving their "soft" progenitors in the wake of history. More
austere methods of thought and writing than heretofore are now required. Prominent among these are those based on modern logico-
semantics, which, as Whitehead observed prophetically many years
back, will proceed to lay the foundations for aesthetics and to "conquer" ethics and theology.

Let us begin with a brief survey of some recent work aimed at har-
monizing metaphysics and theology with the sciences, and then go on
to some general comments concerning certain current and widespread misunderstandings as to the use of logical methods. These latter will focus primarily on the semantic notion of truth and the problem of justification, which problem, it will be contended, is essentially
the same for metaphysics as for the sciences.

In his valuable *Forgotten Truth,* Huston Smith makes much of the
numerical character of mathematics, neglecting perhaps the fact that
in its type-theoretic or set-theoretic format quantity plays a relatively
small role in mathematics.[1] Further, he thinks that "numbers and
their logical operators are the only symbols, or rather signs, that are
completely unambiguous: 4 is 4 and that is the end of the matter." But

---

1. Huston Smith, *Forgotten Truth, the Primordial Tradition* (New York: Harper & Row,
1976), pp. 12–13.

much depends here on the set-theoretic structure provided, each different set theory giving rise to a different characterization of '4', indeed even to different "meanings." And if the underlying logic is taken as a many-valued logic, say, there turn out to be many alternative numbers 4 to consider. Thus the situation in mathematics itself is not quite so clear-cut as Smith would have us believe.

Now "the alternative to numbers is words," Smith contends. "Where numbers are signs, words are symbols, and therefore by their very nature equivocal: their ambiguity can be reduced but never eliminated." Such a contention needs a considerable defense, especially in view of recent work on the logical form of natural-language sentences and the problem of "disambiguation."[2] In fact, it is very doubtful that the language or languages of mathematics, and the "exact" sciences in general, differ very much from natural languages in the use of "signs" rather than "symbols" or in the matter of containing or not containing ambiguous sentences. In each case the ambiguous sentence presents itself for disambiguation — unless of course it is the very richness of ambiguity itself that is desired. The difference between numerals and words is less sharp than Smith would have us believe. Nor is it true that "logicians flee . . . [the] meanderings [of words] in favor of fixed and adamantine glyphs. The despair of logicians is the humanist's glory." In the logical analysis of language the meanderings are squarely faced and codified, and the humanist's glory is thus quickly becoming a subject for the logician's purview. The situation is similar to that concerning the language of mathematics a few generations back.

One of the key differences between what Smith calls 'the primordial perspective' and the contemporary one is, according to him, just that the scientist counts and measures and the humanist, more particularly the metaphysician and theologian, does not. It is now frequently being suggested, however, that the use of numbers in theology is not ill-advised.[3] In fact, their use now leads to a deeper, more subtle, and more sensitive characterization than has been available heretofore of certain topics concerned with the divine will.

Whitehead contended, in a famous adaptation from Walter Pater, that "all science as it grows towards perfection becomes mathematical in its ideal." This is of course very questionable. Let us construe sci-

---

2. Recall some of the material in the author's *Semiotics and Linguistic Structure* (Albany: The State University of New York Press, 1978).

3. See II and III below. Cf. also Frederick Sontag, "Being and Freedom: the Metaphysics of Freedom," a paper read before the Metaphysical Society of America, March 1979.

ence in a broad sense, as with Whitehead, to embrace all domains of systematic knowledge or *Wissenschaften*. A safer historical description would then be to the effect that all *Wissenschaften* as they grow toward perfection become logistical in their ideal, and thus lend themselves to the application of a semantical predicate for *truth*. In particular, then, even the more or less traditional theism, which Smith refers to as the *philosophia perennis*, is of course included here. In VI and XVII below we will attempt to show in detail how some strands of the perennial tradition — the *philosophia perennis* is not just one view but several woven a bit loosely together — may be formulated in a sufficiently precise logistical way to allow a clear-cut notion of truth for the language-system involved.[4] In discussing the forgotten truth of traditional theism, let us be sure not to forget the truth-predicate of modern semantics.

"The multivalence of language enables it to mesh with the multidimensionality of the human spirit," Smith continues, "depicting its higher reaches as numbers never can. Equations can be elegant, but that is a separate matter. Poems cannot be composed in numbers." These are not the words of a poet such as Paul Valéry or John Berryman. Both writers spoke frequently of the *exactitude* in the use of words in poetry — as exact as that of the mathematician in his use of numbers, Berryman once remarked in one of his more sober moments. The multidimensionality of the human spirit need not be neglected if our discourse concerning it is to be suitably formulated or articulated in modern terms.

According to Smith, science, in the narrow sense as practiced by professionals, is limited in its exclusion of discourse concerning *values, purposes, life meanings,* and *quality*. We cannot be sure in advance, however, that sciences allowing such discourse will not develop in the course of time. But even so, theological discourse accommodating such topics can be formulated in a relatively precise, even *wissenschaftliches,* way to some extent as regards values, purposes, and life meanings, as has been shown in the papers referred to. As regards quality, surely the material of Nelson Goodman's *The Structure of Appearance*[5] is an important attempt to subject discourse about quality to cogent logical form. In all of these examples, a theory is formulated with sufficient precision to allow the application of a semantical truth-predicate.

---

4. Cf. the author's *Truth and Denotation* (Chicago: The University of Chicago Press, 1958).

5. (Cambridge: Harvard University Press, 1951).

A similar point has been made by Father Bocheński in his *The Logic of Religion* (pp. 62–63).[6] "But man is constituted in such a way that he always tends to axiomatize his discourse; and the religious man is no exception in this respect. There will be, consequently, a more or less pronounced tendency in believers to order . . . [their religious discourse] by axiomatizing it. Such an axiomatization is the field of what is called 'theology' (or 'Buddhology') in the strict meaning of the term. . . ." Under 'axiomatization' here one can include *partial formalizations* also, about which more will be said below; in any case the applicability of suitable truth-predicates to the sentences of any such theory is assured.

Once these and other such *caveats* to Smith's book have been registered, there is much that is admirable in his discussion of the parallels and divergencies between science and *philosophia perennis* as he conceives it. In calling attention to the parallels, he emphasizes general descriptive similarities rather than specifically methodological ones. In both the parallels and divergencies, (pp. 98 ff.), "things are not what they seem" at first blush unaided. In each "the other-than-the-seeming is a *more*; indeed a stupendous more." In each, "in their further reaches the . . . *mores* cannot be known in ordinary ways" but rather "admit of being known in ways that are exceptional." Further, "the distinctive ways of knowing which the exceptional regions of reality require must be cultivated," and such "profound knowing requires instruments." In science the instruments include both theoretical constructs and telescope, spectroscope, and the like, whereas in the *philosophia perennis* they are the "revealed texts" or scriptures or "ordering myths" of that tradition accepted as definitive. Smith's discussion of these parallels is illuminating and surely on the right track. As we go further along the track, however, sameness of ontology might be discovered, some one basic soul- or mind-stuff of which matter, mind, soul, and spirit are all specific manifestations. But this is for the future perhaps, and Smith finds enough that is striking in restricting discussion to the results of contemporary science.

On the methodological parallels between science and religious discourse, Bocheński is more enlightening. He notes (in *The Logic of Religion*, pp. 61–62) that "from the logical point of view, the situation in RD [religious discourse] is very similar to that which we find in the discourse of natural sciences. The ρ-sentences [the sentences of objective faith directly accepted by the believer] play in RD a role closely similar to that of experimental sentences in those sciences. The only

6. (New York: New York University Press, 1965).

question which may arise in both cases is whether the given sentence really does belong to the class under consideration, that is, whether it really is a ρ-sentence, or a duly established protocol sentence. . . ." Once this is determined, the parallel is evident. Bocheński gives (pp. 64—65) a "comparative table" between methods in physics and theology. The physicist "starts (theoretically) with experimental sentences" just as the theologian "starts (theoretically) with ρ-sentences." The physicist then "explains the experimental sentences by other sentences from which the former may be deduced." The theologian similarly "explains the ρ-sentences by theological conclusions which are such that from them the ρ-sentences may be deduced." The physicist "deduces from the explanatory sentences new ones which may be verified by experiment" just as the theologian "deduces from the theological conclusions new sentences, which may be verified by seeing if they do belong to ρ." Both the physicist and the theologian "explain the first-grade explanatory sentences by further explanatory sentences in the same way" and "verify such sentences by examining their consistency with other sentences in the system." And finally, just as the physicist "introduces new 'theoretical' terms not found in protocol sentences" the theologian "introduces new 'theological' terms not to be found in ρ-sentences."

The various items of this table are not intended to provide an exhaustive, or even wholly accurate, description of procedure in either science of theology. Such a description, it seems, has never been given for either, owing no doubt to the sheer difficulties involved. Nonetheless the table is valuable in calling attention to methodological parallels usually overlooked, and helps to supplement Smith's list of similarities.

In the chapter, "Justification of Religious Discourse," in *The Logic of Religion*, Bocheński considers several theories concerning "the activity by which the acceptance of a (meaningful) sentence [of RD] is justified." These comprise in particular the "blind-leap" theory, the "rationalistic" theory, the "insight" theory, the "trust" theory, the "deductivist" theory, the "authority" theory, and the "theory of the religious hypothesis." It is clearly the last that he favors, but curiously gives it no more space than the others, which for the most part he dismisses as inadequate. Let us glance at Bocheński's theory of the religious hypothesis and then reflect how, one by one, the other theories may be viewed as contributing to it. The comments here, *mutatis mutandis*, concern scientific and metaphysical hypotheses equally well, as Bocheński himself observes.

The gist of the theory of the religious hypothesis is that "the be-

5

liever constructs before the act of faith, as an explanatory sentence, the very BD [basic dogma] of the religion concerned. This sentence — called here '[the] religious hypothesis' — serves to explain his experience." Formally, Bocheński goes on to note, "the procedure by which the religious hypothesis is established is closely similar to that used in reductive [abductive] sciences. The starting point is experimentally established sentences. The hypothesis is such that they may be deduced from it; it permits predictions and can be verified by new experimental sentences." It should be observed, however, as Bocheński notes, that the experimental sentences of a given science form a much narrower class than those relevant to the religious hypothesis, the latter including all manner of sentences concerning the personal life of the believer, sentences concerned with moral, social, and aesthetic values, and so on. All such sentences must be formulated in a sufficiently precise way, for the relevant semantical truth-predicate to apply.

The very breadth of the sentences relevant to a religious hypothesis explains the difficulty of the believer's persuading someone else of its truth or acceptability; the other person's experiences may be very different. "No two persons have the same total experience and, consequently, a hypothesis which seems to be quite plausible to one of them does not need to appear to be plausible to the other. . . ." Also the difficulty in overthrowing someone's religious hypothesis by falsification is due to its very great generality. As Bocheński notes, "one must be very little instructed in the procedures of science to think that a dozen facts inconsistent with a great physical theory will lead automatically to its rejection. But the religious hypothesis seems to be far more general — that is, it covers far more sentences — than even the most general scientific theory. Therefore, it is much more difficult to overthrow it." The generality is not, however, that of containing "more sentences," for in both an infinity of sentences must be allowed. It is rather that the religious hypothesis is more general in its relevancy to more *kinds* of sentences than in a science, or even in all the sciences put together.

Bocheński goes on to reflect upon explanation and prediction on the basis of a religious hypothesis, but no crucial differences emerge as between these and explanation and prediction in the sciences. Of course the vocabulary of the religious hypothesis is broader, and a great deal of work needs to be done to characterize that vocabulary in a logically acceptable way.

There is enough germ of truth in the other theories of justification Bocheński discusses to suggest that some aspects of them may be incorporated in the theory of the religious hypothesis. In the blind-leap theory the believer makes a "leap" from "nothingness to full faith without any logical or experimental foundation." Well, not without *any*, but perhaps with very little. This need not matter once the religious hypothesis is firmly accepted. Some features of a "rationalist" theory are incorporated in the theory of the religious hypothesis, in particular, use of the methods of logical deduction — methods of reduction or discovery also, if reliable rules concerning them should ever be formulated. Once a religious hypothesis is held, there is "trust" in it and in the objects with which it deals. And of course "deductions" are made, in particular from the general hypothesis to further experimental sentences. Also the role of the authority may be helpful to some, in calling attention to relevant experimental sentences, to the very nature and formulation of a religious hypothesis, and to its deductive consequences. In some such ways as these, then, there may be seen to be some little grain of truth in all of the other theories. Bocheński states most of them, it might be thought, in so severe a form as to make them unacceptable.

There is also much in George Schlesinger's recent discussion of theism and scientific method that is admirable.[7] He claims (p. 201) "that the traditional theist need not recoil from examining his basic propositions by a method of inquiry which adopts the standards employed in science. On a correct understanding of the essence of scientific method, Theism does not stand to lose from such an inquiry; in fact it gains, emerging from it with enhanced credibility." The author does not deny that (p. 2) "the classical theistic hypothesis greatly differs from the kind of hypotheses advanced within science. . . . Yet the question whether all the laws of nature and the initial conditions are what they are without there being anything behind them, or that they are what they are because of the will of a minded, very intelligent, and powerful being seems intelligible in a very straightforward manner, no less than many questions asked by scientists and more so than some questions asked by metaphysicians." We are thus invited to view God as somehow incorporating the "laws of nature" and the "initial conditions." Finally, the implicit aim of the author is "to exhibit the richness of the philosophy of religion" and "to show that it impinges upon nearly every important topic in philosophy in general," especially upon some crucial ones in the philosophy of science concerning confirmation and confirmability.

---

7. George Schlesinger, *Religion and Scientific Method* (*Philosophical Studies Series in Philosophy*, Dordrecht: D. Reidel Publishing Co., 1977).

To give an even moderately accurate description of scientific method in all its complexity is no easy task, as already remarked, and Schlesinger does not claim to have done this. His description revolves around two "elementary principles," Principle A and Principle E. The latter (p. 157) is that "when a given piece of evidence E is more probable on H than on H' then E confirms H more than H'." Principle A (p. 161) is that "when H and H' are similarly related to all the available evidence, we regard H as more confirmed than H', if and only, H is more adequate than H'." Much is made of these two "principles," which the author contends "are inevitably to be employed [by scientists] when searching for any hypothesis." It is claimed that they are "justified" and that they characterize the very heart of scientific method. The principles cry out, however, for a clear-cut foundation in which such key terms as 'more probable than', 'confirms', 'more confirmed than', and 'more adequate than' are fully explicated. In view of the immense difficulties encountered by all attempts at characterizing these notions as applicable to scientific language-systems of even comparatively simply a structure, it is unlikely that we should accept Schlesinger's principles at the face value he asks us to. Also they must be intimately related to the detailed characterization of observation, experiment, the making of hypotheses, testing, verification, and so on.

Even if we remain within the domain of scientific languages, we are overwhelmed with the amount of work needed to "justify" these principles. But this is nothing as to what is needed if our language is augmented to enable us to state the thesis of theism. Not only the key notion of God, but such "analogical" words as 'omnibenevolent' and 'omnipotent', need exact definition. One could perhaps reply that — oh well, the tradition tells us perfectly well what these terms mean. But this of course is not the case if the thesis of theism is to be stated in sufficiently precise a way that the exact techniques of logic, semantics, and confirmation theory may be applied to it. Schlesinger frequently uses the terms 'logically compatible', 'logically possible', and the like, in ways that also need further clarification as to just what kind a "logic" is being presupposed. A first-order logic? A higher-order one? One containing suitable meaning postulates?

Schlesinger claims "that by employing the most elementary principles underlying scientific method we may construct certain aspects of the world as constituting empirical evidence confirming Theism." He never states *how much* evidence, however, nor is it clear from his account that the evidence for theism is actually *greater than* for some alternative. Also the use of the truth-predicate is essential in any clear

8

delineation of a theory of confirmation, so that here too we should not attempt to justify "forgotten truth" without at least a passing glance at 'true' in the semantical sense.

In his recent *Atheism and Theism*,[8] Errol Harris also discusses the problem of "The Rational Basis of Theism" in a pivotal chapter with that very title. And although the metaphysical *ambiente* of his discussion is very different from that of Smith, Bocheński and Schlesinger, there is a similar underlying aim. Harris, however, thinks that "formal logic" — and therewith presumably confirmation theory also — is not appropriate for attempting to delineate the rational basis for theism, it being (p. 67) "appropriate to only a certain level of thinking." Another kind of logic is needed "which is universal in its scope" (p. 68) and which "displays itself in specifically different phases of thinking, of which formal logic (in any of its forms) is only one." This universal or "dialectical" logic, Harris thinks, is *sui generis* and cannot be formulated as an applied formal logic in the usual sense; that is, with suitable non-logical constants as primitives and with appropriate meaning postulates concerning them. However, Harris has nowhere, either here or in his other writings, formulated a single rule or principle of such a logic with the necessary rigor in modern terms. Whatever "dialectical" logic is, there is no reason to suppose that it cannot be formulated, along with other metaphysical views, on the basis of formal logic in the modern extended sense. Harris, like Findlay,[9] writes of formal logic primarily in terms of its state of development prior to 1910 or thereabouts. Their strictures are seen to be inappropriate, however, if recent developments are taken into account.

That the techniques of modern logic are an inestimable help to metaphysicians is commonplace among those who use them. Indeed, so great is this help that they wonder how it was ever possible to do without them. Although the use of such techniques is becoming more and more widespread, there are many who resist them and, as already suggested, like Peter Damian see in logic the machinations of the devil himself. Much of this resistance, it seems, rests upon misunderstanding of one kind or another. It is safe to say that no one who takes the trouble to master the intricacies of modern logic continues resisting for very long. But many things stand in the way of being motivated to attain this mastery. Let us reflect for a moment upon the most important of these, with the aim of removing some of the misunderstand-

---

8. Errol E. Harris, *Atheism and Theism* (*Tulane Studies in Philosophy*, Vol. XXVI, 1977).
9. Cf. John Findlay, "Ordinary, Revisionary, and Dialectical Strategies in Philosophy," *Erkenntnis* 11 (1977): 277–290 and VIII below.

ings surrounding philosophic logic, its nature and scope, and the use of logical methods in metaphysics generally. Most of these points have been made elsewhere, but no harm will come from reminding ourselves of them here.[10]

In the first place, we should not think of logic in just the sense of *Principia Mathematica,* say, or of axiomatic set theory. Such "logics," if such they be, are in some respects too restricted and in others, too inclusive. They are too inclusive in embracing vast portions of mathematics in their scope, even some dubious mathematics perhaps, and too exclusive in not embracing logical *semiotics (syntax, semantics,* and *pragmatics),* as well as the *calculus of individuals,* a theory of *intensionality,* and an *event* logic. These latter are the very stuff of which metaphysics is made, the areas of theory most helpful to the philosopher, and curiously, the very ones to which least attention has been paid in recent years.

Nor should we think of logic as being the exclusive possession of logical positivism, as is so often done even now, these many years after the virtual demise of that view. The *subject-matter neutrality* of logic has often been pointed out. It is true, of course, that the positivists were pioneers in using logic for philosophic purposes, and this perhaps is their most lasting contribution, the really positive part of positivism, as it were. But it is also now widely recognized that other kinds of philosophers may reap its benefits also, as has been forecefully emphasized by thinkers so diverse as Gilbert Ryle, Heinrich Scholz, K. Gödel, and Frederic Fitch.[11]

Closely related with Ryle's point is one made by the English mathematician A. B. Kempe as long ago as 1886. "Whatever may be the true nature of things and of the conceptions which we have of them," he stated, "in the operations of reasoning they are dealt with as a number of separate entities or *units.* These units come under consideration in a variety of garbs — as material objects, intervals or periods of time, processes of thought, points, lines, statements, relationships, arrangements, algebraical expressions, operators, operations, etc., etc. . . ."[12] In all discourse, philosophical or otherwise, the entities dealt with are thus to be handled as separate units. Some

---

10. Cf. *Truth and Denotation,* Chapter I, and the author's *Logic, Language and Metaphysics* (New York: New York University Press, 1971), Chapter I.

11. See especially Gilbert Ryle, *Dilemmas* (Cambridge: Cambridge University Press, 1954), and Heinrich Scholz, *Metaphysik als Strenge Wissenschaft* (Darmstadt: Wissenschaftliche Buchgesellschaft, 1965, but first published in 1941).

12. A. B. Kempe, "A Memoir on the Theory of Mathematical Form," *Philosophical Transactions of the Royal Society,* 177 (1886): 1–70.

of them are given proper names, and usually they are taken as values for variables — or if not, they are handled as constructs in terms of entities that are. That this is the case seems to be a necessity of discourse if the "operations of reasoning" are to take place, and without such operations there can be no philosophy — in our western sense — worthy of the name. Josiah Royce also made essentially the same point in 1914 when he noted that "without objects conceived as unique individuals, we can have *no Classes*. Without Classes we can . . . define *no Relations,* without relations we can have *no Order. But to be reasonable is to conceive of order-systems, real or ideal. Therefore we have an absolute logical need to conceive of individual objects as the elements of our ideal order systems.* This postulate is the condition of defining clearly any theoretical conception whatever. . . . To conceive of individual objects is a necessary presupposition of all orderly [thought and] activity."[13] Again, some of these objects are given proper names, and some surely are taken as values for variables. And these objects are variously grouped into classes; or, as we say equivalently, certain properties are ascribed to them, and certain *relations* hold between or among them, these classes and relations usually being regarded as designated by suitable predicates.

It is often very difficult to be able to decide what predicates are to be taken as *primitives* and which are to be defined via suitable nominal definitions. There is often considerable latitude here and to some extent the choice may be arbitrary. Every predicate occurring in the system must be either primitive or defined — there is no other possibility. Once the primitives are chosen, as a result usually of a good deal of trial and error, the remaining predicates are defined. Although defined predicates *sensu stricto* may always be eliminated, the definitions of them "are at once seen to be the most important part of the subject," as Whitehead noted in 1906. "The act . . . [of giving a definition] . . . is in fact the act of choosing the various complex ideas which are to be the special object of study. The whole subject depends upon such a choice."[14] Here again there are often alternatives, with difficulty in selecting the most suitable.

Once primitives are decided upon, suitable axioms or meaning postulates are needed to characterize them. But before it is profitable to axiomatize, a great deal of analysis and experimentation must take place, presystematically as it were. It is often advisable to try to deter-

13. See *Royce's Logical Essays,* ed. by D. Robinson (Dubuque, Iowa: Wm. C. Brown Co., 1951), p. 350.

14. A. N. Whitehead, *The Axioms of Projective Geometry* (Cambridge: Cambridge University Press, 1906), p. 2.

mine what principles or laws are to obtain, irrespective of which are ultimately suitable as axioms. The problem of axiomatization is often a merely technical or mechanical one once a suitable parade of principles is laid out. Thus we should not disparage what are often spoken of, following Carnap, as *partially formalized systems,* systems in which the full primitive vocabulary is fixed, as well as the formulas and some at least of the crucial rules and principles, but without specification of axioms. We can often make enormous headway with only partially formalized systems. In fact, it is likely that such systems are of greater interest for metaphysics and theology, at their present stages of development, than fully formalized ones. Metaphysics — in its preliminary stages anyhow — seems to have more to do with the basic vocabulary chosen, the kinds of terms and formulas admitted, and general principles characterizing that vocabulary, than in any specific choice of axioms.[15] And *a fortiori* for theology.

Even in partial formalizations a very considerable technicality usually results. But of course technicality is unavoidable nowadays anyhow, whether we use partial formalizations or not. Peirce noted years back that the philosophy of the future would have to employ a "fiercely technical vocabulary." Indeed, it is difficult to see how this can be avoided in an age of highly sophisticated methodologies such as our own. This is a circumstance we must accept and welcome, for fierce technicality is with us whether we like it or not. Gone is the day when philosophy can be done in just common-sense terms with horse-and-buggy procedures. It is interesting to note that the latest word even from Oxford is to this effect.

Those who insist upon keeping metaphysics close to ordinary language must now face the fact that the analysis of ordinary language itself is slowly giving way to the exact study of logical form. The problem of "representing" or mirroring ordinary sentences or texts in exact logical or semantical structures is one of the most important problems in contemporary structural and transformational linguistics. Although still in its infancy, the study of logical form promises to revamp to its very roots the systematic study of language. Enormous progress has been made in this kind of work in recent years, which should not be overlooked by the metaphysician.

Sometimes it is contended that the use of logical methods in philosophy depends too heavily on language, and *how* we say it, than on what is said and on what is being talked about. Language takes over and true philosophy is given short shrift. This contention of

---

15. Cf. *Truth and Denotation*, pp. 17ff.

course misses the point that semantics is now a part of logic, and that semantics is the study of how words relate to objects and how sentences relate to what is meant. Thus there need be no neglect of the objects talked about or of what is intended to be said about them.

Sometimes it is contended that the use of logical methods in philosophy provides a kind of "straight-jacket" or rigid form which does violence to the subtlety of what is intended — the fit is never quite right. Logic distorts, so we had better abandon it altogether. Well, the answer to this kind of objection is a question *tu quoque*. Is the fit ever quite right if natural language is used? A similar point used frequently to be made by Philip Frank about physics, and also by Bocheński, as noted above. No physical theory ever quite encompasses or explains all the phenomena we would like it to. There are always a few recalcitrant circumstances that refuse to fit. Clearly there should be here a two-way adjustment. We must seek ever-more comprehensive theories, which, however, are not to be abandoned, *ceteris paribus*, to fit a few recalcitrant circumstances.

A similar point has been made by H. L. A. Hart (in conversation) about the use of logical systems in the law. If the system is too narrow, let us go on to make every effort to formulate more comprehensive and adequate ones for the purpose at hand.

Another objection frequently brought against the use of logical methods in philosophy rests on the contention that such methods are appropriate only for the sciences and perhaps for the philosophy of science, but not for the more "humane" parts of philosophy such as aesthetics, ethics, theology, and metaphysics. Such a contention is to make a fundamental duality where there is none. Of course there are important differences among these subjects, just as there are important differences among the sciences. Some methods are useful in some and others in others. But logic is common to all of these, being not only subject-matter neutral but closely interwoven with the very texture of language.

It is interesting to recall, looking almost two millenia back, the contention of Plotinus that dialectic is "the precious part of philosophy: in its study of the laws of the universe, philosophy draws on dialectic much as other studies and crafts use arithmetic, though, of course, [italics added] *the alliance between philosophy and dialectic is closer*" (*Enneads*, I.3.5−6). Now semiotics here is in essentials merely dialectic in modern garb. Just as a matter of fact, semiotics is of much greater interest for, and help to, philosophy than mathematics is. The alliance is closer. Mathematics and logic have always been strange bedfellows anyhow, and never stranger than in the recent proliferation of metamathematical and model-theoretic techniques for philosophical purposes.

There is an increasing use of logical methods in analyzing and reconstructing the great historical metaphysical views. Sometimes this is holistic, sometimes piecemeal. Such work can be very illuminating in updating views or arguments that might otherwise remain as mere historical curiosities. The aim of such work is in part historical, to help see precisely what is being said. But it may also be reconstructive and may part in very substantial ways from the historical text. Again, such work may be useful in helping to preserve what is of permanent importance. Inevitably this kind of work will increase in the years to come. The great historical views die hard; rather are they *semper reformanda* in the light of new knowledge.

And of course logic-cum-semiotics is itself also under continual development. We must not suppose it fixed once and for all for a new dogmatic slumber. New methods and formulations should be welcomed in an open-armed, inquiring spirit. But at the same time, progress in logical matters is slow and difficult and not every *nouveauté* can pass the critical scrutiny demanded of it. As a matter of fact there are fewer alternatives than is commonly supposed, once analyzed to their logical bedrock with maximum logical candor.

There is also the "it can't be done" attitude. Logical methods may be suitable for some purposes but not for others. Sometimes the "it can't be done" is insisted upon dogmatically. The Dutch intuitionist Brouwer for years apparently insisted that his mathematical work could not be formalized. Over the years, however, the work of Heyting and others, with ever improved formulations, convinced him that it could be. Of course nothing succeeds like success, and the best way to convince those who think that it can't be done is to go ahead and do it. Often of course a few easy phrases will not suffice for this, but only years of hard work.

Progress in metaphysics is *par excellence* "progress in clarification." Progress in the sciences, or in society, is something else again, to say nothing of progress in the arts if there is any. In metaphysics, however, the great historical views must be continually kept alive by viewing them in the light of what we now know. This is almost always a matter of more adequate formulation of precisely what the view is, of probing more deeply into its foundations, of showing it adequate in this or that respect in which it was previously thought wanting, in showing how it may be brought into accord with modern science, and so on. The conscious use of logic is almost a *sine qua non* for such progress.

14

Some metaphysicians are impatient of logical methods, claiming that they accomplish too little for the effort required. This is rarely the case, however. The situation is rather the other way around; new problems and difficulties emerge with the closer logical look, problems that would not have been seen otherwise. In this way logic is often a means of genuine discovery. Nelson Goodman has pointed out that "I cannot hold the logical philosopher up . . . as a man who has found a magic key to all the riddles of the universe; rather, he seems to have found a way to cause himself a good deal of trouble. It is true, as the unlogical philosopher and the unphilosophical logician often point out, that the way of the logical philosopher is much like that of any transgressor."[16] He transgresses the bounds of conventional philosophy with deeper, more thorough, and more searching formulations, and he insists that "unphilosophic logic" itself be subject to the same philosophic scrutiny as other "logics" are, especially as regards ontic commitment and ontic involvement, this latter being the ontic commitment of the metalanguage.[17]

Throughout by "logic" we have meant, of course, a semiotics based on the standard first-order theory of quantification, as already remarked, without sets, classes, or relations as values for variables in any wise or form. Some logicians find this too severe a restriction and wish to include also a higher-order logic, a set theory, and perhaps also a model theory or semantics of "possible worlds," as well. There are many objections to including these, not least of which is the excessive ontic commitment and involvement. We do not wish "our logic . . . to be responsible for more of our ontology than is the extralogical part of our system," as Goodman put it (*ibid.*, p. 39). "And some of us are *not* willing to countenance . . . abstract entities [such as classes, relations, and sets as values for variables] at all (if we can help it) either because we are nominalists or because, for the sake of economy, we want to commit ourselves to as little as possible. If either nominalism or plain parsimony leads us to insist upon a logic that is not committed to abstract entities, then we shall have to forego a large part of the usual modern logic — namely, most of the theory of classes and relations. This will make the going hard. . . . The difficulty of doing without a philosophically objectionable technique is not, however, any sufficient reason for retaining it." These admirable statements are beyond reproach and totally persuasive. Even so, we should go one

---

16. N. Goodman, *Problems and Projects* (Indianapolis: The Bobbs-Merrill Co., 1972), p. 40.

17. See the author's *Belief, Existence, and Meaning* (New York: New York University Press, 1969), Chapter II.

step further: We do not wish our logic to be responsible for *any ontology at all,* irrespective of whether it be more or less than in the extralogical part of our system. Otherwise we should have to give up one facet of the requirement of subject-matter neutrality.

It is often complained that logical philosophy is excessively complicated, too many symbols are used, the formulas are too long, and so on. But of course, once the new problems are opened up, the unlogical philosopher must now do without symbols and formulas what the logical philosopher can do with them. The situation is thus just the other way around. The problems are there and can no longer be avoided, and nonsymbolic procedures are seen to be intolerably complex in handling them or perhaps not able to do so at all. And in any case, the problems are usually more difficult than the unlogical philosopher supposes, as Russell pointed out at the end of his "On Denoting." "I will only beg the reader not to make up his mind against the view [put forward] — as he might be tempted to do on account of its apparently excessive complication — until he has tried to construct a theory of his own. . . . This attempt, I believe, will convince him that, whatever the true theory may be, it cannot have such a simplicity as one might have expected beforehand."[18]

The historically most famous and influential argument *against* the kind of unification of method advocated here is probably that of Aristotle in 1094[b] of the *Ethica Nicomachea.* "Our discussion will be adequate [Ross translation] if it has as much clearness as the subject-matter admits of, for precision is not to be sought for in all discussions. . . . Now fine and just actions . . . admit of much variety and fluctuation of opinion. . . . And goods also give rise to a similar fluctuation because they bring harm to many people. . . . We must be content, then, in speaking of such subjects and with such premises to indicate the truth roughly and in outline, and in speaking of things which are only for the most part true and with premises of the same kind to reach conclusions that are no better. In the same spirit, therefore, should each type of statement be *received*; for it is the mark of an educated man to look for precision in each class of things just so far as the nature of the subject admits; it is evidently equally foolish to accept probable reasoning from a mathematician and to demand from a rhetorician scientific proofs."

There are several objections to these comments to be voiced straightway. In the first place, it should be asked how the degree of clearness or precision a given subject-matter "admits of" is to be de-

---

18. *Logic and Knowledge* (London: George Allen and Unwin, 1956), p. 56.

termined. The subject-matter does not wear this on its sleeve, and every discipline as it grows to maturity tends to become more precise in its vocabulary. Aristotle goes on to speak of the "fluctuation of opinion" concerning the fineness and justice of actions and concerning the value of possessing goods. In all such matters, of course, as well as in the sciences and humanities alike, there are always many competing views with fluctuations of opinion. Whether there is more, or less, concerning human actions than in the various intellectual disciplines is dubious. In any case, the matter seems never to have been put to the test. Because of such fluctuation, Aristotle goes on, we must be content "to indicate the truth roughly and in outline" only. But even at best this is all we can ever do — or have ever done — anyhow. The very meaning of 'truth' must be relative to a language-system, even if it be a natural language, with its inevitable limitations of expression. The use of the existential quantifier, '(Ex)' or 'there is at least one x such that', enables us to express one kind of restraint. 'Frequently', 'many', 'a few', and so on, are expressions that enable us to state others. Once expressed, however, the resulting statements are either true or false, not just "true for the most part." Such expressions as these enter into discourse in very exact ways with an appropriate logic governing them. Further, the very diversity of opinion, of which Aristotle speaks (concerning any subject-matter whatever) can be handled in systematic pragmatics by explicitly bringing in persons (as users of language) and their opinions. Once brought in, full statements that so and so has such and such an opinion is then true or false, not just true or false "for the most part." And similarly for the conclusions, which are no better or worse in this respect. Also similarly for the receiver or hearer of such statements. The mark of an educated man is thus to look for precisely what it is that is being expressed, to eke out ambiguities and inadequacies in it, to reflect upon alternatives, and so on. Aristotle's contention here is a most unfortunate one and has probably helped block the road to inquiry as much as any other single methodological maxim ever penned.

A word or two now concerning "verification" and "validation." Both topics raise problems of enormous difficulty in the methodology of the sciences and hence *a fortiori* in that of metaphysics and theology. Only a few items need be mentioned here. No easy comments concerning these topics are forthcoming at the present stage of research — there is just too much that we are ignorant of in the methodology of the sciences. However, there is progress in the right direction, it is hoped, to which attention may be called.

The analysis of both verification and validation must be given in

17

terms of truth. To verify is to find that a given sentence is *true*, or at least to come to accept or take it as true. To validate is to verify a sentence of general form, whereas we verify only a singular sentence. Sophisticated methodology of the sciences makes use of the subjective notion of *degree of verification*, the degree of the strength of one's acceptance of an hypothesis as true. As already suggested, there is every reason to think that such a notion will also prove useful in metaphysics and theology.

Variant notions of probability loom large in contemporary methodology of science. For the most part, these are confined to contexts of a purely extensional kind. Methods are forthcoming, however, of handling probability statements in all manner of intensional contexts via the Fregean notion of the *Art Des Gegebenseins,* the notion of an entity's being taken *under a linguistic description*.[19] Thus, instead of speaking of the probability of a class, say, relative to a given reference class, we must speak instead of the probability of that class under a given *Art Des Gegebenseins* relative to that reference class, likewise as taken under a suitable *Art Des Gegehenseins*.[20] The use of probability notions in intensional contexts can be accommodated in this way — subjective probability, confirmation or logical probability, as well as statistical probability.

Finally, it would seem all but impossible to discuss verification and validation — and indeed justification also — very deeply without a theory of human acts or actions, which in turn would rest upon a prior theory of events. We need not take events as the only realities, as the process metaphysicians would have us do. But we must, at least at some stage, recognize events, actions, processes, and states happening or taking place or occurring. And we must recognize that the logical properties of such occurrences differ radically from those of non-eventival entities.

In sum, then, there is no royal road to metaphysical knowledge. The problem of verification and validation for metaphysics presupposes the analogous problem for the sciences, which if anything is more difficult. The domain of principles or axioms required is wider as well as the admitted types of verificatory experiences, as Bocheński has pointed out. Adequate discussion of these topics is thus very difficult and must await adequate solutions to the corresponding prob-

---

19. See *Translations from the Philosophical Writings of Gottlob Frege,* ed. by P. Geach and M. Black (Oxford: Blackwell's, 1952), pp. 11 and 57.

20. See the author's "On the Language of Casual Talk: Scriven and Suppes," in *Pragmatics, Truth, and Language (Boston Studies in the Philosophy of Science,* Vol. XXXVIII; Dordrecht: D. Reidel Publishing Co., 1979).

lems for the sciences. There is no special metaphysical insight here that enables us to skip over the formidable difficulties involved. The situation is rather the other way around. Metaphysical insight itself should help us to find adequate solutions to these problems as confined to just the sciences, which then can be used for the wider purposes at hand.

These various comments are by no means intended to supply a thorough analysis of the role of logical methods in metaphysics and theology, but only as a few reminders of points that are often misunderstood or neglected. Readers familiar with those methods will have found them for the most part superfluous; those who are not are invited to join the sodality of those who are in order to get on with the metaphysical jobs ahead.

CHAPTER II

On God and Primordiality

> For my thoughts are not your thoughts, neither are your ways my ways, . . . For as the heavens are higher than the earth, so are my ways higher than your ways, and my thoughts than your thoughts.
>
> *Is.* 56:8-9

In his *The Meaning of Grace,*[1] Charles Journet comments that "in God there is no past, present, and future parallel to our past, present and future. He is on the mountain of eternity, whence he sees simultaneously the whole sequence of our past, present, and future. In God there is no *remembrance* of things past nor, strictly speaking, *foresight* of things to come. There is in him but one *vision*, a single present and simultaneous look at what, successively, has been, is, will be. From his place of eternity God knows all the free acts his creatures have done, are going, will do; he knows with a knowledge which does not *precede* these free acts, but is *above* them; he knows them not *beforehand,* but *from all eternity.* . . ." This fine passage cries out for a full and explicit logico-metaphysical foundation.

The "mountain of eternity" is very much like the logician's tense of timelessness, so that here there is strictly no temporal meaning for 'simultaneity'.[2] God cannot "see" the whole sequence of our past, present, and future simultaneously, but can do so only tenselessly, so to speak. His remembrance, foresight, and vision — indeed, his whole "knowledge" — must likewise be viewed as atemporal. It is not just that tensed statements concerning his knowledge are false, it is that in the strict sense they are meaningless — meaningless in that such statements are not allowed by the formation rules of the language, and are indefinable in terms of its primitives. Knowledge in the tense of timelessness does not then *precede* temporally the actual events and objects constituting the physical cosmos and its history; it is *above* them primordially, this knowledge itself being one of the creative factors of the cosmos. This knowledge is pretemporal, but contains implicitly the divine, predestined plan for all contingent happenings.

---

1. (Glen Rock, N.J.: Paulist Press, 1962), p. 33.
2. The notion of the tense of timelessness is due apparently to Peirce and Frege.

"We must bear in mind, at the outset," Journet notes a little later on (p. 47), "that in the word 'predestination', as in 'prescience', the prefix 'pre' signifies an anteriority of *dignity and excellence*, not one of *chronology* which would suggest a scenario written beforehand. Predestination is a love-assignment made on high, a supreme divine destination in course of realization, a supreme "prevenience" on the part of Love, a prevenience not [always] refused, but [sometimes] accepted and finally [sometimes] brought to fulfillment." Let us attempt to make logico-metaphysical sense of these and the foregoing remarks on the basis of event logic.[3] Of just what, precisely, does this anteriority of excellence and dignity consist? What, ontologically speaking, *is* the divine knowledge? And precisely who or what is it that has it? To answer this last an exact definition of 'God' is needed and presumably this will have to be given in terms of a Russellian description. "For a clear and precise definite description of God is basic to any discussion of theological language and the first task of natural theology," as Bowman Clarke has so trenchantly remarked.[4]

The primordial knowledge should not be thought of as knowledge in the usual sense, i.e., as true belief on adequate evidence. God is in no way concerned with evidence and to attribute beliefs to him seems somehow beside the point. Even truths, especially factual truths, seem secondary in this context. God's knowledge rather is primarily *valuational*; more particularly, it is of what is valued *in the highest possible sense*, of what is worthy of being *loved* in the highest sense, so much so that it *ought in fact* to be realized on earth as in heaven. This valuational character of God's primordial nature has, of course, been emphasized by Whitehead. But Whitehead is not so clear that the valuations are obligational and of what ought to be. In fact, he nowhere tells us just what valuations are, nor just how they are to be expressed linguistically, nor how they are related to what ought to be.[5] The result is that the primordial nature of God must forever remain rather vague — rather ill-characterized, in fact — unless a good deal of supplementary clarification is forthcoming.

In his *First Considerations*[6], Paul Weiss comments that the "cosmos exists apart from all men only as . . . inseparable from an ideal cosmos embracing the possible unrealized ways in which actualities and finalities could have been together. . . . It is the actualities and

---

3. See especially the author's *Events, Reference, and Logical Form* (Washington: The Catholic University of America Press, 1978).
4. In his *Language and Natural Theology* (The Hague: Mouton and Co., 1966), p. 98.
5. See the author's *Whitehead's Categoreal Scheme and Other Papers* (The Hague: Martinus Nijhoff, 1974), pp. 43 ff.
6. (Carbonville: The University of Southern Illinois Press, 1976).

finalities as maximally together, *together as they ought to be* [italics added]." Weiss is much more explicit here than Whitehead concerning the *ought-to-be,* and also concerning the need for completeness in the description of it. God is complete in a sense that must be provided for in the definite description of him. But he need not be thought of as embracing *all* unrealized possibilities, but only the one ideal one.

Whitehead was not happy with bifurcations in nature, and yet God, according to him, is essentially bifurcated or dichotomous, comprising both the primordial and consequent natures. The "primordial created fact is the unconditioned conceptual valuation of the entire multiplicity of eternal objects. . . . God is the primordial creature; but the description of his nature is not exhausted by this conceptual side of it. His 'consequent nature' results from his physical prehensions of the derivative actual entities, . . ." we are told in *Process and Reality* (p. 46). The question arises as to whether this dichotomy is a happy one and as to whether it is really needed in any essential way. Perhaps the primordial nature suitably embraces the consequent one. If the former is really complete, there will be "knowledge" of all the items in the consequent nature. But these items need not be regarded as *parts* of God's nature; they are "known" by him, but this is quite another matter. In any case, the view to be suggested below will avoid whatever taint of pantheism there is in admitting God s consequent nature, as well as all traces of a bifurcation. Although the point of departure here is thus Whiteheadian to some extent, the position will deviate so completely in details that only some whisps of the spirit, not the letter, or Whitehead's view will remain.

Let us recall that the logico-metaphysical theory of events consists of a first-order logic with identity and non-logical predicates, augmented to include the theory of virtual classes and relations, the calculus of individuals (mereology or theory of the part-whole relation), a theory of temporal flow, the theory of event-descriptive predicates, and a first-order semiotics (syntax, semantics, and pragmatics) including a theory of intensionality handled in terms of Frege's *Arten des Gegebenseins*.[7] Although this technical development is presupposed in what follows, all the relevant details will be explained in context as we go on. Note that classes and relations appear only virtually, not as real entities in the theory. Thus in effect the eternal objects are handled in a manner closer to that of Hartshorne than of Whitehead. As to the

---

7. See especially G. Frege, "Über Sinn und Bedeutung," second paragraph, and his *Begriffsschrift,* §8, or *loc. cit.* On virtual classes and relations see *Belief, Existence, and Meaning,* Chapter VI.

fundamental individuals admitted (as values for variables), there is a choice. We may admit both physical objects including persons — although persons are not therewith handled *merely* as physical objects — as well as events (including states, acts, process, and the like). Or we may take a purely "process" view and admit only the latter, in which case of course there is the formidable problem of introducing adequately names of objects, and predicates applicable to them, in terms wholly of events and the event-descriptive predicates. (It seems unlikely — the third alternative — that event talk could be dispensed with altogether, primitively at least, in favor of physical-object talk.) Whatever choice is made here will affect the details of what follows but not its substance, and thus will not matter too much for present purposes.

Note that the whole logico-metaphysical system contains an object-linguistic part, a metalinguistic semiotics of this part, a metametalinguistic semiotics of this semiotics, and so on. This is in accord with the familiar Tarskian doctrine of the hierarchy of language, which seems to provide the best way of arranging the matter in both metaphysics and the philosophy of language.[8] Note, however, that the semantics involved differs in very basic respects from that of Tarski.[9]

For the theory of the primordial valuations a new primitive is required. Let

(1) $\qquad\qquad$ 'a PrOblgd $e_1, \ldots, e_k$'

express primitively in the metalanguage that the k-place predicate a is primordially obliged (in the valuational sense) to apply to the events or objects $e_1, e_2, \ldots, e_k$ (taken in this order). More fully, (1) expresses that it is valued primordially to the highest degree that a apply to $e_1, \ldots, e_k$, or that it is more eminently desirable or loved that this be the case, so much so indeed that this ought to be the case. The 'e_1', and so on, are variables of the widest range, having as values whatever the fundamental individuals are taken to be. The 'a' is a syntactical variable for the expressions of the language of next lower level in the hierarchy of languages, and in the context (1) a is to be a k-place predicate. The a need not be a primitive predicate but may be a defined one and hence of considerable internal complexity.

---

8. Cf. Zellig Harris, "The Two Systems of Grammar: Report and Paraphrase," in his *Papers in Structural and Transformational Linguistics* (Dordrecht: D. Reidel Publishing Co., 1972) and the author's "On Harris's Systems of Report and Paraphrase," in *Semiotics and Linguistic Structure*.

9. See especially in this regard the author's "Some Reminders Concerning Truth, Satisfaction, and Reference," in *Pragmatics, Truth, and Language*.

Let us observe how (1) can be used to formulate the essential content of the Second Commandment, for example, which presumably is ordained primordially. To avoid any complications arising from the use of the pronoun 'thou' and the use of the imperative mood, let us assume it to be formulated as

'Given any two persons, one is primordially obliged to love the other with a love like that he bears himself'.

This may be rendered — or given a deep structure — as

$$'(p)(q)((\text{Per } p \bullet \text{Per } q \bullet \sim p = q) \supset \text{'}\{rs \ni (r \text{ } Love \text{ } s \bullet (e)(e')$$
$$((<r,\text{Love},s>e \bullet <r \text{ } \text{Love},r>e') \supset e \text{ } Like \text{ } e'))\}\text{' } \text{PrOblgd } p,q)'.^{[10]}$$

Here 'Per' is the predicate for being a human person, and 'Like' is the predicate for a suitable relation of being *like* or *similar to*. The virtual-class abstract '$\{rs \ni -\}$' is said to be primordially obliged to apply to any two persons p and q. The sentential form '$<r,\text{Love},s>e$' expresses that e is a state of r's loving s. Thus the '$(e)(e')(-)$' clause here expresses that any state e of r's loving s must be like any state e' of r's loving himself. Note that this rendition differs from the imperatival form of the Commandment in stipulating not only what ought to be, but in affirming something that is valued to the highest degree primordially.

It is also interesting to explore the deep structure of the First Commandment, which, however, is considerably more complicated.[11]

One of the most important features to observe about (1) is that the a may be of a very considerable internal complexity and also that it must be a *predicate*, not a relation the predicate might be said to stand for. The reason for this latter constraint is that the form (1) is intensional. The use of a predicate captures the essential purport of the *Art des Gegebensein*. It is the relation *under the given linguistic description* that is the carrier of obligation here, not the relation itself.

The words 'obligation' or 'valuation', or the phrase 'valuation obligation', are used here synonymously but 'will' or 'adversion' could be used equally. A primordial valuation is an expression of the primordial will. Some of them perhaps cannot fail to obtain — more will be said concerning these below — but some most certainly do not, and hence the presence of evil. Later we shall distinguish other types of

---

10. The use throughout of special kinds of variables for special sorts of entities is as follows: 'e', 'e''', etc., for events, acts, states, or processes, 'x', 'y', etc., for physical objects, 'p', 'q', etc., for human persons, and 'a', 'b', etc., for the linguistic expressions of the language taken as object language.

11. See *Events, Reference, and Logical Form*, pp. 140ff.

valuations, and 'obligation' will then be used in a somewhat narrower sense.

In terms of (1), it seems, we have a form enabling each and every primordial obligation to be expressed. This does not mean of course that we, finite little creatures that we are, can succeed in expressing all of them or even that we can recognize them once expressed. The contention is only that we gain a language for a natural theology if sentential forms of the form (1) are added to the logico-metaphysical theory, for God emerges then as a suitable construct containing all primordial valuations.

To simplify, let us suppose that some integer n is the degree of the predicate of highest degree entering into any primordial valuation. Thus no primordial valuation will concern a predicate of degree $> n$. Suppose further that for each $k < n$, some primordial valuation concerns a predicate of that degree. In reflecting upon the primordial valuations, then, we need consider only predicates of each and every degree $\leq n$.

Let us collect now all of the primordial obligations together. Strictly an *obligation* here is an *act or state of valuational obligating*. We let

$$\text{`}<a,\text{PrOblgd},e_1,....,e_k>e\text{'}$$

express that e is an act of having the predicate a primordially obliged to apply to e_1, ..., e_k. It is a *pure* act or state uninfluenced by anything whatsoever, except perhaps by other such acts or states of similar kind.

Let 'Obj e' be defined to express that e is an object other than a primordial obliging or sum of such. To define this notion we may proceed as follows. Let 'e P e'' express that e is a *part* of e' in the sense of the calculus of individuals. And let 'e Fu F' express that e is the *fusion* of the (virtual) class F, i.e., the sum of all its members. It is a theorem of that calculus, it will be recalled, that every non-null class has a unique individual as its fusion. Consider now the class

$$\{e' \ni (Ea)(Ee_1)...(Ee_n)(<a,\text{PrOblgd},e_1>e' \text{ v } <a,\text{PrOblgd},e_1,e_2>e'$$
$$\text{v ... v } <a,\text{PrOblgd},e_1,...,e_n>e')\}.$$

Let this be F and let e'' be its fusion. To say that e is an object is to say that then e is not a part of e''. Thus

$$\text{'Obj}\,e\text{'} \quad \text{may abbreviate} \quad \text{'}(Ee'')(e'' \text{ Fu F} \cdot \sim e \text{ P } e'')\text{'}.$$

The primordial obligings are to be only of objects and not of themselves. Consider now the virtual class of all such acts,

(2) $\{e \ni (Ea)(Ee_1)...(Ee_n)(\text{Obj } e_1 \cdot \text{Obj } e_2 \cdot ... \cdot \text{Obj } e_n \cdot (\text{PredCon}_1 a \cdot$
        $<a,\text{PrOblgd},e_1>e) \text{ v } (\text{PredCon}_2 a \cdot <a,\text{PrOblgd},e_1,e_2>e) \text{ v } ... \text{ v}$
        $(\text{PredCon}_n a \cdot <a,\text{PrOblgd},e_1,...,e_n>e)))\}.$

Here 'PredCon$_1$ a' expresses that a is a one-place predicate constant, and similarly for 'PredCon$_2$ a', and so on. This virtual class thus consists of all primordial obligations of one-place predicates of an object, of two-place predicates of two objects, and so on to n-place predicates.

There might be temptation to identify this class with the primordial nature of God, resulting in a somewhat societal conception. Alternatively one may take God as the fusion of this class. We may let

'God'   be defined as   '$(ie \cdot e \text{ Fu G})$',

where G is the class (2). In this way the primordial God emerges as an individual, perhaps even as a personal consciousness of some sort, but including the whole society of the primordial obligations in his "real internal constitution."

It must be assumed at the outset that wherever (1) obtains, a is a k-place predicate and each of $e_1, ..., e_k$ is an object. Thus we have that

P1. $\vdash (a)(e_1)...(e_k)(a \text{ PrOblgd } e_1,...,e_k \supset (\text{PredCon}_k a \cdot \text{Obj } e_1 \cdot ... \cdot$
            $\text{Obj } e_k))$, for each k such that $k = 1, k = 2, ... ,$ or $k = n$.

In view of this principle the expression for (2) above may be simplified. Note that **P1** here is an axiom-schema, specifying a specific axiom for each permitted value of 'k'. The '$\vdash$' is Frege's so-called assertion-sign expressing that the sequence of symbols following it is an axiom or theorem of the system.

The primordial obligings are not to be thought of, of course, as taking place in space or time, or under this or that physical condition. They "precede" all physical happenings, and indeed all mental ones as well, in the sense of 'pre-' suggested above. They take place from all eternity and are, so to speak, of eternal, non-temporal, duration. The objects to which they apply, however, it is to be noted, are the actual objects of the physical cosmos. Thus although the divine nature here is concerned with ideals, with what ought to be, they are always ideals *of* or concerning items in the actual world, including all manner of evil. God is thus by no means completely "other," being concerned par excellence with the immediate here and now as well as with the remote there and then.

The existential quantifiers '(Ee_1)', and so on, in the expression for the class (2) range over all events and objects in the cosmos, and the 'a' over all possible predicates. The class (2) is thus maximally complete in having as members each and every primordial obliging. Every hair on one's head, every whisp of a happening no matter where or when, is given its primordial status. Nothing is left out in the divine dispensation. To assure that this is the case, an axiom-schema is needed; let us call it — for the pleasure of having a label — the *Principle of Primordial Completeness.* It states that given any objects there is at least one predicate primordially obliged to apply to them:

P2. $\vdash (e_1)...(e_k)((\text{Obj}\, e_1 \cdot ... \cdot \text{Obj}\, e_k) \supset (Ea)a\, \text{PrOblgd}\, e_1,...,e_k)$, for k $= 1, 2, ..., n,$ the n fixed as above.

Of course many *specific* axioms are required also, including perhaps forms for the First and Second Commandments, as well as numerous other statements concerning specific predicates and the specific objects to which those predicates primordially apply. Whatever it is that God's will is thought to specify then is given in the axioms and in the theorems that follow from them.

The existence and uniqueness of God may be proved from **P2**. Where '$E!(\imath e \cdot Ge)$' is defined as '$(Ee)(Ge \cdot (e')(Ge' \supset e' = e))$', to express that the one and only object having G exists, we have clearly that

P3. $\vdash E!\text{God}.$

The proof utilizes the theorem from the calculus of individuals mentioned above, that

$$\vdash (Ee)Ge \supset (Ee')(e'\, \text{Fu}\, G \cdot (e'')(e''\, \text{Fu}\, G \supset e'' = e')).$$

All we need now is to prove that

$$\vdash (Ee)Fe,$$

where F is the class (2). But this follows immediately from **P2** and the principle of the existence of an object,

$$\vdash (Ee)\text{Obj}\, e,$$

and the logical Principle of Abstraction, that

$$\vdash \{e' \ni -e'-\}e \equiv -e-,$$

where '$-e'-$' and '$-e-$' are sentential forms differing appropriately from each other. The need for the assumption of the existence of at least one object should not cause any surprise here, for there is always the null individual if no other.[12]

---

12. Cf. the author's "Of Time and the Null Individual," *The Journal of Philosophy* 62 (1965): 723–736.

The primordial obligations or valuations must also be *consistent* one with another, lest the divine nature be a mere jungle. Any predicate 'F' has a negative '-F' defined as '$\{e \ni \sim Fe\}$'. Thus any a has a negative $\ulcorner$-$a$$\urcorner$.[13] The *Principle of Primordial Consistency* is then:

P4. $\vdash \sim (Ea)(Ee_1)...(Ee_k)(a \text{ PrOblgd } e_1,...,e_k \cdot \ulcorner$-$a$$\urcorner \text{ PrOblgd }$
$e_1,...,e_k)$, for k as above.

This too must hold either as an axiom- or theorem-schema.

It is sometimes maintained that God's omniscience and his omnipotence are one and the same. This is doubtful, but in any case they are surely closely related. God is omnipotent in the sense that it is his power to arrange the primordial obligations as he will; but once arranged, they are not to be altered — at least not within any one cosmic epoch. 'Omniprepotent' would perhaps be a better word here. God is omniprepotent in fixing unto eternity once and for all the primordial decrees in just such fashion as he will. In fact he *is*, on the present account, just this fixing in just this fashion.

In what sense may God be said to be omniscient or "omniprescient"? He is surely omniprescient in the sense of containing all the primordial obligings in his nature once and for all. His omniscience, on the other hand, concerns the objects and process of nature. He surely should be said to "know" the objects entering into the primordial obligings. If he did not know them in some sense it would seem impossible for him to ordain anything about them. The word 'know' has not been represented thus far by a technical term. Perhaps we may legitimately introduce the special phrase 'God-Knows' in context as follows.

'God-Knows e'   merely abbreviates   '$(Ea)a$ PrOblgd e'.

It then immediately follows that

$$\vdash (e)(\text{Obj } e \supset \text{God-Knows } e).$$

Even so, God's knowledge in this sense is rather weak, for even though he knows all things, he need not know that the classes (or properties in extension) of which these things are members do actually have them as members. God's knowledge thus in this sense always remains primordial, *de re*, so to speak, and takes cognizance of actual happenings only in so far as there are primordial obligations to cover them.

---

13. Note the need for Quine's quasi-quotes or corners here.
14. See *Truth and Denotation*, especially Chapters III and IV.

It might be contended that God's knowledge *de re* involves also knowledge *de dicto*. To know *e* is to know at least that something or other obtains of *e* — for omniscience this is to know *all* that obtains of *e*. Where 'God-Knows *e,a*' expresses that God knows *de re* and *de dicto* that *a* applies to *e*, we should perhaps have also the principle that

$$\vdash (e)(a)((\text{God-Knows}\,e \cdot a \text{ Den } e) \supset \text{God-Knows}\,e,a).$$

('*a* Den *e*' expresses that *a* denotes *e* in the sense of multiple denotation.[14]) But of course 'Knows' here is not to be taken in the ordinary sense. "For my thoughts are not your thoughts" and God's knowledge is not of the human kind.

(It should be noted of course that the locution 'God-Knows *e*' is *not* an instance of '*p* Knows *e*' for variable '*p*'. It may be read '*e* is God-known' equally well. An alternative method suggests itself, however, by taking 'God Knows *E*' as an instance of '*p* Knows *e*' and, in place of the definition above, adopting the principle that

$$\vdash (e)(\text{God Knows}\,e \equiv (\text{E}a)a \text{ PrOblgd } e).$$

And similarly 'God Knows *e,a*' could be taken as an instance of '*p* Knows *e,a*', with the retention of the *de dicto* principle given written now without the hyphens. In this alternative method, 'Knows' *is* taken in the ordinary sense, but with such special principles concerning God's knowing as to justify the contention that it is not of the human kind.)

The sense in which God is omnipresent, or "omniprepresent," is also clear. He is present in each and every object or occasion in the sense of having placed that object once and for all in its proper setting primordially.

Both the immanent and transcendent characters of God are thus preserved in this account — immanent in the sense that all things and happenings are given their proper role primordially, and transcendent in the sense that the primordial order is atemporal, aspatial, and beyond any possible physical description.

It is tempting to reflect also on the senses in which God may be said to possess the so-called transcendentals, the sense in which he may be said to be *ens, res, aliquid, unum, bonum,* and *verum*. The very brief following comments may not be without interest. He is clearly *ens,* the whole system being arranged to allow for this. He is a *res*, in view of **P3**, in the sense of being an individual admitted as a value for a variable, and *aliquid* — distinct from all objects or everything else — in view of the principle that

P5. $\vdash (e)(\mathrm{Obj}\, e \supset \sim \mathrm{God} = e)$.

Thus far no technical expression has been introduced for the relation of the application of a k-place predicate to its arguments. Such an expression will be needed in what is to follow. Therefore we let

$$\text{'}a\ \mathrm{Den}\, e_1,...,e_k\text{'}$$

express that the k-place predicate a *denotes* the objects e_1, ..., e_k in that order. Thus, for example, 'Loves' may be said to denote persons p and q (in that order) just where p loves q. (The $(k + 1)$-place 'Den' may be defined in terms of the two-place 'Den' if it is assumed that every entity is either assigned a proper name primitively or at least is describable by a Russellian description.)

God is *unum* of course in the sense of being a unique entity defined by a Russellian description. He is *bonum* in the sense that all that is terrestrially desirable or good, in the most fundamental sense, is obliged to be such primordially. The very meaning of 'good' in the highest sense as applicable to acts, events, persons, objects, is to be ascertained by reference to the primordial obligings. God is good as the source of all terrestrial goods. The primal meaning of 'good' then is to be given by the following definition-schema introducing the primordially good:

'$\mathrm{PrGood}\, a, e_1,...,e_k$'   abbreviates   '$(a\ \mathrm{PrOblgd}\, e_1,...,e_k \bullet a\ \mathrm{Den}\, e_1,...,e_k)$'.

It is thus good in the most fundamental sense that a does apply to e_1, ..., e_k just where a is primordially obliged to do so and in fact does. The existence of good in this sense does not follow from any of our principles thus far, however. An additional one is needed to assume this, namely:

P6. $\vdash (Ea)(Ee_1)...(Ee_k)\mathrm{PrGood}\, a, e_1,...,e_k$, for $k = 1$ or $k = 2$
or ... or $k = n$.

Note that the 'or' here is inclusive, so that there might be k-adic good, so to speak, for each k between 0 and n, but this is not required by this *Principle of the Existence of the Primordial Good*. Of course the good here is the highest good always, and neither the principle nor the definition rule out lower or derivative goods or excellences of various kinds.

In what sense now is God *verum*? In the first place, his decrees are true in the sense of the semantical truth-concept for the logico-metaphysical system under discussion. The axioms containing parts of the form '$a\ \mathrm{PrOblgd}\ e_1,...,e_k$' non-trivially are themselves true statements, as of course are their logical consequences. God, however, is not *verum* in the sense that what he decrees always obtains. It may be the case that a PrOblgd $e_1,...,e_k$ without its being the case that a actually applies to e_1, ..., e_k. But *some* of his decrees do issue in truths, as is required by the Principle of the Existence of the Primordial Good. Let 'R' be some k-adic abstract containing no free variables. Concerning k-adic denotation, we have clearly the law that

$$\vdash (a)(e_1)...(e_k) ((a \text{ Den } e_1,...,e_k \bullet a \text{ Des R}) \supset R e_1,...,e_k).$$

And clearly concerning the semantical truth-predicate 'Tr' we have that

$$\vdash (Ee_1)...(Ee_k)Re_1...e_k \supset Tr \text{ '}(Ee_1)...(Ee_k)Re_1...e_k\text{'}.$$

Hence, on the basis of the Principle of the Existence of the Primordial Good and the semantical principle that $\vdash (Ea)a$ Des R, we get that

$$\vdash Tr \text{ '}(Ee_1)...(Ee_k)Re_1...e_k\text{'}, \text{ for at least one } k \text{ where } 1 \leq k \leq n.$$

God is thus *verum* in the sense that some of his decrees issue in existential truths.

If we accept the principle suggested above about God's knowledge *de re* and *de dicto,* there is a third sense in which God is *verum,* the sense in which he knows all truths *de dicto simpliciter.* For from that principle, we can readily prove that

$$\vdash (e)(a)(b)((b \text{ Des } e \bullet \text{PredCon}_1 a \bullet Tr (a ^\frown b)) \supset \text{God-Knows } e,a).$$

This states that if b is an expression *designating* e and the result of *concatenating* a one-place predicate a with b is true, then, to speak roughly, God knows it. But this principle is perhaps dubious, in view of the lack of an adequate characterization of God's knowledge *de dicto*.

Of course in attributing these transcendentals to God, we are stretching language beyond its ordinary bounds. The same is true when we speak of God's knowledge, will, love, freedom, mercy, and tenderness, and the like. Whatever we wish to say concerning God, his characteristics, and his relations to the creatures must, strictly, be said in terms of the exact theological language. "All our difficulties [concerning God's nature and the like] come from representing God's knowledge [and the like] after the fashion of man's," Journet has aptly observed (pp. 39–40). "As soon as we take account of the transcendence of the divine knowledge, will, and freedom, all contradictions disappear; but we are plunged in mystery." Of course the contradictions can disappear only within the confines of a well-knit system — there is no meaning to 'contradiction' otherwise. And the mystery we are up against is then like that which the theoretical scientist is up against all the time. We get at the mystery intellectually by using suitable theoretical constructs in terms of which ever more adequate systems may be formulated explanatory of the phenomena under discussion.[15]

Nothing has been said thus far concerning perfection. But clearly, according to the conception here, God is a perfect being in an appropriate sense. Perfection for objects is determined by the primordial obligations, and hence God himself may be regarded as perfect also in his role as the determiner of such perfection.

In terms of 'PrOblg' a kind of deontic logic may be developed as applied to God's decrees. Thus a predicate a may be said to be *primordially prohibited* if its negative is primordially obliged, of the same objects. Thus

'a PrPrhbtd e_1,...,e_k' may abbreviate ' $\ulcorner \neg a \urcorner$ PrOblgd e_1,...,e_k'.

And a may be said to be *primordially permitted* provided its negative is not primordially obliged, so that

'a PrPrmtd e_1,...,e_k' may abbreviate '(PredCon$_k$ a • Obj e_1 • ... • Obj e_k • ~ $\ulcorner \neg a \urcorner$ PrOblgd e_1,...,e_k)'.

Also a may be said to be *primordially neutral* provided a is neither primordially obliged nor prohibited. Thus

'a PrNtrl e_1,...,e_k' abbreviates '(PredCon$_k$ a • Obj e_1 • ... • Obj e_k • ~ a PrOblgd e ,...,e_k • ~ a PrPrhbtd e_1,...,e_k)'.

Clearly then we would have the law that whatever is primordially obliged is primordially permitted, of the same objects,

P7. $\vdash (a)(e_1)...(e_k)(a$ PrOblgd e_1,...,$e_k \supset a$ PrPrmtd e_1,...,$e_k)$,

in view of the Principle of Primordial Consistency. Also

P8. $\vdash (a)(e_1)...(e_k)((\text{PredCon}_k a$ • Obj e_1 • ... • Obj $e_k) \supset (a$ PrOblgd e_1,...,e_k v a PrPrhbtd e_1,...,e_k v a PrNtrl e_1,...,$e_k))$.

This last, although a mere logical truth in the formalism, is of interest in expressing that all objects and predicates are appropriately encompassed in God's nature. We might dub it the *Principle of Primordial Comrehensiveness.*

Note also that any primordially permitted valuation is either obliged or neutral and conversely,

---

15. For remarks along a somewhat similar vein, see J. Bocheński, *The Logic of Religion.*

P9. $\vdash (a)(e_1)...(e_k)(a \text{ PrPrmtd } e_1,...,e_k \equiv (a \text{ PrOblgd } e_1,...,e_k \vee a \text{ PrNtrl } e_1,...,e_k))$,

and that any permitted one is not prohibited and conversely,

P10. $\vdash (a)(e_1)...(e_k)((\text{PredCon}_k a \bullet \text{Obj } e_1 \bullet ... \bullet \text{Obj } e_k) \supset (a \text{ PrPrmtd } e_1,...,e_k \equiv \sim a \text{ PrPrhbtd } e_1,...,e_k))$.

Also the neutral valuations are just those that are permitted but not obliged,

P11. $\vdash (a)(e_1)...e_k)(a \text{ PrNtrl } e_1,...,e_k \equiv (a \text{ PrPrmtd } e_1,...,e_k \bullet \sim a \text{ PrOblgd } e_1,...,e_k))$.

And as a corollary of **P8** and **P9,** we have that

P12. $\vdash (a)(e_1)...(e_k)((\text{PredCon}_k a \bullet \text{Obj } e_1 \bullet ... \bullet \text{Obj } e_k) \supset (a \text{ PrPrmtd } e_1,...,e_k \vee a \text{ PrPrhbtd } e_1,...,e_k))$.

If the logical properties of these notions were to be examined in full, the two following principles would presumably obtain, concerning logical sums and products of two k-adic relations. Let

$$\text{`}(G \cup_k H)\text{'} \quad \text{abbreviate} \quad \text{`}\{e_1...e_k \ni (Ge_1...e_k \vee He_1...e_k)\}\text{'}$$

and

$$\text{`}(G \cap_k H)\text{'} \quad \text{for} \quad \text{`}\{e_1...e_k \ni (Ge_1...e_k \bullet He_1...e_k)\}\text{'},$$

for sums and products of k-adic virtual relations, respectively. Here again these definition-schemata are to be understood as specifying various definitions, one for each value of k. Then the following principles should obtain:

P13. $\vdash (a)(b)(e_1)...(e_k)((\text{PredCon}_k a \bullet \text{PredCon}_k b) \supset (\ulcorner (a \cap_k b) \urcorner \text{ PrOblgd } e_1,...,e_k \equiv (a \text{ PrOblgd } e_1,...,e_k \bullet b \text{ PrOblgd } e_1,...,e_k)))$

and

P14. $\vdash (a)(b)(e_1)...(e_k)((\text{PredCon}_k a \bullet \text{PredCon}_k b \bullet (a \text{ PrOblgd } e_1,...e_k \vee b \text{ PrOblgd } e_1,...,e_k)) \supset \ulcorner (a \cup_k b) \urcorner \text{ PrOblgd } e_1,...,e_k$.

Thus, to speak loosely, a product is primordially obliged if and only if both its factors are, whereas a sum is obliged if (but not only if) at least one of its summands is.

An immediate consequence of these principles is what might be called the *Modus Ponens Principle* for primordial obligations.

P15. $\vdash (a)(b)(e_1)...(e_k)((\text{PredCon}_k b \bullet a \text{ PrOblgd } e_1,...,e_k \bullet \ulcorner \neg (a \cap_k \neg b) \urcorner \text{ PrOblgd } e_1,...,e_k) \supset b \text{ PrOblgd } e_1,...,e_k$.

33

An immediate consequence of **P13** is that

P16. $\vdash (a)(b)(e_1)...(e_k)((\mathrm{PredCon}_k\, a \bullet \mathrm{PredCon}_k\, b) \supset (\ulcorner(a \cup_k b)\urcorner$
$\mathrm{PrPrmtd}\, e_1,...,e_k \equiv (a\ \mathrm{PrPrmtd}\, e_1,...,e_k \text{ v } b\ \mathrm{PrPrmtd}\, e_1,...,e_k)))$,

and of **P14** that

P17. $\vdash (a)(b)(e_1)...(e_k)((\mathrm{PredCon}_k\, a \bullet \mathrm{PredCon}_k\, b \bullet \ulcorner (a \cap_k b)\urcorner$
$\mathrm{PrPrmtd}\, e_1,...,e_k) \supset (a\ \mathrm{PrPrmtd}\, e_1,...,e_k \bullet b\ \mathrm{PrPrmtd}\, e_1,...,e_k))$.

A good deal more needs to be said concerning the deontic logic of the primordial concepts. The foregoing rudimentary comments provide apparently the first attempt to characterize them in any even approximatively exact way.

It has frequently been remarked that the deontic concepts are intelligible only within the context of a given moral or valuational code — just as the modal ones are intelligible only relative to a given set of principles taken to be "necessary." The code here is of course part of a wider theological one, from which specifically moral and ethical principles are to be derived.

Note that with the admission of the definitions and principles just given, the primordial valuations include now, not only the primordial obligations, as in the preceding sections, but also all primordial permissions as well as prohibitions. It would seem appropriate to include all of these within God's nature. God is now then to be regarded as the fusion of the class of all primordial valuations whatsoever. Thus we let now

'God'   abbreviate   '$((\imath e \bullet e\mathrm{Fu}\,\{e\, \ni (Ea)(Ee_1)\,...\,(Ee_n)$
$(<a,\mathrm{PrPrmtd},e_1>e' \text{ v } <a,\mathrm{PrPrhbtd},e_1>e' \text{ v }...\text{ v}$
$<a,\mathrm{PrPrmtd},e_1,...,e_n>e' \text{ v } <a,\mathrm{PrPrhbtd},e_1,...,e_n>e')\})$'.

Some of the material above must now be reconstrued in accord with this definition. The notion of being an object remains the same, but note that the acts of primordial neutralizing, so to speak, are included as objects. If this is thought undesirable it may be avoided by a suitable technical change. Also note that in the definition just given the clauses containing 'PrPrhbtd' may be dropped, the result being equivalent.

All order in the cosmos is given by the primordial valuations. A distinguished subclass of these consists of the *primordial determinations*, to the effect that such and such *must obtain* in order to have our cosmos at all. Whatever must obtain is obliged to, so that whatever is primordially determined is primordially obliged, but not necessarily conversely.

Let

(3)   '$a\ \mathrm{PrDtrmnd}\, e_1,...,e_k$'

express that it is primordially determined that the k-place predicate a apply to e_1, ..., e_k, in the sense not only that a is primordially obliged to and does, but cannot fail to. Clearly then

P18. $\vdash (a)(e_1)...(e_k)(a \text{ PrDtrmnd } e_1,...,e_k \supset a \text{ PrOblgd } e_1,...,e_k),$

and

P19. $\vdash (a)(e_1)...(e_k)(a \text{ PrDtrmnd } e_1,...,e_k \supset a \text{ Den } e_1,...,e_k).$

The effect of the 'cannot fail to apply' here must be spelled out in suitable detail in any given system. One thing is certain about the primordial determinations, if we think that the laws of logic, mathematics, and empirical science generally give us a true account of the cosmos — namely, they must include the realm of scientific law. In other words, where instances of (3) hold, a is of the form of a suitably established scientific law, either causal or stochastic. Let the class of such admissible laws be L. Thus we have also that

P20. $\vdash (e_1)...(e_i)(Ee_{i+1})...(Ee_k)a \text{ PrDtrmnd } e_1,...,e_i,e_{i+1},...,e_k,$ where a is the form '$\{e_1...e_k\supset(-e_1,...,e_k-)\}$' and '$(e_1)...(e_i)(Ee_{i\ 1})...(Ee_k)(-e_1,...,e_k-)$' is one of the laws of L, and $1 \leqq i < k$ or $k = 1$.[16]

Of course this principle is not very informative without a full specification of L. One of the aims of science, it would seem, is to give such specification.

It seems reasonable to regard scientific truths as primordially determined. They are there somehow, to be gotten at by suitably gifted persons who are willing to do the necessary hard work, and they characterize the cosmos in what — to the late twentieth century mind anyhow — would seem to be the most satisfactory way we have. Whatever order and intelligibility the physical cosmos has is to be ascertained only in this way. And similarly, those primordial obligations that are not determinations are to be known only by persons suitably gifted in another direction who are willing to undergo the necessary discipline — in its highest form, presumably that of sainthood. Viewed in this way, there is no quarrel whatsoever between the aims and methods of science and those of religious practice. In fact, on the view here they are seen in full philosophic detail to be merely different aspects of a common endeavor.

Incidentally, note that more can be said concerning the *verum* once

---

16. Note that the formulation here takes cognizance of the Skolem normal form for first-order quantificational formulae.

the primordial determinations are introduced, if scientific laws are regarded as true. What is primordially determined would then be true. Thus we would have

P21. $\vdash (e_1)...(e_k)(a \text{ PrDtrmnd } e_1,...,e_k \supset \text{Tr } b)$, where a is as in **P20** and b is the corresponding law of L.

Of course, this remark and the foregoing ones scarcely scratch the surface here as to how God and truth are related. One thing emerges clearly, however: the need for the semantic truth-concept in order to give any reasonably precise account. (See also III below.)

Another comment. **P20** is limited to our own cosmic epoch. If there are others, **P20** must be given a much more general form. It would have to take account of laws concerning the coming into being, the regnancy, and the passing out of being of laws themselves. Of course, we cannot at present formulate laws of such vast generality, but their possibility should be allowed for in God's envisagement. Indeed such possibility may be essential, if any rational sense is to be made of the crisis in contemporary physics, which John Archibald Wheeler has described so eloquently.[17]

The primordial obligations that are not also determinations may be thought of as God's *desires*. He desires that they obtain. God's will — regarded as comprising the obligations — is dichotomous, for he presumably wills both his determinations and his desires. Because the determinations cannot fail to obtain, the petition 'Thy will be done' should be understood to apply only to the desires; it is pointless as applied to the determinations.

God's will might also be thought to encompass the primordially neutral, thus extending to all the permissions. This would appear to give us the Augustinian sense of 'will', for then "nothing . . . happens but by the will of the Omnipotent, He either permitting it to be done, or Himself doing it [in the sense of having it done]."[18] 'Thy will be done' would then extend to all that is permitted, even including evil, but not of course the primordially evil. In this case the petition is less imprecatory than it seems; it becomes a quiet benediction poured out upon all terrestrial happenings by means of which evil is absorbed within the primordial permissions.

Some desires are more intense than others, and perhaps a notion of *degree of intensity* should be introduced here, and for the determina-

---

17. In his address at the *Fifth International Congress for Logic, Methodology, and Philosophy of Science*, London, Ontario, Aug. 27–Sept. 2, 1975.
18. *Enchiridion*, XCV.

tions and neutral valuations also. To characterize this latter, probability considerations (in the logical as opposed to stochastic or subjectivistic senses) would have to be introduced. A much more elaborate theology would result, but also one presumably more adequate to the complexities of scientific methodology, on the one hand, and to the delicacies of moral and religious experience, on the other.

Very little has been said thus far concerning evil. But just as good is primordially obliged, evil is primordially prohibited. Of course there may be different kinds of evil just as there are different kinds of good, but in the most fundamental sense evil occurrences may be regarded as those that are prohibited primordially. Thus we may let

'PrEvil $a,e_1,...,e_k$' abbreviate '(PrPrhbtd $e_1,...,e_k \cdot a$ Den $e_1,...,e_k$)'.

The so-called problem of evil would be no problem were it not for the existence of the primordially evil in this highly imperfect world. It seems that primordial evil exists:

P22. ⊢ (Ea)(Ee_1)...(Ee_k)PrEvil $a,e_1,...,e_k$.

This of course is analogous to **P6** for the primordial good.

The cosmos containing a good deal of variety, there exist also objects or occurrences that are neither primordially good nor bad:

P23. ⊢ (Ea)(Ee_1)...(Ee_k)(a PrNtrl $e_1,...,e_k \cdot a$ Den $e_1,...,e_k$),

and hence of course

P24. ⊢ (Ea)(Ee_1)...(Ee_k)(a PrPrmtd $e_1,...,e_k \cdot \sim a$ PrOblgd $e_1,...,e_k \cdot a$ Den $e_1,...,e_k$).

Occurrences and objects that are primordially neutral would seem to constitute the great inert bulk of most of history and the cosmos.

The view here is compatible with the notion that *homo prima causa mali*. "Thy destruction comes from Thee, O Israel; from me comes thy help." Again, Journet has stated the matter with a fine clarity (p. 39): "My sin of yesterday, my sin of tomorrow, it is not that God *saw* or *will see* me committing them; he *sees* me now [in his eternity]: he sees me frustrating the prevenient movements of his grace. He sees this in the eternal present in which he establishes his plan. It is true that the divine plan is immutable, once it is fixed from all eternity. But it is fixed from all eternity only with the free defection of man taken into account. Thus man's sin does not modify the divine plan, but enters into its eternal and determined pattern." Everything said here, it seems, can be spelled out fully and explicitly in terms of the primordial valuations. (See IV below.)

Although the view put forward here makes use of primordial valuations somewhat in the manner of Whitehead, it differs remarkably in allowing no explicit place for his consequent nature of God, as already noted. In this respect the view here is perhaps closer to classical theism than to that of either Whitehead or Hartshorne. Neither of those authors has spelled out in any exact detail the structure of the primordial nature, however. Once this is done, we may see that there is simply no need for the consequent nature, no need for an undesirable bifurcation in God's internal structure. The latter is actually contained in the former, in the sense that all the objects and happenings of the cosmos are items in the primordial envisagement. (See X below.)

The crucial difference between the view here and that of orthodox process theology is, then, just this, that the body of God is not regarded as a *part* of God but rather as something covered distributively, so to speak, in the primordial valuations. This would seem to entail no loss, however, in any essential way, metaphysical, theological, or religious. Whatever there is of significance that can be said of God in the bifurcated sense can be said of him as defined above, it would seem, with the necessary changes of phrase. To substantiate this claim in detail would require of course a fuller discussion than can be given here. By way of summary or outline of such a discussion, let us reflect briefly upon Whitehead's famous six "antitheses" concerning God in the World at the end of *Process and Reality* (p. 528).[19]

"It is as true that God is permanent and the World fluent, as that the World is permanent and God is fluent," Whitehead writes. Clearly 'is as true as' here is not intended to introduce a comparative notion of truth, but to indicate rather that both of the 'that'-clauses are true. God is permanent in view of the unchanging, *tota simul*, primordial valuations, and the World is fluent regarded as consisting of fluent actualities. But the World is also permanent as being just one cosmos, the fusion of the virtual class of all objects. And God is fluent in the sense that each and every fluent object is given a status within the primordial envisagement.

"It is as true to say that God is one and the World many, as that the World is one and God many." Both God and the World are definable by means of Russellian descriptions as being fusions of appropriate non-null virtual classes. And they are both many in the sense that the cardinality of the membership in those classes is very large.

"It is as true to say that, in comparison with the World, God is actual

---

19. Cf. *Whitehead's Categoreal Scheme*, pp. 56–58.

eminently, as that, in comparison with God, the World is actual eminently." Whitehead does not use 'eminently' here as a special technical term. This sentence may best be glossed perhaps by noting that God is more actual eminently than the World in containing the full ideality, the full ought-to-be or "reality," of the latter. But then the World is more actual eminently than God in the sense of containing all actualities, all processes, comings into and passings out of being, and the like.

"It is as true to say that the World is immanent in God, as that God is immanent in the World." The objects and events of the World are essential ingredients in the primordial valuations. But also these valuations are active forces in the World as ideals or standards to be heeded or obeyed. Similarly, "it is as true to say that God transcends the World as that the World transcends God." Surely the former holds, God being the transcendent good, even the "wholly other," although of course concerned with the entities of the World. But the World transcends God in being wholly distinct from it, in containing no primordial valuations whatsoever.

Finally, "it is as true to say that God creates the World as to say that the World creates God." The World creates God in the sense of contributing the entities with which the primordial valuations are concerned. Now, in what sense does God create the World? The word 'creates' has not been introduced as a technical term above. It may be taken here in the loose Whiteheadian sense (essentially that of the *Timaeus*) of 'is one of the creative factors of'. In this sense clearly God creates the World, giving it not only its determinative laws but its ideality as well. This view accords well with the opening lines of *Genesis* in *The New English Bible* (1970) translation: "In the beginning of creation, when God made heaven and earth, the earth was without form and void, . . . God said, 'Let there be light', and there was light; and God saw that the light was good. . . ." Incidentally, it is fascinating to observe — in all seriousness — that *language* must be present "in the beginning of creation," according to this account. It is not just that God said so and so, but that what is said, statements of primordial valuations, themselves contain a linguistic item and are thus metalinguistic.

Bowman Clarke is one of the very few who have reflected upon the Whiteheadian God — or indeed upon any other conception of God — with the necessary logical care.[20] He does this in terms of Good-

---

20. *Op. cit.*, pp. 157 ff.

man's theory of *qualia*[21] using the calculus of individuals. There are points of parallel between his treatment and the foregoing, but there are important differences as well. Clarke accepts the bifurcational view and it will therefore be of interest to compare and contrast his treatment with that above.

Clarke thinks the bifurcational view is needed in natural theology mainly because of a "major difficulty in the classical position" in connection with time and omniscience. "God sees all things together, not successively," according to the *Summa Theologica* (I, q.14, a.7), and "although contingent things become actual successively, nevertheless God knows contingent things not successively, as they are in their own being, as we do, but simultaneously" (I, q.14, a.13). The result is that, according to Clarke, the classical view cannot take time seriously. Note that this criticism does not apply to the view put forward above, however, for a theory of temporal flow is built into the theory fundamentally. Events are interrelated by means of suitable relations, including a relation of *earlier than* or *before than*. But further, the predicates entering into the primordial obligations may themselves be concerned with temporal matters. These predicates, remember, are of the form

$$`\{e_1...e_k \ni (-e_1,...,e_k-)\}`,$$

where '$(-e_1,...,e_k-)$' may contain the symbol for the before-than relation in all manner of ways, specifying how e_1, ..., e_k are temporally related. In this way the primordial valuations may concern time fundamentally. Also, as noted above, 'simultaneous' in connection with the primordial valuations is not to be understood in any temporal sense but only in the Fregean tense of timelessness. Thus time is placed *in* God's envisagement, without making him a temporal entity or locating him in the temporal flow. Similar remarks, incidentally, would apply to space and other physical notions or constructs. Note also that even mention of specific times, or of times relatively specific, may be incorporated in the primordial valuations. In this way primordial valuations concerning even dated occurrences may be expressed.

This is not the occasion to reflect upon Clarke's explication of what is essentially the Whiteheadian God on a Goodmanian basis. But two or three comments are in order. Clarke takes the primordial nature to be the sum of all "eternal individuals" and the consequent nature to be the all-inclusive individual. For the consequent nature, this procedure seems satisfactory. But for the primordial nature, are not the

---

21. N. Goodman, *The Structure of Appearance* (Cambridge: Harvard University Press, 1951).

"valuations" of what ought to be and of waht must be left out of account? It would seem so, and it is difficult to see how they could be accommodated other than within a theory considerably more extended than Goodman's. In particular, processes and acts must be recognized as over and above both concrete individuals and/or qualia, and also a method of incorporating intentionality in the handling of the ought-to-be. (See also X below.)

A few final comments concerning Whitehead. The view put forward above is thought to provide an improvement on his conception in several respects, bringing it closer in spirit to St. Thomas as well as to modern science.

The existence of God, according to Whitehead, is "the ultimate irrationality" (*Science and the Modern World,* p. 256). He notes that "there cannot be value without antecedent standards of value, to discriminate the acceptance or rejection of what is before the envisaging mode of activity [an actual occasion]. Thus there is an antecedent limitation among values, introducing contraries, grades, and oppositions. . . . God is the ultimate limitation, and His existence is the ultimate irrationality. For no reason can be given for just that limitation which it stands in His nature to impose. . . . No reason can be given for the nature of God, because that nature is the ground of rationality."

Now this is curious terminology indeed. Why should the existence of a source for or ground of rationality itself be called "irrational'? One may as well regard the source of the good as an ultimate evil, or the source of all perfection itself as an imperfection. Or the existence of science itself as unscientific. To be sure, there is a shift of level in the use of the adjectives here, but it is eminently natural to apply to the same adjective to the source as to what issues from that source. A person is said to be a kind person if and only if his acts are kind, generous if and only if he performs generous acts, and so on. It seems better then to regard God not only as the source of all rational valuations, but himself as rational in the most fundamental sense.

Once all this is said, the difficult problem remains as to why the primordial envisagement is just the way it is and no other. Perhaps the best we can do here is to make the factual assertion that this is the way it is, so far as we are able to ascertain. There is also the difficult question as to how we know what the primordial envisagement is. Here there is not only our factual and theoretical knowledge to rely on, but also tradition, authority, the scriptures of the given religion, and the teachings of its Church. Any of these may of course turn out to be erroneous and subject to subsequent correction and refinement. And where these leave off, faith may begin. There need be no quarrel amongst these. '*Fides quaerens intellectum*' may as truly be said of a natural theology as may its converse.

Whitehead's failure to give the primordial valuations a suitable moral and religious status — or indeed a scientific one — is due in part perhaps to his assimilation of human persons to sums or nexūs of actual occasions. But the human being is really quite special and needs to be handled with care. His hopes, fears, loves, desires, prayers, sacrifices, adorations, and attempts to discover and formulate scientific laws, to create works of art, and so on, are *sui generis*, so far as we know, and differ wholly from those that might be ascribed to animals, vegetables, and inert (or comparatively inert) actual occasions. In grouping all such entities together, it seems, Whitehead never does full justice to the moral, religious, and noetic differentiae of human persons.

Also the metaphysical underpinning of the theory here of course differs remarkably from that of Whitehead. There are no eternal objects, only virtual classes and relations. There is no theory of prehensions here, only the theory of specific nonlogical relations. There are no "propositions" here but instead a unified semantics incorporating the hierarchy of languages. There are no "actual occasions," but merely the things, events, acts, states, and processes, expressions for which play a fundamental role in the analysis of the structure of our ordinary language.[22] Logic here is exclusively first-order logic, not of higher order. Finally, mathematics is not viewed as a fragment of higher-order logic, as with Whitehead, but *sui generis* and of a more constructivistic kind. The only residue of Whiteheadian doctrine here is in the forms (1) and (3) required for spelling out the primordial valuations, although Whitehead himself nowhere suggests such forms.

The precise temporal status of Whitehead's God is controversial. His consequent nature surely is temporal in the sense of containing all temporal occurrences as *parts*. The conception of God above, like the primordial nature (according to some interpreters at least), is wholly atemporal. This seems a most natural conception, in accord with a great tradition, on the one hand, and with the demands of theoretical simplicity, on the other. It seems rather unreasonable to require God's nature to be any more intertwined with time than with space, temperature, mass, or other items of concern to theoretical physics. It should be intertwined no more, no less, it would seem. If time is given a special status in theology, a very considerable — and indeed undesir-

---

22. Cf. especially *Semiotics and Linguistic Structure*.

able and irrelevant — theoretical complication results. If the foregoing kind of view is tenable, this complication is not needed.[23]

A perennial difficulty with metaphysical theories of the nature of
God is that of connecting them satisfactorily with the object of religious worship, the personal "God we seek" and pray to, the Living God
of the Old Testament. The view put forward above, and indeed
Whitehead's also, are no exceptions in this regard. If we give the divine envisagement an appropriate moral and religious status, however, the basis is laid, it would seem, for bridging this gap. To show
this in detail would be a long, arduous undertaking, and we cannot be
assured of success in advance. Nonetheless, there is good reason to
think that the foregoing account has promise of enabling us to do this
satisfactorily.

Theologians and metaphysicians not fond of modern logic, systematic semiotics, and the like, may think that "it is philistine to lay the
rude hands of logic" (C. I. Lewis's phrase) upon matters so exalted as
the primordial nature of God. But the kind of clarity and exactitude
arrived at here — and indeed aimed at by most of the historically
great writers on this subject who have understood the purport of logic
— cannot be attained in any way other, it would seem, than by pro-
mulgating a logical system. In so doing there is progress in clarification
and explicitness, and the desideratum of "complete humility before
logic" is achieved, to some extent at least. In any case, and whatever
the defects of the foregoing, the "distant future" spoken of by
Whitehead, when an expanded symbolic logic "will proceed to conquer ethics and theology," is already at hand.

---

23. In some basic respects the view put forward here is akin to those of Norris Clarke
and Lewis Ford. See W. Norris Clarke, "A New Look at the Immutability of God," in
God Knowable and Unknowable ed. by R. Roth (New York: Fordham University Press,
1973), pp. 43–73. And also Lewis Ford, "Boethius and Whitehead on Time and Eternity," *International Philosophical Quarterly* VIII (1968): 38–67; "The Non-Temporality of
Whitehead's God," *ibid.* XIII (1973): 347–376; and "The Immutable God and Father
Clarke," *The New Scholasticism* XLIX (1975): 189–199.

CHAPTER III

Some Thomistic Properties
of Primordiality

Stemmata quid faciunt, quid prodest, Pontice, longo, Sanguine censeri?

In trying to *préciser* the character of the primordial God we should realize straightway, it would seem, that no *physical* attributes or properties should properly be ascribed to him. God should be given no spatial location, no temperature, no mass, no density, no coefficient of expansion, or the like. Similarly he should be given no *temporal* location either. He is neither before or after or contemporaneous with this or that physical occurrence in some time-system in accord, say, with the special theory of relativity. Nor is he to be located temporally in accord with any other physical theory of time. This observation might be thought supererogatory, but some process theologians seem to deny it. In some sense surely, we wish to be able to say that God is atemporal or eternal. Even Whitehead, the prince of the process theologians, seems to allow this for the primordial nature.

St. Thomas Acquinas has put the matter well in noting that "eternity is known from two facts: first, because what is eternal is interminable — that is, has no beginning or end (that is, no term either way); secondly, because eternity itself has no succession, being simultaneously whole" (*Summa Theologica,* I, q.10, a.2). This passage is not without ambiguity, however. Are we to understand it as saying that it is *false* that what is eternal has both beginning and end and that it is false that what is eternal has succession? Or are we to understand it as saying that it is *meaningless* even to say so? False statements are not therewith meaningless, it should be recalled. So-called meaningless statements are neither true nor false, nor are they indeed even statements. It will make an enormous difference in our natural theology as to how this ambiguity is resolved. If in the former way, we will have upon our hands the difficult problem of showing precisely and in detail how physical time and the divine nature are interrelated within what, it is hoped, would be the latest and best established contemporary physical theory.[1] And howsoever this would be worked out, God would emerge as an extraordinary entity, an exception to physical laws and to metaphysical principles. It is precisely this that Whitehead wished to avoid. God should not be an exception to but rather the chief exemplification of the metaphysical scheme adapted.

It would seem extraordinary if the very internal structure of natural theology should have to base itself upon the latest achievements of physical science. Whatever God's nature is, it is the same *in principio et nunc et semper et in saeculo saeculorum,* and our view of it should not have to change with every scientific advance. It is rather the other way around in a certain way: the scientific advance is already contained in God's envisagement.

It would seem better then, in view of these considerations, to formulate theology in such a way as to exclude as meaningless all temporal talk from a discussion of God's nature, just as we exclude all talk of physical temperature, mass, velocity, and the like. All temporal or quasi-temporal words should thus be used with caution. Strictly we should not even use the words 'simultaneous', or 'succession', or the like, unless they are explicitly defined in just the sense that is needed. To say that an eternal being is "simultaneously whole" is misleading without an exact definition of the phrase. And howsoever defined it should presumably then follow not only that God is eternal but that he is uniquely so. This will be provable, however, only *after* a theory of time and eternity has been introduced into the system. That theory itself should be of the best scientific provenance available, but subject of course to change and improvement. Hence the theorem concerning eternity will be *relative to a given theory of time* with respect to which 'eternal' is given meaning. Note that this theorem contrasts sharply with the analogous theorem if physical time were built into our theology at the outset, for then some one time-scheme is declared the true or fundamental one.

But we are getting ahead of our story. Let us start with the great *locus classicus* of discussions of God's attributes, the *Summa Theologica* I,i, and reflect upon them one by one. This will be done on the basis of the conception of God as a *fusion of primordial valuations* discussed in II above. This latter results from that of Whitehead's primordial nature of God by giving the primordial valuations an exact logico-metaphysical framework. This framework is thought to be more acceptable than that of Whitehead on several grounds. Note in particu-

---

1. Cf. Paul Fitzgerald, "Relativity Physics and the God of Process Philosophy," *Process Studies* 2 (1972): 251–276.

lar that no place is allowed for the consequent nature of God, which, it is claimed, is not needed. Also eternal objects are rejected in favor of *virtual* classes and relations, a step bringing the theory closer to Aristotle and St. Thomas of course than to Plato.

The logic presupposed is merely that of first order, augmented with the calculus of individuals and a theory of events, states, acts, processes, and the like.[2] It is only with the addition of these latter that modern philosophic logic may be said to have come of age; for it is only with them that we have for the first time a sufficiently pliable logic to be of genuine help in analyzing and clarifying the really important philosophical issues. The mathematical theory of sets has proved to be merely obfuscatory here, even though it has been widely cultivated within recent decades by mathematicians and philosophers alike. Set theory, like that of the Platonic forms, it has been contended, has built "between thought and the world of sense an insuperable barrier of essences, a barrier that the human intellect . . . [is] never able to cross."[3] (Cf., however, XVI and XVII below.)

First let us recall a few principles concerning God's nature and existence that have already been established in the system. The first is that God *exists* as a unique entity, in the sense of 'exists' appropriate for Russellian descriptions.

$$\vdash \text{E! God.}$$

Further God is totally *other* in the sense of being distinct from all objects.

$$\vdash (e)(\text{Obj}\, e \supset \sim e = \text{God}).$$

The objects are regarded as just the entities other than primordial valuations or compounds of them.

A fundamental contention of St. Thomas is that God's essence is the same as his being (q.3, a.3 and 4) and this view is intimately connected with the Aristotelian doctrines of genera, species, causation, and the like. Can we make sense of this contention independent of those doctrines? The "essence" of God is given here by the definition

$$\text{'God' abbreviates '(Fu'F)',}$$

where F is the virtual class of all primordial valuations, and (Fu'F) is

---

2. As in II above and in *Whitehead's Categoreal Scheme and Other Papers, Events, Reference, and Logical Form,* and *Semiotics and Linguistic Structure.*

3. Quoted from Anton Pegis in *Basic Writings of Saint Thomas Aquinas* (New York: Random House, 1945), Vol. One, Introduction, p. xlvii.

the fusion of that class. This fusion might even be said to *be* the essence of God, the membership of F totally determining his nature. The thorem — but not the definition, note — that

$$\vdash God = (Fu`F)$$

then states that God is identical with his own essence. We also have immediately that

$$\vdash E!God \equiv (E\textit{e})e \in F,$$

so that God exists (in the descriptional sense) if and only if the class determining his essence exists (in the sense appropriate to virtual classes), i.e., if and only if F has a member. And note that God is the *only* entity of which this can be said. We may see this as follows.

Consider any individual constant 'j', say, *defined* as '($\imath e \cdot e \in G$)' for some suitable G regarded as determining j's essence. Then it is *not* the case that

$$E!j \equiv (E\textit{e})e \in G,$$

but only that

$$\vdash E!j \equiv (E\textit{e})(e \in G \cdot (e')(e' \in G \supset e' = e)).$$

And if 'j' is a *primitive* individual constant, then

$$\vdash E!j \equiv {\sim} Null\, j,$$

where 'Null j' expresses that j is the null individual. In a genuine sense, then, we see that God is the one and only entity whose existence is equivalent to the existence of its definitional essence.

Let 'Body *e*' express that *e* is a material body, i.e., an object having such and such physical characteristics. God not being an object, he cannot *a fortiori* be a material body, so that (q.3, a.1)

$$\vdash (e)(Body\, e \supset {\sim} e = God).$$

Similarly where 'Move *e*' expresses that *e* is a body capable of motion, we have that

$$\vdash (e)(Move\, e \supset {\sim} e = God).$$

And where 'Mat *e*' expresses that *e* is some portion of matter — whatever that is — and 'P' stands for the part-whole relation between individuals, we have (q.3, a.3) that

$$\vdash (e)(Mat\, e \supset {\sim} e\, P\, God).$$

47

These principles are a bit naive, no doubt, being based on an out-moded physics. Even so, we may let them stand for the moment.

A few metalinguistic properties of 'God' should be noted. 'God' is neither a genus-word nor a species-word (q.3, a.5), these latter being virtual-class expressions. Similarly 'God' is not a non-logical virtual-class expression, and hence not a word for an "accidental." (We may say that 'F' is an *accidental* property-word in 'Fa' provided 'Fa' is true (factually or accidentally true) but not logically so, 'a' here being an individual constant.) And similarly 'God' is not a word for a form or idea, but for an individual. Nor is 'God' a word for a *society* of occasions, but only for the fusion of the appropriate society.

"God is truly and absolutely simple," Augustine noted (*De Trin.*, VI (PL 42, 928)), and St. Thomas carries this over *sans phrase* (q.3, a.7). But note how 'simple' is construed: ". . . there is neither composition of quantitative parts in God, since He is not a body; nor composition of form and matter; nor does His nature differ from His *suppositum*; nor His essence from His being; neither is there in Him composition of genus and difference, nor of subject and accident. Therefore it is clear that God is in no way composite, but is altogether simple. . . ." No difficulty arises in accommodating this contention here. However, there is another sense in which God *should* be regarded as composite, namely, as the logical sum (perhaps even a countably infinite one — perhaps even a non-countably infinite one?) of all primordial valuations. Where $e_1, e_2, \ldots$ is the list of these, we have that

$$\text{God} = (e_1 \cup e_2 \cup \ldots),$$

where '$\cup$' is the sign for the operation of summation. Even so, of course, all the summands here are closely similar in structure, so that God is a sum of similars, not of entities remarkably disparate from one another.

Nothing technical has been said thus far concerning causation. The *secunda via* (q.2, a.3) requires fundamental use of a relation of efficient causation. Let us follow Donald Davidson for the moment in taking tentatively

$$'e_1 \text{ Cause } e_2'$$

to express that event e_1 causes e_2 in the efficient sense.[4] Then of course God may significantly be said to cause or to be caused. Presumably one would have then that

$$\sim (Ee)e \text{ Cause God}$$

---

4. See his "Causal Relations," *The Journal of Philosophy* 64 (1967): 691–703.

and that

$$(e)(\sim e \text{ P God} \supset \text{God Cause } e).$$

However, the key relation of Cause needs a good deal of further analysis before we have any sufficiently clear statements to be adapted here.

God cannot "enter into the composition of anything, either as a formal or a material principle" (q.3, a.8). Clearly

$$\vdash \sim \text{Mat God}$$

and hence

$$\vdash (e)(\text{Mat } e \supset \sim \text{God P } e),$$

where we assume that

$$\vdash (e_1)(e_2)((\text{Mat } e_1 \bullet e_2 \text{ P } e_1 \bullet \sim e_2 = \text{N}) \supset \text{Mat } e_2).$$

Likewise 'God' not being a form-word, expressions of the sort 'God e' are not false but meaningless. ('N' here stands for the null entity.[5])

The meaning of 'perfect' or 'perfection' is to be articulated wholly by reference to the primordial valuations. To say that

$$a \text{ PrOblgd } e_1,\ldots,e_k,$$

for example, is to say that the k-place predicate a is *primordially obliged* to apply to e_1, ..., e_k, as in II above. And to say this is to say that it is *perfect*, or *ideal*, or *good to the highest possible degree*, that a do so. There are accordingly at least four senses of 'perfect' to be distinguished, depending upon whether an *object* e_1 is said to be perfect, a *predicate a*, an *act of obliging*, or *God* himself. For an object to be perfect with respect to predicate a is to have that predicate primordially obliged to apply to it and actually to do so. And then an object e is said to be perfect in all respects provided all k-place predicates primordially obliged to apply to e_1, ..., e_k actually do so and e is one of e_1, ..., e_k. Thus we may let

'PerfObj e' abbreviate '(Obj e • $(a)(a$ PrOblgd $e \supset a$ Den $e) \bullet$ (a) $(e_1)(e_2)((a$ PrOblgd $e_1,e_2 \bullet (e = e_1 \text{ v } e = e_2)) \supset a$ Den $e_1,e_2) \bullet \ldots \bullet$ $(a)(e_1)\ldots(e_n)((a$ PrOblgd $e_1,\ldots,e_n \bullet (e = e_1 \text{ v } \ldots \text{ v } e = e_n)) \supset a$ Den $e_1,\ldots,e_n))$'.

The use of the numerical parameters 'k' and 'n' here is as in II above. We let some integer n be the degree of the predicate of highest degree entering into any primordial valuation. Thus no primordial

<hr>

5. As in "Of Time and the Null Individual." Note that $e_2 = \text{N} \equiv \text{Null } e_2$.

valuation will concern a predicate of degree $> n$. Suppose further that for each $k \leqq n$, some primordial valuation concerns a predicate of degree k. In reflecting upon the primordial valuations, then, we need consider only predicates of each and every degree $\leqq n$. 'Den' here is the predicate for k-place *denotation*, so that 'a Den $e_1,...,e_k$' expresses that the k-place predicate actually does apply to $e_1, ..., e_k$ in this order.

Perfect objects are those perfect in all possible respects in accord with the primordial obligations. It may indeed be questioned whether there ever has been, is, or will be any object perfect in this sense.

But surely there are perfect predicates, namely, those entering into the primordial obligations.

'PerfPred a' abbreviates '$(Ee_1)...(Ee_n)(a$ PrOblgd e_1 v a PrOblgd e_1,e_2 v ... v a PrOblgd $e_1,...,e_n)$'.

Also there are perfect *acts*, and we might think of these as being just the acts of primordial obliging. We might let

'PerfAct e' abbreviate '$(Ea)(Ee_1)...(Ee_n)(<a,\text{PrOblgd},e_1>e$ v ... v $<a,\text{PrOblgd},e_1,...,e_n>e)$'.

But this would not quite do. The primordial valuations encompass more than the primordial obligations. We let

'a PrPrmtd $e_1,...,e_k$'

express, as in II above, that a is primordially *permitted* to apply to $e_1, ...,$ e_k;

'a PrPrhbtd $e_1,...,e_k$',

that a is primordially *prohibited* from applying to $e_1, ..., e_k$; and

'a PrDtrmnd $e_1,...,e_k$',

that a is primordially *determined* to apply to $e_1, ..., e_k$. The primordial permissions include the obligations and determinations, everything (so to speak) being either permitted or prohibited. (Various principles concerning these notions are spelled out in the previous paper.) God's perfection comprises more than merely his act of obliging; it must include all the permissions and prohibitions as well. Thus we must let

'PerfAct e' abbreviate rather '$(Ea)(Ee_1)...(Ee_n)(<a,$ PrPrmtd$,e_1>e$ v $<a,\text{PrPrhbtd},e_1>e$ v ... v $<a,\text{PrPrmtd},e_1,...,e_n>e$ v $<a,\text{PrPrhbtd},e_1,...,e_n>e)$.

It follows then that

$\vdash (e)(\text{PerfAct}\, e \supset e\, \text{P God})$.

Note that the perfect acts are not something that God *does* or performs, they are — taken collectively — what God *is*. Or, put another way, we could say that his being *is* his performance. Thus God is *pure act,* his whole constitution consisting of perfect acts. Of course the sum of any two perfect acts might itself be regarded as a perfect act, in which case God is the one and only *maximal* perfect act. If we require that

$$(e)(e')((\text{PerfAct}\,e \cdot \text{PerfAct}\,e') \supset \text{PerfAct}\,(e \cup e')),$$

presumably then

$$\text{God} = (\text{Fu}'\{e\ni\text{PerfAct}\,e\}),$$

the perfect acts then being just those constituting his essence.

Let hereafter

'$a\ \text{PrVltd}\,e_1,...,e_k$'   abbreviate   '$(a\ \text{PrPrmtd}\,e_1, ...,e_k \vee a\ \text{PrPrhbtd}\,e_1,...,e_k)$',

the valuations consisting of just the permissions (which include both the determinations and obligations) and prohibitions together.

Observe that (q.4, a.2) "all the perfections of all things are in God. . . ." Literally this may be taken to mean that all the perfect predicates of any object *e* are in God in the sense of being predicates of some primordial valuation with respect to *e*. Thus

⊢ $(e)(a)((\text{PerfPred}\,a \cdot \text{Obj}\,e) \supset (Ee')(Ee_1)...(Ee_n)(<a,\text{Pr-}$ $\text{Vltd},e>e'$ v $(<a,\text{PrVltd},e_1,e_2>e' \cdot (e = e_1 \vee e = e_2))$ v ... v $(<a,\text{PrVltd},e_1,...,e_n>e' \cdot (e = e_1 \vee ... \vee e = e_n))))$.

This law is a logical consequence of the Principle of Primordial Completeness. Let us refer to it as the *Principle of Perfection.* (The Principle of Primordial Completeness, it will be recalled from II, is that

⊢ $(e_1)...(e_k)((\text{Obj}\,e_1 \cdot ... \cdot \text{Obj}\,e_k) \supset (Ea)a\ \text{PrOblgd}\,e_1,...,e_k)$, for $k = 1,2,...,n$.)

The primordially good, or good to the highest degree, has been discussed to some extent in the previous paper and need not be repeated here. But "goodness and being are really the same, and differ only in idea" (q.5, a.1) and "in idea being is prior to goodness" (q.5, a.2) in the sense of being definable in terms of it. Further, "any being, as being, is good. For all being, as being, has actuality and is in some sense perfect . . ." (q.5, a.3) This does not say that every being is good or perfect, but only that every being *as being* is *in some sense* perfect. We may interpret this in accord with the Principle of Primordial Completeness to say that every object is covered by at least one primordial obligation; that every object has its perfection, so to speak, at least in God's envisagement if not in actuality.

The notion of a final cause has not been introduced thus far. But clearly God is the final cause of every object and predicate in the sense that that object or predicate is covered by appropriate primordial valuations. More specifically, just these valuations may be said to be the final causes of any object or predicate, and by a kind of summation God himself is the final cause of all objects or predicates (q.5, a.4). Thus

$$'e \text{ FinalCause } e'' \text{ abbreviates } '((Ea)(Ee_1)...(Ee_n)$$
$$((<a,\text{PrVltd},e_1>e \cdot (e' = e_1 \vee e' = a)) \vee (<a,\text{PrVltd},e_1,e_2>e \cdot$$
$$(e' = e_1 \vee e' = e_2 \vee e' = a)) \vee ... \vee (<a,\text{PrVltd},e_1,...,e_n>e \cdot (e' = e_1 \vee$$
$$... \vee e' = e_n \vee e' = a))) \vee (e = \text{God} \cdot (\text{Obj } e' \vee \text{PredCon}_1 e' \vee ... \vee$$
$$\text{PredCon}_n e')))',$$

and

$$\vdash (e')(\text{God FinalCause } e' \equiv (Ee)(e \text{ FinalCause } e' \cdot e \text{ P God} \cdot \sim \text{God P } e)).$$

And of course we must have also that

$$\vdash (e)((\text{Obj } e \vee \text{PredCon}_1 e \vee ... \vee \text{PredCon}_n e) \supset \text{God FinalCause } e).$$

Concerning final causation, there is perhaps no more to be said. It is all contained in this last principle. However, concerning the good, and the varieties of human good, much remains of course to be said. The above must suffice here, however, where we are concerned only with the properties of the primordially good. This latter has to do only with the obligations. To discuss the merely human good, the other primordial permissions and the primordial prohibitions must be brought in fundamentally.

The infinitude of God (q.7) has already been commented upon. But whether this infinitude be countable or non-countable remains an open question.

In what sense now may God be said to be *in* all things (q.8, a.1)? ". . . not, indeed as part of their essence, nor as an accident, but as an agent is present to that upon which it acts. For an agent must be joined to that on which it acts immediately, and reach it by its power . . ." Strictly God does not *act* upon anything at all, but still he may be said to be the *agent* of all primordial goodness or perfection. Since every object is covered by primordial valuations, every object then has God as an agent. And similarly God is in all places (q.8, a.2) and hence everywhere, places themselves being a species of objects, or at least

52

presumably determined in terms of the objects that occupy them. God is in all places in the sense that they too are covered by primordial valuations. And if the handling of efficient and final causality above is sound, God may also be said to be present in all objects in the sense of being their efficient cause, and also their final cause. "Therefore, God is in all things by His power, inasmuch as all things are subject to His power [as efficient cause]; He is by His presence in all things, inasmuch as all things are bare and open to His eyes [or covered by the primordial valuations]; He is in all things by His essence, inasmuch as He is present to all as the [final] cause of their being."

Further (q.8, a.4) God is uniquely the efficient and final causes of all objects, so that

$$\vdash (e)(e')((\text{Obj}\,e' \cdot e \text{ Cause } e') \supset \text{God Cause}\,e'),$$

and of course

$$\vdash (e)((e')(\text{Obj}\,e' \supset e \text{ FinalCause } e') \supset (e')(\text{Obj}\,e' \supset \text{God FinalCause}\,e')).$$

The latter follows immediately from what has already been noted. The former, however, postulates something genuinely new concerning the relation of efficient causation and is perhaps somewhat dubious.

Movement and change in no way pertain to the primordial valuations as such, so that God must be immutable, if mutability is defined in terms of them (q.9, a.1). Thus if 'Mut e' expresses that e is capable of mutability, presumably it would hold that

$$\vdash (e)(\text{Mut}\,e \supset \text{Move}\,e).$$

Hence also

$$\vdash (e)(\text{Mut}\,e \supset \sim e\,\text{P God}),$$

in view of the (naive) principle concerning movement cited above. Further (q.9, a.2), God is the *only* immutable entity, so that we must have also that

$$\vdash (e)(\sim e\,\text{P God} \supset \text{Mut}\,e).$$

The latter is provable from the presumed physical law that

$$\vdash (e)(\text{Obj}\,e \supset \text{Mut}\,e).$$

(This law need not violate the supposed abstract character of mathematical entities, for these may be handled as suitable conceptual constructs and do not require the postulation of a separate realm of immutable beings such as sets, classes, functions, and the like.[6])

_____

6. See "On Mathematics and the Good," in *Whitehead's Categoreal Scheme Etc.*

The atemporal or eternal character of the primordial valuations has been noted above. In the development of time-theory within the system, all objects are to be given suitable temporal location. Thus the primordial valuations and compounds of them would emerge as the only atemporal entities (q.10, a.3).

The unity of God has already been commented on to some extent. It is interesting that (in q.11, a.3) unity is spoken of in three senses, all of them provided for above. First, of course, God exists and "it is impossible that there should be many Gods," so that

$$\vdash \text{E!God.}$$

Secondly, "God comprehends in Himself the whole perfection of being," so that we have both that

$$\vdash \text{God} = (\text{Fu'}\{e \ni \text{PerfAct}\, e\})$$

and the Principle of Perfection cited above. Thirdly, there is the (valuational) unity of the world. "For all things that exist are seen to be ordered [valuationally] to each other since some serve others." This order is given primordially, every object being ordained with respect to a multiplicity of relations to other objects.

Let us turn now to the questions concerning God's knowledge (q.14). "In God there exists the most perfect knowledge. . . . Hence knowledge is not a quality in God, nor a habit; but substance and pure act" (a.1.) According to this God's knowledge, i.e., the kind of knowledge that God has, is of everything covered in the primordial envisagement. It is thus pure act. Further (a.2), "God understands [or knows] Himself through Himself" and (a.3) "knows Himself as much as He is knowable; and for that reason He perfectly comprehends Himself." God's knowledge is thus *sui generis* and hence we may define 'God-Knows e' in its own right, as in II above, and not as an instance of 'e' Knows e' for *variable* 'e'. To accommodate all instances of God's knowledge, we must let 'God-Knows e' express that e is one of the objects or predicates entering into the primordial envisagement in one way or another. Further, it must be defined so as to include God himself among the objects of knowledge. Thus we may let

'God-Knows e' abbreviate '$((\text{E}a)(\text{E}e_1)...(\text{E}e_n)((a \,\text{PrVltd}\, e_1 \cdot (e = e_1 \vee e = a)) \vee ... \vee (a \,\text{PrVltd}\, e_1,...,e_n \cdot (e = e_1 \vee ... \vee e = e_n \vee e = a)))$
$\vee \text{PerfAct}\, e \vee e = (\text{Fu'}\{e' \ni \text{PerfAct}\, e'\})))$'.

Note that we have now as immediate consequences that

$$\vdash (e)(\text{PerfAct}\, e \supset \text{God-Knows}\, e),$$

$$\vdash (e)((\text{Obj}\, e \lor \text{PredCon}_1\, e \lor ... \lor \text{PredCon}_n\, e) \supset \text{God-Knows}\, e),$$

and

$$\vdash \text{God-Knows God}.$$

Also *a fortiori*,

$$\vdash (e)((\text{PerfObj}\, e \lor \text{PerfPred}\, e) \supset \text{God-Knows}\, e).$$

Somewhat similar remarks apply to 'God's intellect' (q.14, a.4). "It must be said that the act of God's intellect is His substance. . . . His act of understanding must be His essence and His being." This seems merely to reiterate that

$$\vdash \text{God} = (\text{Fu'}\{e \ni \text{PerfAct}\, e\}),$$

and 'God's Intellect' is merely another way of writing 'God'.

St. Thomas glosses St. Augustine's 'God does not behold [know] anything out of Himself' (*Lib. 83 Quaest.*, q.46 (PL 40, 30)) by saying (q.14, a.5) that this passage "is not to be taken in such a way as if God saw [knew] nothing that was outside Himself, but in the sense that what is outside Himself He does not see [know] except in Himself . . ." Precisely. All perfect acts and fusions of such, all objects, and all predicates are "in" God in the sense of being covered primordially.

All this is of course concerned with God's knowledge *de re* (of objects) and not *de dicto*. Let us write 'God-Knows$_{Re}$' hereafter to remind us of this. "Proper knowledge," however, is *de dicto* and "to have proper knowledge of things is to know them not only in general, but as they are distinct from each other" (q.14, a.6). But things are distinct from one another in having something true of one but not of the other. All that is desired here may be achieved if we let

'God-Knows$_{Dicto}\, a$' abbreviate '(Sent $a \cdot (e)(\text{God-Knows}_{Re}\, e \supset \ulcorner\{e' \ni a\}\urcorner \text{Den}\, e))$'.

To allow for knowledge *de dicto* (of sentences), this definition can be given only within the metametalanguage, which however contains the metalanguage as a proper part. (Note here of course that the vacuous abstract $\ulcorner\{e' \ni a\}\urcorner$ is universal or null depending on whether the sentence *a* is true or false.) We then have immediately, in view of an appropriate semantical truth-definition — cf. XIII below — that

$$\vdash (a)(\text{God-Knows}_{Dicto}\, a \equiv \text{Tr}\, a).$$

55

And hence in particular of course

$$\vdash \ \ulcorner \sim e_1 = e_2 \supset \text{God-Knows}_{\text{Dicto}} \ \ulcorner \sim e = e_2 \urcorner \urcorner \ ,$$

where in place of 'e_1' and 'e_2' any individual constants are inserted. Thus God knows of distinct things that they are distinct. And likewise

$$\vdash \ \ulcorner (a)(\text{PredCon}_1 \, a \supset (a \ \text{Den} \ e \supset \text{God-Knows}_{\text{Dicto}} \, (a \frown e)) \urcorner \ ,$$

where in place of 'e' an individual constant is inserted. Thus God knows of any particular e precisely the properties (so to speak) that pertain to it. In this way God may be said to know the *essence* of e, that essence being just the predicates that truly apply to it. We may define

$$\ulcorner \text{God-Knows}_{\text{Ess}} \, e \urcorner \quad \text{as} \quad \ulcorner (a)(a \ \text{Den} \ e \supset \text{God-Knows}_{\text{Dicto}} \, (a \frown e)) \urcorner \ ,$$

where in place of 'e' an individual constant is inserted. Whence we have that

$$\vdash \ \ulcorner \text{Obj} \, e \supset \text{God-Knows}_{\text{Ess}} \, e \urcorner \ .$$

And similarly for predicates also.

"In the divine knowledge there is no discursiveness" (q.14, a.7) in the sense of temporal succession, the primordial valuations and the semantical truth-concept being entirely atemporal. "God does not see all things in their particularity or separately, as if He looked first here and then there; but He sees all things [in their parrticularity] together at once" (St. Augustine, *De Trin.*, XV, 14 (PL 42, 1077)). Further, "it is manifest that God causes things by His intellect . . . and hence His knowledge must be the cause of things" (q.14, a.8). Clearly, in view of theorems already at hand, we have that

$$\vdash (e)(\sim e \ \text{P God} \supset (\text{God-Knows}_{\text{Re}} \, e \equiv \text{God Cause} \, e))$$

and

$$\vdash (e)((\text{Obj} \, e \ \text{v PredCon}_1 \, e \ \text{v} \dots \text{v PredCon}_n \, e) \supset (\text{God-Knows}_{\text{Re}} \, e$$
$$\equiv \text{God FinalCause} \, e)).$$

"Whatever . . . can be made, or thought [q.14, a.9], or said by the creature, as also whatever He Himself can do, are all known to God, although they are not actual. And to this extent it can be said that He has knowledge even of things that are not." Now the only thing that is not actual is the null individual, according to the logical theory presupposed here, but it may be spoken of under different linguistic descriptions.[7] The null individual taken under a given description (Fre-

---

7. Cf. G. Frege, "Über Sinn und Bedeutung," paragraph 2, and *Begriffsschrift*, §8, or *loc. cit.*

ge's *Art Des Gegebenseins*) is an intensional object. But these too may be included in the primordial valuations and thus subject to God's knowledge. (The technical details will be omitted.)

"Whoever knows a thing perfectly must know all that can occur to it. Now there are some good things to which corruption by evil may occur. Hence God would not know good things perfectly, unless He also knew evil things" (q.14, a.10). Where 'Evil e' is suitably defined to express that e is either evil primordially (and thus prohibited) or by corruption, we surely would have that

$$\vdash (e) \ (\text{Evil} \, e \supset \text{God-Knows}_{\text{Re}} \, e).$$

That God knows singular things (q.14, a.11) has already been established. And also that he knows infinite things (q.14, a.12), e.g., his own valuations, as well as future contingent things (q.14, a.13).

That "God knows all enunciations that can be formed" (q.14, a.14) is contained in the doctrine of predicates above. The primordial valuations cover in one way or another all predicates, everything enunciable — every sentence — being so by means of predicates.

Just as God is immutable, so is his knowledge (q.14, a.15). Thus not only must we have that each item of God's knowledge is immutable,

$$\vdash (e)(a)(<\text{God-Knows}_{\text{Dicto}}, a>e \supset \sim \text{Mut} \, e),$$

but also that it is immutable as a whole,

$$\vdash (e)(e = (\text{Fu}`\{e_1 \ni (Ea)<\text{God-Knows}_{\text{Dicto}}, a>e_1\}) \supset \sim \text{Mut} \, e).$$

Ideas on the present account are regarded as entities taken under given linguistic descriptions or *Arten des Gegebenseins*. An idea of what is not actual is the null individual taken under a given description. In this way ideas are posited (q.15, a.1) in the sense of being accommodated in the primordial valuations. The desired modes of description may be placed appropriately in the valuational predicates wherever needed. Many ideas are thus present in the divine mind (q.15, a.2), even many ideas of one and the same object. And further, ideas of all things whatsoever (q.15, a.3) are included, even *all* ideas of all things whatsoever, there being no ideas not enunciable.

A few further remarks on truth, which "resides primarily in the intellect, and secondarily in things according as they are related to the intellect as their source" (q.16, a.1). Let us consider only the divine intellect. Recall that

$$\vdash (a)(\text{God-Knows}_{\text{Dicto}} \, a \equiv \text{Tr} \, a),$$

57

and hence (q.16, a.5),

$$\vdash \{a \ni \text{God-Knows}_{\text{Dicto}}\, a\} = \{a \ni \text{Tr}\, a\} = \text{Tr.}$$

If the divine intellect is identified with the virtual class of what God knows *de dicto*, then his intellect *is* simply truth itself. Secondarily, truth "resides in things according as they are related to the intellect. . . ." For a truth to "reside" in a thing is for some predicate to apply truly (denote) that thing. The principle that

$$\vdash \ulcorner (a)(a \text{ Den } e \equiv \text{God-Knows}_{\text{Dicto}}\, (a \frown e)) \urcorner ,$$

together with the observation that

$$\vdash \ulcorner (a)(\text{God-Knows}_{\text{Dicto}}\, (a \frown e) \equiv \text{Tr}\, (a \frown e)) \urcorner$$

show that any given truth concerning a thing e resides in e as related to God, God of course being its "source" as both final and efficient cause.[8]

Truth, moreover, is eternal in the sense of being identical with God's intellect — ". . . because only the divine intellect is eternal, in it alone truth has eternity" (q.16, a.8). And similarly (a.9) "the truth of the divine intellect is immutable." Note how well this latter accords with the modern semantical notion of truth, which likewise is atemporal. This does not mean, of course, that 'true today', 'false tomorrow', and the like, may not be accommodated, but only that they are somewhat secondary, the fundamental notion being atemporal.[9]

The living God "has life most perfect and eternal, since His intellect is most perfect and always in act" (q.18, a.4). In this sense of course life can indeed properly be attributed to God on the basis of the foregoing. Further, "whatever is in God as understood is the very living or life of God. Now, therefore, since all things that have been made by God are in Him as things understood, it follows that all things in Him are the divine life itself" (q.18, a.5). Therefore "all things are life in God." To be life, or living in this sense, then, is merely to be covered primordially.

Just "as God's knowledge is His being, so is His willing" (q.19, a.1). God's will is included in His intellect, so to speak. Further, "God wills not only Himself, but also things other than Himself" (q.19, a.2), just

---

8. The comments here concerning God's knowledge, as well as those concerning efficient and final causation, are of course much more Thomistic than Whiteheadian, and part from the account in II above.

9. As in Tarski's famous *Der Wahrheitsbegriff in den Formalisierten Sprachen*, tr. in *Logic, Semantics, Metamathematics* (Oxfort: Clarendon Press, 1956) and the author's *Truth and Denotation*.

as, in accord with what has been established above, he knows not only himself but other things also. God's will may be wholly characterized in terms of the primordial valuations, just as his intellect is.

There are two senses in which God may be said *necessarily* to will what he wills. "God wills the being of His own goodness necessarily" (q.19, a.3) in the sense of *absolute* necessity. This is the kind of willing that attaches only to the primordial *obligations,* all goodness having their source in them. "But [also] God wills things other than Himself in so far as they are ordered to His own goodness as their end." This kind of willing is necessary *by supposition* and attaches to the primordial valuations that are neutral, so to speak, i.e., those that are neither prohibited nor obliged. (Note that even a prohibition is an obligation with respect to the negation of its predicate.) Thus everything that God wills is seen to be willed necessarily in one or the other of these two senses. And thus (q.19, a.10) God has no free choice with respect to what he wills with absolute necessity, but only with respect to what he wills necessarily by supposition.

Although God, or his intellect or will, is the cause of things other than himself (q.19, a.4), "in no wise has the will of God [itself] a cause" (q.19, a.5), as is evident from the principle above that

$$\vdash \sim (E e) e \text{ Cause God.}$$

Note also that "the will of God must needs always be fulfilled" (q.19, a.6), everything not primordially prohibited being at least permitted (even if not obliged). And of course "the will of God is entirely unchangeable" (q.19, a.7), because both God and his intellect are.

Does the will of God impose necessity on the things willed (q.19, a.8)? On some things, but not all. What is primordially determined is presumably imposed necessarily, but not what is obliged or merely permitted.

The primordially evil — mortal sin — is that which is primordially prohibited. And as we have seen, God should not be said to will this. "He in no way wills the evil of sin" (q.19, a.9). All other evils, however, are embraced in the primordial permissions.

The primordial valuations, it will be recalled, are subdivided into determinations, obligations (including the determinations), permissions (including the obligations), and prohibitions. The obligations that are not determinations are *desires,* and the permissions that are not obligations are primordially *neutral* — 'tolerations', they might be called. There are two kinds of prohibitions, based on either the determinations or the desires. (The predicate a is said to be primordially prohibited of $e_1, ..., e_k$, recall, if and only if its negative $\ulcorner \lnot a \urcorner$ is primordially obliged (determined or desired) to apply to $e_1, ..., e_k$.) Those based on the desires might be called 'detestations', those on determinations 'impossibilia'. But there is no need for the impossibilia, and it is doubtful if there are any. Now the "five signs of will" (q.19, a.12) may all, it would seem, be fitted into this classification. The matter is complex and needs a good deal of spelling out. Very roughtly and preliminarily, the Thomistic *operations* may be identified with the determinations; the *persuasions* with the desires, both (positive) *precepts* and *counsels* being subclasses of these; the *permissions* with the tolerations; and the *prohibitions*, including negative precepts, with the detestations. The structure of the divine will is complex in diverse ways, but can, it would seem, be fully characterized in terms of the foregoing.

There is of course much more to be said concerning the "real internal constitution" of God and of his relation to the creatures. The foregoing must suffice for the present, however, in getting us started in what it is to be hoped is the right direction, using some of the treasures of modern logic and semantics as our guide.

In this brief discussion of some of the primary properties of primordiality, there has been no attempt to push the theory in the direction of St. Thomas, except perhaps in the handling of causation — which no doubt is the weakest part of the foregoing. It is remarkable that, starting with a very different point of view — gained in trying to characterize precisely the logic of the primordial valuations — we end up with a view similar to that of the angelic doctor in some respects. Even so, there are always differences of interpretation. The foregoing is perhaps Thomistic in only a somewhat Pickwickian sense, and in any case puts forward only one possible rendering out of many. Nonetheless, it is almost incredible that St. Thomas could have written with such precision and depth of these primordial properties on the basis of so narrow an Aristotelian logic, on the one hand, and an inadequate physics and cosmology, on the other. The real greatness of the Thomistic conception of God shines forth in spite of the insufficiencies of its scientific and philosophical foundation.

CHAPTER IV

The Human Right
to Good and Evil

Ubi velis volunt, ubi nolis volunt ultra:
Concessa pudit ire via.

At the very end of his little book *God and the Permission of Evil*, it will
perhaps be recalled, Maritain stresses that he has not claimed "to have
furnished a perfect theory, polished, screwed down, and padlocked
on all sides."[1] Even so, he had "confidence that on God and the permission of evil, the paths . . . [he] proposed . . . are good ones" and
that his "masters and friends the theologians will one day embark
upon them," and do "better work" than he. Howsoever this may be,
we surely cannot do better than to follow in the footsteps he has provided. Fundamental theology and metaphysics must be allowed to develop hand in hand, as indeed they have over the centuries. Maritain's
book, of which he was especially fond, raises very basic problems
about the "real internal constitution of God's nature" (in Whitehead's
phrase). Indeed these problems are "particularly crucial," as Maritain
notes (p. viii). And if, he continues, "in . . . [his] philosophical work
there has perchance been some actual contribution . . . to the progress
of thought, and to the researches which announce a new age of culture, it is indeed . . . [he thinks] the one with which this little book has
to deal." In any case, it will surely be agreed that this book is concerned with a most central theological problem, that of God and the
plethora of evil always surrounding us at every turn.

The task before us is to interrelate, as clearly as we can, the notion
of God, his desire for the good, and his permission of evil, with the
subject of human rights. Our topic is thus *the human right to good and
evil*, the characterization of which is to be traced back to the real internal constitution of God's nature. Fortunately we need not start from
scratch, but can stand on the shoulders of giants. We may start with

---

1. J. Maritain, *God and the Permission of Evil* (Milwaukee: Bruce Publishing Co.,
1966), p. 133.

Whitehead and work back to St. Thomas with Maritain as our Virgilian guide.

Right at the start we will do well to avail ourselves of the technical resources of modern logic and semantics. These resources are especially appropriate in these last decades of the twentieth century, a day and age of highly sophisticated methodologies. For one thing, they help us to avoid ambiguity. "Ambiguity is not a philosophical instrument," Maritain himself noted[2], "and the reconciliation of Thomism with certain modern systems would be too dearly paid for were it to be bought at the price of equivocal language." Further, the devices of logic, i.e., quantification theory perhaps with identity, provide the foundation for the so-called "sciences of explanation." "These are sciences that deal with . . . essences *as known*," Maritain has written, "not known in any exhaustive fashion (for indeed we do not know all about anything) but nevertheless known or revealed (by their externals). These are deductive sciences, philosophical or mathematical. . . . In . . . [the philosophical sciences, the mind] does not lay hold of substantial essences by themselves but through their proper accidents and it only proceeds deductively by being constantly revitalized by experience. These sciences are properly sciences of explanation διότι ἐστιν, *propter quid est*. . . . They reveal to us intelligible necessities immanent in the object; they make known to us effects by principles, or reasons for being, by causes. . . . It can happen, it is true, that when confronted by a very exalted reality, one whose essence can be known only by analogy, they must limit themselves (and this is the case of metaphysics when confronted by God) to a knowledge of simple factual (supra-empirical) certitude. . . . [The sciences of explanation] set before the mind intelligibles freed from the concrete existence that cloaks them here below, essences delivered from existence in time. . . ."[3]

Essences here may be thought of as being given by suitable definitions within a proper deductive system. They reveal the "intelligible necessities" of the object whose name or description is being defined. Principles, or meaning postulates, must be laid down concerning whatever terms are taken as primitive, and these must be of sufficient complexity as to assure the existence and uniqueness of the object designated by a suitable description. The situation should be no different when we turn to the most "exalted" reality, "one whose essence can be known only by analogy," lest that reality become an ex-

---

2. *The Degrees of Knowledge* (New York: Charles Scribner's Sons, 1959), p. 429.
3. *The Degrees of Knowledge*, pp. 32–33.

ception to metaphysical principles rather than their chief exemplification. Fundamental principles should be, surely, simple factual certitudes; in any case, it is the metaphysician's prerogative to regard them as such throughout the context of his inquiry.

It might be thought that the fundamental use of modern logic here will do violence to Maritain's intent. To urge that this is not the case, allow me to recall a conversation with him, at Charles Hendel's home in New Haven, in 1941 or 1942, when I was a student at Yale. We were speaking about Father Bocheński's work on analogy in St. Thomas, a topic of course in which Maritain was deeply interested. His reservation about Bocheński's work was fear that something fundamental would perhaps be left out if the formal methods were pressed too far. Of course emotional tone would be left out—Frege's *Befarbung* — but Maritain thought that something more would be missing also, some essential cognitive content. As I recall, not much more than this was said, the conversation then turning to other subjects. My feeling was, however, that Maritain was in no way opposed to the use of modern logical techniques in theology, provided only that they really succeed without losing sight of the essential aims at hand.[4]

We were talking of course of only the logic of *Principia Mathematica,* the logic used by Bocheński as a basis for his work, especially the material concerned with the ordinal similarity of relations. But great strides have been made in the development of logic since 1910–1913, when the great *PM* first appeared. If we take these into account, as indeed we should, we have a much more pliable and subtle guide for our work than Bocheński used in his early papers on analogy. In particular there is the development of semantics and systematic pragmatics, of a theory for handling intensional types of discourse, and, more recently, of methods for handling events, states, acts, processes, and the like.[5] With these available, Maritain's fear can, it would seem, be laid aside, or at the very least, lessened to a considerable extent, and we may return with confidence to the "passion of his youth."

Our first task is to give a suitable definition of 'God', the first and foremost task of any natural theology.[6] To give such a definition is presumably *scire de aliquo an sit* or *scire quid est.* This will be a nominal definition. "In a nominal definition," Maritain noted, "it is already the

---

4. Recall the charming comment in *God and the Permission of Evil,* p. 54, written in the 1960s: "At my age one no longer has time, nor perhaps good enough eyesight, for these works of logical watchmaking with magnifying glass whose importance, however, I in no way deny, and for which I had a passion in my youth."

5. As in *Events, Reference, and Logical Form, Semiotics and Linguistic Structure,* and *Pragmatics, Truth, and Language.*

6. Cf. Bowman Clarke, *op. cit.,* p. 98.

thing that is signified, though in a confused and imperfect fashion. . . . All the more so when we know God by means of created perfections, which . . . stamp a likeness to God in the very heart of things;
we know the Divine Essence, not, to be sure, in itself, *sicuti est*, nor by a
real definition which is indeed impossible, but very truly and very
certainly. . . . And so . . . [we are enabled] to assign — in place of an
impossible real definition — what is, according to our mode of conceiving, the *formal constitutive of the Divine Essence*" [italics added].[7]
Thus we can know at least enough of God's nature to give a nominal
definition within a suitable logico-theological framework, in accord
with Maritain's own account.

Let us turn now very briefly to the nominal definition giving as best
we can, the "formal constitutive" or the "real internal constitution" of
the Divine Nature. For this, we may follow in essentials the material of
the two previous papers, in which God is regarded as the fusion (in
the sense of the calculus of individuals) of the virtual class of all the
"primordial valuations." This last phrase is borrowed from
Whitehead, but he has not given it a very thorough analysis.
Whitehead nowhere tells us just what a primordial valuation is, nor
does he subdivide them in a way that would be fruitful for theology.
This last is a very difficult matter, of course. A suitable classification of
the primordial valuations amounts essentially to a characterization of
the Divine Will. This may be done in many different ways, and
perhaps no fully satisfactory way of doing it has yet been put forward.

Whenever we speak of the Divine Will we are speaking of a *mys-
terium tremendum* always transcending our feeble efforts to grasp or
characterize it. However this may be, one presumably should distinguish the *primordial obligations* from the *primordial tolerations,* these two
together being mutually exclusive but jointly exhaustive of the *primordial permissions*. There are also *primordial prohibitions*, which, together
with the permissions, exhaust the set of primordial valuations altogether. Precisely how these are further subdivided and interrelated
need not concern us for the present.

Howsoever the details are arranged, some distinction between what
God primordially obliges for our good and for the good of the cosmos, and what is merely permitted or tolerated, must be drawn,
perhaps somewhat in the manner of II and III above. The distinction
is essential for present purposes. Also it is necessary to subdivide the
obligations so as to distinguish between the ordination of the reign of
scientific law throughout the cosmos (the primordial *operations* and

---

7. *The Degrees of Knowledge*, p. 230.

determinations) and God's *desire*, between that which is ordained by necessity — even including there perhaps stochastic or probabilistic laws as well as causal ones — and that which is ordained for the good of the creatures by counsel or precept. This distinction is of course implicit in the *Summa Theologica* (q.19, a.12). These latter, i.e., the primordial valuations given by counsel or precept, we may call the primordial *desires* or *desiderata*.

Let

$$\text{'}a \text{ PrDsrd}\, x\text{'} \quad \text{and} \quad \text{'}b \text{ PrDsrd}\, x, y\text{'}$$

express respectively that it is primordially desired that the one-place predicate a denote or apply to the object or event e, and that the object or event x stand in the relation denoted by the two-place predicate b to the object or event y. And similarly for

$$\text{'}a \text{ PrPrmtd}\, x\text{'} \quad \text{and} \quad \text{'}b \text{ PrPrmtd}\, x, y\text{'}$$

for primordial permission. (We need not consider triadic relations here, for methods of handling them are forthcoming in terms of suitable prepositional relations.[8]) A notation for the other primordial notations may be introduced in similar fashion, with

$$\text{'}a \text{ PrVltd}\, x\text{'} \quad \text{and} \quad \text{'}b \text{ PrVltd}\, x, y\text{'}$$

then introduced by summation.

To spell out fully the "formal constitutive of the Divine Essence," one more notation is needed. Let 'e', 'e_1', and so on, be event- or act-variables. God's essence is *pure act* or *state*, namely, that constituted by all of the primordial valuations. Where

$$\text{'}{<}a,\text{PrVltd}\, x {>} e_1\text{'} \quad \text{and} \quad \text{'}{<}b,\text{PrVltd}, x, y {>} e_2\text{'}$$

express, respectively, that e_1 is specifically an act or state that a PrVltd x and that e_2 is an act or state that b PrVltd x,y, we may define

(**D**)   'God' as '$(\iota z \cdot z \text{ Fu } \{e \ni (Ea)(Ex)(Ey)((\text{PredCon}_1 a \cdot$

       ${<}a,\text{PrVltd}, x{>}e) \text{ v } (\text{PredCon}_2 a \cdot {<}a,\text{PrVltd}, x, y {>} e))\})$'.

Note that this definition is in terms of a Russellian description of the one entity that is the *fusion of* the virtual class of all e's where e is an act or state of some primordial *valuating* with respect to a *one-* or *two-place predicate constant*.

In the definiens here, of course, the acts or states e are not tensed. They are given in the tense of timelessness or tenselessness, a "tense" first explicitly noted apparently by Frege. It might also be called the

---

8. See especially *Semiotics and Linguistic Structure*, Chapters X–XII.

tense of eternity. In this way, not the slightest hint of temporality enters into the pure acts constituting God's essence. Of course the objects or events *x* and *y* are in time, some of them anyhow, just as they are in space and possess this or that physico-chemical property. But this circumstance should not lead us to attribute to God spatial or other physico-chemical characteristics. Nor should the temporality of the objects or events primordially valuated lead us to attribute to him temporal characteristics. The real internal constitution of God's nature is given only *sub specie aeternitas.*

In speaking of the tense of timelessness, the tense of eternity, of primordiality, of the divine *"praescitus"* or foreknowledge, one should recall the text of St. Peter Damian (quoted on p. 78 of *God and the Permission of Evil*): "The divine *today* is the incommutable, indefeasible, inascessible eternity to which nothing can be added, from which nothing can be taken away. And all things which here below supervene upon and succeed one another by flowing progressively into non-being . . . are present before this today and continue to exist motionless before it. In that today, the day when the world began is still immutable. And even so, the day is already present also when it will be judged by the eternal judge." It is inconceivable that the divine *praescitus* could be characterized other than in the logical tense of timelessness.

Let us turn now to the problem of moral evil as seen on the basis of the foregoing. In particular, let us follow the discussion in *God and the Permission of Evil.*

Maritain speaks of the *absolute innocence of God* as regards the origins of moral evil. The key text for this is the *Summa Theologica* I-II, 79, 1: *"Deus . . . non potest directe esse causa peccati. Similiter etiam necque indirecte . . . Et sic patet quod Deus nullo modo est causa peccati."* This absolute innocency is provided here in the very nature of the primordial valuations, in particular the desiderative ones, which determine the morally good. The morally good is absolutely innocent of the morally evil, which is activity not in accord with the desiderative will, defection from it however slight, privation of its supremacy as the sole directive of our lives. The desiderative will is the grace of God waiting for us, as it were, waiting for our openness to receive it, to act in accord with it, to make it our very own.

Maritain stresses equally, of course, that *defectus gratiae prima causa est ex nobis.* "The creature has the first initiative of moral evil; it is in the creature that the *initiative* and the *invention* of sin have their origin" (p. 6). Whence else could sin arise? we may ask. Surely not from the primordial operations or determinations. Hence only from the permissions as regards the creatures. God permits the *defectus gratiae* in us, but of course is not the cause of it in the sense of the operations or determinations.

To reconcile these two principles, which are at the very heart of Thomism — indeed (p. 9) "every Thomist theologian, indeed, every Catholic, whether simple man of faith, philosopher, or theologian, is ready to die for . . . [these] two axioms" — Maritain formulates the *principle of dissymmetry*, of "the fundamental, irreducible dissymmetry between the line of good and the line of evil." In the line of good, i.e., in our discussion of the good, "God [p. 10] is the first and transcendent cause of our liberty and of our free decisions, so that the [good] free act is wholly from God as first cause and wholly from us as second cause; because there is not a fibril of being which escapes the causality of God." For *evil* acts, and for decisions leading to them, however, "God is absolutely not the cause of . . . [them]; it is man who is the *first cause* and who has the *first initiative* of moral evil." Maritain does not say here, nor anywhere (I believe), that God is the *secondary* cause of moral evil.

Let us try to be as clear as we can about this principle of dissymmetry, for Maritain was obviously proud of it, regarding it as one of his best achievements. In so doing we must be very careful in our use of 'cause', a very tricky word in theology and the sciences alike. (That this last is the case is witnessed by the voluminous literature about it since the time of Aristotle right down to the very latest talk, in contemporary philosophy of science, of causality as explained away in probabilistic terms for the physical sciences, but irreducibly fundamental (probably in terms of a primitive) for the social and historical ones.)[9]

Let us speak first of causation *of an object or entity* merely as specification in the primordial valuations. Since these latter are all-inclusive, and concern all modes of being whatsoever, there can be "not a fibril of being [or of occurrence] which escapes the causality of God." This is *objectual* or *entitival* causality, the cause of the being of the object *as such*, independent of whether it has such and such a property or stands in such and such a relation. In addition, there is causality *that* an object have such and such a *property* or stands in such and such a *relation*. This we may call *property* causality (provided we realize that *relational* causality is included as well).

God is clearly the objectual cause of all objects whatsoever, good,

___

9. See "On the Language of Causal Talk: Scriven and Suppes," in *Pragmatics, Truth, and Language*.

evil, and indifferent, but he is the property cause of only (primordially) good acts, not of evil ones. How is the latter to be assured? Well, by specifying that the clause '—', when we use 'that —' in a statement of property causality for acts, be of the form 'αe_1' or '$\beta e_1 e_2$', where a designates α, b, β, and a PrDsrd e_1 or b PrDsrd e_1, e_2 respectively. Thus God is the *property cause of e_1's having* α if and only if that e_1 has α is provided for among the primordial desiderata. Finally, we may say that God is the property cause of the *property* α *itself* if and only

$$(e)(\alpha e \supset a \text{ PrDsrd } e),$$

where a designates α. And similarly for a dyadic β.

In some such way as this, we are assured of a precise principle to the effect that God is the objectual cause of all acts, good and evil, but the property cause only of the good, not of the evil.

Let us turn now to human or creaturely causality. The human person is not the objectual cause of any of his acts — or of anything else, for that matter — although he is of course a factor in them. He *does* or *performs* his acts, but this is a very different matter. Only God can cause objectually the being of an act. A person can, however, cause — *person*-cause, so to speak — that an act, his or another's, have such and such a property or stand in such and such a relation. In this way he may be said to cause the property in performing the act. Thus we can say that a human is never an objectual cause of anything, but he is the person- or human-cause of the properties of his acts. And among these properties are good and evil.

We end up then with a principle of dissymmetry rather different from that of Maritain: God is the objectual cause of all acts, good and evil, but the property cause — property-*God*-cause, as it were — only of the good, not of the evil, whereas the creature is never the objectual cause of anything, but is the property human-cause of the good and evil of his acts alike. It is not clear that this principle differs from that of Maritain, however, in any really substantive way. It merely serves to make it more precise and to place it on a more secure logical footing than heretofore.

We should observe that in these statements about causation by God, 'cause' is being used only analogically. In fact whenever we speak of causation by God, the word does not have its ordinary meaning at all, but always a special analogical one. And this analogical meaning is always to be analyzed out in terms of the primordial valuations. This is perhaps a point not always admitted, even by very good Thomists. All use of 'God' is ultimately in terms of its definiens, and its definiens (giving the "essence" of God) is stated wholly in terms of the primordial valuations. This essence wholly exhausts his being, God being the fusion of all the primordial valuations. Thus there is no way of construing statements that God causes so and so other than in primordial terms. The very meaning of 'analogy' is merely this: a term is being used analogically when this use may be defined away wholly in primordial terms.

When we speak of God's knowledge, we must always remember also that we are speaking only analogically. Here too God's *objectual knowledge must be distinguished from his knowledge-that*, his *property* or *relational* knowledge. The one we may think of as knowledge *de dicto*. A good deal has been said about this distinction, and about God's knowledge in general, in the preceding papers.

"In the line of good," Maritain writes (p. 10), "all that which God knows in created existence, He knows because He causes it. His 'science of vision' is the cause of things. . . . [But], in the line of evil, well! the evil accomplished by creatures is known by God, and yet God is absolutely not the cause of the evil, *neither directly nor indirectly*. . . . Evil is known by God without having been in any way caused by God." Here again, everything to be said about God's knowledge must be traced back to the *praescitus* of the primordial valuations. God may be said to "know," analogically, where *a* designates α and *b*, β, that αx or βxy just where *a* PrVltd *x* or *b* PrVltd *x,y*, respectively. And because all that happens (or is) happens (or is) either by God's doing (or creating) it or permitting it to be done, every factually true statement of these forms occurs among the primordial operations or determinations. Thus God knows *de dicto* all factual truths, including those stating that such and such is evil. But this of course in no way runs counter to the principle, mentioned above, that God is in no way the property-cause of evil. It thus in no way impugns the doctrine of the "absolute innocence" of God as regards the origins of moral evil.

The "*defectus*, or free failure which is the *cause* of moral evil without being itself an evil, is the *non-consideration of the rule* — which is not, note well, an *act* of non-consideration, but a *non-act* of consideration" (p. 35). In other words the *defectus* is not, at first anyhow, a deliberate, meditated act of non-consideration. Where '<Cons,*r*>*e*' expresses that *e* is an act or state of consideration of the rule *r*, and 'Act *e*' that *e* is a deliberate, self-conscious act on the part of the agent, a non-consideration of the rule *r* is an *e* such that

$$\sim (\text{Act}\, e \cdot <\text{Cons},r>e).$$

An act of non-consideration, on the other hand, is an e such that

$$(\text{Act } e \cdot \sim \, <\text{Cons}, r>e).$$

These are, of course, very different, as Maritain points out.

The divine desiderata seem to be essentially what Maritain means (p. 38) by a "shatterable motion [,] a divine motion or activation which causes the free agent to tend to a morally good act, but which includes of itself, by nature, the possibility of being shattered" or violated — "it is exactly this that corresponds to a *fallible* human liberty." The violability of the divine desiderata is the price humans must pay for their liberty of free choice.

"You see here another example of the dissymmetry between the line of good and the line of evil [p. 40]. In the line of good the idea of an indeterminate or undifferentiated divine *motion*, which it would depend on created liberty to complete or terminate in one direction or in the other, is an inadmissible idea, since of the smallest *good* determination, God has the first initiative, is the first cause." In other words, no item of good, however small, is omitted from the primordial desiderata. The set of them is fully complete. If this were not the case, some fundamental lacuna would be present in the divine nature, some important good perhaps not properly envisaged. To allow such would of course limit drastically the conception of God put forward above. Further, all the desiderata are fully determinate in the divine nature, in the sense of being explicitly spelled out. Of course *we* are unable to write them down in full detail. To allow this would be presumption on our part. We can never know the divine nature to this extent. But even so, the plenum of desiderata constitutes an essential part of God's nature, even though we cannot know it in its full detail.

"But in the line of evil (p. 40) a *permission*, . . . an indeterminate or undifferentiated divine *permission*, in virtue of which, *if* the creature wishes, shatterable motions will be shattered and fissures or abysses of nothingness, of moral evil, will be introduced into being — such an *indeterminate* divine *permission* is a valid and necessarily required concept, because in the line of nonbeing [or evil] it is precisely the creature, and not God, who is the first cause, and who takes the first initiative." Here again we must allow for the analogical use of terms. Strictly, God takes no initiative other than what is specified in the primordial valuations. In what sense are the divine permissions "indeterminate" or "undifferentiated?" Well, in just the sense of not being spelled out explicitly among the desiderata, operations, or determinations. It is only these latter that may be said to be "determined" and hence of course clearly differentiated from each other, and particular items within each kind clearly differentiated from each other.

One more notion, and we will have the full battery of notions Maritain uses for the discussion of moral evil — save one. "In the theory that I propose," he writes (p. 59), "it is indispensable to posit the existence of a *consequent permissive decree* (consequent to the instant of nihilation or of non-consideration of the rule, where the shatterable motion is shattered)." By 'consequent' here of course nothing temporal is meant. The decree, i.e., the permissive valuation, is consequent upon the free agent's non-consideration of the rule, dependent upon it. Were there no such free act (or rather, *non*-act) there would be no primordial permission concerning it. Maritain differs here from those Thomists who speak instead of an *antecedent* permissive decree. Here too nothing temporal must be read into 'antecedent'. Strictly all it can mean, however, is that the decree is an item in the primordial *praescitus*. Both 'antecedent' and 'consequent' are used here only analogically anyhow, so that nothing much depends on them unless explicitly defined in primordial terms.

One final principle is essential, to complete Maritain's portrayal of moral evil. It is the principle of St. Cyprian (p. 62) that "the adversary can do nothing against us without the prior permission of God." A somewhat stronger statement, but surely not "identical" with it as Maritain suggests, is the Augustinian view that God "would never permit evil if He were not strong enough and good enough to draw good even from evil." Thus, as Maritain words it, "God permits evil only in view of a greater good, that is to say, by referring or ordaining [or purposing] this evil to a greater good." The greater good here, Maritain thinks, is "principally and above all in the order of eternal life, but also, secondarily, in the order of temporal history itself." But all that is in the order of eternal life is presumably already good, even already good to the highest degree. Perhaps the first part of Maritain's statement here can best be glossed by saying that God permits evil in order that the creature will turn to the good, the order of eternal life, and thereafter resolve to make greater effort to conduct his behavior in accord with it. In this way also, then, the good may be made to prevail "in the order of temporal history itself." It is one of the divine purposes that this obtain, according to Maritain, a purpose that in fact is always realized and hence never violated. In this respect the primordial purposes are more like the operations and determinations than the desires.

In the foregoing, the divine purposes have been presumed handled in terms of the primordial desires. But these desires may be violated or "shattered" by the "non-consideration of the rule" and behavior subsequent to it, as already noted. And indeed, in the foregoing, no provision is made for this principle of optimism or amelioration, as it might be called. In order to accommodate it here a new category of *primordial purposes* is needed, a new subdivision among the primordial valuations. We may let

'*a* PrPrps *x*'   and   '*b* PrPrps *x,y*'

be the new sentential forms needed for this, in terms of which such purposings as are thought to belong to the divine essence may be stated.

A technical point is in order. The sentential forms used thus far, for stating the primordial valuations, have all been atomic ones, where, however, *a* and *b* may be either primitive or defined predicates of any complexity. Presumably, then, no technical difficulties will arise in forming any molecular sentences needed for stating the more complex valuations. However, the notation may be made more pliable if we bring in a special relation to handle 'that'. This relation is the relation *that of intensionality*. It is symbolized by 'That$_{Intensional}$' and is to be significant in contexts of the form

'*e* That $_{Intensional}$ *a*',

where *e* is an intensional act or state and *a* is a sentence giving the content, so to speak, of that act. If *e* is a purposing and *e* That$_{Intensional}$ *a*, then *a* is a sentence saying what it is that is purposed. (This that-relation is to be contrasted with the *that-relation of occurrence*, needed for handling

'It was 5 o'clock that Jane arrived from Boston'

and the like.[10]) In place of saying that *a* PrDsrd *x*, for example, we can say that there is a primordial desire that bears the that-relation of intensionality to a sentence to the effect that *a* applies to (or denotes) *x*.

Let '<PrPrps>*e*' express now that *e* is an act or state of primordial purposing, with similar expressions for the other primordial valuations. A more pliable definition may then be given in place of (**D**) above, namely

(**D'**)   'God' abbreviates   '($\imath x \cdot x$ = (Fu'{$e \ni$(E*a*)((<PrVltd>*e* v <PrPrps>*e*) • Sent *a* • *e* That$_{Intensional}$ *a*})))'.

---

10. Cf. "Some Hiżian Heresies," in *Pragmatics, Truth, and Language*.

And of course this definition takes into account the primordial purposes not provided for in (**D**). This definition may thus accommodate suitable principles of amelioration by suitable choices of *a*, both for "creatures individually" and "in the domain of temporal history." There can be no doubt but that Maritain would prefer (**D**′) to (**D**) as approximating more closely to his views.[11]

Let us turn now to the last chapter of *God and the Permission of Evil*, perhaps one of the best in all of Maritain's work, and to the Appendix to the third edition, which contains a splendid suggestion for future work, one also made tentatively at the end of II above.

First let us reflect upon "that metaphysical abomination," as Maritain calls it (p. 69), namely, "a determination of the act of divine knowledge, that is to say, of God Himself, by the creature." We are invited to "suppose that God did not will that things should be; in other words if God had created nothing at all, if there were neither world, nor angels nor men nor saints nor blessed, nor even the sacred humanity of Christ — well [if this were the case] there would be *absolutely nothing changed* in the divine act of knowledge, which is God Himself. Think a little about this," we are urged. "And yet all the things that He has freely decided to create are *truly and really known* by Him, just as they are *truly and really loved* by Him. It is always necessary to have present before the mind such a mystery of transcendence when one is speaking of problems like those of which we are speaking now."

A full explication of this fascinating passage is forthcoming upon the basis of definition (**D**′) above, which brings to the fore the *intensional* character of the primordial valuations independent of actual existence. All reference to objects in the definiens of (**D**′) is in the statements *a* which are *mentioned* there but not *used*. In (**D**), however, objects are referred to fundamentally. But (**D**′) has its force just as well even if *there are no objects whatsoever*. It is God's intensional character that is brought out here rather than his connection with the creatures. In accord with (**D**′) God is in no way determined by the creatures. It is rather that the primordial sentences *about* the creatures determine them. In this way the "metaphysical abomination," of which Maritain spoke, is avoided, and the mystery of transcendence remains intact, but with no loss in God's "knowledge" of and "love" for the creatures viewed analogically.

It was mentioned above that among the primordial determinations may be found probabilistic or stochastic laws, in addition to strictly

----

11. Note that (**D**′) presupposes that the grammar of 'PrVltd' is also handled in terms of 'That$_{\text{Intensional}}$' and not in just summational terms as above.

causal ones. This was not insisted upon but was allowed as a possibility. Whether there is a really basic or fundamental difference between laws of these two kinds is a moot point, in view of some recent attempts to handle causal laws stochastically. At any event probabilistic considerations must surely be introduced at some point in any serious attempt to get at the full characterization of scientific knowledge in modern terms, and its connection with God's nature. Maritain comes close to saying something like this when he invites us to consider an alternative characterization of the divine essence. "Rather than to introduce moments of reason into the establishment of the eternal plan," he writes (pp. 93–94), "it seems to me . . . that one could try, by a sort of back-and-forth movement, to consider created things now according to their own nature, now according as they are established by the eternal purposes." Among the purposes here no doubt we should include all the primordial valuations whatsoever.

From the point of view of the divine plan, everything that takes place does so by necessity *ex suppositione*. When we turn to *our* knowledge of created things, "there are free acts of which, if they are taken *collectively* and *indeterminately,* the occurrence is *certain*. According to the example given by St. Thomas, if all the inhabitants of a town are bilious it is certain that a fight will break out — although one cannot say with certainty that at such or such a given moment this individual and that individual will come to blows. If on the contrary it is a question of a free act *individually* taken, it cannot be foreseen with certainty. . . ." Here we are presumably allowed to assign probabilities to events taken "collectively and indeterminately," in accord presumably with a relative frequency conception of probability. But also Maritain apparently would allow probabilities to be assigned to individual acts or events. This raises difficult technical matters as to how such probabilities are to be assigned, even as to the very meaning of sentences stating them. But never mind. The interesting question arises as to whether probability statements, both general probability laws as well as statements assigning specific probabilities to either individual events or to classes of such, are to be incorporated in the divine plan, or whether they are merely somehow products of human reason and methodology. Maritain almost suggests the former in his mention of the "back-and-forth movement" in the establishment of the eternal plan. The movement is back and forth as between causal and probabilistic laws among the primordial valuations. In the light of recent work on the nature of such laws, such a back-and-forth movement is perhaps to be recommended. Note that the divine *praescitus* includes now all that it did before, but in addition God's knowledge includes all true stochastic statements.

In the section on "Predestination and Reprobation" Maritain calls attention to the scholastic distinction between the antecedent, "primordial and uncircumstanced will" and the consequent, "definitive or circumstanced" one. The former, the antecedent will, is violable or "shatterable" and seems to correspond exactly with the desiderative valuations mentioned above. The "definitive or circumstanced will" seems to correspond with the primordial operations and determinations, which can never be violated. The operations give the so-called "boundary conditions" and the determinations, the whole parade of laws that govern the cosmos including the creatures. These, the cosmos and the creatures, are just the way they are and cannot be altered. The use of 'primordial' throughout this paper is of course essentially Whitehead's and is intended to embrace the whole divine economy, so to speak, whereas for Maritain, the primordial will comprises only the desires or desiderations. Aside from this unimportant verbal difference, however, the scholastic distinction may easily be fitted into the characterization of the divine will suggested above. Of course there are further factors to take into account, the primordial prohibitions, tolerations, and so on. As already suggested, it is not clear that a fully adequate and sufficiently precise characterization of all the factors that must enter into the divine will has ever been given satisfactorily, and on the basis of a suitably secure logic and metaphysics.

Maritain comments (pp. 111−112) that "not only the letter, but also . . . the tone, the accent, the cadence, the *thin edge*" of his views are contained in the declaration of the Council of Quierzy: "Deus omnipotens *omnes homines* sine exceptione *vult salvos fieri* (1 Tim. 2:4), licet non omnes salventur. Quod autem salvantur, salvantis est donum; quod autem quidam pereunt, pereuntium est meritum" (Denz., 318). It is a primordial desideration that all men be saved and led to eternal life, but some (indeed, it would seem, most) are not. That certain ones be saved, this is the "gift" of Him who saves, and is given in view of their *ever-considering the rule and patterning their behavior in total accord with it.* And that certain ones perish is due to their having rejected the rule somewhere along the way. And whether one is saved or not is of course already contained in the *praescitus,* but not in the plan.

A comment concerning this last distinction. The plan, strictly speaking, includes the primordial operations, determination, and desiderations — perhaps also the prohibitions — but not the non-operative, non-determinative, and non-desiderative tolerations and permissions. Again, this may not be the best way to draw the distinction, but it will suffice for the moment.

In the "Appendix Note," in fact, Maritain makes a suggestion, which, if we were to follow it through, would necessitate modifying almost everything said thus far. It is, namely, that we should not speak of the good and the evil, *simpliciter* or in the positive case only, but that some activity is *"less good* than it could have been" (p. 114) or than some other activity in its place. Presumably we should take into account here a comparative notion 'better than' as well as the superlative 'best' or 'good to the highest degree'. A similar point was made in II above, it will be recalled, where, anent the primordial desiderations, it was remarked that "some [of the primordial] desires are more intense than others, and perhaps a notion of *degree of intensity* [italics added] should be introduced. . . . [Some desiderata are no doubt more binding upon us than others.] A much more elaborate theology would result, but also one presumably more adequate to the complexities of scientific methodology, on the one hand, and to the delicacies of moral and religious experience, on the other." Maritain does not quite say this in his Appendix, and perhaps he would not agree with so strong a statement; but clearly there is striking accord between the two passages.

Rather similar considerations should no doubt be brought in to the characterization of the very notion of consideration of the rule. The rule can be considered in different ways and with varying degrees of comprehension on our part. It can be there merely as a back-drop or it can be ever-present to our mind and heart and soul in the maximum sense of which humans are capable. The First Commandment, for example, which (in declarative terms) is surely among the primordial desiderations, cannot be stated other than in terms of a superlative notion of some kind. Also non-consideration of the rule can be of varying degrees and in different ways. The rule may be "considered" or "non-considered" in some one respect but not so in another. Full consideration of the rule presumably entails a total comprehension of, and complete agreement with and complete acceptance of, its content unambiguously construed. But there are lesser ways of consideration, and hence of non-consideration, these latter not necessarily leading to moral evil.

Another comment. Presumably we should always consider the rule maximally, and act accordingly. We should "think of God oftener than we breathe." Any little defection from this results in some little evil creeping into our lives. "To get along in the world, you must cheat a little," it has been said, all such cheating being traceable back to defection in the total, all-absorptive consideration of the rule.

Strictly it is never the consideration of only one rule that is relevant, but of all the desiderative rules together, with emphasis perhaps on one in a given context. The rules "interanimate" each other in very fundamental ways, and one cannot be considered apart from the others and retain its full import. They must be taken together holistically. Thus throughout we should think of 'consideration of the rule r' as construed as 'consideration of all the desiderative valuations with emphasis on the one rule r, in the context of all primordial valuations whatsoever'.

Throughout, moral evil has been spoken of only in terms of one person. It is person p's non-consideration of the rule that may result in his evil act. But actually this is very much oversimplified, as Maritain would of course agree. *Another person's* non-consideration of the rule may lead to my evil act, just as my non-consideration may lead him to evil, even moral evil. Various kinds of evil to the person should be considered here, and ultimately traced back to non-consideration of the rule on someone's part. But also there are evils of various sorts inflicted by the family, for example, or by the social group, the public media, the government, or society as a whole. Can all such evil be traced back to non-consideration of the rule on someone's part? This is a very difficult question. Men collectively commit atrocities they would never dream of doing individually. Where are the gradations here? At just what point do we pass from being moral individuals to committing the collective monstrosities that largely constitute our lives in modern society?

Finally, let us note the connection with human rights, a topic so eloquently discussed by Maritain. The very fundamental right of the human person as such is "the right to existence," and hence of course to all that human existence involves in its experience of good and evil. Indeed, the fundamental right of the human being is to good and evil alike — on the one hand, to follow the desiderative will of God as best he can, and, on the other, to yield to the *defectus* or non-consideration of the rule that may lead to moral evil. The very ground of this doctrine, it is thought, is provided in full detail in the characterization of the primordial valuations. Correlative with human rights are human duties. Theologically speaking, these are of course to mold all our individual and collective behavior in maximal accord to the desiderative will. Indeed, this is what is petitioned the world over whenever the Lord's prayer is made — that we do our duty in helping the desiderative will to be accomplished throughout our history on earth. But to go from this very general statement to a spelling out of rights and duties for each and every individual citizen and for social groups and for society as a whole, is a long, hard process, as we all know. And even if this were done satisfactorily in some way, how could behavior in accord with it be achieved? How could we help people to do their duty and to claim that which is their right? Most people reject the "gift" offered to them, and indeed have done so throughout history. Even so, we may hope, as Maritain wishes us to, that suitable principles of amelioration obtain among the primordial purposes, in accord with which our individual lives may become intrinsically more valuable to ourselves, to others, and to society as a whole.

CHAPTER V

Fact, Feeling, Faith, and Form

Naśyami aham bhû naśyati lóka!
Sruyatâm dharma, Bhagawat.

"What is that, knowing which, we shall know everything?" It is not easy to know the real, internal constitution of God's nature, and perhaps no one has ever known it fully. Perhaps no one has ever known it even partially, although this is doubtful. Beliefs, intimations, surmises, and the like, have often sufficed. No matter, the notion of God should be characterized, it would seem, in so grand a fashion as to contain, in some specific sense, all knowledge of all beings and happenings, here, there, and everywhere, past, present, and future. In particular God's nature should contain, in a most intimate way, it may be thought, all scientific law, both causal and stochastic, as well as all boundary conditions. Hence implicitly it should contain all factually true statements. But God is not merely the repository of truth, but of value, of beauty, and goodness, as well. Science and value, whatever the shortcomings or defects of our knowledge about them, should be properly fused, it would seem, in any satisfactory characterization of the real internal constitution of God's nature. Failure to attain this fusion is to rest content with an only partial and hence inadequate characterization.

The perennial theme "that being is one and identical with God the creator," as Richard Taylor puts it, ". . . is rediscovered in every age and in every corner of the world. It is at once terrifying and completely fulfilling. It will never perish and nothing will ever replace it. Nothing possibly can; its endurance is that of the stars."[1] But even the stars may come and go and still be terrifying. Only if we add the insight of *philosophia perennis,* that being is in its real nature akin to *mind* or *spirit* in some sense, it would seem, do we have the basis for a view of the kind described. Whatever spirit is, being is "identical" with it,

1. Richard Taylor, *With Heart and Mind* (New York: St. Martin's Press, 1973), Proem.

and being *one*, so also is spirit. "There is only one river [p. 142], which here and there assumes new forms or is modified in this way and that, either briefly or more lastingly. Here it assumes the form of a ripple, there of a waterfall, and numberless other forms in other places." Being here and now is a material object, but there and then a mental act perhaps. No matter what forms or shapes it assumes or however it is modified, it still may be regarded as identical in character with God the creator, "that from which the origin, subsistence, and dissolution of this world proceed."

Let 'AS' be a primitive individual constant designating Absolute Spirit or Mind. Immediately we note, as a first metaphysical principle, that AS exists.

Prl. $\vdash E!AS$.

The existence of individuals is handled here predicatively, where

$$\text{'E!}x\text{'}\quad \text{is short for}\quad \text{'}\sim x = N\text{'},$$

N being the null individual.[2]

It is interesting that Hegel, at the very beginning of his *Phänomenologie des Geistes*, differentiates "Subjective" and "Objective" Spirit from the AS.[3] The one is a "manifestation" of AS, the other, we might say, is an "embodiment" of it. The various objects of nature are embodiments, of AS, those of the mental realm, manifestations. Accordingly, two new primitives are needed for these notions. Let us symbolize them by 'Manif' and 'Emb'. Clearly the following principles should obtain concerning these notions.

Pr2. $\vdash (x)(y)((x \text{ Manif } y \vee x \text{ Emb } y) \supset x = AS)$.
Pr3. $\vdash \sim (Ex)(x \text{ Manif AS} \vee x \text{ Emb AS})$.

Thus AS alone manifests or embodies anything, and nothing whatsoever manifests or embodies it. Also nothing is both manifested and embodied by anything.

PR4. $\vdash \sim(Ex)(Ey)(x \text{ Manif } y \cdot x \text{ Emb } y)$.

We may now define

$$\text{'SubjSp'}\quad \text{as}\quad \text{'(Fu'}\{x \ni AS \text{ Manif } x\})\text{'}$$

and

$$\text{'ObjSp'}\quad \text{as}\quad \text{'(Fu'}\{x \ni AS \text{ Emb } x\})\text{'}.$$

---

2. On the null individual, see the author's "Of Time and the Null Individual."
3. §§ 385 and 386.

Thus the realm of subjective spirit is the fusion of (the virtual class of) everything manifested by AS, and objective spirit is the fusion of (the virtual class of) everything embodied by AS. These definitions give a very natural way of providing for the two Hegelian realms. Should they be regarded as mutually exclusive? If so, we would need to postulate that every *part* of a manifested or embodied individual is also manifested or embodied, respectively. Thus, where P is the part-whole relation, we would have also that

Pr5. $\vdash (x)(y)(z)((x \text{ Manif} y \cdot z \text{ P} y) \supset x \text{ Manif} z)$

and

Pr6. $\vdash (x)(y)(z)((x \text{ Emb} y \cdot z \text{ P} y) \supset x \text{ Emb} z)$.

Also it should then obtain that

$$\vdash \sim (\text{E}x)(\sim x = \text{N} \cdot x \text{ P SubjSp} \cdot x \text{ P ObjSp}),$$

that SubjSp and ObjSp have no non-null part in common. If the two spheres are taken to overlap in various ways, these two principles would not be appropriate.

If these two spheres are taken to exhaust the cosmos, we would have a *Principle of Completeness,* that

Pr7. $\vdash (x)(\sim x = \text{AS} \supset (\text{AS Manif} x \text{ v AS Emb} x))$.

Note of course that we are in no way following Hegel here but merely making use of some of his terminology.

But perhaps there are realms of derivative being other than these two, or even altogether different. Perhaps the two Hegelian ones are themselves unjustifiable on the basis of modern science, and constitute an illicit dichotomy. For the moment, we need not attempt to answer these difficult questions but we should note that the foregoing material may easily be extended to allow for any number of derivative realms of being — or even for none at all. But let us assume at least one. And, for the moment, let us speak of manifestation in a wider sense so as to include embodiment, as well as whatever further kinds of process are appropriate for generating the given kinds of entities. Thus we let 'Manif$_1$', 'Manif$_2$', and so on, be primitives, and we let

'U$_i$'   abbreviate   '(Fu'$\{x \ni \text{AS Manif}_i x\}$)'.

Thus the universe of entities U$_i$ is merely the fusion of the entities to which AS bears Manif$_i$, for each i. For each relation Manif$_i$ we then have principles analogous to **Pr2** and **Pr3**, and appropriate extensions of **Pr4** and **Pr7**.

If $i = 0$, absolute monism results. AS is the only reality and there is nothing else except *māyā*. Even the name 'AS', the very inscriptions of **PR1, Pr2**, and so on, would be dropped. They would all be items of *māyā* and thus presumably not worthy of rational discourse. But even if $i > 0$, we could still hold to a form of the doctrine of *māyā* in regarding the entities of U_1, U_2, and so on, as *māyā*-items but allow rational discourse about them. However, if the discourse is to be in accord with modern logic and science, it will quickly be seen to be so important for our human life, and so insistently objective and compelling — and indeed so difficult to come anywhere near getting it right — that the point of talk of *māyā* at all is soon lost. Surely the AS is not the less great, the less worthy of our total and all-absorbing effort to grasp it, if we regard the derivative entities to be genuine in some sense, if only as manifestations of it. In fact, the situation is the other way around. Let us embrace the derivative entities as worthy of our love and respect, and make every possible effort to come to see most intimately how they are interrelated one with another. It is in this way, in part, that we can come to know the grandeur and munificence of the AS itself. However, our "knowledge" of it need not be exhausted therewith, but rather enhanced.

The manifested objects of the U_i's are to comprise whatever it is that our cosmos contains. Precisely how we are to populate them is of course an incredibly difficult matter. Surely they must contain the objects needed for the sciences in their most developed stages. We must not rest content with the ontology of centuries back nor even with the "stale" science of yesterday. But to spell out in detail the ontology of even one science, at its present state of development, would be very difficult and would tax even the greatest practitioners. Nonetheless we may suppose it to consist of a presumably small number of U_i's in terms of which the desired assertions of that science can be made. And similarly for other sciences. And we must never suppose that any characterization of the U_i's needed for science would ever be final or complete. On the contrary, they would always be *semper reformanda,* and would exhibit enormous variation in the hands of different practitioners in the same field even at the same time.

Of particular interest for philosophers of logic and mathematics is the U_i, or the U_i's, needed for both. If logic is taken as standard first-order logic, as throughout this paper, no assumption concerning the U_i's need be made. On the monist view, our only individual is AS, plus the null and world individuals. The latter, however, would be identical with AS, and the null individual N has the property that

$$\sim E!N,$$

that it does not "exist" in the appropriate sense. (Of course N is a value for a variable, but that is something else again.) And if $i > 0$, the U_i's are merely those of the sciences as already provided.

Logic as such has no ontology. For mathematics, however, the situation is very different. Let us think of it set-theoretically, in terms of the Zermelo-Fraenkel-Skolem system.[4] Here two U_i's are needed, one for individuals or *Urelemente* — Zermelo himself insisted upon their admission, it will be recalled — and one for the realm of sets. No harm need arise from admitting the *Urelemente,* the very entities that may be presumed to populate the cosmos. The admission of a domain of sets, however, postulates entities that do not populate the cosmos in any obvious sense. Even so, this matter need not deter us, for we may allow set-theoretic talk about the *Urelemente* in the manner of the "moderate" realism of Duns Scotus.[5] In this way classical mathematics in the set-theoretical sense may be preserved, and used, moreover, as a basis for the other theoretical sciences. For this, of course, a new primitive is needed, and for applications to the sciences, such new primitives as those sciences require.

Once the U_i's needed for the sciences have been arrived at, the question arises as to whether any further ones should be added. Do the ontologies of the sciences suffice for all discourse — other of course than that concerning the AS and its possible manifestations in SubjSp? Well, surely yes, if 'science' is construed widely enough. Note that the question is merely one about *ontologies,* not about the modes of discourse allowed concerning the items admitted in the sciences. One and the same act, for example, may be said to occupy such and such a place-time in one scientific context, but to be immoral or illegal or prohibited or whatever, in others.

Mental entities are the occupants of the realm of SubjSp, and any interesting metaphysical idealism may be presumed to admit such entities. The basic items here are no doubt individual souls or minds, and mental acts are presumably dependent upon these fundamentally. It is a bit mysterious as to just what an individual mind is and how it is to be individuated. You have one and I have one, and they are alike in both being minds. Let yours be m_1, and mine m_2, and let

---

4. For useful expository remarks, see especially H. Wang, *From Mathematics to Philosophy* (New York: Humanities Press, 1974).

5. See the author's "On Common Natures and Mathematical Scotism," in *Peirce's Logic of Relations and Other Studies, Studies in Semiotics,* Vol. 12, ed. by Thomas Sebeok (Nisse, The Netherlands: Peter de Ridder Press, 1978).

m_3, m_4, and so on, be those of others. Then the calculus of individuals allows us to form the "group" mind

$$(m_1 \cup m_2 \cup m_3 \cup m_4 \cup \ldots).$$

Even this group mind does not of course exhaust the AS, the latter being infinitely greater. Is this group mind a *part* of the AS? If so, then each individual mind is also, each being a part of the group sum. Equally difficult is the question as to how the individual souls or selves are related to the mental acts of or pertaining to them. And this in turn leads to the problem as to how such acts themselves are to be individuated.

Individual minds result from the AS by one kind of manifestation, bodies by another. Does the human person, a unique complex of mind and body, result by still a third kind of manifestation? Some idealists might well contend so. To bring then a mind, a body, and a person together, we need the Of-relation of possession.[6] It is not clear whether the mind possesses the body, or the body the mind, or the person the mind, or the mind the person, or the body the person, or the person the body. Perhaps there is possession in all of these ways. In any case, if bodies, minds, and persons result from separate kinds of manifestation, a suitable way of bringing a body, a mind, and a person together must be at hand to provide for a concrete human person.

The idealist, of course, regards minds as *par excellence* the real entities, they being like the AS itself. Rather than to regard the other types of entities as arising by other kinds of manifestation, perhaps they should be regarded rather as the result of the *concentration* of soul-stuff in some particular way or other. Each material object is merely soul *concentrated* in a certain way. The notion of concentration, the very prototype of mental activity, then, would play the role of the relations of manifestation. But concentration is mental in a way in which the relations of manifestation are not. And if "subject" and "object" are alike, both must be mental. Thus the following "principle," where Conc is the relation of concentration, might well hold, namely,

$$\vdash (x)(\text{AS Conc}\, x \supset x \text{ Like AS}).$$

Everything that results from the AS by concentration is itself like or similar to AS. And likewise,

$$\vdash (x)(x \text{ Like AS} \supset x \text{ P AS}),$$

---

6. Cf. the author's "Of 'of'," in *Pragmatics, Truth, and Language*.

that everything like AS is itself a *part* of it. The former principle might well hold without the latter. If the two principles are taken together, a genuine monism, even a pantheism, is achieved. The development of idealism in terms of the theory of concentration would be more Vedantic than Hegelian. Principles akin to **Pr2–Pr3** and **Pr6–Pr7** would obtain, with 'Conc' in place of 'Emb', no change being required in **Pr1** and **Pr5**.

For the purposes of the subsequent discussion, and to simplify, let us presuppose the theory above as developed in terms of the Hegelian 'Manif' and 'Emb'. But whatever modifications of this might be thought desirable can easily be presupposed equally well.

Howsoever the fundamental ontology is arranged, the AS has remarkable tasks to perform and must be given some remarkable properties, akin to those of the Thomistic God and the Whiteheadian primordial nature. To see this let us consider again the primordial valuations constituting this latter, which will be helpful as a heuristic, enabling us to flesh out the theory underlying St. Thomas' "five signs of will."[7]

The five signs of will, it will be recalled, are *operation, permission, precept, counsel,* and *prohibition,* but St. Thomas is not too clear as to precisely how these are to be construed. The words are used analogically. "A man may show that he wills something . . ." by doing it "directly when he works in his own person; in that way the sign of his will is said to be an *operation*. He shows it indirectly, by not hindering the doing of a thing; . . . In this the sign is called *permission*. He declares his will by means of another when he orders another to perform a work, either by insisting upon it as necessary by *precept*, and by *prohibiting* its contrary; or by persuasion, which is a part of *counsel*."[8] St. Thomas goes on to note that "since the will of man makes itself known in these ways, the same five are sometimes called divine wills, in the sense of being signs of that will. That *precept, counsel,* and *prohibition* are called the will of God is clear from the words of *Matt.* vi. 10: *Thy will be done on earth as it is in heaven*. That *permission* and *operation* are called the will of God is clear from Augustine, who says: *Nothing is done, unless the almighty wills it to be done, either by permitting it, or by actually doing it.*" These very significant but difficult comments should be helpful in attempting to characterize the divine will, whether construed Thomistically or not.

---

7. The treatment of the priordial valuations here, although akin to that of II and III above, differs from it in important technical respects.

8. *Summa Theologica,* I, q. 19, a. 12.

Among the operations we should surely include all the manifestations and embodyings. These operations concern only the ontology. In addition, there are the primordially ordained circumstances, laws, and so on. Let

$$\text{'AS PrOp } a, x_1, ..., x_n\text{'}$$

express that the AS *primordially* operates or has it obtain that the n-place predicate a, standing for a virtual class or relation, apply to or denote $x_1, ..., x_n$, in this order.

That the AS is the "creator" of all entities (other than himself) is in effect provided by **Pr7** above. But he is also the ordainer of all scientific, moral, and aesthetic law, and this aspect of the divine activity can be stipulated only by bringing in the relation PrOp. Thus suppose $\ulcorner ax_1...x_n\urcorner$ obtains, for fixed $x_1, ..., x_n$, and a, not just factually but as the result of, or as an instance of, some scientific law. Then it would obtain that

Pr8. $\vdash$ AS PrOp $a, x_1, ..., x_n$,

for such $a, x_1, ..., x_n$. Nor need **Pr8** be restricted to just scientific law. It should be extended to instances of whatever laws are thought to obtain in any of the spheres of knowledge. And if one or more of the x_i's are allowed to be numbers, natural, real, or complex, even laws of a probabilistic kind may also be included here. Think what a staggering principle **Pr8** then is, incorporating as it does all the laws governing the cosmos, construed in the most inclusive possible sense. But surely the AS must be conceived as so great as to incorporate no less.[9]

Clearly also it holds that

Pr9. $\vdash (y)(a)(x_1)...(x_n)(y \text{ PrOp } a, x_1, ..., x_n \supset y = \text{AS})$,

so that the AS is the *only* entity capable of the primordial operations. And also

Pr10. $\vdash (a)(x_1)...(x_n)((\text{AS PrOp } a, x_1, ..., x_n \cdot a \text{ Des}_{\text{VR}} F) \supset Fx_1....x_n)$.

Whatever is primordially ordained to obtain does actually obtain. But the converse need not hold. Not all that obtains is primordially ordained to do so. The 'Des$_{\text{VR}}$' here is the sign for the designation of virtual classes or relations, and if $n = 1$,

$$\text{'}a \text{ Des}_{\text{VR}} F\text{'} \quad \text{is short for} \quad \text{'}(\text{PredCon}_1 a \cdot (x)(a \text{ Den } x \equiv Fx))\text{'},$$

---

9. **PR8** is of course oversimplified, but a more general formulation and discussion is not needed for the present.

'Den' being the primitive for denotation.[10]

The primordial operations need not be confined to just the demands of scientific law, as already noted. Moral and aesthetic laws, if there are such, are included, and even such boundary conditions as might be thought to obtain independent of law. Perhaps even there are miracles in some sense as the direct result of a primordial operation. If so, the stipulation of such is presumed included here.

St. Thomas speaks of prohibition in a somewhat narrow sense, of prohibiting the "contrary" of a precept. Here let us speak rather of prohibiting the contradictory of an operation. Thus we may let

$$\text{'AS PrPrhbt}_{\text{Op}}\, a, x_1, ..., x_n\text{'} \quad \text{abbreviate} \quad \text{'AS PrOp } \ulcorner \neg a \urcorner, x_1, ..., x_n\text{'},$$

where $\ulcorner \neg a \urcorner$ is the negation of a. There are other kinds of prohibition, which we shall meet with in a moment.

The primordial operations concern all objects whatsoever, including human persons, actions, events, states, processes, and the like. The precepts and counsels, on the other hand, may be thought to concern only human beings and their actions. Let 'p' be a variable for persons and 'e' for actions of the kind humans are capable of performing. Let P be a virtual class of persons satisfying such and such conditions, and A a class of suitable actions. Then we may let

$$\text{'AS PrPrcpt 'P', '}\{p \ni (Ee)(p \text{ Prfm } e \bullet A e)\}\text{''}$$

express that it is a primordial precept that persons of the kind P should be persons who *perform* actions of the kind A, under appropriate circumstances. Precepts always seem to be general in this way applying to all persons and actions of given kinds. Counsels, on the other hand, may always be regarded as specific, applying to a given person with respect to a given action.

Are all counsels covered by a precept? It is tempting to think so, whether the precept is explicitly known or exhibited or not. If so, we may let

$$\text{'AS PrCnsl } p, e, \text{'P', 'A''} \quad \text{abbreviate} \quad \text{'AS PrPrcpt 'P', '}\{q \ni (Ee')(q$$
$$\text{Prfm } e' \bullet A e')\}\text{' } \bullet \text{ P}p \bullet Ae)\text{',}$$

so that p is counseled to do e relative to 'P' and 'A' just where it is precepted that all P's do A's and p is a P and e an A.

More general definitions, with variables in place of the constants, may be given by letting

---

10. Cf. *Truth and Denotation*, p. 106.

'AS PrPrcpt a, $\ulcorner\{p\ni(E e)(p$ Prfm $e \cdot b$ Den $e)\}\urcorner$',

and the like, also be significant primitively, and then letting

'AS PrCnsl p,e,a,b' abbreviate 'AS PrPrcpt a, $\ulcorner\{q\ni(E e')(q$ Prfm $e' \cdot b$ Den $e')\}\urcorner \cdot a$ Den $p \cdot b$ Den e)'.

Note that by means of precept the AS in effect "orders" a person "to perform a work" by "insiting upon it as necessary," in some social, moral, or aesthetic sense. And surely some generality must obtain as a condition for the necessity; hence the use of the class terms 'P' and 'A'. Counsel, however, is always specific and "persuasion" is a part of it. Only a person presumably, even a sum of persons, can be persuaded and hence counseled in this sense.

There are relevant kinds of prohibition corresponding with precept and counsel. Thus we let

'AS PrPrhbt$_{\text{Prept}}$'P','A'' abbreviate 'AS PrPrcpt 'P','$\{p\ni\sim(E e)(p$ Prfm $e \cdot Ae)\}$'',

so that persons of the kind P are prohibited in this sense from being persons who perform actions of the kind A. And there are also prohibitive counsels, so that

'AS PrPrhbt$_{\text{Cnsl}}p,e$,'P','A'' abbreviates 'AS PrPrhbt$_{\text{Prept}}$ 'P','A' $\cdot$ P $p \cdot$ A e)'.

More general forms of these definitions, with variables in place of the constants 'P' and 'A', may also be given.

Clearly, corresponding with **Pr9**, we should have that

Pr11. $\vdash(x)(a)(b)(x$ PrPrcpt $a,b \supset (x = \text{AS} \cdot (y)((a$ Den $y \vee b$ Den $y) \supset$ Per $y)))$,

where 'Per' is the predicate for persons.

Also where

$$'p\ \text{Oblg}\ a'$$

expresses deontically that p is *obliged* to be a person of the kind denoted by a, we should have that

Pr12. $\vdash(a)(b)(p)((\text{AS PrPrcpt}\ a,b \cdot a\ \text{Den}\ p) \supset p\ \text{Oblg}\ b)$.

This principle assumes that whatever is primordially precepted, so to speak, is deontically obliged. This at least should hold, but not the converse. There are surely obligatory acts not determined so primordially.

No doubt much takes place in the cosmos that is primordially neutral in the sense of being neither the result of an operation nor operationally prohibited. Thus, where 'PredCon$_n$ a' expresses that a is an n-place predicate constant,

> 'AS PrNtrl$_{Op}$$a,x_1,...,x_n$' may abbreviate '(PredCon$_n$$a$ • ~ AS PrOp $a,x_1,..x_n$ • ~ AS PrPrhbt$_{Op}$$a,x_1,...,x_n$)'.

And similarly for human actions that are neither covered by precept nor precept-wise prohibited. Thus also

> 'AS PrNtrl$_{Prcpt}$ 'P','A'' abbreviates '(~AS PrPrcpt 'P','$\{p \ni (E e)(p$ Prfm e • A $e)\}$' • ~ AS PrPrhbt$_{Prcpt}$ 'P','A')'.

Here too, a more general definition may easily be given.

Note that in the foregoing only 'PrOp' and 'PrPrcpt' have been needed as primitives, in addition of course to 'Manif', 'Emb', and 'AS'. All the other primordial predicates have been defined within the linguistic framework embodying quantification theory, identity, mereology (or the calculus of individuals), and of course some semantics and event theory. The deontic notion 'Oblg' is also presumed available, either primitively or by definition, but it is not a purely primordial notion, being relative always to a given social group and a specific deontic code.

There is also the all-important notion of a primordial *permission*, to which we now turn.

It is clear, if nothing is done other than its being done either by the Almighty or being permitted by him, that the operations and permissions exhaust the divine will and that the other "signs" are to be handled as subdivisions. The operations and permissions are thus to be mutually exclusive and jointly exhaustive. Under the primordial operations are included the manifestations, embodiments, operations proper, and the operational prohibitions. These operations are all such that their results, so to speak, *must* obtain if our cosmos is to be the way it is. All the other primordial notions are included in the permissions, whose results *may* be violated in our cosmos. Note the implicit distinction here between the operations and permissions, on the one hand, and their "results," on the other. The results of the one *must* obtain, but those of the other need not. On the other hand, the operations and permissions themselves constitute the necessary activity of the AS, if our cosmos is to be what it is.

The prohibitions include just the three kinds, operational, preceptual, and counsel-wise, the precepts both the proper and prohibitive ones, and similarly for the counsels. The primordially neutral comprise the operationally neutral and the preceptually so. The primordial permissions, as already noted, then comprise all the primordial activities not included in the operations, i.e., the prohibitions, the precepts, the counsels, and the primordially neutral. These comments may all be summarized by means of three additional definitions. We may let

'PrOp e' abbreviate '$(Ea)(Ex_1)...(Ex_k)(<$AS,Manif,$x_1>e$ v
$<$AS,Emb,$x_1>e$ v $<$AS,PrOp, $a,x_1>e$ v $<$AS,PrOp,$a,x_1,x_2>e$
v ... v $<$AS,PrOp,$a,x_1,...,x_k>e$)',
'PrPrmsn e' abbreviate '$(Ea)(Eb)(Ep)(Ee')(Ex_1)...(Ex_k)$
$(<$AS,PrPrhbt$_{Prcpt}$, $a,b>e$ v $<$AS,PrPrhbt$_{Cnsb}p,e',a,b>e$ v
$<$AS,PrPrcpt,$a,b>e$ v $a,x >e$ v ... v
$<$AS,PrNtrl$_{Op}$,$a,x_1,...,x_k>e$ v $<$AS,PrNtrl$_{Prcpt}$,$a,b>e$)',

and

'PrPrhbtn e' abbreviates '$(Ea)(Eb)(Ep)(Ee')(Ex_1)...(Ex_k)$
$($AS,PrPrhbt$_{Op}$,$a,x_1 >e$ v ... v $<$AS,PrPrhbt$_{Op}$,$a,x_1,...,x_k>e$ v
$<$AS,PrPrhbt$_{Prcpt}a,b>e$ v $<$AS,PrPrhbt$_{Cnsb}p,e',a,b>e$)'.

These definitions introduce the notions of being a primordial operation, permission, or prohibition, respectively.

Note the use of the variable 'e' for an act or state. And recall that the expressions enclosed in the half-diamonds are event-descriptive predicates. Thus '$<$AS,Manif,$x_1>e$', for example, expresses that e is an act or state of x_1's being manifest by AS. Extensive use is made of such predicates within event logic.[11] Note also the special use of the parameter 'k' for the degree of the primitive predicate of greatest degree needed as a primitive, and where there are assumed to be primitive predicates of each degree n where $1 \leq n \leq k$.

The notion of the divine will may be thought to be fully analyzed in terms of the disjunction of these three. Thus

'DW' may be short for '$\{e\ni(PrOp\,e$ v $PrPrmsn\,e$ v $PrPrhbtn\,e)\}$'.

The DW is thus merely the virtual class of all primordial operations, permissions, and prohibitions.

A few principles over and above **Pr1–Pr12** above that should presumably obtain are as follows.

Pr13. $\vdash (a)(x_1)...(x_n)($AS PrOp $a,x_1,...,x_n \supset ($PredCon$_n\,a \cdot \sim x_1 = $AS $\cdot$
... $\cdot \sim x_n = AS)$.

---

11. See *Events, Reference, and Logical Form* and *Semiotics and Linguistic Structure*.

Pr14. $\vdash \sim (Ea)(Ex_1)...(Ex_n)(\text{AS PrOp } a,x_1,...,x_n \cdot \text{AS PrPrhbt}_{\text{Op}}$
$a,x_1,...,x_n).$

Pr15. $\vdash \sim (Ea)(Eb)(\text{AS PrPrcpt } a,b \cdot \text{AS PrPrcpt } a, \ulcorner \text{-}b \urcorner,$

Pr16. $\vdash (a)(b)(x_1)...(x_n)(\text{ASPrOp } \ulcorner (a \cap_n b) \urcorner,x_1,...x_n \equiv (\text{AS PrOp}$
$a,x_1,...x_n \cdot \text{AS PrOp } b,x_1,...,x_n)).$

Pr17. $\vdash (a)(b)(x_1)...(x_n)((\text{ASPrOp } a,x_1,...,x_n \text{ v AS PrOp } b,x_1,...,x_n) \supset \text{AS}$
$\text{PrOp } \ulcorner (a \cup_n b) \urcorner,x_1,...,x_n).[12]$

Pr18. $\vdash (a)(b)(x_1)...(x_n)((\text{AS PrOp } a,x_1,...,x_n \cdot \text{AS PrOp } \ulcorner (\text{-}a \cup_n$
$b) \urcorner,x_1,...,x_n \supset \text{AS PrOp } b,x_1,...,x_n).$

Some of the various principles given may need some modification in the light of a more thorough presentation. The whole theory of primordiality in fact cries out for further elaboration and development, being still in its infancy.

The analysis of the primordial valuations and hence of the divine will, given above, agrees with that of St. Thomas to some extent. A few additional points of parallel are as follows. St. Thomas notes that "there is no reason why the same thing should not be the subject of precept, operation, counsel, prohibition, or permission." Clearly one and the same human act can be the result of a prohibitional operation as well as a prohibitional counsel, and hence of a prohibitional permission. St. Thomas contends also that "God ordains rational creatures to act voluntarily and of themselves. Other creatures act only as moved by the divine operation; therefore only operation and permission are concerned with these." This contention agrees with the foregoing, permission here being taken in the sense of the primordially neutral.

'All evil of sin," St. Thomas notes also, "though happening in many ways, agrees in being out of harmony with the divine will. Hence, with regard to evil, only one sign [of will] is proposed, that of prohibition." The evil of sin is precisely what is primordially prohibited by precept. (There is no sin as the result of a primordial operation, all such operations being included in the primordially good.) "On the other hand," St. Thomas goes on, "good [the humanly good] stands in various relations to the divine goodness, since there are good deeds without which we cannot attain to the fruition of that goodness, and *these are the subject of precept* [italics added]." The primordially good is the subject of precept, and counsel above was taken as instantial of precept. But St. Thomas construes counsel here rather differently, "for there are other goods," he says, "by which we attain to it [the fruition] more

---

12. The '$\cup_n$' and '$\cap_n$' are the signs for the union and intersection respectively of virtual n-adic relations.

perfectly, and these are the subject of counsel." Here counsel seems to be concerned rather with supererogation. But even some precepts might be stipulative of the supererogatorily good, so that even this last remarks could be seen to accord with the foregoing.

Any philosophical discussion of God's will must perforce be speculative, as indeed is the foregoing. There would not seem to be much point in discussing it at all, however, without some analysis of what the phrase is supposed to designate. At best we can merely hypothesize what this might be, and thus we never could be said to know it in any more direct sense. Even so, hypothetical constructs are useful in theology just as they are in theoretical science.[13]

Note that the foregoing hypothetical reconstruction of some features of metaphysical idealism has been given in a semantical metalanguage incorporating a theory of acts. It would seem very doubtful that a more restricted kind of logical framework would suffice for this purpose. Note also that the primordial notions have been handled intensionally. These are given by reference to a *predicate* rather than to a (virtual) class or relation the predicate might designate. The reason for this is the familiar one concerning the intensionality of obligation, to which the primordial notions are akin. It would not do to say, in a deontic logic, for example, that one is obliged to be an F, for F might be equivalent with some G, with respect to which one is not obliged. Reference to the predicate 'F' here instead of to the virtual class F prevents any such unwanted consequence. Hence the intensional treatment, within a semantical metalanguage, of the primordial notions throughout, in terms essentially of Frege's *Art des Gegebenseins*.

An alternative, more sophisticated way of handling manifestation and embodiment, and even some of the primordial relations, suggests itself if a numerical measure is introduced. We may think of the AS as manifesting itself in x *to just such and such a degree*. All entities manifested to the same degree would then be of essentially some same kind. The very difference between manifestation and embodiment could then be handled in terms of difference of degree. Embodiment would be low degree of manifestation. Let

$$\text{'AS Manif}^i x\text{'}$$

express that x is a manifestation of AS to just degree i. If $i = 0$, we could let x be the null entity, and if $i = 1$, we could let x be AS itself. AS

---

13. Cf. J. Bocheński, *op. cit.* See also the discussion thereof in *Whitehead's Categoreal Scheme and Other Papers*, Chapter IX.

then manifests itself to maximal degree. Physical objects have low degrees attached to them, and highly mental ones have high degrees; and similarly for the primordial precepts, some of which are more binding than others. Here too it might be of interest to introduce a numerical degree. Whitehead speaks of the degree of a primordial valuation, as noted above. No one, it would seem, has ever developed such a theory in any detail, however, for natural theology and the use of numerical measures are not ordinarily thought to go hand in hand. A quite sophisticated view would result if a suitable numerical measure were introduced, and no doubt some interesting notions would be forthcoming in terms of it.

Nothing has been said thus far concerning physical time, space, casuality, and the like. Any attempt to locate the AS with respect to any of these is quite foreign to the foregoing. It is rather the other way around, all objects of the physical world themselves being embodiments of the AS. Hence the foregoing theory is all couched in the Fregean tense of timelessness, so to speak, as in that of spacelessness, causalitylessness, and so on.

Of course only the barest logical *maquette* of the full theory concerning AS has been given here. Indeed, to flesh out the foregoing in adequate detail would be a formidable task indeed. Nonetheless, certain general features of what the fuller development would be like should be evident. In particular it would comprise foundations for a theory of objective value as contained in the primordial precepts. Thus, as far as this scheme goes, there is no essential dichotomy between fact and value, but each is handled in its separate way. Nor is there any easy reduction of one to the other. Each is given its proper dignity and the way is left open for discriminating all manner of interconnections between the two. Note also that there is here no illicit dichotomy between reason and faith. Again, it is rather that a rational scheme is available in which a theory of faith may be incorporated. Indeed, it may be that faith, in a suitable sense, is our highest rational activity, for it is always reasonable to let one's mind wander to an *0 altitudo!* The task of natural theology in fact may be thought to be just this.

But faith is nothing if it does not issue in action, as many writers in the tradition of *philosophia perennis* have eloquently affirmed. And indeed the notion of the AS is of such staggering grandeur and magnitude that it seems eminently rational that we should "shape the whole conduct of [our] life . . . into conformity" with it. To do this, in fact, should be our whole aim, everywhere and always, as the great writers of that tradition have been continually affirming across the centuries. "To interpret the absolute we must give all our time to it." The pursuit of science, of beauty, and of goodness are alike here given their proper role in this endeavor.

There is something compelling about human feeling at what we take to be its highest, in the full experience, say, of a great work of art. It is doubtful that such feeling can be suitably and fully explicated on any other basis than one such as the foregoing. We can go a long way in analytic aesthetics without it, but always with a most essential human ingredient left out — the depth and quality of authentic aesthetic feeling at its best.

The positive contribution of the present paper is merely to have made seem tentative suggestions toward giving the *philosophia perennis* the logical backbone it is often thought to lack. Usually in discussions of the AS there is too much logically irresponsible misstatement. But so lofty a topic would seem best served by using such clean-cut logical notions as are now available. Surely we should let idealism, along with other metaphysical views, grow along with the advance of science and philosophic technique.

CHAPTER VI

On the Logic of the
Psyché in Plotinus

Bonus animus in mala re, dimidium est mali.

The primary aim of this paper is to attempt to bring what essentially is the great cosmological vision of Plotinus into harmony with contemporary science, including logic and mathematics. The brief sketch of a logico-metaphysical system to be presented is thus thought to provide an at least rough approximation to some of the basic features of the Plotinic system. We need not worry as to how exact the fit is. No doubt it is very loose in some respects and perhaps too tight in others. Enough will be shown, it is hoped, to suggest that with suitable emendations and extensions, however, the approximateness may be lessened and the fit made more comfortable throughout.

To attempt to get the exact fit, incidentally, is eminently "dialectical" in the Platonic — and no doubt Plotinic — sense. A. E. Taylor commented many years back that "what the *Republic* calls 'dialectic' is, in principle, simply the rigorous and unremitting task of steady scrutiny of the indefinables and indemonstrables of the sciences, and that in particular . . . [Plato's] . . . ideal, so far as the sciences with which he is directly concerned goes, is just that reduction of mathematics to rigorous deduction from expressly formulated logical premises by exactly specified logical methods of which the work of Peano, Frege, Whitehead, and Russell has given us a magnificent example."[1] It is thus eminently dialectical to apply Plato's ideal to the Plotinic system itself.

Recall also Plotinus' own comment (I.3.5-6) that dialectic is "the precious part of philosophy: in its study of the laws of the universe, Philosophy draws on Dialectic much as other studies and crafts use Arithmetic, though, of course, the alliance between Philosophy and

---

1. A. E. Taylor, *Plato, the Man and His Work* (London: Methuen, 1963 (first published in 1926)), p. 293.

Dialectic is closer."[2] Of course we must not force the letter of logical theory-construction upon either Plato or Plotinus, so much as note similarity of spirit across the centuries. Recall also the remarkable comment in I.8.1 where Plotinus writes: "Our intelligence is nourished on the proposition of logic, is skilled in following discussions, works by reasonings, examines links of demonstration, and comes to know the world of Being also by the steps of logical process, having no prior grasp of Reality but remaining empty, all Intelligence though it be, until it has put itself to school." Well, let us put ourselves to school on what is essentially the Plotinic system.

Let 'One' be a proper name for the Plotinic One or Unity, and 'AllSoul' for the *Psyché* or the All-Soul. And let 'Int' be a one-place predicate so that 'Int x' expresses that x is a Form or a member of the Intelligible Realm, of *Noûs*. And let 'Obj x' express that x is an object of the lower Cosmos, of the lower world of Nature or of the Sensibles, among which are included human bodies. Roughly, then, we have these four expressions for the four Plotinic levels; two of them, note, are proper names, and two of them are predicates. The proper names are for the primary unities, and the predicates are for multiplicities, which, however, also have a kind of unity, a secondary unity, let us say. With this notation in mind let us reflect now upon (1) the logic of emanation, (2) the role of modern set theory with sets construed as elements in the Intelligible Realm, (3) how the lower souls may be construed modally as constructs in terms of 'AllSoul', (4) the character of the "Plan contained in the Reason-Principle" whereby the All is governed, and, finally, (5) the notion of the return to the One, the flight of the alone to the Alone.

Let us consider first the logic of emanation, which is no doubt best construed in terms of a dyadic relation. Let 'x Em y' express that x emanates into y or that y is an emanation from x. The exact behavior of this relation is, of course, what we wish now to inquire into. Let us first specify a few very simple principles concerning emanation. First, the relation Em is presumably *totally irreflexive, asymmetric,* and *transitive*. Thus

Pr1. $\vdash (x)\sim x \operatorname{Em} x,$

Pr2. $\vdash (x)(y)(x \operatorname{Em} y \supset \sim y \operatorname{Em} x),$

and

Pr3. $\vdash (x)(y)(z)((x \operatorname{Em} y \cdot y \operatorname{Em} z) \supset x \operatorname{Em} z).$

Clearly also the four realms are *mutually exclusive,* in the sense that

---

2. The translation used throughout is that of McKenna.

Pr4. ⊢ ~ Int One • ~ One = AllSoul • ~ Obj One • ~ Int AllSoul • ~ Obj AllSoul • ~ (Ex)(Int x • Obj x).

And all four domains *exist* in appropriate senses, so that

Pr5. ⊢E!One • (Ex)Int x • E!AllSoul • (Ex)Obj x.

Concerning the One we have some special principles as follows.

Pr6. ⊢ (x)(~ x = One ⊃ One Em x).

Pr7. ⊢ ~ (Ex)(~ x = One • (y)(~ y = One ⊃ x Em y)).

Pr6 states that everything other than the One is an emanation from the One, and **Pr7** states that there is nothing other than the One from which everything other than the One emanates.

Immediate consequences of these principles are:

Pr8. ⊢ (x)(Int x ⊃ One Em x).
Pr9. ⊢ One Em AllSoul.
Pr10. ⊢ (x)(Obj x ⊃ One Em x).

But also the following hold.

Pr11. ⊢ (x)(Int x ⊃ x Em AllSoul).
Pr12. ⊢ (x)(Obj x ⊃ AllSoul Em x).

Every intelligible emanates into the AllSoul and the AllSoul into every object. No object, however, emanates into anything, so that

Pr13. ⊢ (x)(Obj x ⊃ ~ (Ey)x Em y).

Concerning the One, very little can be truly said that cannot be said in terms of 'Em'. Thus

Pr14. ⊢ ⌐~ **F** One⌐ , for most predicates **F** not containing 'Em'.

Of course in a fuller discussion we shall have to be more specific here about the **F**'s, how they are constructed, and so on.

Concerning the intelligible realm, however, a good deal can be said, and it may be of interest to try to view it in terms, partly at least, of modern set theory. Sets are thought by many contemporary theorists to constitute *par excellence* the very prototype of intelligible entities. Some even go so far as to say that they are the *only* such objects, but this contention might seem somewhat extreme. Let us require here only that sets are *included* among the intelligibles but perhaps do not exhaust them.

A clarificatory remark is in order. Note that in including sets among the intelligibles, we are not *using* the notions of set theory in the underlying logic of the theory of emanation. For this latter we are using only the familiar first-order quantification theory with identity. The domain of individuals is taken to consist of all the entities of the four Plotinic realms, including now sets in the intelligible realm. To specify all this we take 'ϵ' for the membership relation and 'Λ' for the null set as primitive. We may then define

D1.   'Set x'   as   '$(x = \Lambda \text{ v } (Ey)y \epsilon x)$',

and stipulate that

Pr15. $\vdash (x)(\text{Set } x \supset \text{Int } x)$.

We also need to specify what the members of sets are to be allowed to be. Clearly the members are to be just the inhabitants of the lowest realm, sets of such, and so on, but not the One nor the AllSoul. If these were allowed membership we should then be *using* set theory to formulate the Plotinic theory, rather than merely allowing sets their proper place in the intelligible realm. Thus we have as additional principles that

Pr16. $\vdash \sim (Ex)\text{One } \epsilon x \cdot \sim (Ex)\text{AllSoul } \epsilon x \cdot \sim (Ex)(\text{Int } x \cdot \sim \text{Set } x \cdot (Ey)x \epsilon y)$,

and, more generally, that

Pr17. $\vdash (x)(y)(x \epsilon y \supset (\text{Set } x \text{ v Obj } x))$,

and hence of course that

Pr18. $\vdash (y)((\text{Set } y \cdot \sim y = \Lambda) \supset (Ex)(x \epsilon y \cdot (\text{Set } x \text{ v Obj } x)))$.

It was remarked that the One and the AllSoul are given primary unity, and that the intelligible realm and the cosmos are multiplicities and have only secondary unity. How then do we handle the individual souls, and the oneness of these realms? To attempt to answer the first question, let us bring in the human body. Let 'HB x' express that x is a human body. What then is the human person or individual soul? If we allow ourselves the logical devices of the calculus of individuals (Leśniewski's *mereology*) — which we shall surely wish to do at some point anyhow — in addition to quantification theory with identity, we may proceed as follows. Let $(x \cup y)$ be the compound or sum individual consisting of x and y together, and let us suppose that we can form the sum of any two entities from the whole Plotinic universe. Also we let 'x Ens y' express that x *ensouls* y, i.e., x enters into or affects y in the appropriate manner. We then may identify the living human person or individual soul-cum-body as merely the compound entity (AllSoul $\cup x$) where x is an HB ensouled by the AllSoul. Thus we may define

D2.   'LPer x'   as   '$(Ey)(HB\,y \cdot x = (AllSoul \cup y) \cdot AllSoul\,Ens\,y)$'.

Then clearly we have that

Pr19. $\vdash (x)(y)(z)((HB\,y \cdot x = (AllSoul \cup y) \cdot AllSoul\,Ens\,y \cdot HB\,z \cdot x = (AllSoul \cup z) \cdot AllSoul\,Ens\,z) \supset y = z)$,

and of course, where P is the part-whole relation between individuals, that

Pr20. $\vdash (x)(y)((LPer\,x \cdot LPer\,y \cdot (Ez)(HB\,z \cdot z\,P\,x \cdot z\,P\,y)) \supset x = y)$.

Note that **Pr19** and **Pr20** are merely logical truths, showing the one-to-one correspondence between living persons and ensouled human bodies. Also clearly

Pr21. $\vdash (x)(HB\,x \supset Obj\,x)$,

but

Pr22. $\vdash \sim(Ex)(LPer\,x \cdot Obj\,x)$.

The use of 'Ens' here for the relation of ensoulment is a desirable extension of our vocabulary. Plotinus explicitly states, in IV.3.9, that "if we are to explain and to be clear, we are obliged to use such words as 'entry' and 'ensoulment', though never was . . .[the] All unsouled, never did body subsist with soul away, never was there Matter un-elaborate; we separate, the better to understand; there is nothing il-legitimate in the verbal and mental sunderings of things which must in fact be co-existent."

Now let us consider the unity of the realm of the intelligibles. This may be taken in terms of the notion of the *fusion* of a class in the sense of the calculus of individuals. Thus we may identify *Noûs* with this fusion. More formally, we may let

D3.   'Noûs' abbreviate   '(Fu'Int)'.

Where $i_1, i_2, \ldots$ is the nonndenumerably infinite array of intelligibles, the entity Noûs is merely $(i_1 \cup i_2 \cup \ldots)$. Of course we can never carry out an enumeration of these intelligibles, their cardinality presumably being beyond all bounds even among the transfinite cardinals.

With the notion of Noûs available as a collective term, so to speak, we may emend **Pr11** above. It might appear too strong to say that each and every intelligible individually emanates into the AllSoul. A weaker and perhaps more acceptable statement is that Noûs as a whole does, that is, that the intelligibles *collectively* emanate into the AllSoul. Thus in place of **Pr11** we might better require that

Pr11′.   ⊢ Noûs Em AllSoul.

Let us try now to justify some of these principles, to some extent anyhow, on the basis of the actual text.

That there is a multiplicity of ideal forms is discussed at some length in VI.7, and in II.4.4 it is commented that "there must be some character common to all [forms] and equally some peculiar character in each keeping them distinct. This peculiar characteristic, this distinguishing difference, is the individual shape. But if shape, then there is the shaped, that in which the difference is lodged. There is, therefore, a Matter accepting the shape, a permanent substratum. Further, admitting that there is an Intelligible Realm beyond, of which this world is an image, then, since this World-Compound is based on Matter, there must be Matter there too."

The feature common to the forms is no doubt that they are instantiable or inherent in something else. This feature is "there," then as characterizing the entities in the intelligible realm. When there is an "individual shape" or character, there also is implicitly that which is shaped or characterized. There is then "intelligible matter" in the ideal realm in just this sense. And note how natural it seems to include sets in the intelligible realm, sets above all having this property of having members — except the null set, which is somewhat adscititious anyhow. It is very interesting too to note that Plotinus, in II.4.5, comments that "we discover these two — Matter and Idea — by sheer force of our reasoning which distinguishes continually in pursuit of the simplex, the irreducible, working on, until it can go no further, towards the ultimate in the subject of inquiry." The irreducible in any inquiry are the notions characterized in primitive terms in just such and such a way, much as subjects (proper names or variables) and predicates, together of course with the basic logical ingredients, are irreducible elements in language-systems.

Definition **D2** is in close harmony with I.1.3−5. Plotinus states that "we may treat of the Soul as in the body — whether it be set above it or actually within it — since the association of the two constitutes the one thing called the living organism, the Animate. . . . Now this Animate might be merely the body as having life: it might be the Couplement of Soul and body: it might be a third and different entity formed from both." Or, we can add, it might be all three. "The truth lies," Plotinus contends, "in the consideration that the Couplement subsists by virtue of the Soul's presence." Plotinus seems to come out here by saying that whatever we wish to say concerning the Animate we can say in terms of the ensouled "Couplement." A most natural interpretation of these remarks is thus in terms of logical sums, as in **D2**. Recall also, in I.7.3, that "life is a partnership of Soul and body; death is the dissolution; in either life or death, then, the Soul will feel itself at home." The AllSoul is clearly "at home" in both itself and any of its couplements.

That a proper name should be taken for the Soul is amply justified in IV.9, in which it is argued that there is but one Soul, although there is a sense in which we may speak of your soul, my soul, and so on. "We are not asserting the unity of soul in the sense of a complete negation of multiplicity — only of the Supreme can that be affirmed — we are thinking of soul as simultaneously one and many, participant in the nature divided in body, but at the same time a unity by virtue of belonging to that Order which suffers no division. . . . These reflections show that there is nothing strange in that reduction of all souls to one. But it is still necessary to inquire into the *mode* and *conditions* [italics added] of the unity," as well of course into the perhaps merely verbal partition of the AllSoul into the celestial and lower souls. It would seem that this all can be done on the basis of the foregoing logical reconstruction, as we shall see in a moment.

Incidentally, the remarkable passage in II.3.13 no doubt gives the key to what remains to be done. "The gist of the whole matter lies in the consideration that Soul governs this All by *the plan contained in the Reason-Principle* [italics added] and plays in the All exactly the part of the particular principle which in every living-thing forms the members of the organism and adjusts them to the unity of which they are portions; the entire force of the Soul is represented in the All but, in the parts, Soul is present only in proportion to the degree of essential reality held by each of such partial objects." How Whiteheadian this sounds, the "degree of essential reality" being akin to the degree of ingression of an eternal object into an actual occasion, and to the extent to which any occasion acts in accord with the vision of it in the primordial nature of God. Should we introduce a numerical measure here? It is tempting to do so, just as it is in the discussion of Whitehead.[3] We might let 'x Em^iy' be taken primitively to express that x emanates into y to just degree i. A much more elaborate theory would result. However, let us not introduce here complications beyond necessity.

---

3. See *Whitehead's Categoreal Scheme and Other Papers*, Chapter I.

The cosmic plan contained in the Reason-Principle will be discussed in a moment.

In IV.3 Plotinus argues "against those who maintain our souls to be offshoots from the Soul of the universe (parts and not an identity *modally parted* [italics added])." On the contrary, "there is one identical soul, *every separate manifestation being that soul complete* [italics added]." Plotinus is sensitive to divergent meanings of 'part', and regards it as false that individuals souls are "parts" of the AllSoul in most senses of that word. However, there is one sense that he does seem to allow. There is the sense of 'part' in which we speak of a theorem as being a part of the entire science to which it belongs. "The theorem is separate, but the science stands as one undivided thing, the separation into theorems being simply the act of making each constituent notion explicit and efficient: this is partition without severance; each item potentially includes the whole science, which itself remains un unbroken total." How now are we to handle the multiplicity of souls so as to assure that there is only one identical soul, "every separate manifestation being that soul complete?" The key notion here is that the individual souls are only "modally parted" from the AllSoul — *intentionally* so, we might say — but not actually so.

To handle intentionality let us adopt Frege's notion of the *Art des Gegebenseins,* or mode or manner of linguistic presentation. Let us consider first the embodied AllSoul as taken under this or that predicate. Let 'F_0' be a predicate-description of entities capable of *intellection,* of intuiting entities of the intelligible realm. Let 'G_0' be a predicate-description of entities capable of *reasoning* in the ordinary sense, and 'H_0' for unreasoning entities (or animals). We can then consider human and animal bodies under these three different predicates, which give, as it were, the three characteristic acts of the lower souls. To provide for the first two, the intellective and reasoning human souls, we form ordered couples of human persons with 'F_0' and 'G_0'. Thus $<x,‘F_0’>$ becomes identified with the Intellective-Soul of person x, and $<x,‘G_0’>$ with x's Reasoning-Soul. Thus in general we may let

D4a. 'IntSoul$<x,‘F_0’>$' abbreviate '(LPer$x$ • 'F_0' Den$x$)',

where 'Den' stands for the relation of multiple denotation between the one-place predicates of the language and whatever objects that language is concerned with. And similarly

D4b. 'ReasSoul$<x,‘G_0’>$' for '(LPer$x$ • 'G_0' Den$x$)'.

And similarly for Unreasoning Souls, *mut. mat.* (**D4c**).

102

Note that the principle of individuation for the multiplicity of intelligible and reasoning souls is the human body, and for the unreasoning souls, the animal body. This would surely seem to accord with Plotinus' intent.

Note the need for the intentional treatment of the lower souls. It might well obtain factually that

$$\vdash (x)(F_0 x \equiv \operatorname{Repr} x),$$

for some 'Repr', expressing, say, that x reproduces its kind by sexual union. But we would not wish then to regard $<x,\operatorname{Repr}>$ or $<x,\text{'Repr'}>$ as an intellective soul. Hence the use of the predicate 'F_0' rather than the property (or class) F_0 as the second item in the couple, which use prevents the replacement of 'F_0' by its factual equivalent 'Repr'. And clearly we would not be tempted to replace the *name* 'F_0' by the name 'Repr', these being very different names.

Now "nothing of Real Being is ever annulled." There is no "bodily partition" among the intelligibles, "no passing of each separate phase into a distinct unity; every such phase remains in full possession of that identical being. It is exactly so with the souls." Recall that **D4a**−**D4c** make of "bodily partition" the principle of individuation for the separate souls. Even so, each separate soul remains in "full possession" of the AllSoul. Note also that, although the whole human person is regarded here as capable of intellection and reasoning, it is only the person *under the given predicate-description* that is regarded as a soul. In this way an intentional multiplicity of individual souls is achieved, so to speak, but with the unity of the AllSoul preserved. All of the lower souls involve, in a suitable way, the whole of the AllSoul, as we see from the definitions. There is thus no actual partition of the AllSoul into a multiplicity, only a modal or intentional one.

No doubt we should distinguish here between embodied and unembodied souls. **D4a**−**D4c** are concerned of course with embodied souls, and it is they to which the predicates 'F_0', 'G_0', and 'H_0' are regarded as applicable. Analogous definitions could be given taking the AllSoul itself under these descriptions. There would then be just three such unembodied souls. The multiplicity can be achieved, however, by taking 'F_0', 'G_0', and 'H_0' more narrowly as descriptive of just the intellective, rational, and unrational capacities and/or activities *of the various individual souls*. We would then have as many 'F_0's as intellective souls. Let 'F_0^a' be the intellective predicate for the AllSoul as ensouling human person a, 'F_0^b' for the AllSoul as ensouling human person b, and so on. Then

D5a. ⌜UnIntSoul<AllSoul,F_0^a>⌝ abbreviate ⌜(LPer **a** • EF_0^a Den **a**)⌝ , where ⌜EF_0^a⌝ is the structural description of the predicate ⌜F_0^a⌝ .

And similarly for the other two, *mut. mat.* (**D5b**−**D5c**). According to these definitions, it is of course the AllSoul that performs intellection or reasoning through or by means of a human person, so to speak.

In this way, then, "the world of unembodied souls" is provided, as well as those "in our world" that "have entered body and undergone bodily division." (4.1.1). Recall that "soul, there without distinction or partition, has yet a nature lending itself to divisional existence; its division is secession, entry into body." Also "the secession is not of the Soul entire; something of it holds its ground, that in it which recoils from separate existence." Thus, although 'AllSoul' occurs essentially in the expansions into primitive terms of the definientia of **D4a**−**D4c**, it is only certain very special "phases" of AllSoul that are considered, not all phases, not all properties ascribable to it. "Thus it is that, entering this realm, it [the AllSoul] possesses still the vision inherent to that superior phase in virtue of which it unchangingly maintains its integral nature. Even here [in the world] it is not exclusively the partible soul: it is still the impartible as well: what in it knows partition is parted without partibility; undivided as giving itself to the entire body, a whole to a whole, it is divided as being effective in every part" — of the body, we should add, as well as being effective in every part of every body.

Again, in IV.2.1, it is noted very explicitly that "the bodies are separate and the Ideal-Form [AllSoul] which enters into them is correspondingly sundered while, still, it is present as one whole in each of its severed parts, since amid that multiplicity in which complete individuality has entailed complete partition, there is a permanent identity;. . . . In whatsoever bodies it occupies — even the vastest of all, that in which the entire universe is included — it gives itself to the whole without abdicating its unity. . . . Itself devoid of mass, it is present to all mass: it exists here [in distinct phases (?)] and yet is there, and this [there] not in distinct phases but with unsundered identity: thus it is 'parted and not parted', or, better, it has never known partition, never become a parted thing, but remains a self-gathered integral, and is 'parted among bodies' merely in the sense that bodies, in virtue of their own sundered existence, cannot receive it unless in some partitive mode; the partition, in other words, is an occurrence in body, not in soul."

Enough now — perhaps too much — on the AllSoul and its various phases or partitions. But not yet enough about its role as the De-miourgos and the Cosmic Plan. How are we to handle this latter? Clearly the AllSoul *orders* of every object and of every intelligible whether that object partakes of that intelligible or not. The Soul governs the All by the plan contained in the Reason-Principle, as was noted in II.3.13. And in IV.3.13, we are told that "the Ineluctable, the Cosmic Law, is . . . rooted in a natural principle under which each several entity is overruled to go, duly and in order, towards that place and Kind to which it characteristically tends, that is, towards the image of its primal choice and constitution. . . ." Are we to regard the Plan, then, as including items provided by metaphysical principles such as **P1–P22**, etc., above or are we to think of it as having to do only with the objects of the lower cosmos? The former, **P1–P22,** etc., are already provided for and stipulate the way the world is, where 'world' is taken in the widest possible sense. And one of the ways the world is, of course, is that the AllSoul plans how "each several entity," including the lower souls, goes "duly and in order to that place and Kind" to which it properly belongs. Thus the Plan seems to have to do primarily with the lower Cosmos, and with the intelligibles only in their relevance, so to speak, to the lower Cosmos. The AllSoul "looks towards its higher and has intellection; towards itself, and orders, administers, governs its lower" (IV.8.3).

The Plan here, incidentally, has some affinity with the primordial valuations constituting Whitehead's primordial nature of God. These are fixed once and for all and concern each and every actual occasion with respect to the ingression in it of each and every eternal object.

Let 'Order' be a new primitive for the dyadic relation of ordering in just the sense that the AllSoul is to be regarded as ordering the lower cosmos. Syntactically speaking, the AllSoul orders that such and such sentences obtain. Some of these sentences are to the effect that

$$x \in y,$$

where x is an object and y is a set of objects. Others of these sentences concern the lower souls, which in the foregoing treatment are regarded as entities taken under a given linguistic description or *Art des Gegebenseins*. Thus the theory concerning Order will be in the *metametalanguage* of that in which sentences concerning the lower souls occur. This is harmless enough, merely a fact to be noted.

A word more concerning the syntactical structure of the sentences concerning the lower souls is in order. Because we are not using set theory here as part of the basic logic of the entire scheme, the ordered couples used for handling the lower souls are merely *virtual*. The no-

tation for them is thus wholly eliminable in favor of a primitive notation in which no ordered couples are values for variables.[4] And the
bringing in of an *Art des Gegebenseins* carries us into the metalanguage,
enabling us to speak of the AllSoul in its various modal or intentional
phases. Expressions for the lower souls are thus significant only con-
textually, more specifically, in contexts in which the AllSoul (in its
entirety, so to speak) is taken under different linguistic descriptions.
Let us call any sentence (in primitive terms) of this kind an *LS-
statement,* a statement ascribing or denying something or other of the
lower souls. Similarly let us call *Obj-statements* sentences of the form

$$\ulcorner x \in y \urcorner$$

where **x** is a constant for an object and **y** for a set. (Note the legitimacy
here of using set theory in speaking about *objects*.) Now the Plan is
concerned in part surely with LS- and Obj-statements, as we shall see
in a moment.

As metametalinguistic principles concerning the Plan, we have then
the following.

Pr23. $\vdash (x)(a)(x \text{ Order } a \supset (x = \text{AllSoul} \cdot \text{Sent } a))$

and

Pr24. $\vdash (a)(\text{AllSoul Order } a \supset \text{Tr } a),$

where 'Tr a' expresses that a is a truth of the metalanguage. **Pr23** here
is a *Limitation Principle,* according to which only the AllSoul orders
anything, and whatever it orders is a sentence of the metalanguage.
Pr24, a *Principle of Cosmic Obedience,* we might call it, is to the effect
that whatever is ordered is true. We may assume also a *Completeness
Principle,* that the AllSoul orders all logical consequences of what it
orders.

Pr25. $\vdash (a)(b)((\text{AllSoul Order } a \cdot b \text{ LogConseq } a) \supset \text{AllSoul Order } b).$

Having built set theory into the lower cosmos, we need to allow the
AllSoul to provide for its axioms, and no doubt for basic scientific law
also. Let 'SetAx a' express that a is an axiom of the set theory assumed,
and 'ScL a' that a is an acceptable scientific law. Then also a *Principle of
Scientific Law* obtains.

Pr26. $\vdash (a)((\text{SetAx } a \vee \text{ScL } a) \supset \text{AllSoul Order } a).$

---

4. On virtual classes and relations, see *Belief, Existence, and Meaning,* Chapter VI and
Semiotics and Linguistic Structure, Chapters I and II.

Provision must also be made for laws governing intelligibles that are not sets. Let 'IntL *a*' express that *a* is such a law. Then also a *Principle of the Intelligible Realm* obtains.

Pr27.   ⊢ (*a*)(IntL *a* ⊃ AllSoul Order *a*).

That this principle is needed is evident from IV.3.13, where it is said that "even the Intellectual-Principle, which is before all the Cosmos, has it also, its destiny, that of abiding intact above, and of giving downwards; what it sends down is the particular whose existence is implied in the law (or decreed system) of the universal; . . ."

Finally, surely, the AllSoul orders all (factually) true LS- and Obj-statements.

Pr28.   ⊢ (*a*)(((LSSent *a* v ObjSent *a*) • Tr *a*) ⊃ AllSoul Order *a*).

This is the *Principle of Factuality*.

Note that **Pr24** provides only that truth is a necessary condition, not a sufficient one, for what is ordered. The preceding principles **P1−P22** (or rather their translations within the metalanguage) are themselves true but not ordered. Note also that all of the Principles, including the Plan-principles **Pr23−Pr28**, are timeless, all being stated in what Frege called the "tense of timelessness." Time, space, and the like, being relevant only for objects of the lower cosmos, are provided in what is ordered, not in the ordering, so to speak.

Another point is perhaps worth making. In taking an entity under a linguistic description, we can of course allow for equivalent descriptions in various ways: in terms of *L-equivalence,* in terms of some suitably defined notion of *synonymy,* or in terms of the linguists' relations of *paraphase* or *translation*. An entity taken under any paraphrastic description is just as good, like a rose by any other name. This point is scarcely worth the making were it not so frequently misunderstood.

The multiplicity, but not the unity, of the lower cosmos has been commented on. How can we handle the unity? Merely as the fusion of the realm of objects. Thus

D6.   'LCosmos' is short for '(Fu'Obj)'.

This definition is of course analogous to **D3** above, of 'Noûs', and makes use of Leśniewski's mereology just as that definition does.

It should be recalled from II.3.13 that the "Soul governs this All by the plan *contained in the Reason-Principle* [italics added] . . . ." Reasoning of course has to do with statements — or propositions if you like — whereas intellection has to do only with the pure apprehension of the intelligibles. Intellection is thus not propositional, whereas reasoning is. The Plan is thus given by the AllSoul in its capacity for reasoning, and is stated in terms of statements. It is only statements that are ordered. Of course, reasoning presumably presupposes intellection of that which is reasoned about, just as statements must contain in an essential way names or other expressions for the intelligibles.

A further remark or two now about the One. "That awesome Prior, The Unity, is not a being [in the sense of being an intelligible, the AllSoul, or any object of the lower cosmos]. . . .: strictly, no name is apt to it, but *since name it we must* [italics added] there is a certain rough fitness in designating it as unity [or 'One' as above] with the understanding that it is not the unity of some other thing" (VI.9.5). Without a name for it, any systematic discourse concerning it would presumably be impossible. We could not even state our metaphysical scheme. And although **Pr14** above (that very few interesting properties can be ascribed to the One) does proceed by a kind of *via negativa*, still there is much to say concerning the One as the ultimate source of emanation and as the object of aspiration There — for "There only is our veritable love and There we may unite with it, not holding it in some fleshly embrace but possessing it in all its verity." (VI.9.9).

In all talk of the return to the One, "the flight of the alone to the Alone," the converse of the relation Em, $^\cup$Em, is no doubt the fundamental one. For consider **Pr6–Pr10**, rewritten now in terms of '$^\cup$Em'. These are to the effect that everything other than the One bears $^\cup$Em to it, no second thing does, and thus every intelligible does, the AllSoul does, and every object does. We can read '$^\cup$E' as 'aspires to the condition of', 'desires to return to the purity of', or the like. Note that by **Pr11'**, the Allsoul bears $^\cup$Em to Noûs, by **Pr12**, every object bears $^\cup$Em to the AllSoul, and by **Pr13,** nothing bears $^\cup$Em to any object. All this seems as it should be. Note the analog of **Pr11'** here rather than of **Pr11**. Rather than to say that the AllSoul bears $^\cup$Em to each intelligible, we require only that the AllSoul bears $^\cup$Em to Noûs itself, i.e., to the intelligibles taken collectively, to the Divine Mind. The appropriateness of this gives support to using **Pr11'** in place of **Pr11**. . . . Of course there is much more to be said about the return to the One, the flight of the alone to the Alone, but essential in all such discourse, it would seem, is the relation $^\cup$Em.

It was suggested above that it might be of interest to introduce a numerical degree for emanation so that 'x Em$^i y$' would express that x emanates to y to just the degree i. ('y $^\cup$Em$^i x$' would then express that y aspires to x to just degree i.) The same may be said for the relation Ens for ensoulment. The need for this may be seen as follows. In IV.4.36 we are told explicitly that "we cannot think of the world as a soulless habitation, however vast and varied, a thing of materials easily read off, kind by kind — wood and stone and whatever else there may be, all blending into a cosmos: [on the contrary] it must be alert throughout, every member living by its own life. . . ." Plotinus allows "grades of living within the whole, grades to some of which we deny life only because they are not perceptibly self-moved; in truth, all of these have a hidden life; and the thing whose life is patent to sense is made up of things which do not live to sense, but, none the less, confer upon their resultant wonderful powers towards living. . . ."

To provide for this "hidden life," let 'x Ens$^i y$' express that x ensouls y to just degree i. If $i = 1$, there is total ensoulment. But we would presumably have as a principle that every object is ensouled by AllSoul to a degree, however small, greater than 0.

Pr29.   ⊢ $(x)(\mathrm{Obj}\,x \supset (\mathrm{E}i)(i > 0 \cdot \mathrm{AllSoul\ Ens}^i x))$.

We can then rephrase **D2**, the definition of 'LPer' for living persons, in such a way as to require the ensoulment to be high. If a body is ensouled to a high degree, then and only then is it living. But even dead bodies are ensouled to some very small degree. **Pr29** is thus a kind of *Principle of Panpsychism*.

A few final comments.

The foregoing contains a sketch of the barest beginnings of the Plotinic system. Additional primitives of course are needed, many further principles, much further elaboration. Only the barest logical maquette, so to speak, has been given here. Enough has been shown, however, it is hoped, to enable us to see that the system could be further developed in such a way as to throw more and more light on the full logic of the All-Soul and of the accompanying metaphysical theory. Further, this can be done in such a way, as here, as to bring it into harmony with contemporary scientific theory, both in mathematics and in the empirical sciences. There should be no fundamental conflict, it is contended, between the great Plotinic vision and modern science. But the latter should not be disregarded in our attempt to understand the former. Hence the presence here of set theory and of scientific law as having their proper roles in the entire system. Also it is interesting that in the delineation of the lower souls, an intentional kind of metalogic is needed, and that in the delineation of the Plan, the semantical truth-concept. Without these resources, including of course quantification theory, it is unthinkable that the liaison here could take place. Perhaps this is the reason no one has attempted it heretofore, apparently — the resources were simply not available. In any case, it is hoped that the foregoing helps to show the usefulness of modern logic as a tool of philosophical analysis. Logic should not be seen only as a subject apart, a *logica docens,* having to do just with abstract metamathematical structures, but also as a *logica utens*, helping out not only in the clarification of philosophical problems, but in the analysis of the great historical texts as well.

CHAPTER VII

A Plotinic Theory
of Individuals

Nunquam aedepol temere tinniit tintinnabulum;
Nisi quis illud tractat aut movet, mutum est, tacet.

The metaphysical thesis that individuals are wholly determined in some sense by their properties and relations is an old one and has been espoused in one way or another by many great philosophers. The view has been attributed to Plotinus, and appears rather clearly in St. Basil and Gregory of Nyssa.[1] In the *Enneads,* V.8.7, for example, Plotinus remarks that "all this universe is occupied by forms from beginning to end; matter first of all by the forms of the elements, and then other forms upon these, and then again others; so that it is difficult to find the matter hidden under so many forms. Then matter too is a sort of ultimate form; so that *this [lower] universe is all form, and all the things in it are forms* [italics added]: for the archetype is form: the making is done without noise and fuss, since that which makes is all real being and form." This passage contrasts with others in Plotinus where matter is regarded as absolute formlessness rather than as "a sort of ultimate form." The passage in V.8.7, however, is surely sufficient to justify those who attribute the view to Plotinus that all things are forms, even though this seems not to be the received doctrine. In any case, it is surely consonant with V.8.7.

Interesting as this suggestion is, the question arises as to how it is to be fleshed out into a respectable philosophical theory and formulated in modern terms. The attempt is made to answer this question in what follows.

Let '*F*', '*G*', and '*H*', with or without accents (or primes) or numerical subscripts, he introduced as variables for forms, appropriately construed. Let 'Incld' be the sign for the relation of *inclusion* or *subsumption* between forms, so that '*F* Incld *G*' expresses that the form *F* is included in the form *G*. In addition, a notation must be provided for

---

1. See especially Gregory of Nyssa, *De hom. opificio* 44, 213C Migne.

handling the "mingling" of forms, more particularly, for allowing two or more forms to inhere in the same entity, so to speak. Such a notation will be provided in a moment.

Clearly it will obtain as a principle concerning inclusion that

Pr1. ⊢ $(F)(G)(F$ Incld $G \equiv (H)(H$ Incld $F \supset H$ Incld $G))$,

so that Incld is clearly a totally reflexive and transitive relation. A form is *null* provided it is included in all forms so that

D1. 'Null F' may abbreviate '$(G)F$ Incld G'.

It is interesting that with just this much notation, albeit with a good deal of additional theory yet to be given, we can introduce the notion of the mingling of forms in such a way as to produce an individual. A form, namely, is an individual (or individual-form) provided it is non-null and is included in all the non-null forms included in it. Thus

D1. 'Ind F' may abbreviate '($\sim$ Null $F \cdot (G)((\sim$ Null $G \cdot G$ Incld $F) \supset F$ Incld $G))$'.

To see that F is a form inhering in just one thing, it should be noted that the definiens here stipulates a kind of pinching process, so to speak. Suppose F were a non-null form containing some non-null G, which in turn is applicable to many individuals. F could not then be included in G and be applicable to just one individual. No matter how small G here is taken, so to speak, F must be included in it. But G must be of course non-null. Since F also is non-null and is required to be included in *all* such G, it can apply to just one individual.[2]

Note now that all the forms may be said to exist in the sense that they are admitted as values for variables. But there is another, closely related, notion of being *instantiated*. Let

D3. 'F Instd G' abbreviate '(Ind $G \cdot \sim$ Ind $F \cdot \sim$ Null $F \cdot G$ Incld F)',

so that F is instantiated by G provided F is a non-null form but not an invidual one and G is an individual-form included in F. Then F may be said to be *instantiable* (in the sense of actually being instantiated) provided there is a G that instantiates it.

D4. 'Instble F' abbreviates '(EG)F Instd G'.

---

2. Cf. *DInd2*, p. 43, of *Semiotics and Linguistic Structure*. Cf. also C. S. Peirce, *Collected Papers* (Cambridge: Harvard University Press, 1931–1958), Vol. III, p. 216; A. Tarski, *op. cit.*, p. 334; and the author's "A Homogeneous System for Formal Logic," *The Journal of Symbolic Logic* 8 (1943): 1–23.

Clearly many forms and combinations of them are instantable in this sense. This need not be laid down as a principle for it will follow immediately from other principles.

Many forms that are not individual-forms will have proper names attached to them primitively. Thus 'Horse' might designate the form *horse*, 'Man', *man*, and so on. Those forms that have proper names primitively attached to them will be instantable in the sense of **D4**. Thus

Pr2.   ⊢ ⌐Instbl **F** ⌐, where **F** is the primitive proper name of a non-null form that is not an individual.

Should proper names of individuals be admitted also? No harm will arise from this, although of course all such proper names may be introduced by definition provided suitable predicates are available, via Russellian descriptions. Suppose some proper names of individuals are admitted. Then clearly

Pr3.   ⊢ ⌐$(EG)(\sim \text{Ind } G \cdot \sim \text{Null } G \cdot F \text{ Incld } G)$⌐, where **F** is the primitive proper name of an individual,

and of course

Pr4.   ⊢ $(EF)\text{Ind } F$.

Note that this principle also follows from **Pr2**.

To avoid confusion, let us speak hereafter of individual-forms as *individuals,* and of non-null forms and combinations of such that are not individuals as *proper forms.* Thus

D5.   'PrForm F'   abbreviates   '$(\sim \text{Ind } F \cdot \sim \text{Null } F)$'.

Clearly now

Pr5.   ⊢ $(F)(\text{Ind } F \text{ v Null } F \text{ v PrForm } F))$

and

Pr6.   ⊢ $\sim (EF)(\text{Ind } F \cdot \text{Null } F \cdot \text{PrForm } F)$.

Thus the individuals and null and proper forms are jointly exhaustive of all forms and mutually exclusive of each other.

Many proper forms of course are not instantable in the sense of **D4**, so that

Pr7.   ⊢ $(EF)(\text{PrForm } F \cdot \sim \text{Instbl } F)$.

Such forms are, however, *potentials* for instantiation, we might say. Any two such forms are *compossible* for instantiation should circumstances so arise. This notion may perhaps be defined as follows. Let

D6. 'F Compsble G' abbreviate '(EH)((Ind H v PrForm H) • H Incld F • H Incld G)',

so that compossible forms are those in which some individual or proper form is included. If the H here is an individual, F and G might even be said to be *co-actual*. But if H is itself a proper form and there is no individual H' included in both F and G, F and G are merely co-potential. These two notions themselves seem sufficiently interesting to justify definitions. Thus

D7. 'F CoActl G' abbreviates '(EH)(Ind H • H Incld F • H Incld G)'

and

D8. 'F CoPotntl G' abbreviates '(F Compsble G • ~ F CoActl G)'.

Let us consider now the virtual classes or sets of proper forms that characterize, so to speak, an individual, as well as those that constitute its "essence" in the sense of Whitehead. Whitehead used to refer to the set of *all* properties of an individual as its essence. The essence in this sense includes all, not just some, properties that characterize it. To reflect upon these, a notation for virtual classes of forms, both individual and proper, is needed. Let

D9. 'F ϵ {G⊰−F−}' be defined as '−F−', where '−F−' is a sentential form (or function) of the language containing 'F' as a free variable and 'G' is some new variable not occurring in '−F−', and '−G−' differs from '−F−' appropriately.[3]

The definiendum of **D9** is to the effect that F is a *member* of the *virtual class* of all G's such that −G−. And two virtual classes are *identical* just where every member of one is a member of the other and conversely. Let 'α' and 'β', with or without numerical subscripts, be used hereafter as expressions for virtual classes of forms. We may then define

D10. '$\alpha = \beta$' as '(F)(F ϵ α ≡ F ϵ β)'.

Clearly now a class of classes α is a *Whiteheadian essence* of an individual F just where α is the virtual class of all proper forms in which F is included. Thus

---

3. See *Belief, Existence, and Meaning*, Chapter VI.

D11. 'α WhtdEss F' abbreviates '(Ind $F \cdot \alpha = \{G \ni (\text{PrForm } G \cdot F$ Incld $G)\})$'.

Clearly the following principles hold.

Pr8. ⊢ $(F)((\alpha \text{ WhtdEss } F \cdot \beta \text{ WhtdEss } F) \supset \alpha = \beta)$,
Pr9. ⊢ $(F)(G)((\alpha \text{ WhtdEss } F \cdot G \in \alpha) \supset \text{PrForm } G)$.

Thus far there has been no occasion to speak of the *identity* of forms, but only of virtual classes of such. But clearly identity is to be construed as mutual inclusion, so that

D12. '$F = G$' abbreviates '(F Incld $G \cdot G$ Incld F)'.

Appropriate principles of identity are forthcoming from this definition. And concerning identity as between individuals, it obtains that

Pr10. ⊢ $(F)(G)((\text{Ind } F \cdot \text{Ind } G) \supset (F \text{ Incld } G \equiv F = G))$,
Pr11. ⊢ $(F)(G)((\text{Ind } F \cdot F \text{ Incld } G) \supset (\text{PrForm } G \vee F = G))$.
Pr12. ⊢ $(F)(G)((\text{Ind } F \cdot \text{Ind } G) \supset (F = G \equiv (H)(\text{PrForm } H \supset (F \text{ Incld } H \equiv G \text{ Incld } H))))$.

Another principle concerning Whiteheadian essences is then that

Pr13. ⊢ $(F)(G)((\alpha \text{ WhtdEss } F \cdot \alpha \text{ WhtdEss } G) \supset F = G)$.

Although its Whiteheadian essence α clearly characterizes an individual F, many subclasses of α may do so likewise. Thus F might be the only individual included in the proper forms G_1, G_2, and G_3, say, but also the only member of H_1 and H_2. Yet the virtual class $\{G_1, G_2, G_3\}$, the class whose only members are G_1, G_2, and G_3, clearly characterizes F as $\{H_1, H_2\}$ does. Yet, by hypothesis, these classes are not the same, and neither of them is the Whiteheadian essence, if F is included in other proper forms. Under what circumstances then can a virtual class of proper forms be said to "characterize" an individual F? We let

D13. 'α Char F' abbreviate '(Ind $F \cdot (G)(G \in \alpha \supset (\text{PrForm } G \cdot F$ Incld $G)))$',

so that a class of proper forms α characterizes F just where F is included in every member of α. Then

Pr14. ⊢ $(F)(G)((\alpha \text{ WhtdEss } F \cdot \beta \text{ Char } F \cdot G \in \beta) \supset G \in \alpha)$.

But in general it does *not* obtain that

$$(\alpha \text{ Char } F \cdot \alpha \text{ Char } G) \supset F = G,$$

for one and the same class of proper forms can characterize several individuals. The set of forms {*man,tall,rich*} can characterize many persons. Also it does not in general obtain that

$$(\alpha \operatorname{Char} F \cdot \beta \operatorname{Char} F) \supset \alpha = \beta,$$

for an individual can be characterized by many sets of proper forms. Thus {*man,tall,rich*} and {*English,kind*} can both characterize the same persons without themselves being the same classes.

In addition to **D13**, we may let

D13′. 'α UniqueChar F' abbreviate '$(\alpha \operatorname{Char} F \cdot (G)(\alpha \operatorname{Char} G \supset G = F))$',

to express that α *uniquely* characterizes the individual F.

A few additional principles to be noted are as follows.

PR15. $\vdash (EG)(F)(\operatorname{Ind} F \supset (F \operatorname{Incld} G \equiv -G-))$, where '$-F-$' is any sentential form containing 'F' but not 'G' as a free variable.

This principle will be recognized as the correlate here of Leśniewski's "pseudo-definitions" and of Zermelo's *Aussonderungsaxiom*. Here it is a principle of existence for forms, assuring that there exists a form corresponding to any sentential function '$-F-$'.

Let

D14.   'Univ F' abbreviate '$(G)G \operatorname{Incld} F$',

so that F is *universal* just where every form is included in it. The principle must obtain that there is one and only one universal form.

Pr16. $\vdash (EF)(\operatorname{Univ} F \cdot (G)(\operatorname{Univ} G \supset G = F))$.

An analogous principle also holds concerning null forms.

Pr17. $\vdash (EF)(\operatorname{Null} F \cdot (G)(\operatorname{Null} G \supset G = F))$.

If an infinity of forms is to be assumed, as would seem natural, the following would obtain.

Pr18. $\vdash (F)(\sim \operatorname{Univ} F \supset (EG)(F \operatorname{Incld} G \cdot \sim G \operatorname{Incld} F))$.

Every form other than the universal one is properly included in some form.

In addition to the principles listed, there would be special ones to the effect that certain of the forms are included in others, in particular the proper forms to which names are attached primitively. Thus

Pr19. $\vdash \ulcorner F \operatorname{Incld} G \urcorner$, for some of the primitive proper-form names F and G.

116

Thus far the "mingling" of forms to produce individuals has been discussed, but not much has been said about its co-mingling of forms among themselves. Of course **Pr19** here does specify some of this, specifying that some are included in others. But no doubt we should recognize sums, products, and negation of forms, as well as a universal form. These may all be introduced *in usu* or in context in more or less familiar ways. Thus

D14a. ⌜*F* Incld (*G* ∪ *H*)⌝   abbreviates   ⌜(H_1)(H_1 Incld *F* ⊃ (EH_2)(H_2 Incld H_1 • (H_2 Incld *G* v H_2 Incld *H*)))⌝ ,

D14b. ⌜(*G* ∪ *H*) Incld *F*⌝   abbreviates   ⌜(*G* Incld *F* • *H* Incld *F*)⌝ ,

D15a. ⌜*F* Incld (*G* ∩ *H*)⌝   abbreviates   ⌜(*F* Incld *G* • *F* Incld *H*)⌝ ,

D15b. ⌜(*G* ∩ *H*) Incld *F*⌝   abbreviates   ⌜(H_1)((H_1 Incld *G* • H_1 Incld *H*) ⊃ H_1 Incld *F*)⌝ ,

D16a. ⌜*F* Incld -*G*⌝   abbreviates   ⌜(*H*)((~ Null *H* • *H* Incld *F*) ⊃ ~ *H* Incld *G*)⌝ ,

D16b. ⌜-*G* Incld *F*⌝   abbreviates   ⌜(*H*)((*H*′)((~ Null *H*′ • *H*′ Incld *H*) ⊃ ~ *H*′ Incld *G*) ⊃ *H* Incld *F*)⌝ .

These definitions are actually definition-schemata, note, and hence the presence of boldface letters. They hold only for *specified* **F, G,** and **H,** not for *variable* '*F*', '*G*', and '*H*'. The usual Boolean laws concerning sums, products, and negations are now to hold. And of course many other kinds of co-mingling may be introduced.

No attempt has been made here to axiomatize the theory. Hence the language in which it is couched is merely partially formalized. Also no attempt has been made to specify the primitive names or to characterize the particular behavior of the forms they designate. The aim here is merely to specify the logico-metaphysical foundations on the basis of which such specification and characterization could be given.

Note also that the forms here are regarded as *sui generis* and are not, like classes, wholly determined by their members. Thus in particular it does *not* obtain that

$$(F)(\text{PrForm } F \supset (EG)(\text{Ind } G \cdot G \text{ Incld } F)).$$

For some forms, yes, but not necessarily for all.

Nothing has been said thus far about relations between or among individuals. There are at least four ways of handling these. The first is the method of introducing suitable non-logical primitives for relations, and bringing in the theory of *virtual* relations. Thus, suppose '*R*' is such a primitive, significant in contexts '*F* R *G*'. It would then hold that

$$\vdash (F)(G)(F \ R \ G \supset (\text{Ind} F \cdot \text{Ind} G)).$$

Also suitable meaning postulates would be laid down concerning R. And similarly for all such primitives. Relations, however, in this method, are not taken as values for variables and thus are not regarded as proper forms in any way. Quantification over them is forbidden, relations being regarded as merely virtual. A rather narrow theory of relations would result.

Another method suggests itself by extending the preceding framework in another direction, namely, by recognizing *ordered couples* of individuals as designata of special terms taken as primitives, and then regarding dyadic relations as constituting a species or subclass of the proper forms. More particularly, let

$$`<F,G>`$$

be a term for a form regarded as the ordered couple of F and G. And where H is a dyadic-relation form and F and G are individuals,

$$`<F,G> \ \text{Incld} \ H`$$

then expresses that F stands in the relation H to G. To make this notation work, a good deal of further spelling out of detail is needed, with many changes in the foregoing. However, these are not difficult to supply. To accommodate the full logic of dyadic relations in this way is to provide for the relevant material in *Principia Mathematica* (* 20 ff.) We then would distinguish *monadic* proper forms from *dyadic* ones, by superscripts perhaps. The inclusion sign 'Incld' then takes on a wider meaning than above. 'F Incld G' may hold where F is an individual and G a proper monadic form, or where F and G are both individuals or both proper monadic forms, or where F is an ordered couple and G a proper dyadic form, or where F and G are both ordered couples or both proper dyadic forms — but not otherwise. All of this must be provided by a suitable extension of the material above, including of course additional principles. Further extensions are needed for the theory of triadic relations, and so on, as in *PM* itself. The result is a kind of homogeneous logic of relations, all relations, sums, products, etc., of them being now regarded as items in the realm of forms. On the basis of so powerful a theory, amounting to a full second-order theory of relations, a considerable portion of classical mathematics is forthcoming provided suitable principles are assumed.

Two other methods suggest themselves if either a *type* theory or a *set* theory is brought in in the manner of the Russell-Ramsey theory, on the one hand, or the Zermelo-Skolem one, on the other. In either method, relations may be handled as classes (or sets) of classes (or sets) of individuals in familiar fashion, in terms of the devices of Wiener or Kuratowski. A very strong theory of relations emerges in this way. The price for this, however, is high. Further axioms of great complexity are needed as well as a tremendous extension in the primitive ontology. Some would think that on the basis of either of these theories the realm of forms is stretched too far, not only beyond necessity but beyond credibility. *Incredible incredibilis creditus,* it might be said of either theory.

It might be thought that in all this we have strayed rather far from Plotinus. It is easy to see, however, how this material may be embedded within what is essentially the theory of the preceding paper. But all reference to the objects there must be excised, their role being played by the individual-forms here.

It is also of interest to note that this kind of theory of forms may be made compatible with the theory of Peirce's "Neglected Argument,"[4] and with the idealist theory of V, *mutatis mutandis* in each case. On the idealist view all talk of "embodiment" is now handled of course in terms of "manifestation."

This paper is the result largely of a conversation with Professor John Findlay, one aspect of whose interpretation of Plotinus it attempts to portray in modern terms, however inadequately. The author wishes to thank Professor Findlay for this stimulus.

---

4. See "On the Logic of Idealism and Peirce's Neglected Argument," in *Peirce's Logic of Relations Etc.*

CHAPTER VIII

On Philosophical Ecumenism:
A Dialogue

Crede mihi, miseris coelestia numina parcunt;
Nec semper laesos, et sine fine, premunt.

R.M.M.   Good day, Herr F. It is good to see you again after our meeting in Jerusalem.

F.   Good day. That was a most interesting meeting, wasn't it? What a fascinating city, Jerusalem, and a perfect place for a philosophical meeting. A city of the ages, of all seasons, of all shades of opinions, the most ecumenical of all earthly cities and at the same time a *civitas Dei*.

M.   Yes, and I suppose if philosophical divergences are to be brought into the open, it should be there of all places. I am glad to see you now, for I know you are an admirer of Professor Findlay, and are fond of quoting from his writings. Much of what he said in Jerusalem concerning my paper,[1] you know, seemed to me — and indeed to others too — somewhat distorted and not quite cogent.

F.   I am sorry if you feel that way. Sometimes he does exaggerate a bit publically, you know. He thinks it helps to create an effect and to get people to listen.

M.   Yes, but it can also seriously mislead. In any case, I would like to ask you some questions as to what his views really are, for you of course know them much better than I. To begin with, I would be interested in knowing more clearly just why he laments what he calls 'formal logic' to the extent he seems to, and on every possible occasion seems to derogate its role in philosophy.

F.   He has great respect for formal logic and some of its achievements. What he laments is "tailoring what is [philosophically] worth saying to the limited resources and the artificial rigors of an arbitrarily exact scheme of diction." He applauds "tailoring logic to what is worth saying."[2]

---

1. "On Some Theological Languages," presented at the meeting of the International Society for Metaphysics in Jerusalem, Aug. 18–22, 1977.
2. J. N. Findlay, "Ordinary, Revisionary, and Dialectical Strategies in Philosophy."

120

M.   I think we have no problem as to what is "worth saying," as he puts it. I like him have the profoundest respect for the great philosophic classics, and I want none of them expunged, not even those with which I might not personally agree. The study of the history, the *exact* and highly detailed study of its history, has always seemed to me one of the two chief pillars — the other is logic itself — of philosophic study. Everything important that has been said is eminently worth saying, even though much of it we would now wish to reject. The really important views, I suppose, are those that have either persisted or at least reappeared from age to age, perhaps in almost unrecognizable garb.

F.   The difficulty is that formal logic is so narrow. It condones as valid forms of inference only those so childish and simple that no one ever fails to keep to them, and neglects the really difficult and important forms of inference, which we really wish to know about and which might be really helpful in our philosophical work.

M.   There is truth to what you say. Peirce, you know, said something similar years back. Much depends of course on how widely logic is construed. My fear is that you are construing it too narrowly, and fail to take account of some important recent advances. Logic, like the sciences, is subject to continual growth and development, you know. It never really had the dogmatic slumber often attributed to it, although of course there have been periods during which not much progress was made.

F.   You may be right, but Professor Findlay means by 'formal logic' what is ordinarily meant in the English-speaking world.

M.   So much depends on whom one talks to, and when. A decade ago there was perhaps some agreement, at Oxford, say, about what formal logic is. But the climate has changed and 'formal logic' is now construed there much more broadly, now that they have a real logician, Dana Scott, in their midst. As a friend of mine put it, now at Oxford there is a real logician for the first time since the period of Duns Scotus and Ockham. Logic is an exact *science,* you know. I worry, you see, about your speaking of logic as something being "tailored," in the fashion presumably of a suit of clothes. You tailor it this way or that as fashion or taste dictates. But this is not at all what one does in logic, any more than in physics or biology. It is not *we* who make logic; it is rather that logic is made for us, tailored for us, if you like, by the Supreme Tailor of all. You and Findlay speak of logic as having only "limited resources" and of "the artificial rigors of an arbitrarily exact scheme of diction." Here again, these epithets seem to me rather askew. There is nothing arbitrary about the logical scheme when

properly understood, and its resources are by no means limited —
any more than any science is limited — especially when newer developments are taken into account. In any case, they are much less
limited than you seem to suggest.

F.   What Professor Findlay means is that logic should exhibit "true
neutrality." It [p. 288] "ought to be such that it allows us to think and
talk as unitively or as disjunctively as our empirical and rational insights warrant. It should not evince a prejudiced preference for an
extensionalism geared to a pluralism of sheerly individual objects,
herded at best into sets or classes by synsemantic functions which can
themselves never be independently talked of. The purely descriptive
gossip of ordinary life — 'This house is to the left of that', 'All the
houses in the street are painted white' — fits creakingly into this pattern, but even in ordinary talk our adverbs, our conditionals, our attitudinal expressions, etc., fail to fit it, and the whole of science and
philosophy, including the philosophy of those who formulate such
gossip, cannot be stated in it."

M.   Well, a good deal has been said here, the gist of which I can
agree with. The *way* in which it is said, however, seems to me unfortunate. And on almost every point, it seems to me, grievous blunders are
being made. In the first place, I have been urging for years the neutrality of logic. Ryle did so also, you will recall, in his views of logic as
"subject-matter" neutral. Also Carnap, Gödel, Heinrich Scholz, Fred
Fitch, and others. Indeed, there is an honorable history of this view,
going back to Aristotle. Just *de facto* logic does exhibit true neutrality,
in just Findlay's sense, I think. He speaks of a "prejudiced preference
for an extensionalism," forgetting apparently all the work on non-
extensional logics going back to Frege, as well as all the recent effort
expended attempting to formulate them on a firm extensional basis.
And why is the preference for extensionalism "prejudiced"? Findlay
neglects to note that extensionalism is a view firmly based on certain
desirable principles, including so-called principles of extensionality,
that are so fundamental, basic, and well-entrenched (historically even)
that one does not wish to give them up lightly. Well, this is not the
occasion to present a full-fledged defense of extensionalism, but only
to point out that the most casual glance at the history of logic, especially recent work, would be enough to convince anyone that the view
is not the result of a mere "prejudiced preference."

F.   But there is so much that you simply cannot do just on the basis
of extensions. You must allow for intentionality in the senses of Bren-
tano or Husserl, and accommodate all manner of intentional discourse.

M. Yes, this is true. But much depends on how intentions are handled logically. It was mentioned that extensionalism is firmly "geared to a pluralism of sheerly individual objects, herded at best into sets or classes by synsemantic functions which can themselves never be independently talked of." Now this seems to me clearly in error. Many purely extensional set theories are at hand in which sets or classes are the only entities admitted.[3] Some logicians prefer such theories, in which there is no reference to the contaminate world of "things" in any way whatsoever. And if you don't like set theories, then there is my "homogeneous' logic at hand, in one interpretation of it, in which there are only classes and no individuals.[4] A humble thing perhaps, but mine own. Thus extensionalism is by no means geared to a pluralism of "individuals," nor need it be such that sets or classes cannot be spoken of in them independently. There is still more to say against what you said a moment back. The view that "our adverbs, our conditionals, our attitudinal expressions, etc.," cannot be handled within an extensional logic is also thoroughly mistaken. Please let me call attention to a good deal of recent work in which just this is being done.[5] Of course these matters are not easy, but progress is being made. Some of the work on adverbs, for example, harks back to Reichenbach; that on attitudinals, to Ajdukiewicz. The analysis of conditionals is still highly controversial. But it seems to me premature surely to suggest that the handling of these cannot be made to fit the ordinary kind of logic. You say also that "the whole of science and philosophy [just think what a staggering totality this is!] . . . cannot be stated" in an extensionalist framework. Can you name an intensionalist one in which it can be? Are you not making here an almost preposterous demand?

F. No, I am not demanding too much, nor is Professor Findlay. "One cannot get far in science or philosophy without making intensions (spelled with an *s*), rather than extensions, one's primary theme of reference, and it is further important that they should represent genuine and deep affinities, not superficial alignments dependent on chance usage or the misguided ingenuity of some logic-chopper."

M. I think you are right in this contention in essentials, and I can agree with you while firmly remaining an extensionalist. The whole matter depends on how intensions are introduced and handled. But

---

3. See, for example, the works of von Neumann, Bernays, and Gödel, to mention only a few.

4. "A Homogeneous System for Formal Logic."

5. See especially *Events, Reference, and Logical Form* and *Semiotics and Linguistic Structure.*

you speak of intensions *ex cathedra*, and seem to disregard all the painstaking work that has gone into the attempts to formulate an exact theory of them during the last hundred years. Is all this being dismissed under the grand rubric of "logic-chopping?" If so, just think of the great logicians being dismissed in this way: Frege, Peirce, Russell, Carnap, Church, Tarski, to name only a few. You speak as though these men had never written, and as though you had nothing to learn from them. And you pay no attention to more recent work in which the theory of intensions is put on a more secure logical footing. These great authors do now after all belong to history and their ideas are of contemporary interest only in so far as they can be reformulated so as to meet present standards of rigor, to be of relevance to contemporary structural and transformational linguistics, to be of use in handling problems in the philosophy of science, including the social and humane sciences, and the like. Of course, I would wish to add here aesthetics and systematic theology, but not many of my logical *confrères* would go along with me in this.

F.   What Professor Findlay has in mind is the sort of thing Aristotle did when "he followed his purely formal *Prior Analytics* by the *Posterior Analytics,* which emphasized that the scientific, as opposed to the dialectical syllogism, must always employ genuine universals as middle terms, universals which *Noûs* has picked out, and which are the explanatory essences of the matters on hand."

M.   I have this sort of thing in mind also. Let us word it in more contemporary terms. The narrow formal logic of quantification theory with non-logical constants is to be supplemented with the calculus of individuals, with an event logic, with logical syntax, semantics, and a systematic pragmatics. And of course notions of probability must be brought in also, the various ones clearly distinguished from one another and then suitably interrelated. Here as elsewhere *Distinguuer pou: mieux unir* is the guiding principle. Incidentally, it is very important also to provide for probability sentences in intensional contexts. This is a problem most theorists of probability have almost completely neglected.[6]

F.   Well, suppose we were to grant you that there have been gains in the theory of intensions of which Findlay has not taken account sufficiently. Still, "one [p. 219] ... cannot hope to get far in philosophy, or in the humane or social sciences, without making intentions (spelled with a *t*) one's prime objective of reference, and so

---

6. See especially "On the Language of Causal Talk: Scriven and Suppes," in *Pragmatics, Truth, and Language.*

recognizing as illuminating and informative, and not merely 'opaque', occurrences to which the true-false antithesis is irrelevant, and which, in such occurrences need not have the logical relation[s] that they otherwise would have. For it is unfortunately often as possible to believe in the false as the true, and to see logical connections which are not present, while failing to see connections which in independent contexts would be there. The formalist, like the moral rigorist, hates the probabilism of intentional discourse, for while intentionality involves intelligence, and intelligence will open our eyes to logical connections, it is also a matter of degree, and its exercise therefore a matter of probability. The extensionalist and the rigorist accordingly seek to excise from philosophy and the humane sciences most of what is worth discussing in them."

M. Are you not forgetting here that intentions (with a 't') are a special kind of intension (with an 's') and thus that the logical techniques capable of handling the latter can handle the former also? Much of the motivation for seeking a logic of intensions has been to be able to handle "opaque" contexts of sentences concerning believing, knowing, surmising, enjoying, and the like. There is no doubt but that there are now ways of handling such sentences that are adequate for making the distinctions you are asking for here, in particular to distinguish between the truth and falsity of what is believed, known, or whatever, and distinguishing all these from the truth or falsity of the full sentences stating that belief, knowing, or whatever, i.e., stating that so and so believes, knows, or whatever, such and such. A theory that could not do this would surely not be acceptable. And all such sentences, including those believed, known, and so on, can be "illuminating or informative" quite irrespective of their truth or falsity. What a person does not believe, for example, may be quite as illuminative of his character as what he does. It seems to me that you are quite wrong, however, if you say that the formalist "hates the probabilism of intentional discourse." On the contrary, it is just he who has contributed most to our understanding of the workings of probabilism, which can then be applied to intentional discourse quite as much as to any other. Sentences believed can be themselves probabilistic, as well as the full sentences stating the believing. Of course there are immense difficulties here in being sure of just what notion or notions of probability we are using, of which are the most suitable, of how they are interrelated, and so on. Surely you cannot really think that such eminent writers as von Mises, Reichenbach, Lord Keynes, Sir Harold Jeffries, Carnap, and de Finetti have "excised from philosophy and the humane sciences most of what is worth discussing in them." It is rather that their contributions are paving the way for the techniques by which such matters may be more reliably discussed than heretofore. Again, I am not saying that there are not difficulties here, but rather that there has been real progress you seem to refuse to admit.

F.   But you are neglecting the really important things. "There are [p. 283] other interests than the desire to . . . accord with the exclusions demanded by logic. There is above all the interest in achieving a certain luminous perspicuity and simplicity of vision, and an overriding of the randomly diverse and independent, which is also the inspiration of science. Einstein would never have got far if he had rejected the thesis of the unsurpassable, yet finite velocity of light, or the conception of a universe finite yet unbounded. In the same way an idealism like Berkeley's, Fichte's or Husserl's, courageously rejects the intuitive thesis of the independence of physical objects from the subject who perceives them or otherwise intends them, and makes them all no more than a very special sort of intentional object, with their own unique manner of constitution."

M.   I see no reason why the exclusions demanded by logic — sloppy formulation and invalid reasoning — rule out "luminous perspicuity" and "simplicity of vision" in either science or philosophy. On the contrary they are quite essential to both. As concerns Berkeley's idealism, you will perhaps recall my little paper of some years back, "On the Berkeley-Russell Theory of Proper Names," which tried to provide a suitable logical basis for it.[7] Just recently an eminent Berkeley scholar said to me that this paper had helped him very much over the years. I was glad to be told this, never having been quite sure whether that paper had really hit its mark or not as regards Berkeley. Russell too, you know, strove valiantly with this problem, and it has always seemed to me that Findlay has not paid enough attention to the relevant chapters in *An Inquiry into Meaning and Truth*. English philosophers of his generation have tended, I think, to condemn Russell for his more popular writings, and have failed to give him credit for his real achievements. The best of Bertie, don't forget, is very good indeed.

F.   But Findlay has in mind something more, "of framing concepts that . . . [he calls] 'iridescent', in that they involve a systematic shift through several antilogistic positions, conceiving things in terms of the shift rather than the single vision. . . . An iridescent concept is . . . one that manages genuinely to reconcile different members of an an-

---

7. *Philosophy and Phenomenological Research* 13 (1952): 221–231.

tilogism, so that one manages to understand how, in their mutual tension, they are nonetheless complementary 'sides' of the same situation. It is here all-important that we should distinguish a spurious iridescence in which no genuine concept emerges ... to the case where the philosopher, by a judicious use of language, really pushes us over the borderline, so that we are really able to see how positions we took to be irreconcilable, really fit in with one another. Such an insight of course modifies the positions in question, since there can be no greater modification than one which changes irreconcilables into reconcilables, but such a modification in a sense also preserves what it modifies, since its sense depends on the original exclusion which it in turn transcends. The concept of iridescence is, in short, itself a case of iridescence, since it preserves in its sense the exclusiveness that it also excludes."

M. Well, the whole point of the reconciliation is, I suppose, that what is at first a contradiction is so modified as no longer to be one. A "spurious" iridescence is one for which such reconciliation cannot be given. I like the phrase 'by a judicious use of language', which is no doubt supposed to include the elimination of ambiguity, of any apparent contradiction, and so on. Perhaps too, as Findlay suggests, the notion of iridescence is itself iridescent, although probably one has to move into a metalanguage to say this, so that we need also a notion of *metairidescence*. It is also interesting that only *concepts* are iridescent, not things, according to this account. This raises of course the very different problem as to how concepts are to be handled in any exact way, once we get beyond the level of common talk and vague historical jargon.[8]

F. Findlay's plea is "for the re-introduction of a logic of aspects." Iridescent concepts contain many aspects. Consider an example from Aristotle. "There are few expressions more frequently used by Aristotle than the adverbial form ᾗ, Latin *quā*, English 'as', or 'in so far as'. Thus a line can be considered *as* the boundary of one region and also of another, and while *as* bounding one region it may be concave, *as* bounding the other it will be convex. The convex and the concave are not only different but opposed aspects, and yet we understand perfectly how they complete one another, and are in fact the same line differently regarded. In the same way a thing may be one thing *quā* constituent stuff and another *quā* organized unity, and again we see just how these aspects fit together and complete one another.... Again Aristotle readily conceives that a given motion or state may be

_____

8. Cf. *Events, Reference, and Logical Form,* pp. 15 ff.

at once an action for A and an undergoing for B." There are many other examples of similar kind. "Aristotle in these teachings is not merely conflating disparate functions without showing how they can belong together: he is challenging us, not always with perfect success, to grasp their necessary mutual completion in the same way in which the simpler geometrical structures are to be found in the more complex ones."

    M.   I am glad you explicitly bring up the word 'quā', the logic of which has only quite recently, I think, been formulated. Frege seems to have been the first to have sensed what this is, in essentials anyhow, in his notion of the *Art des Gegebenseins*.[9] One and the same entity may be taken under different *Arten des Gegebenseins*, the totality of which perhaps may be regarded as the *Sinn* or sense of the name of that entity.[10] Of course it is difficult to be sure of precisely how Frege here should be interpreted, but this comment is not an unreasonable way of construing the *Sinne*. It seems to me that what you want as a "logic of aspects" can be fully handled in terms of the *Art des Gegebenseins*. To carry this out in detail, of course, we must go way beyond Frege and bring in all manner of delicate logical matters that have been clarified since his day.

    F.   Well, if that is the case, all to the good.

    M.   Of course there are many technical refinements to be made in all that I have said, but we need not go in to them here. Let us stick only to the essentials. Bearing all that we have been saying in mind, I would like now to ask you about some of the things Findlay said at Jerusalem in criticizing my paper. He began, you will recall, by expressing due respect for the achievements of modern logic, and he said right at the start that he thought that some of the historically great metaphysical views do permit of a logical reconstruction in modern terms. He mentioned Proclus, St. Thomas, and Christian Wolff as typical philosophers whose views he thought could very likely be given such a reconstruction. He failed to point out, however, that this has never been done. Not even the first steps have been taken in reconstructing these views in any adequate fashion — except for Father Salamucha's pioneering work on the *ex motu* argument in St. Thomas mentioned in my paper. He doubted, however, whether this kind of thing is worth doing. But if not, then I have difficulty in seeing how his respect for logic is any more than lip-service. It is quite

---

    9. See especially "On Sense and Reference," second paragraph, and §8 of the *Begriffsschrift*, or *loc. cit.*

    10. See "A Reading of Frege on Sense and Designation," in *Pragmatics, Truth, and Language.*

clear from his comments in Jerusalem that he was not taking into account the material I have drawn attention to above. He did not mention, incidentally, Salamucha's work, which is generally regarded as a landmark in the history of this sort of thing.

F.   He does not object if you want to play silly games with symbols, but you can never express more in them than you can express in our ordinary language. This is one of the things he said, you will recall.

M.   Yes, I recall very vividly his saying this, and it seems to me a pity that he did. I agree with Findlay, in having the highest respect for our ordinary language. My respect here is probably even greater than his, for I have been making a real effort recently in studying logical forms for various kinds of ordinary sentences and the transformations taking us from the forms to the sentences and back again.[11] No one can do very much of this sort of work without realizing how incredibly complicated our natural language is, and how within it in a few short words we can, almost miraculously, be able to say so much. The further we look into the complex structure of language, the greater our respect for it. The business of the logical analysis of language, as I see it, is not to compete with it, to "regiment" it, or anything of the kind, but to analyze it and to attempt to formulate the rules governing sentence construction in terms of certain basic linguistic particles. Of course it should do a good deal more also, but at least this much. The work here is not dissimilar to that of any scientist confronted with the complex data he wishes to study. The important thing in the logic of a language is not what we express, but *how* we express it. Perhaps every sentence in a natural language can be "represented" in a logical form — many linguistis think this and carry out their professional work in accord with it. They study the sentences of a natural language by means of their forms, and the sentences then *mean* whatever their forms do. The point of seeking the forms is not to express *more* than can be done in ordinary language, but to be able to say it better, in a logically responsible way, to say it unambiguously, to say it in the light of the whole, incredibly complex structure that the whole of language exhibits. And so on. Findlay's comment seems to me based on a total lack of interest in, and respect for, all the progress that has been made in structural and transformational linguistics during the past century or so.

F.   Perhaps he does not care about all this new "smart aleck" pseudoscience. In any case, he did call it that at Jerusalem, you will

---

11. See "Some Protolinguistic Transformations," in *Pragmatics, Truth, and Language*.

remember. His disparagement of logic is concerned primarily with its use in philosophy.

M.   Yes. But, as it goes in the theory of logical form for sentences of a natural language, so it goes with the sentences of a metaphysical system. The attempt to subject the system to a logical reformulation helps us tremendously to come to understand better what that system really is, and what is said within it. There is an enormous literature on this subject. You will recall the splendid things Frege has to say about it, and Russell of course, and Whitehead, and Woodger the biologist, and Nelson Goodman, to mention only a few. It seems to me that Findlay has failed to understand the important role logical reconstruction must play in metaphysics, taken either historically or systematically. I for one welcome the increased minding of one's p's and q's in the detailed study of specific texts from Plato, for example, on the part of younger scholars. There is no doubt but that the future will see a great deal more of this in the study of all the historically great philosophers.

F.   Even if one were to succeed to some extent with some philosophers, Findlay said, you remember, there are others for whom it cannot be done. He was thinking especially of Plotinus and Hegel.

M.   Yes, I recall that he objected violently to my suggestions concerning Plotinus. He especially objected to the principle, **Pr6** in my paper, that

$$\vdash (x)(\sim x = \text{One} \supset \text{One Em} x),$$

that the One emanates into everything other than itself. He objected that the principle is no "clearer" than the ordinary English statement. He called it in fact 'meaningless gibberish', but I do him the courtesy of not thinking that he meant this to be taken very seriously. The statement is no more gibberish than the natural-language original. Making the statement in this exact logical way helps us to understand the vocabulary of the reconstructed Plotinic language as a whole, to see how sentences are formed out of that vocabulary, to understand the definitions of the theory, and the basic principles of it. He seemed to think that the sole merit claimed for my statement of this principle is that it is "clearer" than its original. Well, it is surely as clear anyhow. But everything done with symbols can be done more cumbrously without them, so there is not much point in complaining about the use of symbols. The important role of this formula, and of the others, is to make explicit and concise the salient fundamental principles of the system. His objections to **Pr6** are akin to those who object to the famous formula *110.643 in *Principia Mathematica*. Why go through all that rigamorole of symbolization, they ask, merely to prove what we already know, that $1 + 1 = 2$? Clearly such an objection is beside the point and rests upon a misunderstanding of the aims of the whole enterprise.

F.   But you brought in mathematical set theory. For this Findlay has no use whatsoever; he thinks it a lowly subject, almost beneath contempt. Also it is quite foreign to Plotinus, who emphasizes the *instantiability* of the intelligible, and this has nothing to do with your new-fangled sets.

M.   Yes, I recall that he expressed contempt for set theory. Again, I am not sure how seriously he intended this. Much of the history of mathematics of the last 150 years is intimately concerned with sets and their interrelations. Unless one can provide a viable alternative, if one excises sets from mathematics he will not have much left. Now of course it is true that sets in the modern sense play no role in Plotinus. But many regard them as the modern prototype of the intelligibles, the *eidé*. This view was well said some years ago by Paul Bernays, you will remember. Please recall that part of the aim of my paper was to bring Plotinus up to date and to try to show that his great vision is in harmony with modern mathematics and science. The use of set theory is not the only way to do this, of course; I chose it because it is the most widely accepted way of providing foundations for mathematics and the one *prima facie* closest to Plotinus. And of course I was not concerned literally with just Plotinus, but rather with Plotinus in modern garb. All of the historically great metaphysical views should, in my opinion, at some point be viewed systematically in the light of modern knowledge, as well of course as viewed historically in terms of their own time. Now as to instantiability. My reading of Plotinus is that the world of objects, of nature, is really a part of the cosmos, and hence that for him objects do really exist, albeit in a kind of inferior way. If I mistake not, this is the view of Hilary Armstrong and of John Anton, two of our finest Plotinus scholars. Thus we can say that object x is an instance of *eidos y*, both objects and *eidé* being values for variables. If Findlay wishes to allow only *eidé* and to regard objects as *eidé* "thisified, thatified, or thotified," as he puts it, he has quite a job on his hands to formulate just what he means. Thisification presumably involves a kind of ostention, or a notion somewhat akin perhaps to *haecceity*. I do not believe that he has anywhere formulated the logic needed to govern such notions, in the necessary detail and in accord with present-day standards of rigor.

F.   Perhaps not. I recall also that he thought that what you said about $^{\cup}$Em, the converse of the relation Em of emanation, was preposterous. You claim that by means of it we can handle the notion of the "return to the One," of the aspiration of the *Eide* and of the *Psyché* to return to the purity of the One. A great deal more is involved in the theory of the return than can be gotten out of this very narrow relation.

M. But please recall accurately what I said, that the "Plotinic theology is implicit in the theory concerning Em and $^\cup$Em as regards the One." Of course additional *meaning postulates* in Carnap's sense must be added concerning $^\cup$Em not provable from the postulates concerning Em. Also further primitive notions may be needed with postulates interrelating their designata with Em. In all this, however, $^\cup$Em is clearly the fundamental notion.

F. But your handling of Plotinus leaves out completely the "dialectical" character of his thought, Findlay said, the tentative, visionary groping after fundamental truth, even if it should lead to contradiction. This you will never be able to supply within your exclusivist, formalist, extensionalist framework.

M. I am glad you mention this, for this is one very important point we neglected a few moments back in speaking of iridescent concepts. Everything said about them is now relevant to our discussion of Plotinus. Findlay insists that we distinguish between cases of "spurious" iridescence and real iridescence, cases of the latter enabling us "to see how positions we took to be irreconcilable really fit in with one another." Now surely most of the iridescent concepts he finds in Plotinus are real and not spurious. But here is something we neglected above. Perhaps we should say that cases of spurious iridescence belong to what Reichenbach, you recall, dubbed 'the context of discovery', whereas cases of real iridescence belong to the context of justification or of assertion. Contradictory aspects are useful for discovery, for the dialectical or visionary entertaining of one possible hypothesis after another, some of them perhaps contradictory. But in the final reconciliation, these various aspects are harmonized satisfactorily within an all-embracing vision formulated in terms exclusively of mutually consistent *Arten des Gegebenseins*.

F. Well, even if you were to succeed to some extent, there is Hegel, whom your methods cannot possibly touch. You made some ridiculous comments about Hegel, in your talk about manifestation and embodiment, Findlay thought.

M. Please recall that I made no claims about Hegel whatsoever in my Jerusalem paper. I merely took the liberty of borrowing two of his terms in attempting to bridge the seeming gap between absolute monistic idealism and our modern scientific knowledge. However, I am challenged by this point about Hegel. Others have told me essentially the same thing, in particular Errol Harris. It is a matter I would like to inquire into. I cannot, in my heart of hearts, think that Hegel cannot be approached *logistice*, to use Wilfrid Sellar's word, in some appropriate fashion. No doubt to do so will be difficult, but I for one would like to see what could be done here. So far as I am aware, no competent logician has attempted the task, so it seems to me a bit premature to say that it cannot possibly succeed. In any case, Findlay has no respectable *proof* that it can't. We should never contend *a priori* in advance that something cannot be done. This is to block the road inquiry, one of the worst methodological sins, according to Peirce.

F. In spite of what you say, Findlay deplores the superficiality of most of what logicians do. In his paper on "Time and Eternity," presented at the Jerusalem conference, you will remember, he deplored "the objections of logicians [p. 10] to changing truth-values, or to an unsettled alternativity which . . . would violate the Law of Excluded Middle." In fact, logicians have refused "to take time seriously," and "though in some ways deeply contemptible," this does "bear witness to an obscure understanding and taste for the Eternal." All your logic is of no help in trying to do what he was trying to do in that paper. He is (pp. 8−9) "in quest of . . . something that can in some manner be superimposed upon temporal matters, that can be predicated of the being of individuals as they arise, last, change, and pass away in time, and that can be predicated of what they do and undergo at various points in their history, and that can even be predicated in some higher-order fashion of the very time-modalities of their doing and undergoing. It must in some sense be an eternal matter of fact that Buddha is *possibly about* [italics added] to receive enlightenment or Christ to die upon the Cross; it must also be in some sense an eternal matter of fact or truth that Buddha *is* receiving enlightenment or that Christ *is* dying on the Cross . . . and it must in some sense be an eternal matter of fact that such an enlightenment or such a passing occurred many, many centuries ago. It is clear that we are in some manner able to give sense to a being-the-case which does not side-step or ignore, but brackets without altering the facts of development in time, that we can in some sense conceive even temporal matters under a certain species of Eternity, as Spinoza first taught us to do and say. How can we explain this understanding of even a higher-order modality which can be superimposed upon, without destroying, the ordinary time-modalities, but which also utterly transcends any form of direct ostension or illustration?"

M. I find these comments, and in fact Findlay's whole paper, fascinating, but he is really playing right into my hands unwittingly. His talk of Eternity fits in beautifully with the logician's tense of timeless-ness, of which Frege and Peirce were perhaps the first to call attention to. But they did not connect this "time" with Eternity in the almost theological sense in which Findlay speaks of it. Please let me comment on his points one by one. I think it quite wrong to say that logicians do not take time seriously. Peirce and Frege were perhaps the first explicitly to introduce variables for times and to quantify over them. They both did this by assuming first that sentences can be formed tenselessly. The tense of timelessness is prior to the introduction of specific deictic expressions for the handling of the ordinary tenses. And to this of course a good deal of additional material concerning actions, their completion, and so on, must be added to handle the aspectual character of verbs. Once all this is done, there is no diffi-culty about the law of excluded middle, at least in the form

$$'(x)(t)(Fxt \text{ v} \sim Fxt)',$$

that for all x and all time t, either Fxt or not. What Findlay is in quest of seems to me precisely what logicians are eager to provide him with. In the tense of timelessness, the very tense of the law just stated, properties can be predicated of individuals at different stages of their careers. And if the resources of event logic are available, predication may be made of what they *do* and *undergo*, and of the times or events of these doings and undergoings. In the tense of timelessness, it may be said that Buddha at a certain time is possibly about to receive en-lightenment, that at a slightly later time he is receiving enlightenment, and that that time is now several centuries back. In no way do any of these statements side-step or ignore the facts of development. All this is logical commonplace if suitable expression for times or events are introduced and characterized by appropriate meaning postulates. It remains of course to connect this with Eternity, with the vision of the cosmos *sub specie aeternitatis.* I think I have done this, to some extent anyhow, in my paper and in the previous papers therein referred to. Starting with Whitehead's primordial valuations, you will recall, stated of course tenselessly but embracing all time and becoming in their scope, I worked back to the great discussion of God's nature in St. Thomas. And lo and behold, much of that takes on a new clarity — and magnificance, be it said — if viewed in somewhat Whiteheadian terms. Of course one must go way beyond Whitehead to do this. One must distinguish various kinds of "valuations," and one particular way of doing this leads one directly to St. Thomas' "five signs of will." (I have not mentioned Boethius, nor does Findlay, but we should not neglect him in this context.) In a similar vein all discourse about Eternity in the literature of Absolute Idealism can, I think, be handled, stripped of course of purely literary embellishments. The purely literary is something we must all seek to avoid in philosophy, as Whitehead used to emphasize. To be able to write too well is a kind of philosophical curse: one tends to let pretty words and phrases take the place of depth of thought. Too much musical talent is a kind of curse too, for the performer, ease of achievement taking the place of depth of mastery of the several styles.

F.   Perhaps your philosophical views are closer to mine than I had thought. The "metaphysical age into which we seem to be moving," Findlay has said, will be more ecumenical than that of "the bright, brittle, fragmented thinking of the age which is passing."[12] He believes that there are "several modes of thought-approach" and that three of these anyhow "represent essential sides of philosophy, which we must try to practice conjointly." These are what he calls "the austerely analytical, the speculatively systematic, and the iridescent or dialectical." If what you have said is viable, then of course logic, in the broad sense in which you speak of it, has much to contribute to all three approaches.

M.   Yes, I think so. But allow me to strengthen Findlay's plea somewhat. I would urge that we should practice these three approaches not just conjointly but *cooperatively*. It is a pity we all work in so fragmented a fashion when there is so much we can learn from one another. I think it a pity also that Findlay has used his high eminence to vituperate against logic, rather than to have called attention to its value. If he had done this latter, philosophers would perhaps have been more encouraged to undergo the hard labor of mastering logic and of keeping up with newer developments of relevance, so that we could all get ahead more readily with the job to be done. And whatever one individual's views may be, let me recall Whitehead's prophesy — one of my favorite quotes — made many years back. "We must return to my first love, Symbolic Logic," he said. "When in the distant future the subject has expanded, so as to examine patterns depending on connections other than those of space, quantity, and number — when this expansion has occurred, I suggest that Symbolic Logic, the symbolic examination of pattern with the use of . . . [bound] variables, will become the foundation of aesthetics. From that stage it will proceed to conquer ethics and theology."[13]

F.   What an extraordinary statement. I have no doubt but that

---

12. "Ordinary, Revisionary, and Dialectical Strategies ...." p. 275.
13. In *Essays in Science and Philosophy* (London: Rider, 1948), p. 99.

Whitehead is a great philosopher, so I suppose we should take this statement seriously.

Ml.   Yes, I think we should, and Findlay should too. There is much we can learn from so seminal and original a mind as Whitehead's. Findlay has some very interesting metaphysical views of his own, you know, and they are much too important to be allowed to languish about in merely metaphorical terms. They should be formulated in accord with contemporary technical standards, it seems to me. Well, do not let me detain you any longer. It has been a pleasure talking with you, and I hope we shall be able to chat again on another occasion, more deeply and more cooperatively.

F.   I too. Good day.

CHAPTER IX

Some Musings on Hartshorne's Methodological Maxims

Vetera extollimus recentium incuriosi.

In his paper presented at the meeting in Düsseldorf of the International Society for Metaphysics in 1978, Hartshorne comes out for a definition of metaphysics as the *theory* of concreteness.[1] This, he suggests, is in accord with the Aristotelian-Whiteheadian "ontological principle" that "the abstract is real only in the concrete" and that "if we understand concreteness, we also understand abstractness, and hence that a proper theory of concreteness will sum up metaphysical knowledge." Further, "since we can give meaning to 'real' or 'concrete' only by their illustrations in experience, and since an experience includes whatever is given in it so far as given, theory of concreteness coincides with theory of experience. This is what idealists of every type (but hardly materialists or dualists) have seen, however unclearly. The problem is to clarify the insight."

One can agree with the spirit of this contention without wholly subscribing to its letter. Surely the theory of concreteness, including that of the relations between the concrete and the abstract, is of fundamental importance in metaphysics. Unfortunately, one will look in vain for an adequate discussion of the subject in accord with modern standards of rigor. The clearest statement of what "abstract" objects are seems to be in terms of classes, relations, properties, and the like, as opposed to the "concrete" individuals or *Urelemente* of set or type theory. The requirement that 'concrete' has "meaning . . . only by . . . illustrations in experience," however, is a questionable addendum. It leaves out non-experienced, and perhaps non-experienceable, items that play an important role in the theoretical sciences. It may also leave out the very stuff of idealism, whatever this is taken to be, which

---

1. Charles Hartshorne, "Some Principles of Procedure in Metaphysics," to appear in the proceedings of the congress.

is not "experienced" in any obvious sense of that word. In any case, the exact relations between the experienced or experienceable and the fundamental entity or entities of idealism, whatever these are taken to be, need careful exploration. Also, methodologically speaking, much depends on what one takes as values for one's variables of quantification in the underlying logico-linguistic framework.

Hartshorne contends that the objection to metaphysics "that there may be several systems all equally clear and consistent in themselves but incompatible with one another . . . rests on a myth. The sufficient reply is: Show us *two* such systems." Or even *one*, for that matter, done up properly and with the necessary rigor and attention to detail. Further, Hartshorne's objection here could be used against the sciences also, or any systematic area of knowledge, in which alternative, consistent, but incompatible "ways of world-making" are available.

"Metaphysical questions are conceptual, and conceptual analysis must answer them. Linguistic analysts are right in this. . . . Also, conceptual and linguistic are not in all respects synonymous." Quite, but for the clarification of the conceptual, a linguistic factor, it seems, must be brought in.[2] The conceptual is a combination, as it were, of a linguistic and a non-linguistic factor. Even so, it is an extreme view that metaphysical statements are *merely* conceptual ones. There is no doubt that many different types of metaphysical statements are to be discriminated and classified in various ways. Once this is done, some may turn out to be conceptual in a suitable sense, some perhaps not.

Hartshorne goes on to enunciate fourteen "maxims of metaphysical method" that he finds "useful." On the whole, these maxims, which are in imperatival form, are interesting and suggestive, being based on a lifetime of deep metaphysical concern. They merit a more considerable discussion that can be given here. But let us muse a little upon them, one by one.

Maxim 1 urges us to "take human experience as the initial sample of concrete reality or actuality, and try to explain the abstract or potential in terms of concrete experience." The use of 'initial' here is significant, but in order not to run counter to what Hartshorne has already said in his opening remarks, it should not be construed in such a way as not to allow anything later to be admitted that is not a human experience or somehow constructible in terms of such. The use of 'or' in 'abstract or potential' also is to be noted. The word 'or' occurs here, not 'and'. Is the potential to be construed, essentially as with Whitehead, in terms of the abstract, or are these two domains

---

2. See *Events, Reference, and Logical Form,* pp. 15 ff.

quite separate? Or are there two domains here that yet overlap in some fashion? The problem of fashioning the abstract out of the concrete is very different from fashioning the potential out of the concrete or out of the abstract, or out of the concrete and the abstract together in some fashion. In any case, as already suggested in part, we must be sure that whatever we take as our initial samples of concrete reality be of such kind as to be in harmony with the vast edifices of modern mathematics and theoretical science, on the one hand, and with the most delicate insights arising from our most lofty experiences in artistic, religious, and humane matters, on the other. Let us be sure to include here at least the very highest experiences of which man is capable.

Maxim 2. "Look to practical life and its most general presuppositions for the indispensable ideas and ideals philosophy, including metaphysics, is to clarify and purify." This again seems too humdrum a requirement. The lowest types of human experience assert themselves willy-nilly in human life and need no special boost from the metaphysician. It is the highest that are often given short shrift and concerning which it is very difficult to build a theory to explain. Yet it is just this that is a main task of metaphysics. Maxim 2 seems somewhat out of keeping with much of what Hartshorne has emphasized in his writings heretofore. On the other hand, of course, the common items of practical life are not to be neglected but should be given their proper place.

Maxim 3. "Trust terms in ordinary (or, in some science or nonphilosophical discpline, standard) language — for their ordinary or standard purposes; trust terms standard for some schools of philosophy only so far as they prove explicable by ordinary or truly standard terms, together with examples from direct experience of practical life." Actually here there are several quite conflicting maxims, one as concerns ordinary language, and several as concern whatever science (or sciences) or nonphilosophical discipline (or disciplines) are taken as standard. How is the choice to be made among these? The vocabulary trusted in one may be suspect from the point of view of the other. From the metaphysical point of view *all* such vocabularies are suspect until given an adequate founding. The real gist of Maxim 3 would seem to be that the vocabularies in the various scientific and nonphilosophic disciplines are not only to be taken seriously by the metaphysician but are to be regarded as part and parcel of his main concern. Metaphysics is not something wholly *sui generis* but should involve itself severally with all domains of human knoweldge, and not just abstractly so but as regards full delineation of all relevant details. Part of its task is the study of the interrelations of these various domains, of just how one "presupposes" another, of which are more fundamental or "prior" in some sense than others, and so on. The terms in the several sciences and disciplines are thus to be "trusted" not at face value but only as items in need of clarification and incorporation within the general scheme.

Maxim 4. "Do not overestimate the ease with which the metaphysical import of experience and practice is to be discerned, considering (a) that it is the unusual, not the universal or essential, aspects of experience which stand out; and (b) that there is no reason to think that our human awareness can ever be without qualification "clear and distinct," like that theologians attribute to deity; also, (c) that consciousness is selective, and hence, without suitable guiding ideas as to what to look for in experience we are likely to miss much that is relevant to our quest." All philosophy is the explanation of the most obvious aspects of experience, Whitehead used to say, and this maxim echoes the point. To get at the most pervasive traits of experience — or of physical nature, for that matter — requires a considerable imaginative effort, the most general categories being just those that often elude our grasp. Even so, this maxim expresses only half the truth. The unusual aspects of experience do not stand out with any peculiarity unless something forces us to note them. Often they are merely disregarded, or simply not seen, by the insensitive observer. The same holds true of recalcitrant phenomena in the sciences, which are often dismissed or passed over until some compelling reason emerges for the scientist to take them into account. And surely *some* objects of human awareness are clear and distinct enough for *some* human purposes, perhaps even the notion of deity, if a really serious logical effort were made to clarify it. Of course consciousness is selective and whatever one does as a metaphysician, one inevitably passes over some items of possible relevance to some inquiry (or situation) or other. The best one can hope to do in this regard is to be as all-inclusive as possible, within the inevitable human limitations.

Maxim 5. "For such guiding ideas look from the outset to formal logic, as (however successfully or otherwise) Peirce did in his categories of First, Second, Third, and Aristotle did in his use of the distinction between substance and property as analogous to that between subject and predicate." Yes, *total humility before logic* must be exercised at all times. The metaphysician must continually be on his toes in this respect, as has been emphasized in the foregoing papers. Hartshorne gives five examples: "(a) take relations of dependence to be of primary importance, since all inference turns on them; (b) interpret symmetrical relations as special cases, as equivalence (biconditioning) is a special case of one-way conditioning or dependence; (c) look for ontological correlates of the modal terms *possible, necessary, contingent*; (d) distinguish levels of abstractness or logical strength, and avoid the fallacy of misplaced concreteness; (e) avoid fallacies of division . . . and fallacies of composition. . . ."

Hartshorne has made much of relations of dependence in his previous writings. The validity of inference does not turn on them, however, but rather upon the properties of the logical connectives and quantifiers. Hartshorne wants a notion of dependence between entities x and y such that x may be said to depend on y but not y on x, a key instance being where y is deity itself but x is not. A good deal of semantical spelling out of such a relation, or relations, is needed, which seems not to have been fully supplied.[3] Symmetrical relations (all of them?) are somehow supposed to be "special cases" of such relations, just as equivalence is a special case of the one-way conditional. These contentions are obscure at best. Equivalence is not a special case, in any usual sense anyhow, of the conditional, but is defined rather as the *bi*-conditional, the conditional going both ways, so to speak. And surely the relation of *being the same age* as, say, is not a special case of any "dependence" relation, in any obvious sense anyhow.

It is also highly dubious that the modal notions should be given ontological correlates, as Hartshorne urges. Although there has been purported progress in recent years, in attempting to clarify the "meaning" of the modal operators, most of it, it is to be feared, has been pseudoprogress only, but with much attendant uproar and confusion. In any case, the basic metaphysical ontology surely should not be *increased* in order to provide such correlates, if the modal notions may be satisfactorily handled otherwise — which in fact they can be. Further, the modal notions themselves are not very interesting philosophically, an explanation for their purported uses always being forthcoming in other, more basic ways.[4]

Levels of abstractness are presumably provided by the different levels in the hierarchy of languages, each level having greater "logical strength" than its predecessor. The distinctions between object- and metalanguage, between a metalanguage and *its* metalanguage (a

---

3. Cf., however, the discussion in *Whitehead's Categoreal Scheme and Other Papers*, Chapter II.
4. Cf., for example, Ruth Barcan Marcus, "Dispensing with *Possibilia*," *Proceedings and Addresses of the American Philosophical Association* XLIX (1975–1976): 39–48 and the author's "On *Possibilia* and Essentiality," in *Pragmatics, Truth, and Language*.

metametalanguage), and so on, are now almost universally recognized as very basic distinctions beyond reproach. Methodologists have recognized for many years their importance and utility, and structural linguists are at long last recognizing that natural languages themselves contain in some fashion their own hierarchy of metalanguages. It is not quite clear, however, whether Hartshorne's (5d) is to be interpreted in just this way. Perhaps he has in mind something more like the theory of types, which, however, is much more dubious, and not quite in keeping with much of what Hartshorne has written elsewhere concerning eternal objects, for example. (Recall the "ontological principle" mentioned above.) As to avoiding fallacies, surely all purely *logical* ones are to be avoided, but not everything that is called 'a fallacy' is really one. The so-called fallacy of misplaced "concreteness" is not strictly a logical matter, but depends very much on very special views as to what is "concrete" and what is not.

Maxim 6. "Seek formally exhaustive divisions of possible doctrines (employing less crude devices than mere dichotomies, rather at least trichotomies, thus *all, some, only,* and *none*), and search for principles by which to eliminate all but one possible doctrine." This maxim reads well in principle, but will rarely be helpful in practice, except in very simple cases. Any well-articulated view is apt to be much too complicated to fit into any simple classification. Also, the very notion of a "possible doctrine" is not very clear. No matter how one were to circumscribe a set of such, someone might well come along with a doctrine just different enough not to fit. Any non-simplistic "principles by which to eliminate all but one possible doctrine" would have to be of staggering generality, themselves in need of justification and surely transcending the kinds of requirements laid down in the earlier maxims. Hartshorne probably thinks of such principles as *logical* principles, but that this is the case is doubtful. In any case, they need careful statement.

Maxim 7. "With contrary doctrinal extremes (e.g., all relations external, all internal) look for an intermediate position combining the advantages and avoiding the disadvantages of both extremes." Yes, but even so one should not aim merely at an eclectic mish-mash. And in many kinds of doctrines, the extremes will not be compatible. The real point here is that one should always seek to accommodate whatever is valuable in the various alternative positions available, and to be sure that it is not omitted or merely glossed over. Often much must await future research. One may see advantages in an alternative approach, but also recognize that the price is too high, the disadvantages too great. If one cannot easily at first incorporate the advantages, he may hope to succeed later with greater effort. Or he may come to think that the advantages are not so great as at first appeared.

Maxim 8. "Use experiential falsifiability (Popper) not verifiability as primary criteria of the "empirical" or non-metaphysical." This again is a special maxim, the content of which has been under intensive discussion for several decades. This is not the occasion to take sides concerning it. It is, at best, doubtful, however, whether any such maxim properly demarcates between the "empirical" and the "metaphysical." In fact, it may be questioned as to whether any such demarcation is possible, on the one hand, or even desirable, on the other. All knowledge is of a piece, with only artificial barriers drawn here or there for some human convenience. In any case, the barriers are not very important, it would seem, essentially the same methods being applicable throughout.

Maxim 9. "Be cautious about asserting the zero cases, as in 'such and such is not experienced'; remembering that while observation of X as present may establish its presence, inability to detect a presence is not always equivalent to detecting the corresponding absence. . . . Not to *know* that we experience something is not the same as not to experience it. Negative introspection is even more fallible than positive introspection." This maxim could be suitably generalized to urge caution in all assertions, not just those concerning experiencing and what is experienced. Strictly all that "observation of X as present" establishes is observing-of-X-going-on. It is quite an inference from this to the presence of X as such. Some prior delineation of what the X's are — of one's ontology — and as based on sound reasons, would seem essential here.

Maxim 10. "Honor the principle of contrast, avoid saying that absolutely "everything" is such and such — unless you want the such and such to be as devoid of distinctive character as the most general idea of entity, in contrast to bare nothing." This maxim may perhaps be clarified as follows. Let 'Ent x' express that x is an entity in the metaphysical language, where the predicate 'Ent' is taken in the broadest possible sense to be applicable to everything admitted in the given theory. Then, of course, everything is an entity, '(x) Ent x' holds, and the predicate 'Ent' is devoid of distinctive character. But there will be many metaphysical principles of a general character laid down, and these too will involve the universal quantifier. They will say that absolutely everything is such and such, and yet this such and such will have a very definite distinctive character. Without such general laws, a metaphysics is unthinkable. In fact, such vast generality is one of the ways in which metaphysical laws might be distinguished from scientific laws, the latter always having hypotheses to the effect that the entities considered in the context are of such and such a physical, chemical, or biological (etc.) kind. Even so, the principle of contrast among the merely metaphysical laws is not violated, each law contrasting suitably with the others in its very statement — otherwise, we should have only one law, not several.

Maxim 11. "Since metaphysics is searching for the most general meaning of 'concrete', try to find ideas applicable to everything conceivable as concrete . . . though not to absolutely everything, singular or collective, concrete or abstract." The contrast between the singular and collective here is interesting. The only known means of achieving this in a logically sound way is apparently by means of the calculus of individuals. This is a brand of logic that would seem indispensable for Hartshorne, yet one to which he has given very little lip-service, if any. Just how the contrast between the abstract and the concrete is to be drawn is an open matter, as already suggested above. A considerable portion — but not all — of discourse about the abstract can be handled in terms of the theory of virtual classes and relations, together with a suitable semantics concerning them. But more is needed for mathematics and the theoretical sciences.[5]

Maxim 12. "Expect such ideas [i.e., ideas applicable to everything as concrete] to be variables with uniquely great ranges of values, rather than constants or definite values under a variable. (Example: causal determination of events by previous events, and creative transcendence of such determination, may be viewed as matters of degree, whereas classical determinism takes the determination to be absolute or infinite and the creativity to be zero. The absolute degree and the zero degree are, at best, infinitely special cases, not general principles. They are, therefore, suspect as metaphysical. And it is a matter of logic that they could not be established empirically.)" Are not category mistakes involved here, in the literal statements — that between an idea and a variable or constant (these latter being merely linguistic), that between variables and the numerical degree of such and such a phenomenon, and that between the metaphysical and the logical? What Hartshorne wishes to say here is perhaps that in metaphysics the use of quantitative (and no doubt comparative) notions is preferable to that of merely classificatory ones. This is a point usually accepted for the methodology of science, and it is good to have it emphasized here for metaphysics also.

---

5. Cf. "Common Names and Mathematical Scotism," in *Peirce's Logic of Relations and Other Studies.*

Maxim 13. "Since universal ideas must be variables not constants, and since deity is a universal idea (knowing all, influencing all, etc.), expect God to be a variable with infinite range of possible values, not a mere constant — in some sense the most flexible and alterable of all realities, in spite of being the most secure of identity and permanence. . . ." Here "variables" and "constants" seem to have to do with change and alterability, but of course there may be variables over either alterable or unalterable entities, and there may be constants designating one kind, other constants the other. This maxim, again, is not strictly methodological, but rather one leading directly to Hartshorne's own conception of God.

Maxim 14. "Keep the lines of communication open with various forms of philosophizing, and with various religious, scientific, aesthetic specializations: also, look for rational grounds for agreeing or disagreeing with other philosophers, living or dead. . . ." Yes, by all means. But do more than merely this: try to *learn* from other philosophers and forms of philosophizing and give them *maximum credit* for what it is that they accomplish. Then be sure that your own style of philosophizing is such as to accommodate whatever of value you find. In fact, try to have your style of philosophy do it even better, if possible. And the same with the material arising from the various "religious, scientific, aesthetic specializations." In practice, of course, this maxim imposes extreme difficulties upon the metaphysician, and never more so than in the late twentieth century, with its babel of voices and conflicting views, its stupendous specialized scientific achievements, and the incredible confusions that seem to be shaking the very foundations of the arts, to say nothing of morality and the interpersonal relations between "I" and "Thou."

Valuable as Hartshorne's maxims are, there are many others that suggest themselves immediately, a few of which be listed as follows. Some are "Do's" and some are "Don'ts." Some even veer off into matters of professional conduct:

Maxim 15. Atomize as far as possible and then recognize the importance of logical constructs.

Maxim 16. Use quantification theory and generalize as far as possible. Do not ride in a horse and buggy.

Maxim 17. Do not over-mathematize. Do not regard modern metamathematical model theory as the only metaphysical method worth the using. Keep in mind always the difference between mathematization and logicization.

Maxim 18. Learn "to value highly the little unpretentious *cautious* truths, arrived at by rigorous methods, than . . . vast, floating . . . generalities" that often veil more than they express.

Maxim 19. Do not be afraid of being too preoccupied with language. Remember with Lichtenberg that "unsere ganze Philosophie ist Berichtigung des Sprachgebrauchs" and with Condillac that "une science n'est qu'une langue bien faite."

Maxim 20. Be careful not to write too well. "Words are wise men's counters; they do but reckon by them," as Hobbes noted.

Maxim 21. Do let metaphysics grow with the advance of scientific and technological knowledge.

Maxim 22. Be of your times but always be beyond them. Like St. Theresa, be half in and half out of doors.

Maxim 23. Always teach the old dog new tricks and do not block the road to inquiry.

Maxim 24. Do not ride your hobby-horse to death.

Maxim 25. Don't follow fads. Don't bask under the shadow of a great name. Stand rather on the shoulders of giants to see further than they.

Maxim 26. Don't play professional politics, which are always dirty and demeaning and deter the pursuit of truth. Do not condemn a fellow philosopher just because he belongs to the "wrong" faction. Do not condemn him without at least doing him the courtesy of reading and understanding what he writes.

Maxim 27. Always prefer the abstruse and difficult philosophy to the easy and obvious. It is very likely to be the more worthy object of your wholehearted devotion.

Maxim 28. Never forget the human person, his essential dignity, and his important and special place in the metaphysical cosmos.

Maxim 29. Do not forget that man is a social animal and that much of one's work should be directed toward trying to understand how an appropriate human society can be achieved.

Maxim 30. Never forget the fundamental values of truth, beauty, and goodness, and that much of one's effort should be directed toward formulating a theory in which they may be fully incorporated.

Maxim 31. Not only let your mind wander to the *O Altitudo*, incorporate it fully in your work — as well as in your every thought, word, and deed.

Maxim 32. Never forget the unified character of all knowledge, and of methodology in general.

Some of these maxims are close in spirit to some of Hartshorne's, serving to make some of them a little more precise.

Maxim 15 calls attention to the need for recognizing some entities as the fundamental ones. By mere logical devices other kinds of entities may then often be accommodated as constructs, perhaps by means of contextual definitions. These observations are of course reminiscent of Russell's logical atomism, but have a methodological significance far beyond the confines of that doctrine. In fact the observations are completely general, applying wherever modern logic is used seriously.

Quantification theory in its modern form was discovered — or invented — just a hundred years ago, in 1879, with the publication of Frege's *Begriffsschrift*. Frege himself was sensitive to the metaphysical significance of the quantifiers. He berated the attitude of "Metaphysica sunt, non leguntur" as well as that of "Logica sunt, non leguntur." Curiously, however, metaphysicians have not been quick to absorb quantification theory and to recognize the very fundamental role it must play in metaphysics. Indeed, in metaphysics we can do no better than to follow the advice of Simmias, that one "should persevere until he has achieved one of two things: either he should discover or be taught the truth; . . . or, if this be impossible, I would have him take the best and most irrefragable of human theories, and let this be the raft upon which he sails through life — not without risk, as I admit, if he cannot find some divine word which will more surely and safely carry him."[6] Now quantification theory is the best and most irrefragable logical doctrine we have, in which perhaps even the divine word itself may be suitably couched.

The explicit use of quantification theory is the essence of logicization as contrasted with mathematization. In the latter, fundamental use of numbers and of quantitative technics in general appears, or else model- or set-theoretic principles in terms of which all manner of numbers (even transfinite ones) may be accommodated. Well, number theory and the metamathematical theory of models have their own interest. In both instances a great deal more than the logical theory of quantification is involved. Such material belongs to mathematics as generally conceived. Metamathematics, either as a subject-matter or as a technique, has no more relevance to metaphysics than any special domain of science does. The point may seem so obvious as to be scarcely worth making, were it not for a widespread contemporary view to the contrary.

Maxim 18 is due to Nietzsche, but it harks back to Goethe and to many writers in the French Enlightenment. This maxim of course does not exclude rational interest in the emotions nor emotive joy in

---

6. *Phaedo*, 85.

the exercise of reason. Don't forget also that *la raison a ses raisons que le coeur ne connaît pas*, a point surely well known to Pascal *quā* geometer.

Twentieth-century philosophy has made "the linguistic turn" and this we should all learn to welcome, in accord with Maxim 19. And on the whole this has been the right turn to have made. One need not, however, having made the turn, lose sight of the old way of things. The linguistic turn now embraces semantics fundamentally, the study of how words and entities are interrelated. Condillac's "langue bien faite" may perhaps best be thought of as "logical perfection" in roughly the senses of Frege and Russell. In any case, the greater the metaphysician's preoccupation with "une langue bien faite" the more likely nowadays he is to make some contribution of permanent value.

On the other hand, preoccupation with language should not be construed in terms just of good style. Like the pursuit of success, good style is often a "bitch goddess," to use William James' phrase. *It* takes over and leaves what is to be expressed to fend for itself. Hobbes' comment about "reckoning" has a surprisingly modern ring, reckoning being construable in terms of a logical system.

That metaphysics should be allowed to grow with the advance of scientific and technological knowledge is part of Hartshorne's Maxim 14. It might seem unnecessary even to mention it again, were it not for widespread views to the contrary. In this respect what Hartshorne has elsewhere called "the method of convenient ignorance" should not be followed.[7] "Scientia non habet inimicum nisi ignorantem." Even so, it becomes increasingly difficult for even the most enlightened not to be placed here with the "ignorantem."

The contention of Baudelaire that "il faut d'être de son temps" needs a considerable discussion, and at best incorporates a half-truth as regards metaphysics. One is tempted to say that metaphysics abosrbs its history in a way rather different from other disciplines, but this is dubious. On the other hand, the history of metaphysics is a part of metaphysics in a way in which the history of physics, say, is not a part of physics.[8] The metaphysician must both be and not be "of his time" but in different senses. The matter is very complicated and need not be considered further here.

Maxim 23 is of course due to Peirce and is wholly convincing, and hence needs no elaboration.

---

7. Cf. Charles Hartshorne, *Creative Synthesis and Philosophic Method* (London: The SCM Press, 1970).

8. Cf. E. Gilson, *The Unity of Philosophical Experience* (New York: Charles Scribner's Sons, 1937).

Most metaphysicians do tend to ride their hobby-horses to death. Having discovered or found what they believe to be a good thing, they go on repeating it *ad nauseam*. Of course truths bear repeating, rephrasing, being seen from alternative points of view, and on. But some genuine new insight should always be forthcoming, some new intellectual adventure of ideas, some new, deeper interrelation seen or grasped, some further step in the clarification of fundamentals.

Philosophy tends to live on the fads of the moment. Never perhaps has this been more the case than in our present mass, technologically oriented, materialist, "sensate" society. Many conflicting philosophies are clamoring for attention, and the best way to be heard is to join one of the leading fashions. But fashions change as frequently in philosophy as in *haute couteur*. It is sometimes said that vanity is the *sine qua non* for a philosopher to be influential. The philosopher of influence tends then to seek disciples to enhance his own position. All such temptation must be resisted on both sides, and thus also all temptation to join one of the leading cliques — or claques. The metaphysician worthy of his name must always go ahead in his own way and at his own pace. The whole enterprise is essentially a lonely one.[9] Thus professional politics in all its forms is assiduously to be avoided.

Maxim 27 is of course due to Hume, and Maxim 28, to the host of philosophers starting at least with Protagoras, who have emphasized the metaphysical importance of the person. Neither surely needs defense here.

Having recognized the dignity of the human person, one must go on to the theory of society and of social action. Or conversely: having attempted to formulate a theory of society, one must be sure that the essential dignity and uniqueness of the person have not been lost sight of. In either way, there are enormous metaphysical problems and difficulties to be faced, which surely must be accounted among the most important of our time. Especially significant here are the difficulties connected with maximizing the good for each and every individual and at the same time preserving the maximum welfare and moral good for the society as a whole.[10] The problems here are very basic, and probably not enough attention is being given to them from a theoretical and systematic point of view — in which purely logical considerations have to play a leading role.

---

9. Cf. Paul Weiss, *op. cit.,* p. 24.
10. Cf. Reinhold Niebuhr, *Moral Man and Immoral Society* (New York: Charles Scribner's Sons, 1932) and K. Arrow, *Individual Choice and Social Value* (New York: McGraw-Hill Publishing Co., 1951).

The age-old triumvirate of truth, beauty, and goodness is often given short shrift by contemporary writers. Yet 'truth' is ever with us in contemporary semantic considerations, beauty is already creeping back in aesthetics[11], and goodness is ever present in ethical and meta-ethical discussions. Thus the time is perhaps ripe for a reconsideration of a unified theory of value, 'axiology' it used to be called, in accord with the new standards of rigor. If this were to be carried out thoroughly, with a view also to formulate a systematic theology — as in II, III, and V above — it would no doubt be in accord with Sir Thomas Browne's maxim (31).

Maxim 32 is a Whiteheadian principle. It is no doubt an exaggeration to say that any particular branch of philosophy is easy and that only their unification is difficult. No, each field has its own separate difficulties. But still the unification is more difficult, combining as it does not only the separate difficulties of the several fields, but the difficulties attached to the unified formulation as well. But metaphysics should always aim at the unified view. Metaphysical method, moreover, should be a unified method, not differing in any fundamental ways from that of the sciences.[12]

These additional maxims are listed almost at random, and many further ones could be given. Still, they, together with those of Hartshorne, sum to a compelling view as to what metaphysics is. They also incorporate methodological suggestions that may not be without value in the methodological chaos of our time. Above all, the metaphysician should keep his mind open to new knowledge and seek to incorporate it in his view — *Ignoti nulla cupido*. The whole enterprise is in practice well nigh impossible, but still one of the highest of which man is capable. Of this enterprise Hartshorne in his many writings has been an eloquent champion for many years, albeit on the basis of an inadequate logical foundation.

---

11. Cf. recent papers by Mary Mothersill.
12. For some pertinent remarks on a related point, see Nancy D. Simco, "Rationality, Scientific Rationality, and Philosophical Problems," *16th World Congress of Philosophy, Section Papers* (Düsseldorf, 1978): 577–580.

CHAPTER X

On the Eliminability
of God's Consequent Nature

Coepisti melius quam desinis. Ultima primis cedunt.

The Whiteheadian God is genuinely dipolar in comprising two separate "natures," the primordial and the consequent.[1] It is not too clear, however, precisely how these are to be distinguished. Bowman Clarke is the first to have put forward a logical rendition of the distinction, and this is done on the basis of Goodman's theory of qualia.[2]

Very roughly, Clarke's definition is in terms of two "individuals," the *aii* or *all-inclusive individual,* and the *uei*, the *unique eternal individual.* The expressions for these are defined in Goodman's vocabulary, in terms of 'O' for the relation of *overlapping,* 'A' for the relation of being *affiliated with* in a suitable sense, and 'T' for being a *time*. The *uei* is the one individual that overlaps with all and only the individuals that overlap with some individual that is discrete (does not overlap) with all times, and the *aii* is the one individual that overlaps with all and only the individuals that overlap with some temporal individual. A temporal individual is one that some time "qualifies," that is, the time is a proper part of it, where it is a "complex," a complex being in turn an individual whose parts, if non-overlapping, do not overlap with it but are affiliated with it. God in his total fullness is then, for Clarke, the individual overlapping with just those *y*'s that overlap with either the *uei* or the *aii*. It is then shown that God as thus conceived exists uniquely, the proof utilizing only logical principles plus the descriptive or non-logical axioms needed to characterize Goodman's primitives.

Although this characterization is of considerable logical interest in its own right, it will not do as a rendition of the dipolar God of

---

1. A. N. Whitehead, *Process and Reality* (New York: The Macmillan Co., 1939), especially Chapter II.
2. See B. Clarke, *Language and Natural Theology,* pp. 157 ff and Nelson Goodman, *The Structure of Appearance*.

151

Whitehead. Too much is left out. No provision is made for the "primordial valuations" constitutive of the primordial nature, nor is the notion of God in any way integrated with the theory of prehensions and the theory of "concrescence" that are at the very heart of the Whiteheadian cosmology. Further, the notions defined seem devoid of theological interest. Although the *aii* may well mirror the consequent nature to some extent, the *uei* is woefully inadequate for the primordial nature. It is far removed from "the unconditioned conceptual valuation of the entire multiplicity of eternal objects," taken either as such (in terms of "pure" conceptual prehensions) or with respect to their ingression to some degree into each and every actual occasion (in terms of "impure" conceptual prehensions). In fact, the removal is so considerable that little resemblance remains.

An attempt to portray the Whiteheadian God in what is thought a more fruitful way is made in the author's "On the Whiteheadian God."[3] There, it will perhaps be recalled, the favored definition of a name for the primordial nature is to the effect that this latter is the fusion of the class of all conceptual prehendings (to some degree) of eternal objects with respect to all the objects in which they ingress, these prehendings all being "valuations." Thus, where

(1) $\qquad\qquad$ 'e Prhd$_i$ $\alpha, e_1, ..., e_n$'

expresses that e prehends to degree i ($0 \leq i \leq 1$) the n-adic eternal object α as holding among actual occasions $e_1, ..., e_n$, and where

(2) $\qquad\qquad\qquad$ '$e \in$ Val'

expresses that e is an act or state of valuating (in just whatever sense Whitehead intends — he never quite tells us),

(3) $\quad$ 'png' may abbreviate '$(Fu'\hat{e}(E\alpha)(Ee_1)...(Ee_k)(Ei)((<e,\text{Prhd}^i,$
$\alpha, e_1 >e$ v ... v $<e, \text{Prhd}^i, \alpha, e_1, ..., e_k >e) \cdot e \in$ Val $\cdot 0 \leq i \leq 1))$'.

Here the forms '$<e, \text{Prhd}^i, \alpha, e_1>$', and so on, are *event-descriptive predicates*. Note also the use of prehensions that are their own subjects, so to speak, that is, prehensions where one and the same entity *does* the prehending and *is* the prehending. This usage may seem perhaps somewhat *outré*, but is here a mere harmless technical device. The 'k' in the definiens is the degree of the eternal object of highest degree a name for which is admitted as a primitive.

Note the really stupendous all-inclusiveness of the *png*. Every hair of one's head is primordially "valuated" with respect to every eternal

---

3. In *Whitehead's Categoreal Scheme and Other Papers*.

object, and this to just such and such a degree. The fundamental meaning of 'ought' is presumably provided for here. Every actual occasion ought to have just the properties, to speak loosely, ascribed it in the primordial valuatings. The *png* is thus more the source of value, however, than of fact or of scientific law. It might be thought then that the definition is too restricted, not providing the *png* with sufficient breadth or power. It is all-inclusive with respect to value, but that is all. No provision is made for the reign of scientific and other types of *law* within the cosmos, no provisions for divine *intervention* in the stream of affairs other than as a "lure for feeling," no distinction is made between the divine *desiderata,* on the one hand, and divine *permissions,* on the other, no allowance is made for a doctrine of *prohibition,* no status is given the notion of divine foreknowledge or *praescitus,* and so on and on. The *png* is a rather weak entity, actually, it is to be feared, as construed on a Whiteheadian basis.

In addition to the primordial nature, of course, there is the consequent nature, the body of God, so to speak. This was introduced, in "On the Whiteheadian God," as the fusion of everything in the cosmos other than the primordial valuations. Thus

(4)   '*cng*'   was taken as   '$(Fu'\hat{e}\sim(E\mu)(png = Fu'\mu \cdot e \in \mu))$',

where 'μ' is a class variable, classes being included among the eternal objects. God in his total fullness is then merely the logical sum of these two natures, 'sum' here being taken in the sense of the calculus of individuals. Thus

(5)   'God'   is taken as short for   '$(png \cup cng)$'.

Some interesting objections against this definition have been put forward by Clarke in a recent paper.[4] "In speaking of the subject of the primordial valuations," he notes, "it is strange for Martin to write: . . . Whitehead nowhere stipulates . . . just *whose* valuations constitute the primordial nature. . . . God [italics added] is the subject of the primordial valuations." Accordingly, Clarke proposes the following definition:

(6)   '*png*'   for   '$(Fu'\hat{e}(Ei)(E\alpha)(Ee_1)...(Ee_k)((<God,Prhd^i,\alpha,e_1>e$ v ... v
        $<God,Prhd^i,\alpha,e_1,...,e_k>e) \cdot e \in Val \cdot 0 \leqq i \leqq 1))$'.

The consequent nature, he says, analogously, would turn out to be characterized as follows:

---

4. "R. M. Martin on the Whiteheadian God," *The Southern Journal of Philosophy* XVI (1978): 293–305.

(7)   '*cng*' for '$(Fu'\hat{e}(Ee_1)<God,Prhd,e_1>e)$'.

Concerning these definitions Clarke remarks that "they both presuppose that the term 'God' is taken as primitive or has previously been introduced by a definite description. Since for Whitehead, God is a derivative, rather than a primitive notion, this latter alternative [of defining 'God' via a definite description] would be the one to pursue." But how would one pursue it? If 'God' were taken as a primitive, an axiom to the effect that

(8) $God = (png \cup cng)$

would perhaps be in order. But this would seem to make 'God' a fundamental notion, not a derivative one. Unless we are told precisely what definite description 'God' is short for — in which of course no reference can be made to either the *png* or the *cng* — Clarke's proposal remains hanging in mid-air.

In answer to the question: Whose valuations constitute the primordial ones? the answer is, of course: God's. But a technical point here is not to be overlooked, that if 'God' is to be introduced by summation as the sum of the two natures, as seems natural, and indeed in accord with Clarke's own earlier account in terms of qualia, then each nature must be introduced by definitions whose definientia do not contain 'God' in their primitive expansions. Otherwise of course the definition of 'God' would be circular. To avoid this, prehensions having themselves as their own subjects are introduced and made to serve just the purpose intended.

One could, if one wished, introduce

(9)   'PrPhPrhn' as '$\hat{e}(Ee_1)(Ei)(<e,Prhd^i,e_1>e \cdot 0 \leqq i \leqq 1)$'

and

(10)   'PrCptlVal' as '$\hat{e}(E\alpha)(Ei)(Ex_1)...(Ex_k)(<e,Prhd^i,\alpha,e_1>e$ v ... v
$<e,Prhd^i,\alpha,e_1,...,e_k>e) \cdot e \in Val \cdot 0 \leqq i \leqq 1)$'.

These define respectively the notions of being a *primordial physical prehension* and a *primordial conceptual valuation*. Then

(11)   '*png*' could be short for '$(Fu'PrCptlVal)$'

and

(12)   '*cng*' for '$(Fu'PrPhPrhn)$',

and then by summation

(13)   'God' could be short for '$(png \cup cng)$'.

In this way Clarke's suggestion can be accommodated without circularity and without having to bring in 'God' as a primitive name. And note that no harm can arise from allowing certain prehensions to be their own subjects, such prehensions having no role elsewhere in the theory. We pay them overtime, so to speak, and make them do what we wish.

The essential purport of Clarke's definition, that it is *God* who performs the primordial valuations, so to speak, could then be forthcoming as a principle. It could be required that

(14) $\vdash(\alpha_j)(e_1)...(e_j)(Ee')(Ei)(0 \leqq i \leqq 1 \cdot (<God,Prhd^i,\alpha,e_1>e' \text{ v } ... \text{ v } <God,Prhd^i,\alpha,e_1,...,e_j>e') \cdot e' \in PrCptlVal)'.$

Similarly,

(15) $\vdash(e)(Ei)(0 < i \leqq 1 \cdot God \, Prhd^i \, e).$

(These principles are essentially those given on p. 47 of *Whitehead's Categoreal Scheme*.)

Clarke would still object that (6), (10), (11), and hence (13), are based on "impure" conceptual prehensions rather than "pure" ones, and apparently thinks that the primordial nature should be construed wholly in terms of the latter. A key text for this construal is found on p. 70 of *Process and Reality* where Whitehead remarks that in conceptual prehension "there is no reference to particular actualities, or to any particular actual world." Also, in "his conceptual envisagement of eternal objects" God "is not thereby directly related to the given course of history." In accord with this, in place of (1) above, Clarke suggests, forms such as

(16)   '$e \, Prhd^i \, \alpha$'

should be allowed. And to handle relations between or among eternal objects, we should need also

(17)   '$e \, Prhd^i \, \alpha,\beta_1,...,\beta_n$',

that e prehends to degree i that the n-adic eternal object α holds among the eternal objects β_1, ..., β_n. Clarke suggests that this latter form is needed for handling pure conceptual prehensions, but so presumably is (16).

In terms of (16) and (17), the notion of being a pure primordial conceptual valuation could be introduced as follows:

(18)   'PurePrCptlVal' for '$\hat{e}(E\alpha)(E\beta_1)...(E\beta_n)(Ei)((<e,Prhd^i,\alpha>e \text{ v } <e,Prhd^i,\alpha,\beta_1>e \text{ v } ... \text{ v } <e,Prhd^i,\alpha,\beta_1,...,\beta_n>e) \cdot e \in Val \cdot 0 \leqq i \leqq 1)$'.

155

If the definiens of (11) were taken as '(Fu'PurePrCptlVal)', the resulting notion of *png* would be based wholly on "pure" primordial conceptual valuation and thus presumably "not . . . directly related to the given course of history."

A purely technical point. The hierarchy of eternal objects might be arranged to accord with the simple theory of types. If so, dyadic relations could be regarded as classes of ordered couples, triadic relations as classes of ordered triples, and so on. (The well-known definitions of Wiener or Kuratowski could be used.) In (18), then, *n* could always be taken as 1, without loss of generality.

The *png*, if introduced by (18) or (11), however, would seem to be a rather dull and uninteresting entity. The way in which the eternal objects are interrelated amongst themselves is wholly contained in a kind of mathematics, if the hierarchy of them is arranged in accord with type theory — or even an axiomatic set theory, for that matter. Perhaps Whitehead had in mind some other kind of ordering, but this seems doubtful. Whitehead was too much a mathematician to blur over this point. And if memory serves, Whitehead did answer a question put to him by a student on one occasion, that: yes, the eternal objects could be viewed as hierarchically arranged in a suitable mathematical way. If so, then, the *png* as construed in the way Clarke wishes, in accord with (18) or (11), is concerned wholly with pure mathematics, and in no way presumably with the world of process, with the creatures, with the physical cosmos. With so paltry a *png*, the *cng* is surely needed. "By reason of its [God's] character as a creature, always in concrescence and never in the past, it receives a reaction from the world; this reaction is its consequent nature." Without the *cng* there would, on the Whiteheadian basis as construed by Clarke, be no "reaction from the world" in the divine nature. The *png*, as conceived in Clarke's way, is "wholly other," too remote from the field of our sorrow to be concerned in any way with either our individual lives or with the stream of history.

Whitehead is not unambiguous, however, that the primordial nature of God is to be construed in terms wholly of pure primordial conceptual valuations. Many passages can be cited to support the view taken in *Whitehead's Categoreal Scheme,* that the *png* is best introduced via a definition in terms of "impure" conceptual prehensions rather than pure ones. Whitehead speaks (on p. 373) of the "inevitable ordering of *things* [italics added], *conceptually realized* [valuated] in the nature of God," these things surely being the actual occasions taken with respect to the eternal objects characterizing them. Also (p. 522) the "conceptual feelings which compose . . .[the] primordial nature, exemplify in their subjective forms their mutual sensitivity and their subjective unity of subjective aim. These subjective forms are valuations determining the relative relevance of eternal objects *for each occasion of actuality* [italics added]." And again (p. 134), Whitehead comments that the *png* is "the concrescence of an unity of conceptual feelings, including among their data all eternal objects. The concrescence is directed by the subjective aim, that the subjective forms of the feeling shall be such as to constitute the eternal objects into relevant lures of feeling *severally appropriate for all realizable basic conditions* [italics added]." Such passages suggest strongly that the *png* cannot be characterized in terms of "pure" conceptual feelings, as Clarke would have us do.

Let us turn now to Clarke's comments concerning II above, "On God and Primordiality." He reads this paper as "an attempt to put Whitehead's conception of God on a nominalistic basis." This is not an accurate description of that paper, however, which departed almost completely from Whitehead. It was explicitly remarked, it will be recalled, that "although the point of departure here is . . . Whiteheadian to some extent, the position will deviate so completely in details that only some whispers of the spirit, not the letter, of Whitehead's view will remain." Clarke comments that the difference between the material of "On God and Primordiality" and that in *Whitehead's Categoreal Scheme* "is due to Martin's nominalistic inclinations." In part, yes, but the main reasons seem to have escaped Clarke's notice: the *intensional* treatment via the Fregean *Arten des Gegebenseins* of the primordial notions, and the subdivision of the latter into obligations, permissions, determinations, prohibitions, and so on. The nominalism is only subsidiary, as Clarke himself notes. "We could," he writes, "lay aside Martin's nominalistic niceties, and bring this later formulation closer in line with the Whiteheadian one by allowing 'a' to range over eternal objects, or properties or relations, or sets."

Clarke objects to taking a primitive such as 'PrOblgd', for example, in the latter paper, in place of 'Prhd' and 'Val' in the earlier one, on the grounds that the former "applies uniquely to God," whereas the latter have universal applicability. The "very aim of natural theology," he thinks, is "to characterize God in terms which we use to characterize nature." He cites some of the traditional proofs for God, as based on such "natural" relations as *is the mover of* (St. Thomas), *is the efficient cause of* (St. Thomas), and *is greater than* (St. Anselm). Thus in place of writing

$$\text{'}a \text{ PrOblgd } e_1,...,e_k\text{'},$$

as in II above, Clarke urges that we write

$$\text{'}<a,\text{Oblgd},e_1,...,e_k>e \cdot \text{Pr } e\text{'},$$

where 'Oblgd' is a universally applicable predicate for obligation, and 'Pr e' states that e is primordial. Thus Clarke wishes 'PrOblgd' to be systematically unpacked in terms of 'Oblgd' and 'Pr'. Well, yes, one could do this. But is 'Pr' itself then a "natural" predicate? No, for it is applicable only to the divine acts or states of obliging, etc.

Further, it may be questioned why we should attempt to characterize God in terms used to characterize nature, and even whether this is altogether possible or desirable. The view underlying "On God and Primordiality" is just the other way around in a certain sense. God is characterized by predicates used for no other purpose, *all further talk of God being then carried out in terms of them.* All further predicates used in discourse about the divine nature are to be defined analogically in terms of the primordial primitives, so to speak. And in the case of a notion such as 'obligation', lesser obligations are to be traced back to the primordial ones — obligations other than those explicitly laid down on the basis of some kind of conventional moral or social code. And similarly for scientific law, stipulated by the primordial determinations. All talk of the reign of law in the cosmos reduces ultimately to talk of the determinative will, and the search for scientific law, presumably the chief aim of science, becomes the search to understand a part of God's real internal constitution.

Clarke remarks that "the consequent nature of God, as conceived by Whitehead, is already built into . . .[the] characterization of God" in "On God and Primordiality." But this is not the case in any literal sense. There is no doctrine of prehensions in this paper, without which the notion of the consequent nature is unthinkable. Clarke comments that "valuations involving time are the concern of the consequent nature" whereas in "On God and Primordiality" time is placed *in* God's envisagement, some of the primordial valuations being concerned with time fundamentally. "The problem here," Clarke remarks, "stems not only from [Martin's] faulty conception of the Whiteheadian consequent nature of God, but also from a faulty conception of the Whiteheadian primordial nature of God." In the first place, it is difficult to see how use of 'faulty' here is justified, this paper not being really concerned with the Whitehead natures at all. The consequent nature is dropped altogether, so that there is no conception of it here to be found fault with. Secondly, even in Whitehead's primordial nature, as construed in accord with Clarke's own suggested definition, (6) above, there is presumably envisagement of time. Amongst the eternal objects, suitable temporal relations, for example, *before-than* relations in accord with special relativity theory, are to be found, these being interrelated by means of higher-order eternal objects to other eternal objects. Thus it does not seem correct to say, as Clarke does, that for Whitehead "valuations involving time are the concern of the consequent nature." In fact, this contention is, strictly, not even meaningful, "valuations" for Whitehead being the concern of the primordial nature only.

In view of these various observations, Clarke is clearly in error when he suggests that the purported "difficulties" he finds "in Martin's characterization [in *Whitehead's Categoreal Scheme*] of . . .[the] two natures . . . stem from a fundamental difficulty in his treatment of Whitehead's categories, particularly the categories of actual entities and prehensions. It will be remembered that Martin blurs the Whiteheadian distinction between actual entities (subjects of prehensions) and prehensions, taking acts of prehending to be merely a special kind of actual entity, as well as blurring the distinction between actual entities and fusions of sets of actual entities (or nexūs). All of those are treated similarly . . . and taken as values of the event variables. There is no doubt that all three of these . . . would be taken by Whitehead as events. . . . Nevertheless, only actual entities can properly be subjects and they are atomic." This "blurring," if such it be, is quite separate from the purported "difficulties" in the characterization of the two natures, as we have seen.

Clarke goes on to say that "it is the Whiteheadian principles of causation and atomism which distinguish actual entities [from prehensions] and which are missing from Martin's logical construction." Now this is not an accurate statement. The notion of final causation is explicitly provided for in the notion of subjective aim (pp. 19–20 of *Whitehead's Categoreal Scheme*), defined in terms of a primitive 'Purps$_e$'. Atomism is likewise provided for those e's that are in fact actual occasions. The notion of 'Purps$_e$' here, however, it is true, is more inclusive than is perhaps needed. Even prehensions and fusions of such are given purposes, in accord with Whitehead's own tendency to generalize to the hilt. In terms of 'Purps$_e$' everything that needs to be said about final causation, however, can be said.

Clarke goes on to suggest that "what is needed here to distinguish prehensions, actual entities, and fusions of sets of actual entities is something analogous to Nelson Goodman's distinction in *The Structure of Appearance* between complexes, concreta and compounds, where complexes are parts of concreta and concreta, although not parts of

159

other concreta, can along with complexes be parts of compounds."
This is an interesting suggestion. In a footnote Clarke notes that a
primitive predicate 'W' for the *with*-relation could be introduced so
that 'e_1 W e_2' would express that e_1 and e_2 are prehensions or complexes of such and that e_1 concresces with e_2. An actual entity then
could perhaps be regarded as a complex of prehensions that con-
cresce with no other. Perhaps we should say here rather that an actual
entity is the fusion of a class of prehensions any two of which bear W
to each other. Or perhaps 'AO' should be taken as a primitive for
actual occasions, so that an e is a prehension (or sum of such) just
where it is not an AO. An atomic or minimal prehension would then
be one that is part of all its parts. Still another possibility is systematically to restrict the values of 'e' in 'Purps$_e$' to AO's, so that

$$\text{'}e \in \text{AO'} \quad \text{becomes short for} \quad \text{'(E}e'\text{)}\,e' \in \text{Purps}_e\text{'.}$$

The meaning postulates concerning 'Purps$_e$' would then be framed in
such a way as to reflect this restriction. This last method would require no increase in the fundamental vocabulary.

In various such ways, no doubt, prehensions and AO's could be
distinguished. Only minor changes would then be needed in the
material in *Whitehead's Categoreal Scheme,* mostly insertions in the formulas restricting the category of objects talked about to be either AO's
or prehensions or suitable sums of such. Such changes would perhaps
approximate Whitehead's intent more closely.

Let us summarize now the situation as regards the eliminability of
the *cng*. There was no attempt to eliminate it in *Whitehead's Categoreal
Scheme,* even with the *png* defined by (3). If it were eliminated, however, the "reaction" from the world is already provided for timelessly
in the primordial valuations concerning each and every actual occasion. But if the *png* is introduced in terms of pure primordial conceptual valuations as defined by (18), the *cng is* surely needed fundamentally, if some reasonably close approximation to Whitehead's conception of God is to be achieved. In "On God and Primordiality," where
we part company with Whitehead almost entirely, nothing even re-
motely resembling the *cng* as a separate "nature" or part of God is
needed at all.

Another remark concerning (18) is in order. Actually this definition
embraces two kinds of pure primordial conceptual valuations, which
should perhaps be separated from each other, those of the form (16)
and those of the form (17). Are the latter really needed, as Clarke
suggests? The *png*, as the "unconditioned conceptual valuation of the
entire multiplicity of eternal objects" construed on the basis of (18),

has no commerce strictly with how the eternal objects are interrelated, but only with the "valuation" of each and every one in and for itself. Some of these are relational as between other eternal objects, but they are already included in the totality. In other words, the *png*'s conceptual valuations construed on the basis of (18) are not propositional, but only evaluative of each and every eternal object separately. The definition of '*png*' as utilizing the forms (16) and (17) can thus perhaps be simplified, only those of the form (16) being needed.

Once all this is said and done, the inadequacy and limitedness of the Whiteheadian God remain, as pointed out in "On God and Primordiality." A God concerned only with value and nothing else is too paltry for serious theology, or indeed even for a serious metaphysics or cosmology also. We should be grateful to Whitehead for calling attention to the primordial valuations, but lament that he told us so little about them. Nor of course did he subdivide them in any way, into the desiderations, determinations, permissions, prohibitions, or whatever, some such subdivision being fundamentally needed in discussion of the divine will, of the reign of scientific law in the cosmos, and so on. These comments of course presuppose that the primordial valuations are handled propositionally, so to speak, in terms of (1) or (10). If they are handled rather in terms of (16) and/or (17), however, it is difficult to see how a characterization of the divine will is possible. In any event it seems not to have been supplied. If the primordial valuations are handled merely in terms of (16) and/or (17), Whitehead's contributions to theology are much less important and interesting than process theologians would have us believe. Only if the primordial valuations are handled propositionally, as in (1) or (10), can we move on to the really important problems, not only about God's real internal constitution, but about his relations to the creatures and theirs to him.

The foregoing discussion of how best to handle the Whiteheadian God is an interesting example of the use of logical method in metaphysics and theology. We think we know what Whitehead's conception is, until the kinds of problems and difficulties discussed here are raised. But such knowledge is illusory, for once these points have been raised they become absolutely fundamental and must be "solved" or adjusted in one way or another before going on. We can no longer say we understand what Whitehead's God is without taking them into account, and to return to naive ways of thinking without doing so is to flaunt the almost ubiquitous need in philosophy for conceptual clarification. The methods of modern logic are of course essential for this. Whitehead himself, incidentally, was one of the first to call attention to this need, and regretted that he came to professional philosophy too late in his life to take on the taxing difficulties the use of logical methods involves. Once all this is said, we must be wary lest we think we have achieved in the foregoing more than we have. For the most part only definitions have been given and only rarely an axiom or meaning postulate or principle. But the two of course go hand in hand, the postulates chosen influencing the form the definitions must take and conversely. Until a full axiomatization is given the definitions are left in mid-air, as it were. And so it is, unfortunately, with the foregoing.

Finally now a word about the "mystery" of it all. Clarke objects to taking as primitives expressions such as 'PrOblgd' and so on, in "On God and Primordiality," on the grounds that the notions involved are "somewhat mysterious." In that paper it was remarked that "the mystery we are up against [in using such primitives] is . . . like that which the theoretical scientist is up against all the time," in using theoretical constructs. Clarke, as already mentioned above, wishes natural theology to be formulated "in terms which we use to characterize nature," including the theoretical constructs of science if need be, which have applicability beyond theology. The primordial notions of course have application only in theology. But is either kind of expression more mysterious than the other? Both transcend our feeble human efforts, even at their best, to grasp them. (Whitehead in his classes used often to exclaim that oh! if we only had the *ability* to see into these matters more deeply, gently tapping his head with the fingers of his right hand indicating our feebleness in this respect.) Even the little blade of grass is a great mystery, both in itself and in its relation to everything else. Tillich used to say that being itself is the only real mystery. The contention here anyhow is that theoretical science is no less mysterious than theology, the former in fact receiving its primary *raison d'être* in helping us to fathom certain aspects of the divine will.

A final technical point. Even in the treatment of conceptual prehensions here there is strictly "no reference to particular actualities or to any particular actual world," but only quantifiers over such actualities. There is not reference to them in the sense of naming them. Nor is God "directly related to the given course of history" in his "conceptual envisagement" of eternal objects if only his desiderations, say, are considered. Whitehead, however, neglected to include other aspects of God's envisagement needed for any adequate theology.

CHAPTER XI

Of Spiders and Bees:
One Logic, not Two

Ubi mel, ibi apes.

The human person has the remarkable capacity to perform the characteristic activities of both spiders and bees. On the one hand, like spiders, he "spits and spins wholly from himself, and scorns to own any obligation from without," in the words of Jonathan Swift.[1] With "an overweening pride, feeding and engendering on . . . [himself, he] turns all into excrement and venom, producing nothing at all but fly bane and a cob-web. . . ." And on the other, like bees, he is "but a vagabond without house or home, without stock or inheritance . . . [,] born to no possession of . . . [his] own, but a pair of wings and a drone-pipe. . . . [His] livelihood is a universal plunder on nature, a free booter over fields and gardens." He is "that which by a universal range, with long search, much study, true judgment, and distinction of things, brings home honey and wax." On this account, we should no doubt tend to opt for the bees and to be "content . . . to pretend to nothing of our own beyond our wings and our voice: that is to say, our flights and our language. For the rest, whatever we have got has been by infinite labor and search, and ranging through every corner of nature; the difference is that, instead of dirt and poison, we have chosen rather to fill our hives with honey and wax; thus furnishing mankind with the two noblest of things, sweetness and light."

Let us think of the bees as humanists, and the spiders as mathematicians and scientists, as Henry Veatch invites us to do. In his *Two Logics, The Conflict between Classical and Neo-Analytic Philosophy*,[2] in fact, he argues for the recognition of two distinct kinds of logic, "a bee-logic and a spider-logic," regarded as the characteristic instruments for effecting "the more traditional humanistic or philosophical knowledge on

---

1. *A Tale of a Tub to which Is Added the Battle of the Books* (Oxford: Clarendon Press, 1958 ed.), p. 213 and pp. 228–235.
2. (Evanston: Northwestern University Press, 1969).

the one hand, and the newer-fashioned scientific knowledge on the other."

At the very beginning, Veatch asks: "Has it never struck anyone as passing strange that the logic of *Principia Mathematica*, for all of its elaboration, provides no means either for saying or for thinking what anything is?" The reason *PM* contains no such means, it is contended, is that "the subject-predicate schema . . . of modern logic does violence to the logical grammar of 'is', or the 'is'-relationship. For there is just no way in which this relationship can be extended beyond the original schema of one-predicate-one-subject and be made to embrace the whole hierarchy of sentential schemas involving one predicate and many subjects." Here is the pivotal point of Veatch's plea for two logics, upon which the entire discussion of his book seems to rest.

Let us consider Veatch's examples, which help to clarify his contention. The sentence

(1)   'Bertrand Russell is a man of some philosophical capacity'

can be construed as an answer to a question of the general type 'What is x?' But

(2)   'Bertrand Russell is superior both as a man and as a
           philosopher to A. N. Whitehead'

cannot be construed "as a statement in which the predicate provides an answer to the question 'What?' with respect to the subjects. In other words, if 'Bertrand Russell' and 'A. N. Whitehead' are the subjects, then 'being superior as a man and as a philosopher to' can hardly be regarded as stating what Russell and Whitehead are."

The answer to this objection is to be sought, not in *PM* itself, but in a suitably framed *logic of questions*. Elsewhere it has been suggested that a form such as

'p Asks-What a,q'

is appropriate for handling some kinds of what-questions, where a is the proper name of an individual.[3] This form enables us to express that person p asks person q what the individual designated by a is. And for handling answers to such questions, the form

'p Answer b,q'

is appropriate, expressing that p answers b to q, where b is a *one-place*

---

3. See *Semiotics and Linguistic Structure.*

Veatch thinks that there are "fruits of intelligibility . . . associated with the use of a what-logic, as over and against those of mere predictability that . . . [are] associated with a relating-logic." On one construal of the meaning of 'intelligibility' surely the more predictability, the greater the intelligibility. But in any case, Veatch's contention here is quite independent of which kind of logic is presumed to be employed. Surely some predictability is forthcoming on the basis of a purported what-logic, for example, that Thomas Wentworth's pride was sure to lead to his downfall.

Veatch goes on to chastise the *PM* kind of logic on the grounds that it cannot deal with answers to what-questions of the form 'What is an F?' or 'What are F's?' where 'F' is a one-place predicate. Consider the question

'What is a modern logician?'

and the purported answer

'A modern logician is human',

rendered in the *PM* form as

(4)   '$(x)(x$ is a modern logician $\supset x$ is human)'.

"A little reflection," Veatch writes (p. 69) "should convince us that in the one case no more than in the other [considered earlier] does *PM* logic provide us with a means for asserting what things are."

Here again, the logical grammar of 'What is an F?' is relevant. Here the question-answer forms needed are similar to those for handling 'What is an x?' The questions are handled by

(5)   'p Asks-What a,q'

and the answers by

(6)   'q Answer b,p',

where *both* a and b are one-place predicates. Thus to the query 'What are modern logicians?', the answer 'Humans' might be appropriate in some circumstances. But so surely is (4) above, so that

'q Answer $\ulcorner(x)(ax \supset bx)\urcorner, p$'

should also be permitted.

Veatch would perhaps allow (5) here but would object to (6) on the grounds that the truth or falsity of the answer "can only be determined by a consideration of the subject-matter, or of the content of the statement, or of what in the statement we are talking about. In contrast, in the standard form [(4)] in which such a statement is rendered in *PM* logic . . . the truth or falsity of the proposition is supposed to be determined not by the content of the proposition, but by the purely formal (in the sense of truth-functional) relation between the 'if' and the 'then' clauses." Several comments about this contention are in order.

The notions of the truth or falsity of a sentence are to be distinguished sharply from matters concerned with how they are "determined" or come to be known. The latter notions are not strictly logical notions at all, and therefore play no role in the system of *PM*. But no matter. The "content" of (4) — whatever it is — surely may be allowed somehow to depend on the contents of the predicates. Even in the Aristotelian A-form of 'All S are P', the content is determined in some fashion by the content of 'S' and 'P'. Veatch thinks the problem reduces to the fact that "the term 'formal implication' signifies no more than a summation of a number of material implications." Yes, but think of how great the number, that of all the entities over which the variables of quantification are taken to range. Perhaps this totality is of a transfinite cardinality. Thus the logical force of the formal implication is much stronger than Veatch supposes. The truth of a sentence of the form (4) could never be "determined" by going through all of its instances, if the number of them is transfinite. And even if finite, such an enumeration procedure would be impracticable. No, the truth of a sentence of the form (4) is arrived at by reference to relevant verified or previously accepted general statements, to appropriate dictionary entries, or to (usually tacit) meaning postulates governing the key terms, and so on.

When a sentence of the form '$(x)(Fx \supset Gx)$' is taken as an answer to 'What is an F?', the answer may be a logical or factual truth in essentially Carnap's sense. Veatch seems to argue against the possibility of its being either, but not on the basis of clear-cut definitions of the kinds of truth-predicates — 'L-True' and 'F-True' — required. He thinks that answers to this kind of what-question are neither analytic nor synthetic, "but [p. 105] present themselves to us as necessary truths; and yet just as unmistakably they present themselves as truths about the world. Accordingly, this can only mean that, logically considered, such statements must be subject to a dual criterion, as far as the conditions of their truth are concerned. It is only through their being verified in experience that we can claim them to be truths as to what things in fact really are, and it is only through their own self-evidence that we can recognize them to be truths as to what these things are necessarily; each condition, therefore, is necessary for the truth of such a statement, and neither condition is sufficient." Of course 'verified in experience', 'self-evident', 'claim to be true', and 'recognize as true' are pragmatical terms, and a good deal of spelling out of their meaning and of their semantical relations with 'L-True' would be needed before Veatch's claim here could be properly assessed.

Veatch invites us (p. 120) to recall the scholastic distinction of the first and second intentions of terms and of the statements containing them, so that "when we make statements about red and green, they are of first intention; and we make statements about how the terms 'red' and 'green' are to be used, they are of second intention." He argues (p. 123) that "there is a clear priority of first-intentional use of logico-linguistic devices over the second-intentional rules and regulations governing such use." The "fallacy of inverted intentionality" stems from the denial of this priority. But modern semantical theory recognizes both kinds of intention and allows full scope for the characterization both of their properties and interrelations. Thus, although the situation Veatch laments — exclusive attention to the "formal mode of speech" — has been a real one in recent decades, it would scarcely seem to be one any longer. In any case, the existence of this "fallacy" cannot be used as an argument against modern logic in its extended semantico-pragmatical form, nor hence as an argument in behalf of two logics rather than one.

Veatch makes much of the *prima facie* differences between scientific and ordinary languages, when he contends (p. 133) that "what may well be true of the mathematized and formalized language of physics need by no means be true, and in a measure cannot be true, of the language we use when playing backgammon with our friends." Clearly there is much in common here between these two languages, and much not, but no support is therewith given of the existence of two logics for these respective languages rather than one. The rules of backgammon no doubt can be fully formalized, and even the exact sentences of physics can be stated in natural language. And natural language has its own incredibly complex logical structure, which at long last the new logico-linguistics is beginning to uncover.

The real nitty-gritty of Veatch's view emerges, however, only with his discussion of essences and substantial forms. Aye, there's the rub. A what-logic is concerned fundamentally with essences whereas a relating-logic is not. Aristotle, St. Thomas, Leibniz notwithstanding, no really clear or acceptable notion of what an essence is ever emerges in Veatch's discussion, nor is any space devoted to the recent logical literature on the subject. Given the notion of L-truth, perhaps a suitable notion of essence is forthcoming. Other characterizations have to do with properties such that, when an object ceases to have them, that object ceases to exist.[5] An historically older notion of essence, as construed on the basis of the logic of *PM*, is that of Whitehead, mentioned in VII above. The essence of an entity is the class of all classes of which it is a member, or the class of all properties it exemplifies. (Note that on this view, the essence of x, $\hat{F}Fx$, has as members all manner of classes constructed in terms of relations also, so that even the resources of a relating-logic are needed here to spell out x's full essence. That x bears such and such a relation to entities a or b or whatever is for x to be in a certain class or to have such and such a property.) No doubt there are many further alternatives here also. In any case, it seems clear that the prospect of accommodating successfully a suitable theory of essences within the confines of modern semantics is not a hopeless one.

The various technical points raised here can be settled, of course, on the basis of the *PM* kind of logic only with the addition of some specific non-logical constants with suitable meaning postulates upon them. In fact to presuppose here the full resources of the kind of extended logic used in the papers above is perhaps desirable. But with the various extensions involved in this, no new kind of basic logic need be envisaged, the extensions all being of the standard first-order theory of quantification.

Veatch goes on to discuss his two-logics view with the topics of induction, with deductive explanation in the sciences, with historical explanation, and with ethics. Here and throughout he makes many challenging observations and cogent criticisms of various current philosophical views, on the basis of his admirably broad humanistic and cultural outlook. Many of these are acceptable if properly reformulated. Veatch's discussion is a pioneering work in the logic of the humanities, a much-neglected subject in need of development in modern terms.

---

5. Cf. R. B. Marcus, "Dispensing with *Possibilia*," and the discussion thereof in *Pragmatics, Truth, and Language*.

CHAPTER XII

On Intensions and Possible Worlds

Non necesse habes aurum in luto quaerere.

This book[1] is, in effect, a sequel to the author's *Models for Modalities* (1969) and purports to carry forward the case for the feasibility of a "possible-worlds" semantics. The main contention of the book is that such a semantics has its chief application in the study of *propositional attitudes*. But a good deal more than this is claimed, namely, applicability to the study of *epistemic notions* in general, to the study of *causality* and the *language of the sciences,* to the exact study of *phenomenology,* to *linguistics,* to the problem of *"representation"* in the arts, and even to the foundations of *statistics* and *probability theory*.

The book consists of eleven papers, all of which have appeared, or will appear, elsewhere. The first is concerned with a survey of the problems considered together with some comments of a general kind. The second deals especially with the semantics of the *modal notions,* and the third, with the objects of *knowledge* and *belief* and of other *intentional* relations. *Information, causality,* and *perception* are discussed in Chapter 4, and *Carnap's heritage,* or rather legacy, in semantics occupies Chapter 5. Chapter 6 is a dialogue with Quine on *"quantifying in,"* a kind of *causerie du lundi.*

The logic of *questions* and *answers* is discussed in Chapter 7 in the light (or Dunkel, as the case may be) of possible worlds. Some borderline problems between *grammar* and *logic* are discussed in Chapter 8, and the so-called *conservation laws* for the logic of belief and knowledge are rephrased and defended in Chapter 9. The connection of possible-worlds semantics with the phenomenological doctrine of *intentionality* is considered at some length in Chapter 10. And, finally, in

---

1. Jaako Hintikka, *The Intentions of Intentionality and Other New Models for Modalities* (Dordrecht: D. Reidel Publishing Co., 1975).

Chapter 11, the problem of representation in *cubist painting* is discussed and a purported liaison with phenomenology pointed out.

This book is of value primarily for those already convinced of the viability of possible-worlds semantics as a philosophic guide. Those not so convinced will probably wish to turn elsewhere.

In a work covering so many topics, only a few of them can be commented upon here at any depth.

Hintikka notes right at the beginning that there are many "shortcomings" in the approach via possible-worlds semantics "so far." "For what people actually traffic in are not meaning functions or abstract mathematical entities (infinite classes of pairs of correlated argument-values and function-values)," the stock-in-trade of the possible-worlds semanticist, "but suitable 'algorithms' or 'recipes' [laws or principles] for as it were actually finding the function value [or otherwise stating certain regularities]. Even more importantly, the meaning functions seldom depend as their argument on the *whole* possible world, fully analyzed, in which the reference (the value of the function) is located. The relevant arguments must somehow be only certain 'parts' or 'aspects' of the world in question. But, if so, some of the 'parts' we have to take into account may be impossible to extend to a consistent 'whole world'." To an unbiased observer, these two shortcomings would seem formidable indeed, and not just shortcomings of the theory "so far." They are so fundamental and pervasive that it seems doubtful that they ever will be overcome in any but a highly artificial way.

It is a commonplace observance that any language concerned with a subject-matter employing one-many or functional relations can easily be reformulated in the function-value terminology. Thus all talk of fatherhood can be based on expressions such as

$$'x = f(y)',$$

f being the function father of. But anthropologists, kinship-theorists, and we common folk do not "traffic" in such terminology, nor does our common language. The importation of the mathematical vocabulary is not illuminative prior to the recognition, for example, of a general law, to the effect that

$$(x)(y)(z)((x\,F\,y \cdot z\,F\,y) \supset x = z),$$

where F is the *relation* of being the father of in the strict biological sense. This is not, of course, to object to the functional vocabulary, but merely to call attention to the need for prior principles on which it rests. In areas other than mathematics (more specifically, other than

172

areas of mathematics especially concerned with functions), interest focuses upon such principles, their discovery, proper formulation, and so on, prior to their functional representation. Functions are, after all, merely a special kind of relation, nothing more, nothing less.

The second shortcoming is, as Hintikka suggests, the more important, for the characterization of "parts" and "aspects" of possible worlds is very difficult indeed. In fact, they are the crux of the matter, and all reference to "possible worlds" as wholes turn out to be unnecessary. To see that this is the case, let us turn directly to Hintikka's comments concerning the verb 'know'.

A form such as 'p Know a'[2] may be taken to express, according to Hintikka, that "a is known to be true by person p," and this, in turn, is explicated by saying that "a is true in all possible worlds compatible with p's knowing what he in fact knows." But this explication itself is rather involved, employing not only the notion of all possible worlds (as wholes) satisfying a given condition, but the notion of "compatibility," of what one "in fact" knows, as well as the notion of being true in a possible world. This is thus at best a rather gnarled explication, each item of which is in turn in need of explication. It is not clear whether the a here is to be a sign-design or a sign-event, nor is it clear whether the notion of 'true' is to accord with the semantical notion applicable to expressions. Here, too, it makes a good deal of difference whether a semantics based on sign-designs or on sign-events is employed. These are very fundamental matters that should be suitably arranged right at the beginning.

Hintikka thinks that his way of handling 'know' is helpful, perhaps even indispensable, in distinguishing the following various uses of it:

"(1) Knowing that versus knowing how,
(2) Knowing that versus knowing whether,
(3) Knowing that versus such constructions as knowing what, knowing who, knowing when, knowing where, etc.,
(4) Knowing that, or some construction which is like the second part of (2) or (3) in that it involves a subordinate clause, versus knowing plus a (grammatical) direct object (e.g., knowing someone). We might call these the that-construction, the interrogative constructions (or *oratio obliqua* constructions), and the direct object construction, respectively,
(5) Knowing that . . . a_1 . . . (where 'a_1' is a singular term) versus such constructions as knowing of a_1 that . . . he (she, it). . . .

---

2. The variable 'p' is used here for persons and 'a' for statements, an incidental departure from Hintikka's notation.

There is a related contrast between the construction 'it is known that . . .' and 'someone is known to . . .', for instance: it is known that . . . a_1 . . ., and a_1 is known to be such that . . .he (she, it). . . ."

Let us first consider (1), the difference between 'knowing that' and 'knowing how'. Contexts containing these are, of course, contexts containing 'know', some containing 'that' in addition, the others containing 'how' in its place. Hintikka, following Ryle, takes 'knowing that' and 'knowing how' as indissoluble wholes, treating 'that' and 'how' syncategorematically. But these little words have a dignity all their own and may occur in all manner of other contexts and combinations. Each has its own "logic" to be investigated quite independent of its occurrence immediately to the right of 'know'. And similarly, for the other *wh*-words, 'whether', 'when', 'which', 'why', and so on. We must thus part company with Hintikka straightaway and seek a logical framework in which *each word may be studied in all possible contexts of its use; the logic of these contexts should then be forthcoming in terms of the logic of the components.* Such procedure is standard in logic itself for the strictly logical words, and there is no reason to think that it should be abandoned when we turn to the logic of natural language.

It has been suggested elsewhere that the (non-demonstrative) 'that' of intentionality be handled as a relation between an intentional act or state e and an inscription giving the "content" of e.[3] This may be expressed by 'e That$_{Content}$ a'. Thus 'know that' is handled by a conjunction to the effect that

$$<Know>e \cdot e \text{ That}_{Content} a,$$

where '$<Know>$' is an event-descriptive predicate. More specifically, the tenseless form

$$'p \text{ know that } a'$$

is handled or "represented," to use the technical term of generative semantics, as

$$'(Ee)(e \text{ By}_{Agent} p \cdot <Know>e \cdot e \text{ That}_{Content} a)'.$$

Here, the 'By$_{Agent}$' stands for the by-relation of *agency*. To capture the present tense, an additional clause

$$'e \text{ During } now'$$

---

3. See especially *Pragmatics, Truth, and Language*, Chapters XVIII and XIX.

174

is needed to express that *e* takes place during what the speaker takes as now. Still, more specifically,

> 'John knows (now) that Mary (now) loves Tom'

is represented as

> '(E*e*)(E*a*)(*e* By$_{Agent}$ John • <Know>*e* • *e* During *now* • *e*
> That$_{Content}$ *a* • '(E*e'*)(*e'* By$_{Agent}$ Mary • <Love>*e'* • *e'* During *now*
> • *e'* Of$_{Object}$ Tom)'*a*)'.

The final clause here expresses that the inscription *a* is of the appropriate shape (or sign-design) to give the content of what John is said to know (now).

The 'that' of intentionality or content is to be distinguished from the 'that' of occurrence, as in

> 'It was at 5 o'clock that Mary arrived',

and both of these from the 'that' used in sentences such as

> 'It is a fact that Mary loves Tom',
> 'It is true that Mary loves Tom',

and so on. A full classification of all the kinds of 'that' in English and a logical study of their occurrences in all possible contexts is very much needed.

Similar considerations apply to 'how', which may occur in all manner of contexts other than 'knows how'.

Let us go on to item (2) in Hintikka's list, the difference between 'knowing that' and 'knowing whether'. He notes (p. 4) that '*p* knows whether *a*' is "equivalent to"

> '(*p* knows that *a* v *p* knows that not-*a*)'.

If this construal of 'whether' is sound, we could more generally define

> '*e* Whether *a*' as '(*e* That$_{Content}$ *a* v *e* That$_{Content}$ ('~'⌢*a*))'

within the framework here. Contexts containing 'knows whether' can then be provided for, but also other contexts containing 'whether', such as

> 'John wonders whether Mary loves Tom',
> 'John asks whether Mary loves Tom',
> 'Whether Mary loves Tom is questionable',

and so on. This analysis of 'whether', however, does not provide for uses of the word in the sense of 'which of the two', as in sentences such as

> 'He has not decided whether he will come by plane or by boat',
> 'Whether it is fair or whether it is wet, he pursues his labors with equal success',

and so on.

For the discussion of (3), detailed analyses of contexts containing the other *wh*-words are needed, along lines similar to those involving 'how' and 'whether'. Hintikka's syncategorematic treatment of these words will not suffice for any sophisticated grammar of English.

Hintikka makes much of the distinction, under (5), between expressions such as

$$(6) \qquad\qquad \text{'(E}x)p \text{ knows that a}_1 = x\text{'}$$

or

$$(7) \qquad\qquad \text{'(E}x)(x \text{ is a person} \cdot p \text{ knows that a}_1 = x)\text{'},$$

where 'a$_1$' is a proper name of a person. These forms are supposed to capture the "logical force" of

$$(8) \qquad\qquad \text{'}p \text{ knows who a}_1 \text{ is'}.$$

These two forms, however, fail to provide a full theory concerning 'who' in all possible contexts. Further, the role of identity in these forms is such as not to provide an analysis of (8). To say that there is something (or someone) x whom p knows a$_1$ to be identical with is surely not the same as to say that p knows who a$_1$ is. (Similarly, to say that there is a *person* x such that p knows that a$_1$ to be identified with x is not to say that p knows who a$_1$ is.) When George II asked his famous question as to who Scott is, an answer of the form (6) or (7) would scarcely have sufficed. If I ask 'Who is a$_1$?' and someone tells me 'Jones knows who a$_1$ is', I would not rush to ask Jones the content of his knowledge in this regard if it is merely that there is something (or some person) whom he knows a$_1$ to be identical with. No, sentence (8) states a good deal more and is to be analyzed in terms of a special relation Who such that

$$\text{'}e \text{ Who } q\text{'}$$

expresses that e is an act or state (a knowing, a questioning, or whatever) concerned with the who of q. A sentence of the form (8) may then be analyzed as

$$\text{'(E}e)(Eq)(e \text{ By}_{\text{Agent}} p \cdot <\text{Know}>e \cdot e \text{ Who } q \cdot \text{a}_1 = q)\text{'},$$

and the question 'Who is a_1?' as

$$\text{'(E}e\text{)(E}q\text{)(}<\text{Ask}>e \cdot e \text{ Who } q \cdot q = a_1\text{)'}$$

To answer a question of this kind is usually to give either an indefinite or a definite Russellian description. The answer to 'Who is a_1?' is then usually of the form 'a so and so' or 'the so and so', or stated in a full sentence, 'a_1 is a so and so' or 'a_1 is the so and so'.

The use of '=' in these forms incidentally is very different from Hintikka's use of '='. Here '=' is subject to all the standard logical laws and its use, although not strictly necessary, helps to account for the presence of 'is' in the original or parent English sentence. Logical forms for many English sentences may be arranged in such a way that uses of 'is' may be handled in terms of '=', or the 'is' of identity.[4]

Let us consider next a general sentence. Hintikka construes

(9)   'Doctor Welby knows who has pneumonia'

as either

(10)   '$(p)(p$ has pneumonia $\supset$ Dr. Welby knows that p has pneumonia)'

or

'$(\text{E}p)(p$ has pneumonia $\cdot$ Dr. Welby knows that p has pneumonia)'.

Let us disregard for the moment the "quantifying in" here, to note that there are other readings of (9) to be provided for, readings under which it would ordinarily be taken as true, readings such as

> 'Dr. Welby usually (frequently, usually, habitually) knows who has pneumonia'.

And even the quantifying in here can easily be avoided in terms of the construction 'knows of'. Thus (10) becomes

> '$(p)(p$ has pneumonia $\supset$ Dr. Welby knows of p that the predicate 'has pneumonia' applies to p)'.

Forms for the readings in terms of 'frequently', 'usually', and so on, are more complex, but not beyond the resources at hand.

Hintikka puts forward a bold thesis concerning all of the constructions (1)−(5), namely, that "as far as the basic logical force of the different constructions is concerned, they can all be characterized or 'defined' in terms of the construction *knowing that*, with the exception of one somewhat dubious sense of the construction *knowing how*." He has

---

4. See again *Pragmatics, Truth, and Language*. Chapter XVIII.

given several "arguments" for this thesis. But arguments, however persuasive, do not take the place of actual definitions — or characterizations (whatever these latter are supposed to be). If the given *wh*-word is a *primitive* of the language, then of course it is not defined but will be characterized by meaning postulates. Hintikka suggests occasionally a formula that might be construed either as a definition or as a meaning postulate, but he rarely, if ever, tells us which. And such formulas as he does suggest are always too restricted, covering only the very special cases under review. To establish, with the kind of rigor required now in logico-linguistics and on the basis of suitable empirical evidence, that all of the *wh*-words as occurring in the phrases of the form 'knows wh-' in all their possible contexts of use (saving, perhaps, the one "dubious" use of 'how') are "definable" — 'or characterized' here must be omitted — in terms of 'knows that' would be a formidable task indeed. It would be interesting to have this established, not merely argued for, with explicit definitions of each *wh*-word for all possible relevant contexts involving 'knows'. At best, then, the contention seems premature and must remain a mere conjecture at the present stage of research.

The phrase 'all possible contexts of use' here is of course quite innocent of all talk of possible worlds or of modal operators. The reference instead is to all *inscriptions* of an appropriate kind. And one can of course impose further restrictions if needed to just actually uttered inscriptions, or to just actually uttered inscriptions up to a certain time or by some one person or persons, or to just persons in some one social group, and so on.

Consider next

(11)   'p sees q'

and

(12)   'p sees who q is',

construed respectively by Hintikka as

(11')   'There is a visually individuated individual (call it x) such that p sees that $q = x$'

and

(12')   'There is a physically individuated individual (call it x) such that p sees that $q = x$'.

Let us not worry here over the import of 'visually' versus 'physically' but over the much more fundamental matter that neither (11') nor

178

(12′) come anywhere near to capturing the "logical force" of (11) or (12). In 'Peek-a-book, I see you' there is no individual whom I see as identical to you, but a mere, perhaps a very small, part of some individual. That it be only a part is the whole point. Much talk about parts and wholes is needed that Hintikka fails to bring in. To use '=' in (11′) is foreign and would require a very special meaning for 'see' that may or may not obtain. In any case, there are all manner of sentences of the forms (11) and (12) not logically captured by (11′) and (12′), respectively. Further, both (11′) and (12′) employ 'sees that', the analysis of which should reduce to one for 'sees' and one for 'that'. Thus 'sees that' should be handled as a construct, not as the fundamental locution.

It has been suggested elsewhere that the basic sentential forms needed for handling the logic of 'see' are something like

$$\text{'}p \text{ See } x,a\text{'}, \text{'}p \text{ See } q,a\text{'}, \text{ and } \text{'}p \text{ See } e,a\text{'},$$

that person p sees object x, person q, or event e *as taken under the predicate-description a*. The great pliability of these forms is such that the tremendous diversity of sentences concerning seeing may be handled in a very natural way.

Possible-worlds semantics is a demanding and selfish mistress, extracting her price. The laws of quantification, fundamental laws of logic of otherwise universal generality and applicability, must be given up, and restricted substitutes instituted in their place. "These [general quantificational] laws fail as such [p. 39] as we are considering several possible worlds in their relation to each other and thus considering individuals as they appear in these different possible worlds." Thus they are allowed to hold only under supplementary conditions. A high price indeed, but a price that once paid leads down the primrose path. Everything is then seen in the light of possible-worlds theory, not only the theory of the attitudinal and epistemic notions. In a footnote (p. 40) Hintikka remarks that "it is instructive to see how pervasive and how unavoidable precisely analogous considerations are in the foundations of statistics, and how commonplace and innocent some of the intended applications of these concepts are." He cites Leonard Savage's *The Foundations of Statistics* as an example. "An ontological standard which (in the name of science (?)) tries to exorcise possible worlds from our conceptual system is likely to make shambles of statistics and applied probability theory." But it is doubtful that such "analogous considerations" are as pervasive as is contended, and no satisfactory evidence has ever been given that they are "unavoidable." Nor are such applications "innocent" in any clear sense. Savage's work is notoriously lacking in logical rigor and attempts to construe it in terms of possible worlds are not to be held up in any way as paradigmatic in this respect. Further, intentional methods for handling applied probability, and probably therewith the foundations of statistics as well, are forthcoming without the use of possible worlds.[5]

Hintikka's handling of (11) and (12) does, of course, require fundamentally "quantifying in," and this is a technically dubious procedure, as Quine and others (including even Hintikka himself) have frequently pointed out. Hintikka defends it here on the grounds that it may be satisfactorily clarified in terms of possible-worlds theory. Even if so, and this is at best doubtful, the price is high, as already noted. The question also arises as to why one should wish to "quantify in" in the first place. *Why not put the intentional talk in the metalanguage, where it belongs anyhow?* — in accord essentially with a great tradition going back to the medieval period. Hintikka contends that Quine and others (p. 103) "have not given a single objective reason yet why concepts like 'necessarily', 'known', or 'provable' cannot be accommodated in our object language, no matter what else it contains." Well of course, they can be so accommodated to some extent, but not fully without too high a price. Here is the real point that seems not to have been discussed very deeply.

Metalanguages are now universally recognized as subject to exact logical rule, and in fact themselves often function as object-languages. More importantly, it is now commonly recognized by structural linguists that natural languages themselves contain their own metalanguages. The analysis of some even very simple English sentences, for example, shows that they are in disguise metalinguistic sentences, and can be given only in a metalanguage of higher level than one might suppose. This level is not picked in advance, each sentence requiring its own level due to its internal structure. There is thus no prior preference for any one level picked in advance and insisted upon throughout. *A fortiori,* of course, for the object-language. There is thus no motive whatsoever for trying to force everything into it, a metalanguage for it being needed at some point anyhow. In fact, the very distinction between object- and metalanguage is no longer important. It is their unification at any needed level in the whole hierarchy of languages that is to be sought. The insistence upon quantifying in is thus seen to be adscititious, at best generating uninteresting and

---

5. Here also see *Pragmatics, Truth, and Language,* Chapter XV.

unnecessary problems of its own, and diverting attention from more suitable and fruitful methods.

Hintikka thinks, and rightly so, that (p. 115) "there is no getting around the fact that there is more to meaning than actual reference," and that this something more is to be handled in terms of "as it were potential references in a number of unrealized situations." Clearly, in order to handle this "something more," we may let

(13)   'p Ref a,x,b'

express that p takes inscription a as occurring in the sentential context b to refer (uniquely) to object x (with corresponding other forms for persons and events). In terms of such a locution, all manner of possibilities may be handled, the variation in 'a' and 'b' here being as wide as the language can handle, and 'p' ranging over all possible users of the language.

Hintikka makes a good deal (p. 115) of Frege's *Sinne* and the *Art des Gegebenseins*. Frege tried to express, as Hintikka words it, how the referent of a term "is picked out, what rule or function takes us from the term to its reference [referent] . . . by means of his notion of *Sinn* which according to him includes, over and above the reference of a term, also the way in which the reference is given *(die Art des Gegebenseins)*. Now the crucial insight here is that all such talk of rules or ways of being given is functional. To specify a rule (a 'how') is to specify the function which gives us the reference, depending on circumstances." Well, this is perhaps one way of interpreting Frege, but not one justified by the text. Frege does not specify that the referent of a term is "included" in the *Sinn*, nor does he say that the "way of being given is functional." (Hintikka himself seems to admit this last point, in footnote 37, p. 135, where he says that "it is fair to conclude that Frege did not after all fully grasp the function-like character of his *Sinn*." And again (on. p. 81) "there does not seem to be an inkling of this idea in his [Frege's] writings.") Further, Hintikka contends (p. 99, footnote 13) that "senses were for him [Frege] non-linguistic entities. In *Über Sinn und Bedeutung* [p. 27, original printing] he emphasized that *Sinn* is independent of language and can be shared by different expressions in one and the same language." Again, this is not an accurate account of what Frege wrote. It is not at all clear that for Frege *Sinne* *must* be construed as non-linguistic entities; this is not explicitly stated and hence surely not "emphasized." All Frege tells us about the inner structure of the *Sinne* is that they are something "*worin die Art des Gegebenseins enthalten ist*," something wherein the mode of presentation is contained. One way of construing the *Art des Gegebenseins* is as a linguistic entity, more particularly, as a referring expression. One and the same *Sinn* can then be "shared" by several such expressions, even by ones in different languages, all of them referring to the same entity. This is not the only way of providing for the *Sinne*, but it appears a viable one. Hintikka thinks that such a construal "is surely completely foreign to Frege's intentions," a contention, however, that is not established. Further, he thinks that on this view, "Frege's very first puzzle about the epistemic difference between '*a* = *a*' and '*a* = *b*' would have been vacuous. . . ." But this is, of course, not the case, '*a*' and '*b*' here themselves being distinct *Arten des Gegebenseins* of one and the same entity.

The discussion of Carnap's heritage in semantics concentrates almost exclusively upon the material of *Meaning and Necessity,* to the neglect of the earlier *Introduction to Semantics* and to the later *Replies* in the Schilpp volume in *The Library of Living Philosophers.* Much of the material in both of these is much superior to that of *Meaning and Necessity,* as Carnap himself was wont to admit. If this latter book, in the words of David Kaplan, "represents the culmination of the golden age of (logical) semantics," one shudders to think of what its bronze age must have been like. Further, Hintikka views even the material of this book as important primarily as a precursor to the possible-worlds view, to the neglect of the material in no essential way connected with that view. Such a one-sided reading ill serves a volume replete with manifold suggestions if not much actual achievement.

In the dialogue with Quine, as already remarked, it is urged that "no objective reasons why concepts like 'necessity', 'known', or 'provable' cannot be accommodated in our object language, no matter what else it contains, have been given." But, as already suggested, Hintikka in turn nowhere gives convincing reasons as to why it is thought desirable that such notions *should* be accommodated in an object-language. The need for metalanguages arises whenever the semantical notion of truth (for a given language) is defined. Now necessary truth is a particular kind of truth, and to know is (according to some analyses anyhow) to know something that is true. The most natural, and indeed desirable, way of seeking to handle notions such as 'necessarily' and 'known' is thus within a metalanguage accommodating a semantical truth-predicate. And indeed recourse to a metalanguage is essential if a principle to the effect that whatever is necessary is true (in the semantical sense), and one to the effect that whatever is known (in the sense of 'known that') is true (again in the semantical sense), are to be forthcoming. Such principles seem not only desirable, but very fundamental in any technically adequate theory of knowledge. The situation concerning 'provable' is, of course, entirely different, this notion being a purely syntactical one.

Hintikka carries his campaign for possible-worlds semantics into the arena of grammar. Here he thinks that many problems (p. 162) became "predictable — and solvable — as soon as it is acknowledged that in modal (or other intentional) contexts more than one possible world is inevitably at issue." Consider the sentence

(14) 'John lost a black pen yesterday and Bill believes that he has found it today.'

This sentence, Hintikka contends, "canot be dealt with in terms of coreferentiality in the actual world or in the kind of world the speaker is assuming." One reason, he thinks, is "that the speaker may know that Bill is mistaken in his belief and has not found John's pen — perhaps he has not found anything at all." Hintikka overstates his case here. More than one possible world is not "inevitably" at stake, nor is it the case that (14) "cannot be dealt with in terms of coreferentiality in the actual world," which incidentally is usually "the kind of world the speaker is assuming." We may see this by giving a logical form to (14) as follows.

The fundamental relation needed is Ref, and contexts of the form (13), in terms of which, together with the other devices of the semiotics of language, the complex referential and other features of sentences may be fully spelled out by clauses to the effect that such and such is taken to refer to such and such.[7]

A form for (14) is, without more ado,

$$'(Ex)(Ee)(Ee')(Ea)(Ec)(\text{BlackPen } x \cdot <j,\text{Lose},x>e \cdot e \text{ During}$$
$$yesterday \cdot <b,\text{Blv},a>e' \cdot e' \text{ During } now \cdot e' \text{ That}_{\text{Content}} a \cdot$$
$$'(Ee'')(<b,\text{Find},it>e'' \cdot e'' \text{ During } today \cdot e'' \text{ Before}_{\text{Time}} now)'a \cdot$$
$$'it'c \cdot sp \text{ Ref } c,x,a)'.$$

The speaker's referential use of the occurrence of the pronoun 'it' is spelled out in full in the last three conjuncts. Note that Hintikka's objection to a referential handling does not obtain. The speaker may know that Bill is mistaken in his belief and has not found John's pen. Moreover, if Bill has not found anything at all, he would clearly be mistaken in his belief that he had found John's pen.

---

6. Cf. Chapter XVI of *Pragmatics, Truth, and Language.*
7. For further details, see *Semiotics and Linguistic Structure.*

Further, as Hintikka points out, "coreferentiality may hold independently of referentiality." An example is the "text"

(15) 'John was trying to catch a fish. He wanted to eat it for supper.'

(This "text" could equally well be construed as a conjunction.) Here Hintikka thinks that "it is very hard to see the connection between the 'logical' forms and the 'grammatical forms' of the sentence in question." Of course it is, especially if no rules of transformation between the two are formulated, a quite separate matter.[8] "Prima facie," Hintikka contends of an allied use of 'it', "all talk of coreference is here vacuous," the 'it' in the second sentence not referring to any one particular fish rather than another, or perhaps to no fish at all if John caught none. For the text (15), we may proceed essentially as for (14), but handling the reference of the inscription b for 'it' by a disjunction to the effect that either j (John) succeeds in catching a fish and the speaker uses b to refer to that fish (assuming there was only one) or j did not succeed in catching a fish in which case (a) the speaker uses b to refer to no fish or (b) to the null individual or (c) there is no y such that sp Ref b,y,a for the appropriate a. Here we merely spell out *with maximum logical candor* the full complexity required in the referential situation at hand, *leaving nothing relevant unspecified*. If this is done always and systematically, reference to possible worlds may always be circumvented. And not only that — there is great gain in clarity and explicitness, to say nothing of a more restricted ontic commitment and involvement.[9]

Hintikka contends that the ambiguities in

(16) 'John wants to marry a girl who is both pretty and rich'

and in

(17) 'John believes that the richest man in town is a Republican'

are best revealed by distinguishing *de re* and *de dicto* readings in terms of possible worlds. But clearly the form

'$(Ee)(Ea)$(j Wants $e \cdot e$ That$_{\text{Content}} a \cdot$ '(Ep)(Girl $p \cdot$ Pretty$_{\text{Girls}} p \cdot$ Rich$_{\text{Girls}} p \cdot$ j Marry $p)$' a)'

provides the *de dicto* reading in an especially simple and straightforward way. 'Pretty$_{\text{Girls}} p$' expresses that p is pretty in the manner appropriate for girls, a notation (or one like it) needed for the analysis of

---

8. *Pragmatics, Truth, and Language.* Chapter XVIII.
9. Cf. *Belief, Existence, and Meaning,* Chapter II.

adjectives, whose behavior, incidentally, is considerably more complicated than is usually thought. The *de re* reading has as a consequence a
sentence stating the existence of such a girl, and is rather

$$\text{'}(Ep)(Ea)(Eb)(Ee)(\text{Girl}\,p \cdot \text{Pretty}_{\text{Girls}}\,p \cdot \text{Rich}_{\text{Girls}}\,p \cdot j \text{ Wants}\,e \cdot e$$
$$\text{That}_{\text{Content}}\,a \cdot b \text{ Des}\,p \cdot \ulcorner j \text{ Marry}\,b \urcorner a)\text{'}.$$

Note the need here for the use of Quine's device of quasi-quotation
and of the relation Des for designation. The ambiguity in (17) may be
brought out in similar fashion. (Note also that no specific clause is
present for handling 'who' in (16), which, strictly, should be provided.)

Hintikka's approach to the logic of questions is also based on epistemic logic and the theory of possible worlds, as one might expect.
Also, fundamental use is made of an *imperative* or *optative* operator, in
effect, a locution 'Bring it about that'. The logic of questions is thus
made to depend on that of imperatives. A more direct, pragmatic
analysis of questions and answers has greater pliability, being less
idealized and closer to actual usage. Such an approach is based on
locutions such as

$$\text{'}p \text{ Ask}\,a,q\text{'},$$

that person p asks (timelessly) person q whether the statement a obtains or not,

$$\text{'}p \text{ AskWho}\,a,q\text{'},$$

that person p asks q for a name of some member of the virtual class
designated by a,

$$\text{'}p \text{ AskHowMuch}\,a,q\text{'},$$

that p asks q how much of the entity designated by the mass-term a is
desired or needed or whatever in the circumstances, and so on for the
other types of *wh*-questions. In a similar way, forms, such as

$$\text{'}p \text{ Answer}\,a,q\text{'},$$
$$\text{'}p \text{ AnswerWho}\,a,q\text{'},$$

and so on, are introduced to handle answers. Some of these forms are
of course definable by means of others. In terms of them, a vocabulary is available for the study of questions of all manner of complexity,
as imbedded in all manner or contexts, linguistic and otherwise.

The general thesis of generative semantics, according to George
Lakoff, is that "the rules of grammar are identical to the rules relating

surface forms to their corresponding logical forms."[10] Lakoff himself has not put forward a notion of logical form of sufficient breadth or precision to give this thesis much content. Nor have transformational rules of suitable generality yet been adequately formulated so as to provide a delineation of what grammatical rules actually look like. Nonetheless, sufficient progress has been made to give Lakoff's thesis considerable cogency. Hintikka (pp. 159 ff) does not come out squarely for or against this thesis, but suggests rather two restraints upon it that he thinks needed. One is (p. 170) that "there are surely features of grammar (in any reasonable sense of that word) which have little logical interest." So, the thesis should claim only that "all or at the very least all really interesting factors of the logical behavior of natural language can be turned into" rules of the kind of which Lakoff speaks. The second is that the thesis "must presuppose some idea [of] what the rules of grammar are independently of the re-quirement that they match (or can be interpreted as) rules of logic. For, if there is no such independent criterion, Lakoff's thesis can be satisfied trivially, simply by taking some suitable formulation (if any) of the relevant aspects of logic and postulating grammatical relations and rules to match these. The real question, it seems to me, is not whether this is possible, but whether such an attempt to satisfy Lakoff's thesis is likely to produce results that have some independent grammatical significance."

The first restraint here rests upon an unanalyzed notion of what "logical interest" is, which should not be construed too narrowly. Is there a single word or phrase of a natural language that does not have its own logically interesting behavior? "Every sentence of natural language is a lesson in logic," Mill noted long back, and he should have added that every *word* is also. There would seem to be no *a priori* notion of what logical interest is that Hintikka can invoke here. No, the notion must emerge *in usu* as fruitful applications of logic prolif-erate.

The second restraint similarly presupposes a notion of what "inde-pendent grammatical significance" is. It is doubtful that there is any such significance at all, the structure of natural language being shot through and through at every point with, as well as being fundamen-tally dependent upon, either overt or disguised logical notions. In-deed, natural language is like an iceberg, the greater part of its logical features being hidden beneath the surface waters. It is thus quite

---

10. *Linguistics and Natural Logic,* Vol. 1 (Ann Arbor, Mich.: Studies in Generative Semantics, 1970).

groundless and beside the point to claim that without such an inde-pendence criterion the whole matter of grammar is "trivial," consist-ing merely of postulating "grammatical relations and rules" matching natural and logical forms. On the contrary, a tremendous amount of non-trivial empiricial work is needed here, not only to formulate a system of forms, but then to formulate painstakingly grammatical rules in Lakoff's sense. If this is ever to be accomplished successfully, there will remain little if any connection with traditional grammar, with its outmoded doctrine of the parts of speech. In short, Hintikka's conception of what is logically interesting is too narrow and a prioris-tic and reveals too much respect for the vagaries and obscurities of traditional grammar.

In the discussion of the so-called conservation laws concerning knowledge and belief, Hintikka modifies his previous stand (in his *Knowledge and Belief*, 1962) to the effect roughly that "whenever one knows (or believes) anything, he knows (or believes) all its logical con-sequences," a stand well contested in much recent literature. In any case, the stand is surely too *a prioristic*, laid down *ex cathedra logicae*. Rather, it should hold (if it does) only as the result of *independent criteria* for knowing (or believing). The stand is interesting only in the presence of such criteria, and otherwise (to use Hintikka's own com-ments anent Lakoff) "can be satisfied trivially" simply by postulation. Hintikka has not apparently anywhere put forward such criteria. For a satisfactory formulation of them, no doubt the detailed help of the psycho- and socio-linguist is needed. The problems to be met with in such formulation are simply too complex for the philosopher alone.

Hintikka modifies his previous conservation laws concerning knowl-edge and belief by adapting from von Neumann a notion of arithme-tical depth, dubbing it 'quantificational depth'. The notion is not rigorously defined but only sketched. The main use of it is to suggest a characterization of what we might mean when we say we "under-stand" a sentence or proposition. "Surely the most concrete sense im-aginable of understanding what a first-order proposition p says [p. 189] is to know which sequences of individuals in which combinations one can expect to hit upon if it is true — sequences no longer than those already considered in p. Now this is just what the distributive normal form of p (at the depth of p) spells out as fully as possible." One then reformulates the conservation laws to require that knowl-edge and belief be invariant with respect to those logical equivalences (and material implications) necessary for understanding what is being believed.

Hintikka's suggestion here is not convincing; too many difficulties remain. It is doubtful that understanding is a merely semantical notion, pragmatical ingredients being needed fundamentally. Also, surely before a sentence is understood, its constituent *predicates* must be. The understanding of predicates does not rely wholly upon the individuals or sequences of such to which they apply, as Frege was one of the first to point out. Also no provision is made for understanding sentences of higher order, nor apparently for metalinguistic sentences. In any case, Hintikka's sense of 'understanding' needs much further discussion and is surely far from "the most concrete sense imaginable" for that notion.

This is not the occasion to develop any further the alternative approach to the logic of belief and of knowing in terms of patternization, suggested some years back.[11] In this approach, no *a priori* conceptions are involved. Belief and knowledge are given independent empirical criteria in terms of actually devised empirical tests of some kind, on the basis of which an individual's doxastic behavior is suitably *classified*. If his behavior, in fact, turns out at a given time to be of such and such a kind, his beliefs (or knowledge) are said to exhibit such and such a kind of pattern for belief (or knowledge); and if not, not. There are many interesting kinds of patterns here to be reflected upon, some of them "rational" patterns in an appropriate sense or senses. In some of them, suitable conservation laws may obtain. This kind of approach, which has not been developed very extensively, contrasts sharply with that of Hintikka in lacking all taint of the *cathedra logicae* and in making fundamental use of testing procedures in empirical science, and in exhibiting desirable sensitiveness to ontic commitment and involvement.

The essay on phenomenology and the intentions of intentionality raises many problems and the subject of their interrelations cries out for a discussion in clear-cut logico-experimental terms. Hintikka contends (p. 195) that "possible-worlds semantics is the logic of intentionality, and [the] intentional is what calls for possible-world semantics." Here, too, no doubt, the cart is being coupled with the horse a bit too readily. A clear discussion of intentionality *independent* of possible-worlds theory is needed in order to see that promising alternative approaches are available.[12] Further, the internal difficulties within possible-worlds theory, including problems concerned with individuation, with trans-world lines, with meaning, and the like, are formida-

---

11. Especially in *Belief, Existence, and Meaning.*
12. Cf. "On Gurwitsch's Theory of Intentionality," in *Whitehead's Categoreal Scheme and Other Papers.*

ble indeed, as Hintikka himself admits. There is no need to discuss the inner jargon of the theory here. At best, the possible-worlds approach to the exact study of intentionality is merely one among many, to be judged ultimately by its fruits, its comprehensiveness, its simplicity, the kinds of logical devices it employs, and so on.

In spite of all the propaganda on behalf of the possible-worlds view, the following points should be noted before allowing too much enthusiasm for it to develop. Hintikka, as already suggested, shows little sensitiveness to the postulational foundations required. His view has not been developed sufficiently far as yet to know specifically what primitives, if any, are required over and above those of some set theory. Postulates, in addition to those of the set theory, are then needed. (There is more to this observation than might appear, if one bears in mind that even Gödel numbering or the assignment of entities to expressions, is a semantical procedure requiring its own vocabulary and axioms.) If the view is developed without additional primitives, then the set theory must, of course, be extremely elaborate with many dubious assumptions. The axiomatics of the view should be brought out and faced up to squarely. Further, as already suggested, Hintikka takes no account of inscriptions or sign-events, concentrating only on shapes or sign-designs, the former, however, constituting the really concrete "stuff" out of which languages are built. Hintikka has not developed the theory of logical form very far, being contented here with rather too narrow a conception. And, similarly, for grammatical transformation, which he seems nowhere to have considered. It is not clear how Hintikka proposes to handle the truth-concept for either eternal or occasion sentences (to use Quine's terminology). No direct or explicit way of handling talk of events is forthcoming, nor is any provision made for mereology or the calculus of individuals. Without these latter, or suitable surrogates for them, it is not clear that much real progress can be made in the logical analysis of language.

In the last essay Hintikka argues that the cubism of Braque and Picasso has more than passing kinship with Husserl's phenomenology and even with Frege's doctrine of *Sinne*. Any such attempt to defend a thesis of this kind is fraught with difficulties. Hintikka contends in italics that these painters *"were representing* [Husserlian] *noemata, not objects."* However, precisely how the cubes, volumes, and so on, of cubist paintings are correlated, or even related in some one-to-one or recognizable fashion, with noemata we are not told at all. Hintikka agrees (p. 235) that "neither the general concept of meaning [or *Sinn*] nor its particular explication in the phenomenological concept of noema is unproblematic or even clear." How, then, can any reasonably interesting correlation be set up between them and the very precise painterly items in the cubist technique? Here Hintikka leaves us rather in the dark as to detail. In many passages he talks about what the cubist painters said that they *intended* to accomplish rather than what they actually did. Talk about artistic intentions is dangerously close to the Wimsatt-Beardsley "intentionalist fallacy," which still has a grain of validity to it, even though much buffeted in the critical literature. Also, there is so vast a gap between what artists say about their work and what they actually achieve that it is in general unwise to pay too much attention to the former or to give it much credence.

Hintikka seems to think it a discovery that these cubist artists (p. 237) "were not depicting objects and individuals by means of their appearances or looks, but by means of the properties they are known or thought to have," as though no other artists in the whole of history had ever done this. What properties? *Essential* ones, we are told, "the properties a given individual or object cannot lose without thereby losing its identity, becoming another object or individual." The exact characterization of such properties is by no means easy[13], and even if there are such it is doubtful that the cubists alone were concerned with them or with them only.

With only slight verbal changes, but with none of essential content, Hintikka's entire paper on representation could be transformed into a paper concerning many other styles of painting. It thus throws no special light upon cubism. All painters are concerned to depict noemata in one way or another, even those who do *not* aim at representation, so that Hintikka's contention is vacuous for other kinds of painting as well. Further, it is a considerable oversimplification to contend that even representational painters aim at "depicting objects and individuals by means of their appearances or looks." Representation is a much more complex affair than this, the full theory of which needs a considerable spelling out.[14]

The very last sentence of this last paper is unfortunate indeed. "The spirit of problem-solving," he writes (p. 249), "the sense of addressing oneself to specific tasks instead of lofty ideals which is reflected in Picasso's words is shared by much of the best modern philosophy." Would it not be more fitting here to extol addressing

---

13. Cf. *Pragmatics, Truth, and Language*, Chapter XIV.
14. Cf., for example, *inter alia,* R. Bernheimer, *The Nature of Representation* (New York: New York University Press, and N. Goodman, *Languages of Art* (Indianapolis: The Bobbs-Merrill Co., 1968) and *Ways of Worldmaking* (Indianapolis: (Hackett Publishing Co., 1978).

oneself to specific tasks *in the service of* high ideals? Problem-solving is important only where the problems are important. The "words" of Picasso referred to are the famous ones reported by Kahnweiler to the effect that the pre-cubist painters "whose pictures are hanging in the Louvre" or on the walls of the Sistine Chapel did not solve problems. "What would you say of a mathematician who wrote down a string of figures and giving no solution to a problem?" Picasso asked. Failing this, what is left? "Nothing but charm. The charm of a prostitute."

Art, as well as philosophy, when divorced from its role as serving high ideals, become churlish, insipid, and barren. Likewise, high ideals not served by adequate techniques and probing methods of analysis in accord with high humane, scientific, or other standards, are likely to perish and to lose their importance as guides to human endeavor. At this late date, it is *retardataire* indeed to extol without reserve the art of Picasso or to regard his comments about it as in any way definitive.

Hintikka's infatuation with possible worlds, as evidenced in all of his writing, is to be lamented. Even so, we must be grateful to him, here and elsewhere, for his many incisive insights and valuable suggestions, for his calling attention to interesting interconnections, for his all-too-brief historical asides, and for his persistence in carrying his views at certain points (but, alas, not always) beyond the confines of mere programme. It is a pity, however, that he has not felt the need to develop less objectionable analytic procedures on the basis of a more secure technique.

CHAPTER XIII

On Virtual-Class Designation and Intensionality

Incipe quicquid agas: pro toto est prima operis pars.

One of the most important problems any logico-linguistic theory must face is that of how best to handle *intensional* discourse. There are many alternative theories of intensions on the market clamoring for attention. All of these, however, contain what many regard as excessive ontic commitment and involvement, as well as insufficient postulational economy. In the present paper a treatment of intensions of extreme sparseness is proposed in what is thought to be the logically simplest way yet developed. The leading idea is an adaptation of Frege's *Art des Gegebenseins.*

It is now universally agreed upon that a one- or many-sorted quantification logic of first order with identity, and with suitable non-logical primitive predicate-constants, provides a very powerful framework for the systematic formulation of scientific and philosophical theories. The presence of primitive individual-constants is of course optional, in view of Russell's theory of descriptions. The predicates are presumed applicable to the entities over which the variables of quantification are taken to range. In all interesting cases, these entities are the actual entities the given theory is concerned with, and in the case of philosophical theories these entities are usually presumed to be those of the one actual world constituting our cosmos and everything it contains. The semantics of such languages or formalized systems then characterizes the relations between their categorematic expressions, i.e., the predicate- and the individual-constants (if any), and the actual entities they are taken to stand for or represent (or whatever). There is a long tradition to the effect that the study of such relations constitutes the central core of semantics, and hence is of central importance for logico-linguistics.

One semantical relation of interest is that of *multiple denotation,* in accord with which a one-place predicate constant is said to denote severally the entities to which it applies.[1] Another important relation is that of *designation,* in accord with which a one-place predicate-constant is said to *designate* the class (or property taken in extension).[2] The theory of denotation may be formalized within a first-order semantical metalanguage, whereas that of designation ordinarily requires a metalanguage of *second* order, with variables over classes of expressions in addition of course to the (syntactical) variables over the expressions of the language.

The contrast between denotation and designation centers mainly around what may be called the "principle of unicity."[3] Let '*a* Des *F*' express that the expression *a* designates *F*, where *F* is a class, perhaps a merely virtual one.[4] The principle of unicity for designation is, then, the principle that

$$(a)((a \text{ Des } F \cdot a \text{ Des } G) \supset F = G).$$

But the corresponding principle clearly fails for denotation. Let '*a* Den *x*' express that *a* denotes *x, x* being perhaps merely *ex pluribus unum.* Then it obtains that

$$\sim (a)(x)(y)((a \text{ Den } x \cdot a \text{ Den } y) \supset x = y),$$

in all theories in which there are assumed to be at least two entities. The result is that a semantics based on Des must be very different from one based on Den, as concerns its basic laws, even if we disregard the difference between the first- and second-order kinds of framework needed.

There seems to be a kind of unwritten law that the principle of unicity *should* hold, in accordance, presumably, with the 'Fido'–Fido notion that a given name stands for one and only one object. What holds for names is then thought to hold for all signs. It seems never to have been stated quite why this principle should obtain, other than as making explicit a widespread, rather vague, feeling about how signs do, in fact, behave — at least some of them. No doubt this feeling stems from the behavior of a proper name, which does, after all, stand uniquely for the entity of which it is a name.

For the present, we shall be concerned only with the designation of

---

1. See especially *Truth and Denotation,* Chapters IV and V.
2. *Ibid.,* Chapter VII.
3. Cf. R. Carnap, *Meaning and Necessity* (Chicago: University of Chicago Press, 1967), p. 98. The *Principle of Univocality* combines the Principle of Unicity and a Specificity Principle. Cf. **DesR2** and **DesR3** below.
4. On virtual classes, see especially *Belief, Existence, and Meaning,* Chapter VI.

predicates, not of proper names or individual-constants, designation for these latter being definable, as we shall see in a moment.

There is a certain kinship between a semantics as based on Den (i.e., with 'Den' as the sole semantical primitive) and the traditional doctrine of "common" (as contrasted with "proper") names.[5] Frege, in his critique of Schröder, has some interesting things to say against the doctrine of common names. "The author [Schröder] confuses . . . two cases when he calls 'nothing' and 'round square' alike senseless, nonsensical, or unmeaningful names (pp. 50, 69 [of the *Vorlesung der Algebra der Logik*]). His 'nothing' is in many cases . . . a proper name without any reference, and hence logically illegitimate. 'Round square', on the other hand, is not an empty name, but a name of an empty concept, and thus one not devoid of reference. . . . The word 'common name' is confusing here, for it makes it look as though the common name stood in the same, or much in the same, relation to the objects that fall under the concept as a proper name does to a single object. Nothing could be more false! In this case, it must, of course, appear as though a common name that belongs to an empty concept were as illegitimate as a proper name that designates nothing."[6]

Of course, Frege no doubt has in mind here that 'nothing' is to be handled quantificationally, and hence not as a "proper name without . . . reference." 'Round square', on the other hand, does have reference, namely, the "empty concept." We need not literally follow Frege here, but instead may say that 'round square' *designates* the null class (or virtual class) and has the "empty concept" as its meaning or intension (in some precise sense to be specified). To call 'round square' a common name is surely awkward, however, there being no entities among which it can be "common." If one objects to the use of "common names" here, one might be tempted, more or less *pari passu,* to object also to the semantics based on 'Den'. For when we say that *a* Den *x, a* here is dangerously close to a common name.

Another reason for interest in a semantics based on designation as over and against one based on denotation is, again, a widespread (and somewhat vague, perhaps) feeling that the ontology of a system should include, in addition to the entities taken as values for the variables of quantification, *the designata of its primitive and defined predicates.* These designata themselves need not be values for variables, and indeed *cannot* be so, if the logical framework is of first order. The desig-

---

5. But cf. the author's "On the Semantics of Common Names" and "On Common Names and Mathematical Scotism" in *Peirce's Logic of Relations Etc.*
6. *Philosophical Writings of Gottlob Frege,* pp. 104–105.

nata are then merely virtual, i.e., virtual classes or relations of what-soever degree. The feeling is somehow that these classes and relations are as much a part of the ontology of the language as their members or relata. Perhaps we should distinguish two senses of ontology here, and recognize that both are useful and legitimate notions.

Still a fourth reason for interest in a semantics — we are speaking throughout only of semantical metalanguages of first order — based on designation is the desire to achieve as weak a theory as possible, capable of providing a full-fledged notion of truth. In other words, a definition of 'Tr *a*', where '*a*' is a *variable* for expressions, should be forthcoming on the basis of the simplest kind of theory we can think up. The semantics based on denotation is one very simple theory, but one based on designation might be thought still simpler if it could be formulated on a first-order basis. This we shall attempt to do in a moment. Of course, one could take 'Tr' itself as a primitive, as has often been done, but then the intimate connection between truth, on the one hand, and designation or denotation, on the other, is not brought out. Further, truth is thought to be a derivative semantical notion, depending fundamentally on the more basic semantical relations. It is these latter that are of primary interest, and it has turned out to be a mere happy accident that the semantical truth-predicate is definable in terms of them.

If we wish a semantics based on designation for predicates, the technicalia required are not so obvious as might appear. Virtual-class expressions may be wholly eliminated primitively, if desired, in the semantics based on denotation, where '*a* Den *x*' is the basic locution, with *a* a one-place predicate. But not so, if our interest is in designation. Here '*a* Des *F*' is the basic locution and is not significant unless '*F*' is already primitively available as a virtual-class (or perhaps virtual-relation) expression. The underlying logic with primitive expressions for virtual classes is surely no more (or less) objectionable than that in which they are defined.

In order to distinguish virtual-class designation from the designation of individuals, let us now write 'Des$_{VC}$' for the former and 'Des$_{Ind}$' for the latter. This latter will be defined in terms of the former in a moment.

The Rules of Designation, for the semantics with 'Des$_{VC}$' as the sole semantical primitive and with virtual-class expressions as primitives in the object-language, are as follows:

DesR1.   ⊢ ⌜(*a*)(*a* Des$_{VC}$ *F* ⊃ PredConOne *a*)⌝ , where in place of '*F*' any virtual-class expression is inserted,

DesR2. $\vdash \ulcorner(a)((a \text{ Des}_{VC} F \cdot a \text{ Des}_{VC} G) \supset F = G)\urcorner$, where in place of 'F' and 'G' any virtual-class expressions are inserted,

DesR3. $\vdash \ulcorner a \text{ Des}_{VC} F\urcorner$, where in place of 'F' any virtual-class expression is inserted and in place of 'a' its structural description.

Here **DesR1** is the *Limitation Principle,* that only one-place (primitive or defined) predicate-constants (PredConOne's) bear Des$_{VC}$ to anything, **DesR2** is the *Principle of Unicity,* that expressions bear Des$_{VC}$ to at most one virtual class, and **DesR3** is the *Principle of Specificity* (a restricted 'Fido'—Fido Principle), that certain one-place predicate constants bear Des$_{VC}$ to certain virtual classes. Note that '=' is being used ambiguously throughout as the sign for identity either between individuals or between virtual classes.

If the system contains one or more individual-constants as primitive, we may define

'$a \text{ Des}_{Ind} x$' as '(PrimInCon $a \cdot$ (Eb)(Vbl $b \cdot$ $(LB\frown b \frown invep \frown$ $b \frown id \frown a \frown RB)$ Des$_{VC} \{y \ni y = x\}))$'.

Here 'Prim$\frown$In$\frown$Con a' expresses that a is a primitive individual-constant, and 'Vbl b', that b is a variable. 'LB', '$invep$', 'id', and 'RB' are respectively the structural-descriptive names of '{', '$\ni$', '=', and '}', where '$\{y \ni y = x\}$' is the expression for the virtual class of all entities y such that $y = x$. A primitive individual-constant a is said to bear Des$_{Ind}$ to an individual x, then, according to this definition, just where a predicate-constant or virtual-class expression $\ulcorner\{y \ y = a\}\urcorner$ bears Des$_{VC}$ *to the virtual class* $\{y \ni y = x\}$. The various laws concerning the designation of individuals, including those analogous to **DesR1**– **DesR3**, are immediate consequences.

In terms of 'Des$_{VC}$' a truth-definition for all sentences of the object-language is immediately forthcoming. We may let

'Tr a' abbreviate '(Sent $a \cdot$ (Eb)(Vbl $b \cdot$ $(LB \frown b \frown invep \frown a \frown RB)$ Des$_{VC} \{x \ni x = x\}))$'.

Thus a sentence a is true just where some vacuous predicate constant of the form $\ulcorner\{x \ni a\}\urcorner$ bears Des$_{VC}$ to the universal class. This provides, of course, a definition of 'Tr a' for variable 'a' and thus should serve for most (at least) of the purposes for which a semantical truth-predicate is needed. Further, the definition may be proved *adequate* in the sense that

$$\vdash \ulcorner\text{Tr}\, a \equiv \text{———}\urcorner ,$$

where in place of '———' any sentence of the object-language is inserted and in place of 'a' its structural-descriptive name. And finally, the various fundamental semantical theorems concerning truth as thus defined are now readily provable from **DesR1−DesR3**.

This semantics based on 'Des$_{VC}$' with virtual-class expressions as primitives is then an acceptable alternative to that based on 'Den' (either with or without virtual-class expressions as primitives). Such a semantics might even be thought preferable in view of the four points — albeit perhaps not compelling ones — already given, the one concerned with the principle of unicity, Frege's point concerning "common names," the desire to use 'ontology' to include the designata of the primitive predicates, and the interest in seeking as weak a semantics as possible. There is still another, concerned with *intensionality*.

It is interesting to observe that, with virtual-class and -relation predicates taken as primitives, a powerful theory of semantic intensions is also forthcoming in a very direct way. The leading idea here will be akin to Frege's notion of the *Art des Gegebenseins*, for which a new semantical primitive is needed. Let 'F Under a' express that the virtual class or relation F is taken *under* the linguistic description a. For the present and to simplify, let us consider only virtual *classes*. The handling of virtual relations is then similar.

Concerning the relation Under, the following Rules may be postulated.

UnderR1.   ⌜$(a)(F$ Under a ⊃ PredConOne $a)$⌝, where (etc., about 'F').

UnderR2.   ⌜$(a)((F$ Under a • G Under $a) ⊃ F = G)$⊆, where (etc., about 'F' and 'G').

Here again, the first Rule is a *Limitation Rule*, that virtual classes are taken only under one-place predicate-constants, and **UnderR2** is the *One-Many Rule*, that the Under-relation is a one-many relation.

A kind of synonymy relation, or one of sameness of descriptivity, is provided by defining

$$⌜F \approx G⌝ \quad \text{as} \quad ⌜(a)(F \text{ Under } a \equiv G \text{ Under } a)⌝ .$$

Thus if F and G are taken under just the same predicate-descriptions, F and G are said to be descriptively identical. Clearly descriptively identical virtual classes are to be identical, so that we have also that

UnderR3.   ⊢ ⌜$F \approx G ⊃ F = G$⌝ , where (etc., about 'F' and 'G').

And finally, certain virtual classes are always taken under the very description under which they are taken.

UnderR4.   ⊢ ⌜F Under a⌝ , where in place of 'F' a virtual-class

197

expression is inserted and in place of '*a*' its structural-descriptive name.

Two additional interesting semantical notions are immediately definable, the (total) *designational essence* of *F* and the (total) *descriptive essence* of *F*. Thus

$$\ulcorner \text{DesigEss}'F \urcorner \quad \text{may abbreviate} \quad \ulcorner \{a \ni a \; \text{Des}_{VC} F\} \urcorner$$

and

$$\ulcorner \text{DescrEss}'F \urcorner \quad \text{may abbreviate} \quad \ulcorner \{a \ni F \; \text{Under}\, a\} \urcorner \,.$$

The designational essence of a virtual class is the virtual class of all expressions that designate it, and its descriptive essence is the virtual class of all expressions under which it is taken. Note the harmlessness of the use of 'essence' here, the essence being merely a given totality of one-place predicates having nothing to do with "essential properties" or any other entities equally obscure.

When *a* Des$_{VC}$ *F*, *a* designates *F* truly, so to speak, as provided either by **DesR3** or in view of factual meaning postulates or boundary conditions. But it might obtain that *F* Under *a*, even if *a* does not truly designate *F*. *F* is in such a case merely described wrongly. Virtual classes may be taken under incorrect or erroneous descriptions, for there are false beliefs, superstitions, and the like, which may enter into the descriptive essence of the relevant virtual class. We might also speak of the *veridical* descriptive essence of *F* as consisting of just those one-place predicates under which it is taken that do, in fact, designate it. Thus

$$\ulcorner \text{VerDescrEss}'F \urcorner \quad \text{could abbreviate} \quad \ulcorner \{a \ni (F \; \text{Under}\, a \cdot a \; \text{Des}_{VC} F\} \urcorner \,.$$

The veridical descriptive essence of a class is of interest in singling out just the "correct predicates" applicable to it and under which it is taken.

One of the most important facts about language is that its users use certain expressions to *paraphrase* others, to say or write in other words what they mean or intend. It is difficult to get very far in the exact study of language without a notion of paraphrase, as prominent linguists such as Harris and Hiż, have been telling us for years. Let '*a* Prphrs *b*' express that *a* is a legitimate or linguistically proper paraphrase of *b*. The relations of Prphrs and Under are interrelated by the following *Under-Rule of Paraphrase*.

PrphrsR1. ⊢ $\ulcorner (a)(b)((a \; \text{Prphrs}\, b \cdot F \; \text{Under}\, a) \supset F \; \text{Under}\, b) \urcorner$, where (etc., about '*F*').

There is also a *Designational Rule of Paraphrase*:

PrphrsR2. ⊢ ⌜$(a)(b)((a$ Prphrs b • a Des$_{VC}$ $F) \supset b$ Des$_{VC}$ $F)$⌝ , where (etc.).

By the *sense* of a predicate-constant, let us mean the virtual class of all paraphrastic predicate-constants.[7] Thus

'Sns'a'   may abbreviate   '$\{b \ni b$ Prphrs $a\}$'.

Then clearly

$$\vdash \ulcorner(a)(F \text{ Under } a \supset \text{Sns'}a \subset \text{DescrEss'}F)\urcorner$$

and

$$\vdash \ulcorner(a)(F \text{ Under } a \supset \text{Sns'}a \subset \text{DesigEss'}F)\urcorner,$$

in view of the two Rules of Paraphrase. The sense of a predicate-constant may be regarded as a *concept*. Following Frege in essentials, we may then say that the predicate 'RS' for round squares has the virtual class of predicates paraphrastic with it as its concept and yet designates the null (virtual) class. In some way as this, then, the foundations for a rather far-reaching theory of semantical concepts may be laid.

Note that no requirement of consistency is laid down for 'Under'. It is allowed that F be taken under inconsistent descriptions. People do, after all, describe wrongly, and even inconsistently. However, there are alternative ways of handling erroneous description, so that we could construe 'Under' more strictly. Let us consider one such alternative.

In place of **UnderR1** above, we could require that

UnderR1′. ⊢ ⌜$(a)(F$ Under $a \supset a$ Des$_{VC}F)$⌝ , where (etc.).

UnderR2 is then provable from **DesR2**. The *Principle of Consistency*, that

$$\vdash \ulcorner(a)(F \text{ Under } a \supset {\sim} (Eb)(\text{Vbl } b \bullet F \text{ Under } (LB \frown b \frown invep \frown$$
$${\sim}\frown a \frown b \frown RB)))\top, RB)))\urcorner,$$

is then provable from the corresponding Principle of Consistency for designation. (Here, of course, *'tilde'* is the structural-descriptive name of '~'). **UnderR3** and **UnderR4** are retained. The descriptive essence of F then becomes a subclass of the designative essence, and the verid-

---

7. Frege, *op. cit.*, pp. 10–12 and p. 57. Cf. "A Reading of Frege on Sense and Designation," in *Pragmatics, Truth, and Language*.

ical descriptive essence becomes the same as the designative one. This second way of characterizing 'Under' is in accord with only "correct" usage and hence useful in characterizing only a limited kind of linguistic behavior. The wider construal of 'Under' thus leads more readily into the discussion of pragmatics below.

Having achieved a semantics as simple and economical as the foregoing, we might go a step further. Recall that in 'a $Des_{VC} F$', 'a' is a variable and 'F' an expression for a virtual class. The 'a', of course, may be quantified over, but the 'F' cannot be. Even so, a strong semantics is forthcoming, including a theory of intensions with 'Under' and 'Prphrs' as new relational primitives, as we have seen. The question arises as to whether we really *must* allow quantification over the 'a'. If we forego even this, using only structural-descriptive names in place of the syntactical variables, can we formulate a semantics of any interest? Of course, a *syntax* for the object-language is presumed available, as throughout, as well as the modes of expression of the object-language (or translations of such in the meta-language). We thus have considerable means at our disposal. We can straightaway define, again schematically,

$$\ulcorner Tr\, a \urcorner \quad \text{as} \quad \text{`----'}$$

where in place of '----' a sentence of the object-language is inserted and in place of 'a' its structural-descriptive name. These provisos are precisely those of the Principle of Adequacy above.

The predicate 'Tr' here is not genuinely a semantical one, however, for it is not given in terms of a relation between expressions and objects, but rather, in terms of the correlation between specific object-language expressions and their structural-descriptive names. Still, this is enough for the purpose at least of providing the foregoing definition, which is the pivotal one in the so-called "no-truth" theory of truth. That theory seems never to have been formulated with any exactitude. It would seem to consist merely of the foregoing definition-schema, together with the Principle of Adequacy, which of course follows immediately.

It is often remarkable how much can be accomplished with schematic definitions and axiom-schemata, if a serious effort is made. The situation here is similar to that of an arithmetic without variables (and hence quantifiers) over numbers but with only *numerals*. Such formulations of arithmetic are much more interesting than might be expected. But even so, they are severely limited in crucial respects. One can never state laws of conditional existence; for example, one cannot quantify over all numbers, there are many proofs (e.g., in analytic number theory) that cannot be carried through, and so on. And analogously in the semantics without variables over expressions. Without these, there are many sentences of a natural language for which logical forms cannot be given. But even so, the method of achieving generality of statement by means of schemata can often be shown sufficient for certain restricted purposes.

A kind of "no-intensions" theory of intensions could also be formulated. ⌜*F* Under *a*⌝ would be taken to express that *a* is one of the purported structural-descriptive names of the virtual-class expression put in here in place of '*F*'. And ⌜*a* Prphrs *b*⌝ would express that whatever is put in in place of the structural-descriptive name '*a*' is taken as a paraphrase of whatever is put in in place of the structural descriptive name *b* . Likewise, ⌜*a* Des$_{VC}$ *F*⌝ , where in place of '*F*' a predicate-constant is inserted and in place of *a* a structural-descriptive name of a predicate-constant, could be taken as significant. Some of the preceding theory would then be forthcoming without too much impoverishment. The supposition is that if this theory were worked out in full detail, it would seem to be much more powerful and interesting than appears at first sight, just as arithmetic with only numerals is.

This "no-truth" theory of truth with the "no-intensions" theory of intensions is to be contrasted with the still weaker theory kind of theory based on what Carnap called "absolute" concepts.[8] We may provide for these latter by defining

$$\text{'Tr} \underline{\quad\quad} \text{'} \quad \text{merely as} \quad \text{'} \underline{\quad\quad} \text{',}$$

without distinguishing use and mention. The definiendum can be read: It is true that ——. And we might let

$$\text{'}F \text{ Prphrs } G\text{'}$$

express that to say that something is an *F* is a paraphrase of saying that it has *G*. In effect, we read these in terms of 'that'-clauses. Again, with these absolute concepts, more may no doubt be achieved than appears at first blush. But even so, this theory is much too restricted for the general purposes of providing logical forms for the sentences of a natural language, which in general are much more complex (and thus interesting) than logicians have for the most part supposed.

Let us return now to the full-fledged semantics as based on 'Des' and 'Under' with expression-variables (and virtual-class expressions)

---

8. See R. Carnap, *Introduction to Semantics* (Cambridge: Harvard University Press, 1946), especially p. 89.

as arguments. The theory of intension provided therein, if it may be so called, is *synchronic,* in the sense that a given F is taken or not once and for all under a given description. The relation Under could be construed *diachronically,* however, by adding another argument. Let 'F Under a,t' express now that F is taken under the predicate-description a at time t. One and the same class is then allowed to be taken under a at one time, but perhaps not at another, and of course under varying descriptions at different times. Also, in terms of this diachronic construal of 'Under', a basis is provided for the semantical study of *conceptual change.* Such change is nothing mysterious transcending the bounds of exact study, as some have supposed, but merely one more item to be brought within the purview of logico-linguistic consideration.

The sensitive reader will perhaps have observed that in taking 'Under' (with or without a parameter for times) as a special primitive, we have in effect already transgressed the borders of semantics. In the foregoing, there has been almost a total disregard of the *users* of language — it has been assumed either that there is just *one* user, or that all users are *alike* as to their linguistic behavior as regards 'Under'. Both these assumptions are legitimate for the purposes of a restricted theory. But of course there are many users whose linguistic behavior is not alike. And, of course, it is the users of language who, on given *occasions* of utterance or assertion or writing, or whatever, take given virtual classes under given descriptions. It thus seems eminently natural, and indeed desirable, to make all this fully explicit by bringing in variables for both persons and for their occasions of using language — their *speech-acts,* as it were. If we do this, we land straightaway in the domain of pragmatics and event-logic. And this is a good place to land, it is thought, for features hidden in the foregoing semantics can then be brought to light explicitly. But gain in explicitness is bought only at a price; there is also gain in complexity. The theory of intensions becomes much more complex, being now not only diachronic but relativized to the individual (and even group) users of language as well. The diachronicity can easily be handled in terms of the temporally varying occasions of use.

Let 'p Under F,a' express that user p takes F under the predicate a. Reference to the occasion of use is then forthcoming where

$$\text{'}<p,\text{Under},F,a>e\text{'}$$

expresses that e is an occasion of p's taking F under a. Clearly this pragmatical Under-relation is more useful and pliable than the semantical Under-relation considered above. Above all, there is gain in "logical candour," to use Ryle's happy phrase.

Even designation itself may be pragmatized, so to speak, to good effect. Indeed, such pragmatization is needed if the egocentric or deictic expressions are to be handled appropriately, and a notion of truth for so-called occasion sentences provided for, occasion sentences being those containing, in a fundamental way, one or more such expressions. And, similarly, paraphrase may differ from person to person. Thus we need forms, such as

$$\text{'}p \text{ Ref } a,b,x\text{'} \quad \text{or} \quad \text{'}p \text{ Ref } a,b,F\text{'}$$

and

$$\text{'}p \text{ Prphrs } a,b\text{'}$$

to express that person p uses the expression a as occurring in the sentence b to refer to x (or F) and that p paraphrases a as b. Here, too, the specific occasions of use may be brought in by writing

$$\text{'}<p,\text{Ref},a,b,x>e\text{'} \quad \text{or} \quad \text{'}<p,\text{Ref},a,b,F>e\text{'}$$

and

$$\text{'}<p,\text{Prphrs},a,b>e\text{'}.[9]$$

These two methods, the semantical and the pragmatical ones, are typical of two approaches to logical analysis in general. In the one, there is always abstraction from the full complexity of the material in order to gain a certain simplicity and manageability. The simpler forms are easier to grasp, easier to study, easier to axiomatize, less cumbrous to handle. Such forms are appropriate, especially at the beginning stages of research. And, indeed, the study of semantics has preceded by many decades the exact study of pragmatics. From the point of view of the latter, however, there is too much abstraction in the approach of the former. There is packing too much in the primitives required that needs unpacking. There is too much taken for granted that should not be so, too many covert assumptions that should be brought out into the open. Necessary parameters are missing that should usually be present. Also, the axioms (or axiom-schemata) given are usually oversimplified and, at best, hold for only some special, albeit perhaps interesting, cases. In the semantical method there is thus too much concealment of material that should be

---

9. Cf. *Semiotics and Linguistic Structure*, pp. 121 ff.

considered explicitly. In short, the pragmaticist approach wins hands down, but at the cost of greater caution.

The pragmaticist is more wary than his semantical confrères in his choice of fundamental logical forms. He tries to include all relevant parameters in order to gain the simplest forms possible. He is wary of too simple axioms and seeks rather to characterize general linguistic or other *patterns* rather than to postulate that all users of language behave essentially in the same way.[10] And, above all, he does not theorize *ex cathedra* but looks continually to empirical or experimental science for help in clarifying his fundamental ideas. Pragmatical research is a continuation of scientific research and, ideally, should take place cooperatively. The semanticist tends to hold his head rather above the level of empirical research, with the result often, of course, that his work is too *a priori* and not sufficiently based experimentally.

Note again that all the foregoing theories are concerned with the one actual world and they then contrast sharply with the so-called *possible-worlds* semantics in current fashion. It is difficult enough to characterize our one world and the language we use to describe it. And as John Austin might have said, "there will be time enough to consider the possible worlds once we have gained some little modicum of clarity about the one actual world we inhabit." Further, in taking predicates *under a description*, whether we do this semantically or pragmatically, we gain the effect of being able to talk of all possibilities in *so far as they can be discussed in the language at hand*. Thus let it not be said that the kind of approach here excludes discussion of possibility.

Also, it should be observed that the foregoing has been written from the point of view of *classical* syntax, i.e., syntax in which expressions are construed as shapes or sign-designs rather than as inscriptions or sign-events. A more pliable and adequate theory would be forthcoming in terms of inscriptions. Also observe that the foregoing theory of intensions is given within a wholly extensional metalanguage. We have here a *wholly extensional theory of intensions*. Such a theory is seen to be possible only by bringing out into the open all semantical or pragmatical factors otherwise hidden in the choice of obscure primitives.

The pragmatical forms introduced for 'Under' and 'Prphrs' make use of a parameter for human persons. Should parameters for *social groups* be introduced also? Logical foundations for *sociopragmatics* are as much needed as for the pragmatics of the individual. The difficulty is that the latter does not easily generalize to the former. We cannot

---

10. Cf. *Belief, Existence, and Meaning*, pp. 79 ff, 112 ff, and 272 ff.

correctly state that to say that the group behaves or does such and such is the same as saying that each and every member of the group does. For the pragmatics of the group, *logical sums* of persons may be introduced and made to play the role of the group. Thus, for example, if p is now such a sum, 'p Prphrs a,b' may express that the group as a whole takes a as a paraphrase of b, and this may obtain even if some persons who are parts of p do not.

A central plea of this paper is that all semantics should be pragmatized, and that pragmatization should be extended to the social group. But there are enormous difficulties in this extension, the exploration of which spills over into the very foundations of the social sciences.

CHAPTER XIV

On the Language
of Music Theory

Incipe; dimidium facti est coepisse. Supersit dimidium; rursum hoc incipe, et efficies.

Let us agree straightaway with Milton Babbitt's contention that "statements about music must conform to those verbal and methodological requirements which attend the possibility of meaningful discourse in any domain."[1] Just how such requirements are set up, however, is a difficult matter and has by no means been settled by structural and transformational linguists or by philosophers of language, those above all best equipped to delimit the areas of meaningful discourse. What Babbitt has in mind, of course, is the further and perhaps more specific requirement that (p. 4) "a musical theory . . . should reduce to . . . a formal theory when uninterpreted predicates and operations are substituted for the terms and operations designating musical observables." In this sense a music theory is "statable as a connected set of axioms, definitions, and theorems, the proofs of which are derived by means of an appropriate logic."

Many readers and commentators have found Babbitt's statements too narrow, contending that they exclude much that one might wish to include under the rubric of 'music theory'. Still others have found reason to invoke the "principle" or pseudoprinciple (whichever it is) that (p. 7) "musical theory must not precede musical practice," contending that at best then theory is a matter of *ex post facto* explication and thus not of fundamental interest as a guide for the composer. This is not the occasion to take up this dispute in any detail. Instead let us attempt to outline on a firm logical basis — but still very tentatively and in an exploratory fashion — a conception of what music theory should be conceived to be.

---

1. Milton Babbitt, "Past and Present Concepts of the Nature and Limits of Music," in *Perspectives on Contemporary Music Theory,* ed. by B. Boretz and E. T. Cone (New York: W. W. Norton Co., 1972), p. 3.

On the whole, Babbitt has been interested primarily in systems dealing with music based on the twelve-tone system. Such systems must be allowed to overflow their banks, however, if the full resources of the electronic media are to be provided for, with their (p. 9) "precise measurability and specifiability of frequency, intensity, spectrum, envelope, duration, and mode of succession. . . ." For these latter, a system incorporating the full *real-number* system would seem needed, the means therewith being provided of giving precise measurements to all possible "intervals" in frequency, intensity, and so on, that are of any musical relevance. After all this is done, we would be in a better position to discuss the relative priority of music theory with the actual practice of composing.

Let us attempt then to sketch a completely general theory in which whatever one might wish to say about music of any kind as far as concerns *structure* can be said. No definition of 'structure' will be attempted, nor for that matter will any attempt be made to delimit the field of music itself. The theory, in fact, will consist of a kind of logical system concerning the relevant aspects of sound, but with the admission of specific predicates whose applicability is in fact to just the kinds of sound (i.e., *sound-events*) that enter into music. Thus where e is a simple or complex vibratory occurrence in physical nature of some kind or other, 'MidA e' or 'A^4e' may express that e is recognizable as consisting of just 440 (or 445 or whatever) vibrations per second, and thus as a middle-A or A^4 event having a certain location on the diatonic scale in a given system of tuning. Many further predicates are needed of course for the further description of e, its timbre, intensity, length of duration, and so on.[2]

What are the ultimate units of musical structure out of which combinations are built? One is tempted to say: *discernible* sound-events — Babbitt's musical observables — but such an answer raises difficult problems concerning what is discernible and what is not. In actual practice the specific predicates used will ordinarily be such as to apply only to discernible or discriminable sound-events, but there is no need to restrict the theory to such only. An electronic "ear" can hear much more than the unaided ear can. Also, there are many sound-events that enter into some kinds of music that cannot explicitly be registered on the diatonic scale, so that it would not be desirable to restrict the ultimate units to just those that can be. Examples are chirps, meeows, flutters, and the like, to say nothing of the vast galaxy of other sounds

---

2. Cf. the author's "On the Proto-Theory of Musical Structure," *ibid.*, pp. 91–96, for some additional introductory remarks.

now regarded as commonplace in even non-electronic music. The ultimate units then are to be taken as all sound-events together with all possible combinations of them, spread out before us, as it were, in full view. Such entities are to be the values for the variables of the theory and are thus to constitute its *universe of discourse* or *ontology*.

Immediately the question arises as to how the combinations are to be built up. Well, for this the devices of the so-called *calculus of individuals* are useful.[3] This calculus provides the theory of the *part-whole* relation, or *mereology*, as Leśniewski called it, in accord with which one sound-event e_1 may be said to be a *part* of a sound-event e_2. Each separate sound-event entering into a chord or density, for example, is a part of the total chord. Or e_1 may be a part of e_2 in the physical sense in which the frequencies for the partials in the overtone series may be said to be a part of the fundamental. The calculus of individuals may be formulated in many ways. One convenient way is to regard it as a straightforward *Boolean algebra* with all manner of sums, products, and negatives admitted, as well as a universal and null element.

Given sound-events e_1 and e_2, the *sum* $(e_1 \cup e_2)$ is the sound-event consisting of the sound-events that are part of e_1 *or* e_2 *or both*. The *product*, $(e_1 \cap e_2)$, is the sound-event consisting of all sound-events that are parts of *both* e_1 and e_2. The product of a major third based on a tonic with the minor third based on the median is just the median, being common to both. The negative $-e$ of a sound-event e is the sound-event consisting of all sound-events (or occurrences of frequencies) *not* contained in e. A *null* element is total silence throughout a given duration, the null element being the sum of all the silences. The *universal* element contains all occurrences of admissible frequencies, and presumably has some kinship with "white noise." By far the most important of these are the sums, products, and null elements. Concerning all of these notions the various laws of Boolean algebra apply appropriately.

Thus far nothing has been said of the spatio-temporal ordering of sound-events. Clearly, explicit provision must be made for both spatial and temporal factors. Usually only temporal considerations are taken into account, but clearly spatial ones are essential also in the arrangement of the players in an orchestra, in quadraphonic sound, and so on. All the sound-events considered are to be discernible to the listener — in principle anyhow. A sound-event taking place in Symphony Hall, for example, cannot be combined with one taking place,

---

3. See especially N. Goodman and H. S. Leonard, "The Calculus of Individuals and Its Uses," *The Journal of Symbolic Logic* 5 (1940): 45–55.

either simultaneously or successively, say, in the Grosser Musikverein-saal in Vienna, with the resulting sum being an item in any musical composition in the usual sense. Just how one lays down such spatial constraints on the sound-events admitted is not perhaps a problem of major difficulty, but still it must be done at some point. In the literature, much more attention has been paid to the temporal ordering in terms of a relation of occurring *before-than*. It seems likely that everything we may wish to say about temporal structure in music, in fact, can be said with the help of such a relation. An analogous comment about logico-linguistics can be made, incidentally, provided means are at hand for handling the deictic or "egocentric" word 'now'.[4]

With the introduction of the temporal *before-than* relation, a distinction may be made between *simultaneous* and *successive* (or non-simultaneous) sound-event combinations. All elements of a simultaneous combination *e* last throughout the entire time-span of *e*, although of course with perhaps changing intensity, timbre, and so on. In a successive combination at least one part of at least one element takes place outside the combination, so to speak. Note that if sound-events e_1 and e_2 are simultaneous but distinct, their sum is the chordal combination of the two. The simultaneous negation of a sound-event *e* is almost total cacophony, consisting of all admissible frequency-occurrences other than *e* but simultaneous with it. The simultaneous universal sound-event is total cacophony throughout its duration. The most interesting and useful of these notions, here also, are no doubt the sums and products.

Thus far we have been speaking only of the sound-events, but not of classes of such. All sound-occurrences of the same frequency may of course be grouped into a class, but they may also be summed to form the one total occurrence of all occurrences (throughout the whole of space and time) of that frequency. The former may be called a *pitch-class*. (Or the pitch-class be regarded as including all discernible sound-events at octave intervals, two-octave intervals, and so on.) The latter, the universal successive sum of all sound-events of the same frequency, seems not to have been given a label. The reason, no doubt, is that reference to the pitch-class, handled by means of a predicate, is more convenient. But clearly any member of a pitch-class determined by a frequency *r* is itself both a sound-event of frequency *r* and a part of the universal successive sum of all sound-events of frequency *r*, and conversely. This is analogous to saying that an object

---

4. *Semiotics and Linguistic Structure, passim.*

x is a member of the class of men if and only if x is a man-part, so to speak, of the universal sum of all men, past, present, and future.

In speaking of all frequency-occurrences, sound-events of all possible, but discriminable, intensities, timbre, duration, and so on, are being included, the 'and so on' here being short for the list *all* physical factors of musical relevance. Has this list ever been spelled out in full detail and with the necessary rigor and precision, and for all possible kinds of music known to us? Probably not. The aim here is to provide a basis for *comparative* music theory, in which all kinds of music whatsoever may be systematically discussed and compared. In this respect, the attempt is similar to that of Cogan and Escot.[5]

Let us consider now how to handle the measurement of intervals of the various relevant physical factors. For this a very considerable theory of measurement is, of course, needed. (It is not clear, incidentally, that such a theory has been adequately developed even for the purposes of physics.) To simplify, let

$$\text{`int}_{\text{fr}}(e_1, e_2) = r\text{'}$$

be introduced to express that the frequency-interval between e_1 and e_2, for appropriate e_1 and e_2, is given the real number r. *And similarly for the other factors* or combinations of such. The use of real numbers rather than the rationals may not be altogether necessary, but can do no harm. They will enable the assignment of measures to irrational magnitudes, should this ever turn out to be needed. (Should the system of *complex* numbers, including the so-called imaginaries, ever turn out to be needed, suitable extensions would have to be made to provide for such.) Concerning each interval-function suitable principles must be forthcoming appropriate to the physical theory concerning that factor, i.e., concerning intensity, spectrum, envelope, duration, and mode of succession. From the linguistic point of view, nothing very difficult in principle emerges here.

Let us reflect now a little on matters concerned with notation. And because of the complexities involved, let attention be confined solely to what Erhardt Korkoschka calls 'präzise Notation'.[6] This includes, of course, most of the notation in current use — as contrasted with mere directives to do such and such — outside of the electronic realm. Just as sound-events are distinguished from classes of such, so *note-events* must be distinguished from *note-types*. (The word 'note'

---

5. Robert Cogan and Pozzi Escot, *Sonic Design, The Nature of Sound and Music* (Englewood Cliffs, N.J.: Prentice-Hall Inc., 1976).

6. Erhardt Korkoschka, *Das Schriftsbild der Neuen Musik* (Celle: Moeck, 1966).

here is being read in a purely syntactical way, and not in the strictly scientific sense, according to which a note consists of a fundamental with its retinue of partials and a *tone* as a sound-event without its accompanying partials.) The distinction is analogous to Peirce's distinction between tokens and types, or that between sign-events and sign-designs in logical syntax. A middle-C or C⁴ note-type is the class of all middle-C note-events.

Now the logical syntax of language, just as a matter of fact, was developed first in terms of sign-designs. Such a treatment, however, is clearly too narrow, for it cannot accommodate the egocentric expression 'I', 'you', 'he', 'she', 'here', 'now', and the like, the referents of which vary with varying occasions of use. Different sign-events of the shape 'I' may thus refer to different persons. If we remain with purely syntactical matters, concerned solely with words or signs and combinations of them, this limitation is not very serious. But syntax is of interest primarily as a prelude to semantics, in which signs are related to the objects they *denote* or refer to or stand for in one way or another. The semantical properties of the egocentric words cannot be studied on the basis merely of a syntax of sign-designs, but need the wider resources of one based on sign-events.

There are other reasons for preferring a syntax based on sign-events over one based on sign-designs. Much of the effect of the latter may be achieved in terms of the former, but not conversely, if the devices of using virtual classes and relations are used.[7] Further there is a simpler kind of ontology presupposed, one dealing only with "concrete" events rather than with "abstract" shapes, in accord with a principle of parsimony. In music theory the situation is similar as regards ontology and parsimony, even though there appear there to be no bothersome egocentric elements to worry about. Even so, music is a *performative* art, its flesh and blood being found in discernible sound-events, and not in anything more abstract; hence the emphasis throughout on sound-events rather than on sound-shapes or sound-patterns. And similarly now in matters concerned with musical notation, where the concern will be with note-events, of which note-types are merely classes or virtual classes.

Combinations of sound-events are handled by means of the sums and products of the calculus of individuals. How are the corresponding combinations of note-events to be handled? By means of *horizontal and vertical juxtapositions or concatenations* of note-events on the musical autograph or score or printed page. Thus *two* kinds of concatenation

---

7. See *Belief, Existence, and Meaning*, Chapter VI.

relations are needed, one for *simultaneous* sound-events, the other for *successive* ones. Let

(1)   '*a* SimulC *b,c*'

express that the note-event or combination *a* is the simultaneous (or vertical or chordal) concatenate of note-events *b* and *c*. Similarly let

(2)   '*a* SucC *b,c*'

express that *a* is the successive (or horizontal or linear) concatenate of *b* and *c*. In (2) the *b* and *c* may themselves be either single note-events or simultaneous or successive concatenates of note-events, whereas in (1) the *b* and *c* are to be either single note-events or simultaneous concatenates of note-events but *not* successive ones. In this way the notation provides for concatenates of chord-events (densities), so to speak, but not for chord-events of concatenates. Further, where (1) obtains the tone-events indicated by *b* and *c* are to *start together* simultaneously, but need not be of the same duration. 'Simultaneous' is thus taken here in a somewhat special sense. Of course we are speaking here only of the notation, and not of the densities or chordal combinations that simultaneous concatenates are supposed to indicate. When we speak of note-events, then, we mean either single ones or simultaneous or successive concatenates. And throughout, of course, when we speak of sound-events, we mean either single ones or any combination of such, however complex.

The abstract theory of musical notation is concerned primarily with the laws governing these two concatenation relations. A specific notation is given by all manner of additional apparatus providing for the various clefs, signatures, and the conventions regarding them. Some of these may be introduced by definition. Still further specificities are needed to handle rhythmic matters, most of these being merely conventions concerning the relative temporal lengths of the sound-events provided for. And similarly for matters of phrasing, intensity markers, and other notational items. A good deal of spelling out of the details of all this is needed of course, but the foundations for it all seem to be provided by the two basic relations. The situation is similar to that in linguistics, in which the theory of the concatenation relation provides the foundation for all of syntax.[8]

Among the note-events admitted are a special kind called 'rests'. Let 'Rest *a*' express that *a* is a rest. A rest may be of long or short duration, it may be linearly concatenated with other note-events either simul-

---

8. See *Truth and Denotation,* Chapters III and XI.

taneously or successively. The duration of rests likewise may be indicated once a suitable notation for durations is introduced.

In speaking of these relations of concatenation, we have been speaking of the general system of "präzise Notation" for most types of music; in other words, of the *logical syntax* of the notation, the metanotation, as it were. Strictly speaking, the notation is a mere *diagram,* making no statements or assertions that may be regarded as true or false. The hallmark of a statement, it will be recalled, is that it is the sort of thing that is true or false — even though we may not know which, and even though no one is, or ever has been or ever will be, able to know which. Strictly speaking, the diagrammatic notation states nothing. There are no subjects, no predicates, and hence no statements. Even so, the diagram does have a *semantic* role to play, to which let us now turn.

A relation of *denotation* is a fundamental relation of logical semantics and of the semantics of natural language.[9] Here too a relation of denotation is needed to be able to say that a given note-event of a given score stands for a sign-event. Let

$$\text{'}a \, \text{Den}_b \, e\text{'}$$

express that note-event a as occurring in the score b denotes sound-event e. In terms of 'Den' the kind of correspondence between notation and actual (or even imaginary) sound-events is established, and without it (or some alternative) there would seem to be no way of interrelating the two. There would be no connection between scores and performances.

Let '$e_1 \, \text{B} \, e_2$' express that sound-event e_1 is *wholly before* e_2 *temporally,* and '$e_1 \, \text{Simul} \, e_2$' that they take place *simultaneously,* each beginning but not necessarily ending together. Then it should presumably obtain that

L1. $\vdash (a)(b)(c)(d)(e_1)(e_2)(e_3)((a \, \text{Den}_d \, e_1 \cdot b \, \text{Den}_d \, e_2 \cdot c \, \text{Den}_d \, e_3 \cdot e_3 = (e_1 \cup e_2)) \supset (e_1 \, \text{B} \, e_2 \equiv c \, \text{SucC} \, a,b))$

and

L2. $\vdash (a)(b)(c)(d)(e_1)(e_2)(e_3)((a \, \text{Den}_d \, e_1 \cdot b \, \text{Den}_d \, e_2 \cdot c \, \text{Den}_d \, e_3 \cdot e_3 = (e_1 \cup e_2)) \supset (e_1 \, \text{Simul} \, e_2 \equiv c \, \text{SimulC} \, a,b)).$

These *principles of correspondence* help to make precise the fundamental relations and are interesting as samples of the kinds of principles in

---

9. *Ibid.,* Chapters IX and XI. See also *Semiotics and Linguistic Structure.*

which music theory as conceived here abounds. **L1** states that, where e_1, e_2, and e_3 are note-events denoted in a given score and e_3 is the logical sum of e_1 and e_2, e_1 bears the before-than relation to e_2 if and only if the note-event denoting e_3 is the successive concatenate of the note-events denoting e_1 and e_2 taken in that order. And **L2** similarly for simultaneous note-events and simultaneous concatenations. Further principles concerning both concatenation and denotation will be given a little later.

Nothing has been said thus far concerning the use of *instruments* for the production of the kinds of sound-events that constitute music. Ontologically speaking, such instruments are concrete physico-temporal *objects*, so that our theory must be extended to provide for such. Thus we need not only the variables for *sound-events* '*e*', '*e*₁', and so on, and '*a*', '*b*', and so on, which have been used for the syntactical *note-events*, but also, say, '*x*', '*y*', and so on, for the *physical objects* that either are or are parts of or are appurtenances to musical instruments. And of course human *persons* (to say nothing of their *actions*) must be admitted, as well as the *real numbers*. Thus for the full theory of music, at least these six types of entities must be admitted and re-garded as values for variables. Logically speaking, we need then a *six-sorted* logic with six different styles of variables. (Of course these sorts may be unified, if desired, and the effect of their separation achieved by suitable predicates.)

At the point at which the human person is introduced, especially in his role of composer, performer (either single or as a member of a group-sum), or listener, we enter musical *pragmatics*, the most com-plex and difficult of the three areas of semiotics. Here all manner of relations are studied, relations between the persons (or sums of per-sons) and the other objects of the theory. Especially important are relations concerned with performing, with the physiology of hearing, and the psychology of musical perception, but all manner of other relations (including social ones) are admitted as well. Musical pragma-tics veers off of course into the study of musical performance and into empirical science and must base some of its results on the history of the former and on advances in the latter. At the same time, as in the pragmatics of natural language, a good deal of interesting material might emerge from purely logical investigations if a serious effort were made. Unfortunately, very little work of a thorough, systematic kind in this area seems to have been undertaken to date.

A word more now about the ontology admitted. In some ontologies *atomic parts* are recognized, and it is interesting to ask what atomic parts (if any) are to be recognized in music. In general terms, an *atom*

214

of a system is any non-null entity that is a part of all its non-null parts.[10] This definition of course characterizes atoms in terms of the part-whole relation available. We must now inquire more deeply than above into the part-whole relation needed for music.

Clearly if the temporal duration of e_2 includes that of e_1 but not conversely, and where no temporal part of e_1 temporally precedes e_2 and no temporal part of e_1 temporally succeeds e_2, then e_1 is a part of e_2. Here e_2 is merely of longer temporal duration. There is also a purely spatial sense. Consider two violins playing together, one giving forth sound-event e_1 and one sound-event e_3. Let $e_2 = (e_1 \cup e_3)$. Sound-event e_1 occupies (or at least originates from) a different spatial area than e_3 does. The spatial area of e_2 is the combined spatial area of $(e_1 \cup e_3)$. Clearly we would wish to say here that both e_1 and e_3 are parts of the sum e_2 in this spatial sense. Given these two senses of 'parts of', there is then a combined sense of 'spatio-temporal part of' to be characterized, just as in the theories of space and time generally.

There is also the sense in which a pure or fundamental tone or any of its partials are said to be parts of the sum of the fundamental with all its partials. Similarly, any sum (spectrum) of partials is a part of any sum of partials including that sum. And so on, where both spatial, temporal, and spatio-temporal considerations are also brought in.

If these reflections are sound, we should recognize as the atoms of our theory just pure or fundamental sound-events having one place of origin, of minimally discernible temporal duration, and of some given intensity. In addition, of course, all discernible combinations or sums are admitted as values for variables as well.

In music based on the 1400 or so discernible pitch-types, all admissible sound events may be regarded as built out of the atoms. Even *glissandi* and the like here can be accommodated as successive sums of atoms. Even so, there is no reason our theory *should* restrict itself to just the atoms and their combinations. With electronic devices a "fluid continuum" of sound-events is available, it is often said, to which with time our ears become sensitized. Is this actually the case, or is this merely a manner of speaking? Are there really frequencies measurable only by means of irrational numbers? No, presumably the rationals alone suffice for this purpose. The fluid continuum here is thus perhaps not a real continuum in the strict mathematical sense, but forms only a dense series, with a frequency between any two but such

---

10. Cf. C. S. Peirce, *Collected Papers*, Vol. III, p. 216; A. Tarski, *op. cit.*, p. 334; "A Homogeneous System for Formal Logic," p. 8; and VII above.

that its constituent frequencies can be put into one-to-one correspondence with the positive rationals including 0.

Is there also a fluid continuum here of intensities? And of tone colors? Yes, presumably, only a small fraction of which are usually used. Nonetheless, they should be provided for in the theory should they ever be needed — and they may well be for the music of the future. The situation is similar to that in mathematics generally, with its non-denumerable totality of real and complex numbers, whereas in many applications to science the rationals alone may be made to suffice. But it is good to have the real numbers available, should they ever be needed, as already suggested.

Let us go on now to a few topics of a somewhat controversial nature.

Semantics thus far has been spoken of only in the sense of the theory of denotation as between note-events and the sound-events for which they stand. Another branch of semantics is concerned with *meaning,* and thus a branch of musical semantics should be concerned with musical meaning. In logico-linguistics the status of the semantics of meaning is at best controversial. Some contend that meanings may be handled wholly in terms of denotation (or perhaps designation), and hence that meanings are constructs of a suitable kind. Others recognize the theory of meaning as a separate branch of semantics, but much more complicated than one based merely on denotation. Still others place a curse on both these kinds of theories and wish meanings to be handled wholly in *pragmatical* terms. To "search not for the meaning but only for the use" becomes the leading maxim for such a view. In fact, the whole field of the logico-linguistic theory of meaning is so fraught with difficulties and controversies at the present time as scarcely to provide any secure guidance when we step to the theory of music. Perhaps, at the moment anyhow, we had better not say very much about it at all until such time as a vocabulary is available in which we could discuss it clearly and responsibly.

Of course human beings in given societies *respond* to suitable structures of musical sound in diverse ways. The full study of this response would cover not only its history, but the psychology and sociology of music as well. Also there are the varying fads and fashions that make up the history of taste. Can we cut through all this and make some statements true of all times and styles? Only by making statements of vast generality but perhaps not much content.

Edward Cone, in his analysis of Vermeer's *View of Delft*, has written eloquently of principles of "polar tension," of "fusion by mutual anal-

ogy," of "textural complexity," and "saturation."[11] Each of these notions needs no doubt a considerable analysis. Collectively they call attention to features of western music of *high quality*. The mere mention
of quality, comparative quality, makes us realize the great distance we
must traverse, from the foregoing kind of language in which structure may be discussed in an exact terminology, to a language in which
the full work of art can be systematically compared and contrasted
with another, and finally judged as to quality.

It is a bit old-fashioned perhaps to speak of quality, in our purported democratic age in which everything is supposed to be as good
as any other, the marketplace alone being the sole arbiter. Even so,
high artistic quality is the one thing the creative artist is continually
seeking, and the item above all that the aesthetician and the historians
of any or all of the arts are interested in. Jakob Rosenberg, in his
Mellon lectures, has written a rather notable book on the subject.
Quality is something we should make more of an effort to inquire into
in an exact way than is usually done, for it is the one item that really
counts for those who love the arts.

Let us return now to the question with which we began, whether or
in what sense knowledge of music theory can or should be used as a
guide in musical practice, i.e., in composing, performing, and listen-
ing. Well, the first thing to say is that one can never know too much of
a good thing. Secondly, as Whitehead put it, one can never know too
much of methods one is always employing, whether consciously or
not. The relevant gloss of Whitehead's comment is that one can never
know too much of the foundations, of the structural principles, underlying the subject at hand. That this is the case for the listener goes
without saying. The deeper his knowledge of all relevant factors, the
deeper is his enjoyment in the richest sense. Coleridge's comment that
poetry gives most pleasure when only generally but not perfectly understood, holds of only the pleasure of an English dilettante.

For the performer, the situation is similar, his analytic knowledge
determining the character of his performances in very fundamental
ways. Different methods of analyzing a score result in very different
conceptions and hence of kinds of performances, and the deeper the
performer's analytic knowledge, the more authentic his performances
are likely to be, *ceteris paribus*. It is often said that composers alone

---

11. E. T. Cone, "Music: A View from Delft," in *Perspectives on Contemporary Music
Theory,* pp. 57–71, p. 59.

have this kind of knowledge and hence are the best performers. Schnabel was an example of an outstanding performer-composer; Prokofiev another (at least of his own works), to say nothing of Alfredo Casella and Georges Enesco — to mention four of the idols of my youth.

When we turn to composing, the most creative and fundamental kind of activity in music, the situation is more complicated. Here it is not a question of something spread out before one in advance that one is to perform or to listen to, but of something to be brought into being almost *ex nihilo*. The logic of 'to compose', so to speak, is very different from that of 'to perform' and from that of 'to listen', as our Oxford friends might tell us. Unfortunately, it is to be feared that the logics of none of these words has been looked at very carefully or deeply.

Edward Cone has written perceptively on this topic, in his "Beyond Analysis," which originated as a paper given at the Berkshire Music Center some years back.[12] In this paper he takes Schoenberg to task for the contention that "the unity of musical space [or of a given composition] demands an absolute and unitary perception," and it is assumed that this perception may be fully and unambiguously made manifest in a set of "analytic principles" fully determinative of the composition at hand. Cone's discussion revolves primarily around Schoenberg's further comment[13] that "in this space . . . there is no absolute down, no right or left, forward or backward. Every musical configuration, every movement of tones has to be comprehended primarily as mutual relation of sounds, of oscillatory vibrations, appearing at different places and times. . . ." Actually the main thrust of Cone's discussion is against the first comment. He argues against the contention of an "absolute and unitary conception" of a composition, and to the effect that a composer's concrete choices among conceivable alternatives (p. 82) "are determined by what may be called *absolute decisions*, i.e., decisions for which no analytical reasons can ever be adduced." He thinks (p. 83) that "there is, and can be, no analytical grounds for concrete musical choices, i.e., no grounds within the internal structure of the music itself; yet . . . these choices are crucial in determining musical values, i.e., salient characteristics that afford a basis for distinction, comparison, and judgment." More emphatically, a composer's reasons for his choices are "beyond analysis." Moreover,

---

12. *Ibid.*, pp. 72–90.
13. From Schoenberg's *Style and Idea* (New York: Philosophical Library, 1950), p. 113.

(p. 90) "the single most important thing any one can say about any composition is beyond analysis; namely, "I like it"."

There is apparently a failure in Cone's comments to distinguish *reasons* for choices from analytical *principles* determinative of structure. These are by no means the same and cannot even be made in the same overall parts of the theoretic language. A discussion of structure is couched wholly in the syntactical-semantical part of the language, whereas all discussion of "reasons" belongs to pragmatics, more particularly, to the biography or autobiography of the composer. And both of these are to be distinguished from the choice of a set of analytical principles laid down prior to composing, and from the discernment of them *ex post facto* by analysis of the structure of the composition once written.

Cone does not contend that analytical principles are beyond analysis, but only the "reasons" for the choice of one set of them over another. But here he would seem to be on dangerous grounds. To contend that anything whatsoever is "beyond analysis" is to block the road to inquiry, the worst of all methodological sins according to C. S. Peirce, that greatest of all methodologists. Suppose one's reasons are pressed back even as far as the "I like it." Are there no reasons ever to be adduced as to *why* I like it? Surely there are, always, whether we are consciously aware of them or not. Is Cone not claiming too much in saying that expressions of liking are the single most important things to be said about a composition? More important surely are the *reasons* for our liking or disliking, especially when they are good reasons based on thorough knowledge and deep experience.

As to the relative priority of theory and practice, the situation seems rather analogous to that in the methodology of sciences generally. Reichenbach, it will be recalled, used to distinguish between the context of *discovery* in science and that of *justification*. We know a good deal about justification, that is, about *deductive* inference, and a little bit about *induction* and *statistical* inference generally. But unfortunately we do not yet know very much about *discovery*, the theory of which is sometimes called 'abduction' or 'retroduction'. Some methodologists believe that such a theory is possible, but in the absence of any compelling data there is not much evidence for such a belief. It is very difficult to say with any precision *beforehand* how a scientist should go about to discover or invent a new hypothesis. If he succeeds in doing so, a good deal can be said about it afterwards. He saw some hitherto unseen connection, he noticed something heretofore neglected, he made a daring assumption no one had made, he questioned a fundamental assumption universally accepted, and so on. But none of these descriptions need suffice as recipes or injunctions to go and do likewise with assured success. Similarly, given a set of determinative analytical principles in advance, the composer is not assured of coming out with a work of art merely by their use. Such principles, so to speak, do not provide an adequate set of abductive premisses. Given the completed work of art, however, we must never rest content until every item of relevant structure is explained as fully as possible. If we stop somewhere along the line here, or fail because our theoretic vocabulary is too narrow or its fundamental assumptions inadequate, we can rest assured that someone else will come along to complete the task. No item of structure is beyond analysis. And similarly with "reasons." In principle no reason for any human choice is beyond past finding out, although in practice this may often be very difficult or impossible to achieve.

Once analytical principles are laid down, how rigidly must they be adhered to? Schoenberg, you will recall, is interesting on this point. In speaking of some of his own works, he commented that "it will be observed that the succession of the tones according to their order in the [basic] set has always been strictly observed. One could perhaps tolerate a slight digression from this order (according to the same principle that allowed a remote variant in former styles) in the later part of a work, when the set had already become familiar to the ear. However, one would not thus digress at the beginning of a piece."[14] According to this, analytic principles may occasionally be violated, but not too much, and not at the beginning. For each such violation, each composer will have his own reasons. After all, in the context of discovery or creation, *le coeur a ses raisons que la raison ne connaît pas* — until afterwards perhaps, in the context of justification.

The question as to whether music is a language has often been discussed, but perhaps never quite satisfactorily. The system sketched above is of course not for music but for the *theory* of music and of "präzise Notation." The theory of music, like any theory, must be couched in language. But how about music itself? Is it a language? A language or language system, in the strict sense, consists of *terms* (proper names or variables) regarded as *subjects, predicates*, and the *logical connectives* and *quantifiers*. The notions of being a *well-formed formula* and a *sentence* must be defined for the language. And certain *semantical rules* must be given stating just how the terms and predicates are related (by designation, denotation, or whatever) to the (usually non-linguistic) entities the language talks about. (If the entities are

---

14. *Ibid.*, p. 117.

themselves linguistic, i.e., signs or symbols of some kind, the language is a metalanguage.) In the case of music theory all of these requirements are easily met. But can they be met for music itself, or for its notation, regarded as object-languages?

The fundamental entities of music, as suggested, are sound-events and their combinations, so that, if music were a language, these very entities would have to be the subjects of sentences. *Of what sentences?* Well, the sentences would have to be complex sums of the sound-events. Of just what sums? Those in a single chord, those in some fixed array, those in some whole composition? These subdivisions seem purely arbitrary and no useful notion of 'sentence' in any strict linguistic sense seems forthcoming. Further, what are the *predicates* of music? There are predicates we use to talk *about* music, of course, but *there is nothing in music itself for a predicate to stand for.* That a given sound-event is a middle-C event is not something ever "stated" in the performance of a musical composition. A listener with absolute pitch or a well-trained ear may recognize it as a middle-C event, of course, but this recognition is not a part of the music itself. Similarly one sound-event may be of greater intensity than its neighboring sound-event. This would be a fact about these sound-events, not something literally stated in the performance of the composition itself. In short, music has nothing corresponding to predicates and nothing corresponding to sentences, and thus should not be regarded as a language in any strict sense. At best, it may be regarded as a kind of pseudolanguage, lacking crucial syntactically and semantically determinative features of language itself.

The very notion that anything is ever "stated" — or questioned or commanded or exclaimed or subjunctivized — in music is at best obscure. People respond to music in certain ways, as already suggested; they "like it" or don't as the case may be, they react with powerful feelings to it or not, they rejoice in the discernment of interesting structure, and so on. But from these rather vague facts it would be difficult to construct any very clear theory concerning the stative or assertory character of music, to say nothing of any interrogative or subjunctive character, except perhaps metaphorically. It is better no doubt to study the emotive and other types of response to music *in their own terms* rather than force the discussion into an ill-fitting vocabulary appropriate only to linguistics.

Music itself is to be contrasted, in one important semantical respect, with musical scores. The ultimate foundations of notation in music are to be found in the theory of simultaneous and successive concatenation, as already suggested. Further, the note-events of a score are

regarded as denoting the appropriate sound-events of any performance of which that score is the score, as already noted. A score itself
is a given sum of note-events appropriately ordered by the
concatenation-relations, and a particular performance (or instance of
the score) is the sum of all the sound-events denoted by the successive
note-events of the score as a whole. Increasingly larger concatenates,
simultaneous or successive, denote increasingly larger sums of the
performance as a whole. In a natural language only some of the concatenates are well-formed and hence are sentences capable of being
truly asserted or denied or questioned or whatever. In the musical
notation *all* of the concatenates are meaningful, significantly denoting
the corresponding combinations of sound-events. (One could call all
such concatenates 'sentences' if one would wish to. Not much would
be gained, however, for there would be no non-sentences — other
than atomic sound-events perhaps — to contrast them with.) Also, all
of the note-events are of the same logical types, so to speak, so that in
the notation, as in the performances themselves, there are no predicates in any strict sense. Thus we had better say that the notation
contains no sentences either, and thus like performances themselves,
fails to have the minimal syntactical requirements of a language in any
strict sense, namely, that it contains predicates and sentences. The
notation, however, as already suggested, is like a diagram, and has a
denotative role to play. The notation is thus in this respect closer to
language than is music itself, which has no denotative function in any
strict sense. Both music and its notation are sharply to be contrasted,
then, with language: Music itself lacks both the syntactical feature of
having predicates and has no semantical, denotative function; musical
notation has no predicates but does have denotative function; a
natural language has both.

Nothing thus far has been said about the axioms or theorems of the
theory of musical structure and notation being discussed. To list even
a moderately complete set would be a formidable task. They would be
of wide generality, covering all kinds of music in the same system.
Cone, incidentally, seems to suggest (on p. 83) that tonal music requires one system, anti-tonal music another, and that for the choice of
axioms some "proof" is needed. Of course one cannot "prove" axioms
but one can justify them in the sense of giving some good reasons as to
their choice. It might be of interest, in closing, to glance at a few of the
different kinds of axioms or theorems needed, without going into the
purely technical details involved in choosing specific ones as axioms,
and without attempting to justify them other than their intuitive acceptability in the light of what has already been said. Such axioms or

theorems are called 'laws'. Two of them, **L1** and **L2** have already been given above.

The theory here is formulated in terms of the two concatenation relations and the relation of contextual denotation — contextual because of the presence of a variable or name for the appropriate compositional context. Let us consider first some laws concerning SucC, which is rather analogous to the concatenation-relation required for the syntax of inscriptions. First it is an *asymmetric* and totally *irreflexive* relation in certain senses appropriate to triadic relations.

L3. $\vdash (a)(b)(c)(a\ \mathrm{SucC}\ b,c \supset\ \sim a\ \mathrm{SucC}\ c,b)$.

L4. $\vdash (a)\sim a\ \mathrm{SucC}\ a,a$.

Also it is *intransitive* in a strong sense.

L5. $\vdash (a)(b)(c)(d)(a')((a\ \mathrm{SucC}\ b,c \bullet (b\ \mathrm{SucC}\ d,a'\ \mathrm{v}\ c\ \mathrm{SucC}\ d,a')) \supset (\sim a\ \mathrm{SucC}\ d,a' \bullet \sim a\ \mathrm{SucC}\ b,d \bullet \sim a\ \mathrm{SucC}\ b,a' \bullet \sim a\ \mathrm{SucC}\ c,d \bullet \sim a\ \mathrm{SucC}\ c,a'))$.

And the relation is *associative* in a suitable sense.

L6. $\vdash (a)(b)(c)(d)(b')(c')((c\ \mathrm{SucC}\ d,c' \bullet b'\ \mathrm{SucC}\ b,d) \supset (a\ \mathrm{SucC}\ b,c \equiv a\ \mathrm{SucC}\ b',c'))$.

Further, the following *limitative* law holds.

L7. $\vdash (a)(b)(c)(a\ \mathrm{SucC}\ b,c \supset (\sim a = b \bullet \sim a = c \bullet \sim b = c \bullet \sim a\ \mathrm{SucC}\ a,b \bullet \sim a\ \mathrm{SucC}\ a,c \bullet \sim a\ \mathrm{SucC}\ b,a \bullet \sim a\ \mathrm{SucC}\ c,a \bullet \sim a\ \mathrm{SucC}\ b,b \bullet \sim a\ \mathrm{SucC}\ c,c \bullet \sim b\ \mathrm{SucC}\ a,c \bullet \sim b\ \mathrm{SucC}\ c,a \bullet \sim b\ \mathrm{SucC}\ b,c \bullet \sim b\ \mathrm{SucC}\ c,b \bullet \sim b\ \mathrm{SucC}\ a,a \bullet \sim b\ \mathrm{SucC}\ c,c \bullet \sim c\ \mathrm{SucC}\ a,b \bullet \sim c\ \mathrm{SucC}\ b,a \bullet \sim c\ \mathrm{SucC}\ c,a \bullet \sim c\ \mathrm{SucC}\ a,c \bullet \sim c\ \mathrm{SucC}\ a,a \bullet \sim c\ \mathrm{SucC}\ b,b))$.

We must stipulate also that the two kinds of concatenation never *coincide*,

L8. $\vdash (a)(b)(c)(a\ \mathrm{SucC}\ a,b \supset\ \sim a\ \mathrm{SimulC}\ a,b)$,

and further that they are distinguished from each other in other significant respects also by laws of *conditional non-existence* such as

L9. $\vdash (a)(b)(c)(a\ \mathrm{SucC}\ b,c \supset\ \sim (\mathrm{E}d)(\mathrm{E}a')(d\ \mathrm{SimulC}\ a,a'\ \mathrm{v}\ d\ \mathrm{SimulC}\ a',a))$

and

L10. $\vdash (a)(b)(c)(d)(a')((a\ \mathrm{SimulC}\ b,c \bullet (d\ \mathrm{SucC}\ a,a\ \mathrm{v}\ d\ \mathrm{SucC}\ a',a)) \supset\ \sim (\mathrm{E}b')(a'\ \mathrm{SimulC}\ b,b'\ \mathrm{v}\ a'\ \mathrm{SimulC}\ c,b'))$.

How now precisely are we to construe simultaneously concatenation? No orientation here seems needed as between up and down, so that SimulC is appropriately symmetrical.

L11. $\vdash (a)(b)(c)(a \text{ SimulC } b,c \supset a \text{ SimulC } c,b)$.

Any orientation needed is supplied by the relative pitches of b and c. Also SimulC can be taken as totally irreflexive in the sense of **L4** and intransitive in the strong sense of **L5** (call these laws **L12** and **L13**) and associative in the sense of **L6** (law **L14**). In place of **L7** the following *limitation law* obtains.

L15. $\vdash (a)(b)(c)(a \text{ SimulC } b,c \supset ({\sim} a = b \bullet {\sim} b = c \bullet {\sim} a = c \bullet {\sim} a$
$\text{SimulC } a,b \bullet {\sim} a \text{ SimulC } a,c \bullet {\sim} a \text{ SimulC } b,b \bullet {\sim} a \text{ SimulC } c,c \bullet$
${\sim} b \text{ SimulC } a,c \bullet {\sim} b \text{ SimulC } a,b \bullet {\sim} b \text{ SimulC } a,a \bullet {\sim} b \text{ SimulC } c,c$
$\bullet {\sim} b \text{ SimulC } b,c \bullet {\sim} c \text{ SimulC } c,b \bullet {\sim} c \text{ SimulC } c,a \bullet {\sim} c \text{ SimulC}$
$a,a \bullet {\sim} c \text{ SimulC } b,b \bullet {\sim} c \text{ SimulC } a,b))$.

This law is a little simpler than **L7** owing to the symmetry of SimulC.

Let us consider now a few laws concerning denotation. This relation, it will be recalled, is relativized to the score, so that a given note-event as occurring in a given score is said to denote the corresponding sound-event as occurring in a performance of that score. (We cannot, however, define 'Score a' as '(Ee)a Den$_a$ e', for to do so would entail that every score is performed. On the other hand, we can define

'e PrfmScore a'   as   'a Den$_a$ e',

that e is a performance of the score a if and only if a Den$_a$ e. No harm will arise from restricting attention for the most part to performed scores.) This relativized relation seems more fruitful as a primitive than one not so relativized.

First there are obvious laws of *univocality* or its lack.

L16. $\vdash {\sim} (a)(b)(c)(e)((a \text{ Den}_b e \bullet c \text{ Den}_b e) \supset a = c)$,
L17. $\vdash (a)(b)(c)(e)((a \text{ Den}_b e \bullet a \text{ Den}_c e) \supset b = c)$,

and

L18. $\vdash {\sim} (a)(b)(e)(e')((a \text{ Den}_b e \bullet a \text{ Den}_b e') \supset e = e')$.

Let 'a PrSeg b' express that a is a *proper segment* of b, that is, a consecutive part of b without gaps. Similarly let 'e_1 PP e_2' express that e_1 is a consecutive *proper part* of e_2. Then the following obtain.

L19. $\vdash (a)(b)(e)((a \text{ Den}_b e \bullet {\sim} a = b) \supset a \text{ PrSeg } b)$,
L20. $\vdash (a)(b)(e)(e')((a \text{ Den}_b e \bullet b \text{ Den}_b e' \bullet {\sim} a = b) \supset e \text{ PP } e')$.

These principles assure respectively that only proper segments of scores denote within a score (other than the score itself) and that everything that denotes within a score (other than the score itself) is a proper segment of any performance of the score.

L21. $\vdash (a)(b)(e)(e')((a \ \mathrm{Den}_b e \cdot e' \ \mathrm{PP} e) \supset (\sim a \ \mathrm{Den}_b e' \cdot (\mathrm{E}c)(c \ \mathrm{PrSeg} a \cdot c \ \mathrm{Des}_b e')))$.

L22. $\vdash (a)(b)(c)(e)((a \ \mathrm{Den}_b e \cdot c \ \mathrm{PrSeg} a) \supset (\sim c \ \mathrm{Den}_b e \cdot (\mathrm{E}e')(e' \ \mathrm{PP} e \cdot c \ \mathrm{Des}_b e')))$.

These last two laws incorporate also principles of *conditional existence*.

Finally, we need some laws over and above **L1** and **L2** above, inter-relating denotation with concatenation. Let '$e_1 \ \mathrm{ImB} e_2$' express that e_1 is *immediately* before e_2 in the sense that nothing falls between them, that is, that

$$(e_1 \ \mathrm{B} \ e_2 \cdot \sim (\mathrm{E}e_3)(e_1 \ \mathrm{B} \ e_3 \cdot e_3 \ \mathrm{B} \ e_2)).$$

Then clearly

L23. $\vdash (a)(b)(c)(d) (e_1)(e_2)((a \ \mathrm{Den}_b e_1 \cdot c \ \mathrm{Des}_b e_2 \cdot e_2 \ \mathrm{ImB} e_1 \cdot d \ \mathrm{SucC} \ c,a) \supset d \ \mathrm{Den}_b (e_1 \cup e_2))$,

L24. $\vdash (a)(b)(c)(d)(e_1)(e_2)((a \ \mathrm{Den}_b e_1 \cdot c \ \mathrm{Den}_b e_2 \cdot e_1 \ \mathrm{ImB} e_2 \cdot d \ \mathrm{SucC} \ a,c) \supset d \ \mathrm{Den}_b (e_1 \cup e_2))$.

The twenty-four laws are stated here tentatively and may need revision before being wholly acceptable. Similar remarks apply of course to the whole framework. The more precisely one tries to formulate the theory, the more difficult it becomes, and the more do seemingly unimportant details loom large.

Some readers in fact may question the detailed use here of the methods of logical analysis in music theory. Too many trees for the forest, they say, too much elaboration of unimportant detail, and so on. Well, it is a fact concerning the various fields of human knowledge that the deeper one probes into them, the more puzzling and difficult, and indeed the more detailed, they become. Much depends also on the degree of sophistication of one's probing. For beginners in music theory, the details here are not especially interesting perhaps. But as one delves further into the subject, the larger they loom. *Gott wohnt im Detail,* an old German saying has it — more particularly, in *logical* detail, one should add. Also the attempt to characterize the logical structure of a theory is a great aid to coming to *understand* it, as all who have done so well attest. There is a great deal of contemporary philosophical discussion concerning *hermeneutics,* the general theory of what it means to understand things, sentences, texts, poems, works of art, and so on. Now nothing can take the place of detailed logical analysis as an aid to understanding — indeed this is its whole *raison d'être*. Unfortunately, most of the writers on hermeneutics have failed to avail themselves of the advantages of such analysis, and somehow find themselves opposed to it. They tend to mistake logical analysis for whatever it is that is analyzed, and contrast the one to the other unfavorably. But the two are so different as to be scarcely comparable. The waves of the sea are very different from the mathematical theory of Fourier series, and no one would condemn the one for not being the other. And although the waves of the sea are seemingly unruly and amorphous, this does not mean that the mathematical theory concerning wave phenomena in general need be — otherwise the science of mathematical physics would be impossible.

Enough now of these lucubrations concerning method and the logical structure of music theory. At this point one may well feel as Walt Whitman did at the lecture of the learn'd astronomer:

> When I heard the learn'd astronomer:
> When the proofs, the figures, were ranged in columns before me;
> When I was shown the charts and diagrams, to add, divide, and
>   measure them;
> When I, sitting, heard the astronomer, where he lectured with
>   much applause in the lecture-room,
> How soon, unaccountable, I became tired and sick:
> Till rising and gliding out, I wonder'd off by myself,
> In the mystical, moist night-air, and from time to time,
> Looked up in perfect silence at the stars.

Well, let us not mistake the marvelous enjoyment of looking at the stars with the great scientific achievement that constitutes modern astronomy — nor the wonders and greatness of music with the attempt to get an exact theory concerning it.

CHAPTER XV

On Worldmaking and
Some Aesthetic Relations

Omnium rerum principia parva sunt.

What emerges is Nelson Goodman's *Ways of Worldmaking*[1] can perhaps be described, we are told (p. x), as a "radical relativism under rigorous restraints, that eventuates in something akin to irrealism." The question immediately arises: irrealism with respect to what? With respect to essences, real classes and relations, angels, Homeric gods and goddesses, all abstract objects generally, real numbers, the theoretical constructs of mathematical physics: yes. But with respect to *some* ontology taken as fundamental: no. Some individuals there must be as values for the variables to range over, some entities for Goodman's quantifiers to cover, some (virtual) classes or relations for the predicates to designate (in the sense of XIII above). To determine with any precision just what sorts of entities, to say nothing of the virtual classes and relations, are needed here is by no means easy. One sort is clearly indispensable, however: acts of worldmaking, acts of delineating (p. x) "the structure of the several symbol systems of the sciences, philosophy, the arts, perception, and everyday discourse," in other words, acts of formulating constructional systems or something closely akin to them. With respect to such acts Goodman's view is as realist as can be, as he would no doubt admit. Perhaps also it is realist with respect to a good deal else, as we shall consider as we go on. Meanwhile note the staggering variety of worldmakings allowed, embracing the systems of the sciences (including mathematics), of the arts, of alternative philosophies, of theories of perception, of conception too (regarded as symbol systems and thus presumably metalinguistic in some sense[2]), and, finally, of the system(s) of everyday discourse (presumably natural languages *in use*). Such breadth of scope is of the kind every true philosopher should aim at, and not just prog-

---

1. (Indianapolis: Hackett Publishing Co., 1978).
2. Cf. *Events, Reference, and Logical Form,* pp. 15ff.

rammatically in general outline but with as much attention to detail as possible, within the inevitable limitations of his knowledge and understanding of these several fields.

The very title intrigues. Note the gerundive 'worldmaking' and note that it is one word, not two. And note that it is not 'making of a world' or 'making of worlds', for these latter would presumably involve the existence of that which is referred to as made or being made. 'Ways of' is presumably paraphrastic of 'in the manner of'. Thus where

$$\text{'}{<}\text{Worldmake}{>}e\text{'}$$

express that e is an act or process of worldmaking, the virtual-class expression

$$\text{'}\{e \ni (\mathrm{E}e')(e \text{ In}_{\text{Manner}} e' \cdot {<}\text{Worldmake}{>}e')\}\text{'}$$

stands for or designates the virtual class of the processes taking place in the manner of some worldmaking. 'Way(s) of' may be represented by a special *Of-relation,* that of *manner or way,* so that the "principle" (if such it be)

$$\text{'}(e)(e')(e \text{ Of}_{\text{Way}} e' \equiv e \text{ In}_{\text{Manner}} e')\text{'}$$

expresses the paraphrasis mentioned. Even if this should not hold in general, it surely holds for suitable e and e'. A closer represenation of the title is then

$$\text{'}\{e \ni (\mathrm{E}e')(e \text{ Of}_{\text{Way}} e' \cdot {<}\text{Worldmake}{>}e')\}\text{'}.$$

Or, if 'Way' be taken predicatively, so that 'Way e' expresses that e is a way-state or -process, and 'Of$_{\text{Kind}}$' stands for the *Of-relation of kind*[3],

$$\text{'}\{e \ni (\text{Way } e \cdot e \text{ Of}_{\text{Kind}} \{e' \ni {<}\text{Worldmake}{>}e'\})\}\text{'}$$

gives a still closer representation of the title.

These considerations are not mere *bagatelles*, as they might appear to be to the uninitiate, but have immediate relevance in helping us to grasp the real logical content of Goodman's view. The theory they are contained in, a kind of event-logic, will help us step by step to ferret out the very considerable richness of Goodman's ontology as well as to get at the logical character of the basic classes and relations being employed. No reading short of this is worthy of a work by the author of *The Structure of Appearance,* a landmark in the development of applied logic in a philosophical domain.

---

3. Cf. "Of 'of' " in *Pragmatics, Truth, and Language.*

A philosopher can be judged by the character of his metavocabulary, including as it does that of all lower levels. Sparseness, *ceteris paribus,* is an important factor determinative of its character, although of course not the only one. Goodman is noted for his sparseness, but there appears less of it here than in his earlier writings. There is a greater leniency, the emphasis shifting from the character of the world built (the nature of the constructional system formulated) to the acts of building (formulating) it. "If I ask about the world [pp. 2–3], you can offer to tell me how it is under one or more frames of reference; but if I insist that you tell me how it is apart from all frames, what can you say? We are confined to ways of describing whatever is described. Our universe, so to speak, consists of these ways rather than of a world or of worlds." *Our* universe, note, not *the* universe — our human universe of conceptual activity, of metalinguistic symbol-system building, of worldmaking or worlddescribing. This is all straightforward enough, unless we go to the extreme of *denying* the existence of any world or parts thereof, to describe. If we do this, as Goodman comes close to doing, an "irrealism" with respect to the existence of worlds develops, but not with respect to worldmakings, as already suggested.

Goodman's main concern here is in symbol-systems for the arts. He embraces an out and out pluralism and shows little interest in bringing them all together into a unified whole. Although those required for the sciences are given short shrift, "the pluralists' acceptance [p. 5] of versions other than physics implies no relaxation of rigor but a recognition that standards different from yet no less exacting than those applied in science are appropriate for appraising what is conveyed in perceptual or pictorial or literary versions." A chief difference between science and the arts revolves around *truth*. In the nonverbal arts there is great freedom (p. 17) "to divide and combine, emphasize, order, delete, fill in and fill out, and even distort," but little if any concern for truth. But even (p. 18) "the scientist who supposes that he is single-mindedly dedicated to the search for truth deceives himself. . . . He seeks system, simplicity, scope; and when satisfied on these scores he tailors truth to fit. He as much decrees as discovers the laws he sets forth, as much designs as discerns the patterns he delineates." By 'truth' here of course is meant literal truth, truth of "what is said literally," not metaphorically, and "in a scientific treatise literal truth counts most."

The question immediately arises as to whether "literal truth" is to be handled by means of the semantical predicate for truth, and if so, which one — for there are many competing ones on the marketplace.

Goodman's use of 'true in an actual world' is sufficiently close to the semantical notion to justify the supposition of an affirmative answer to this question. But truth is subsumed under a more general notion of "rightness of fit." We are told (p. 132) that "a statement is true, and a description or representation right, for a world it fits. And a fictional version, verbal or pictorial, may if metaphorically construed fit and be right for a world. Rather than attempting to subsume descriptive and representational rightness under truth, we shall do better, I think, to subsume truth along with these under the general notion of rightness of fit."

It is not clear just why such a procedure would be "better" so far as concerns the sciences. The semantical notion of truth is an extremely helpful one, fully and clearly characterized in appropriate metalanguages for given constructional systems. In fact it can be regarded as a veritable paradigm notion, of a kind rarely attained in philosophy or methodology. The semantical theory concerning it, likewise, is a paradigmatic kind of theory in comparison with which most other theories fall far short. As over and against this notion that of "rightness to fit" seems rather underdetermined. In particular, we are told too little about it to be confident that any such notion can be given a sufficiently precise characterization even for the methodology of the sciences. The sheer generality required of it is staggering. Too much seems subsumed too quickly under too a broad a rubric for very much explanatory theory to emerge.

The converse procedure is perhaps preferable. Use such well-entrenched and clear notions we have, especially those of logic and semantics, as our best guides to forage our way into the difficult problems concerning descriptions and representations of all kinds, verbal and other, metaphorical, fictional, and so on. We should realize straightaway the great power of the semantical truth-predicate as regards the enormity of the kinds of sentences to which it is applicable — to all sentences of a natural language, provided these are properly arranged hierarchically in some fashion to include also metalinguistic sentences, metametalinguistic ones, and so on.[4]

For example, suppose we were to spell out in full detail just what it means for a pictorial style to "fit" — to "worldfit," no doubt, we should say. The style must exhibit a suitable design, use of color and shape, organization, and so on, in accord with whatever the determinative characteristics of that style are taken to be. In any particular instance, *a very deep and detailed characterization of the style by experts is*

---

4. Cf., e.g., Zellig Harris, *op. cit.*

needed. For a given painting to "fit" that style is then for it to exhibit some at least of those determinative characteristics. No doubt it would be better to use here a *comparative* notion of *fits-more-than*. But in any case, enough of the determinative characteristics would be exhibited either to say that the painting fits or to say that it does not. "Rightness of fit" may thus be described harmlessly in terms of the truth of sentences concerning fit. The painting has rightness of fit to a given style provided the sentence that says that it fits the given style is true. Rightness of fit or the relational *fits-more-than* should no more be subsumed under truth than the other way around. Truth is with us willy-nilly, along with the other basic notions of logic. Any attempt to circumvent the very fundamental character of the truth-predicate is thus as unwise as any attempt to avoid using the truth-functions and quantifiers themselves would be. Truth is an essential notion of semantics, semantics being now almost universally regarded as a part of logic writ broadly.

Goodman puts forward what amount to three objections to the classical truth-notion just discussed (pp. 120 ff.). "First, and of least importance," he says, "the familiar dictum " 'Snow is white' is true if and only if snow is white" must be revised to something like 'Snow is white' is true in a given world if and only if snow is white in that world,"...." (It would be better here perhaps to write "true-in-world-W" so that nothing concerning the existence of W is presupposed, in accord with Goodman's intent.) Such a revision is not needed, however, the semantical truth-predicate having *always* been relativized to a language- or constructional system. Such systems are always taken, in the context of some inquiry or discussion, as providing a "true version." Goodman goes on to note that his "revision" of the instance concerning snow of the original Tarski paradigm "in turn, if differences between true versions cannot be firmly distinguished from differences between worlds, amounts merely to " 'Snow is white' is true according to a true version if and only if snow is white according to that version." Yes, of course, in view of the comment just made. Thus no revision is needed on this score either.

A second objection is that because truths conflict, we are reminded "effectively that truth cannot be the only consideration in choosing among statements or versions. . . . Some truths are trivial, irrelevant, unintelligible, or redundant; too broad, too narrow, too boring, too bizarre, too complicated;" or too ambiguous in the given context of use; and so on. There is shift here from talk of truth to talk of "choosing" among statements (or versions) presumed true. Of course, in *choosing* among truths for some given purpose all manner of criteria may be used. Criteria for choosing are not criteria for truth and are irrelevant for the latter, but not conversely. Note the epistemic character of the items in Goodman's list: 'trivial', 'unintelligible', and so on, which properly should be relativized to a given *speaker* or user of language, and perhaps even to a given *context*. A statement may of course be unintelligible to a person at one time but not at another.

"Further, we no more characteristically proceed by selecting certain statements as true and then applying other criteria to choose among them rather than by selecting certain statements as relevant and serviceable and then considering which among them are true." Well, the temporal order here is not important, so that, although "this account does not deny that truth is a necessary condition," it by no means follows that it "deprives it of a certain preeminence." Further, pragmatical criteria for "selecting statements" are relative to a given purpose or inquiry, those for truth being always for the purpose of selecting truths. And "how we characteristically proceed" is not necessarily to be recommended, it being almost always haphazard, unruly, and hit or miss, usually miss. The key item of *success* in characteristic procedure is left out here, the analysis of which presumably would require fundamental reference to truth.

More important is Goodman's third objection, that "truth is no more a necessary than a sufficient consideration for a choice of a statement. Not only may the choice often be a statement that is more nearly right in other respects over one that is the more nearly true, but where truth is too finicky, too uneven, or does not fit comfortably with other principles, we may use the nearest amenable and illuminating lie. Most scientific laws are of this sort: not assiduous reports of detailed data but sweeping Procrustian simplifications."

Whether truth is a necessary criterion or not for selecting reports of data and general hypotheses in science has been much debated, but there seems to be almost universal agreement that downright falsehood (if known) is to be avoided wherever possible. Note also that the contention here rests fundamentally upon a kind of Popperian notion of *more-nearly-true-than,* the very meaning of which is in considerable doubt.[5] Also the relation of being *more-nearly-right-than,* called attention to a moment back, is employed here, rather than out and out rightness to fit. Of neither of these, unfortunately, is any suitable analysis given. And on Goodman's own grounds, would it not seem unwise to contend that scientific generalizations are simplifications?

---

5. See especially Herbert Keuth, *Realität und Methode* (Tübingen: J. C. B. Mohr (Paul Siebeck), 1978).

Of what? one may ask. For him such statements are specific items in ways of worldmaking, to be accepted or rejected in much the same way as one would accept or reject a painting as fitting or not fitting a given style. Scientific generalizations even stochastic ones, may indeed be simplifications, but Goodman seems to have no right, not even the vocabulary, to make the contention.

The only predicates Goodman, as an arch-nominalist and a hyperextensionalist, admits are those for virtual classes and relations, as already suggested. The usual principles of extensionality and of the identity of indiscernibles hold for such entities, so that virtual class F is identical with virtual class G, for example, if and only if every member of F is a member of G and conversely. Note, however, that Goodman speaks of "characteristics" and even of "properties" of a work of art without apology and without suggesting how the identity of such entities (or pseudoentities) is to be handled. This is surely not in accord with his avowal of "no relaxation of rigor" when we turn from the symbol-systems of science to those of the arts.[6] The method of treating them metalinguistically is of no avail, for expressions for the work of art and for its properties must be accommodated in the same language. In any case, the point needs clarification.

A related problem concerns the individuation of acts of worldmaking. Under what circumstances can a worldmaking e_1 be identical with the worldmaking e_2? Also, worldmakings are not indivisible wholes, but allow of decomposition into *parts* in various ways. No doubt the calculus of individuals is needed for this. What then, are the parts of a worldmaking e, and how do we recognize them? A considerable discussion of this would seem needed, especially as regards worldmaking for the arts. For the sciences the situation is somewhat clearer, but even here fraught with difficulty. To be sure, Goodman does not explicitly speak of *acts* of worldmaking, but to do so is eminently natural and does no violence to the essentials of his view.

Almost nothing has been said thus far concerning nominalism, other than the suggestion that the primitive predicates needed for the theory of worldmaking be regarded as standing for virtual classes or relations rather than real ones. Goodman comments (p. 95) that "in this general discussion of worldmaking I do not impose nominalistic restrictions, for I want to allow for some difference of opinion as to what actual worlds there are." Note here the ambiguity as to where nominalistic restrictions might be imposed: upon the general theory of worldmaking itself, or upon the devices needed to make some par-

---

6. Cf. *Ways of Worldmaking*, p. 95.

ticular world or kind of world. For the former, we may suppose that nominalistic restrictions are to remain intact, but not for the latter in view of the "differences of opinion as to what actual worlds there are."

The question arises as to whether such a neutral position is possible, however, in view of the metacharacter of the semantics involved for a platonistic system. Consider the worldmaking of some branch of mathematical physics in which, say, the full real-number system is needed fundamentally. Any resulting system would presumably be a platonistic one. Now any general theory of worldbuilding that would include that particular case would presumably be couched in a metalanguage containing that system (or a translation of that system into the metalanguage) as a part. Hence it would have to be platonistic in at least that part. But the metalanguage also must be "essentially richer" (in Tarski's telling phrase) than the object-language in some crucial respects. The usual way is to countenance variables of still higher logical type. Thus if the semantics is of this usual Tarskian kind, it must be platonistic in this second way also. Thus if we assume the general theory of worldmaking to meet nominalistic requirements, it seems, we must impose such restrictions also upon all the worldmakings countenanced in that theory.

It was mentioned above that Goodman comes close to denying the existence of the worlds made. "We do better," he writes (p. 96), "to focus on versions rather than worlds. Of course, we want to distinguish between versions that do and those that do not refer, and to talk about the things and worlds, if any, referred to; but these things and worlds and even the stuff they are made of . . . are fashioned along with the things and worlds themselves. Facts . . . are theory-laden; they are as theory-laden as we hope our theories are fact-laden." If there are no things or worlds to be referred to, however, it is not clear how words or phrases can be used to refer to them. All talk of reference should be revamped, to accord with Goodman's account, in terms of suitable predicates rather than in terms of a relation of reference. Just as we could say that some inscription of 'Pegasus' is a Pegasus-referring expression, so we now say that a proper name, say an inscription of 'Boston', does not refer to the home of the bean and the cod but rather is a Boston-referring expression. Every occasion in which Goodman uses 'refers' or 'reference' should be revamped accordingly. At best this would result in extremely awkward locutions and may not even be theoretically possible, given the incredibly complex ways compound names may be built up. And similarly for compound predicates for virtual classes and relations.

Note the jump, in the passage just quoted, from talk of facts and theory-ladenness to talk of things and worlds. Facts may be theory-laden and theories fact-laden, but are things and worlds (if any) then fact- and theory-laden without facts and theories being thing- and world-laden? What is the connection anyhow between fact or theory and thing or world? Does Goodman have any right here to use either 'fact' or 'theory' other than as standing for suitable inscriptions, which in turn are results of inscription-making?

Worlds are not "built from scratch. We start, on any occasion, with some old version or world that we have on hand and that we are stuck with until we have the determination and skill to remake it into a new one. . . . Worldmaking begins with one version and ends with another." The obvious comment is of course that somehow the ball does have to get started rolling, and incipient worldmakings may be so neanderthalic as scarcely to be worthy of being called such at all. A moment's glance at the historical actualities of either the sciences or the arts, or of language, should suffice to convince us of this. But, on the other hand, this contention does call needed attention to the historical continuity of activity in these fields and that, in each, development proceeds, either gradually or "catastrophically," by absorbing in one way or another what has preceded.

Goodman's main contention throughout — an admirable one — is that exclusive emphasis on semantical truth or (p. 102) "versions [of worldmaking] that are literal, denotational, and verbal," . . . "leave out perceptual and pictorial versions and all figurative and exemplificational means and all nonverbal media. The worlds of fiction, poetry, painting, music, dance, and the other arts are built largely by such nonliteral devices as metaphor, by such non-denotational means as exemplification and expression, and often by use of pictures or sounds or gestures or other symbols of non-linguistic systems." This emphasis is surely all to the good, as serious contemporary students of the arts will agree. Also it calls attention to the fact that such relations as *representing, exemplifying*, and *expressing*, among others, to say nothing of relations needed for the analysis of metaphor, should be studied with greater rigor and in greater detail than heretofore in the contexts of their use in the theory of the several arts. Also it is good to emphasize (again, p. 102) that "the arts must be taken no less seriously than the sciences as modes of discovery, creation, and enlargement of knowledge in the broad sense of advancement of the understanding" — again, a point well recognized by sophisticated critics, aestheticians, and artists alike. Less well accepted is the contention (p. 107) that "even if the ultimate product of science, unlike that of art, is a literal verbal or mathematical, denotational, theory, science and art proceed in much the same way with their searching and building." It is emphasis upon this last that is probably the most original feature of Goodman's view. Heuristically this is a most valuable point, but still, by way of substantiation, a detailed analysis of ways of science-building and of ways of art-making are needed as a prelude to some systematic comparison of the two. Undoubtedly there would turn out to be much in common, but also much not.

Goodman uses 'denotation' in a broad sense in accord with which a painted portrait of a person, for example, may be said to denote uniquely the person portrayed and pictures in an ornithological guide-book to denote generally the birds pictured. The distinction between unique and general (or singular and multiple) denotation here is important. Even so, there is a long tradition that 'denotation' be taken more narrowly to stand for a relation only between word and object, and not between a nonlinguistic entity and an object. For this latter 'represents' can be used equally well, and in effect Goodman does use it so. The behavior of 'denotes' is subject to exact semantical rules just as 'truth' is. At this stage, it would seem unwise to run counter to such well-entrenched usage and rules. We should go on to see rather what rules are needed to characterize 'represents', 'expresses', and so on, in the most satisfactory way for theory-of-art-building. Some of these may of course turn out to be analogous to those concerning 'true' and 'denotes'; but no matter, they are to be distinguished from them nonetheless. The situation is similar to that in quantitative mathematics, where

$$`(1 + 1) = 2'$$

holds for natural, rational, real, and complex numbers. Still there are four quite distinct laws here, and very different as to content.

The theory of worldmaking in the arts is best seen then, perhaps, as the study of certain specifically aesthetic *relations,* the full theory of which is still in its infancy. Important among these are those to which Goodman calls attention, but there are probably more, and many gradations among those he considers. As already suggested, *comparative* relations here are perhaps more interesting than the positive ones. Relations such as *exemplifies-more-than, expresses-more-than,* and even *represents-more-than* are perhaps more useful than the positive cases of them. In any case, the positive cases are presumably definable in terms of them, but not conversely.

Every philosophical or other paper or book is an exercise in worldmaking. Goodman's book is such, and so is this present paper. Some worldmakings are more programmatic than others. Goodman's book is perhaps best viewed as calling our attention to an important kind of work in the theory of the arts yet to be done than as a finished statement of what is already accomplished. As such it is extremely important. The tasks ahead of us, however, are formidable, and will revolve around attempting to characterize the fundamental aesthetic relations in as precise a vocabulary as we can.

Let us consider first, say, the positive case of representation as between the painted picture (or part of such) and the object or objects pictured. Representation in this sense is to be distinguished sharply from denotation, as already suggested, this latter being reserved for its primal role in the analysis of natural language. Representation, like denotation, however, may — if regarded as a dyadic relation — be singular or multiple; it is neither a one-many nor a many-one relation; presumably it is irreflexive, asymmetrical, and intransitive; and so on. Being theory-laden and intentional, however, it is probably best handled by means of the Fregean *Art des Gegebenseins*[7] and hence as a *triadic* relation. Let

(1)   'α Repr x,a'

express (primitively) that picture or picture-part α represent the object or event x as taken under the linguistic description a, where a is a one-place predicate. (One-place predicates of course *designate* virtual classes (as in XIII above), or, alternatively, *denote* just the members of them.) A fundamental *Rule of Representation* is then that

ReprR1. $\vdash (\alpha)(x)(a)(\alpha$ Repr $x,a \supset x$ Under $a)$,

where 'x Under a' expresses that x is taken under the one-place predicate a (again, as in XIII). Let 'Pict α' express that α is a picture or painting and let 'Obj x' and 'Ev x' express respectively that x is an object or an event. 'PredConOne a' expresses that a is a one-place predicate-constant, and 'P' stands for the relation of part to whole. The fundamental *Limitation Principle* for Repr is then that

ReprR2. $\vdash (\alpha)(x)(a)(\alpha$ Repr $x,a \supset ((\text{Pict } \alpha \text{ v } (E\beta)(\text{Pict } \beta \cdot \alpha \text{ P } \beta)) \cdot (\text{Obj } x \text{ v Ev } x) \cdot \text{PredConOne } a))$.

Also there is a great multiplicity of accepted *Specificity Principles* stating that given pictures do in fact represent given objects or events in specific ways (or by means of given predicate-descriptions). These are provided schematically thus:

---

7. See G. Frege, Begriffsschrift, §8 and "Über Sinn und Bedeutung," second paragraph, or *loc. cit.*

ReprR3. ⊢ ⌐α Repr x,a⌐ , where in place of 'α' names or
(Russellian) descriptions of certain pictures or
picture-parts are inserted, in place of 'x' certain names
or Russellian) descriptions are inserted,
and in place of 'a' certain structural- (or shape-)
descriptive names.[8]

The list of statements given by **ReprR3** is of especial importance, on which the whole empirical part of the theory is based. **ReprR1** and **ReprR2** are more or less logical principles, so to speak. **ReprR3** purports to tell us *specifically* what objects are represented, as well as what they are represented as. This list is of course incredibly long, even if attention is confined, say, to modern Western painting within just a few centuries. And the list is long even for any *one* painting that contains any representative parts at all. One and the same man can be represented in the same portrait, for example, as an Englishman, as a musician, as wealthy, as tall, as snub-nosed, as clear-skinned, and so on and on. It is by means of the multiplicity of such statements, accepted or taken as true, that the full empirical "meaning" of 'Repr' is revealed.

Of the three principles, **ReprR1** is the least satisfactory. Let us recall (from XIII) that a pragmatized Under-relation is for general purposes more satisfactory than the semantical one used in **ReprR1**. In general it is better to use

$$\text{'}p \text{ Under} x,a\text{'},$$

expressing that *person p* takes x under the predicate-description a, in place of 'x Under a'. Perhaps then it would be desirable to reconstrue Repr itself as a pragmatical relation, by bringing in the person (painter or beholder) according to whom the painting is said to represent so and so. Thus we may let

$$(2) \qquad \text{'}\alpha \text{ Repr}_p x,a\text{'}$$

now be the favored form. In place of **ReprR1** we might now assume that

ReprR1'. ⊢ $(p)(\alpha)(x)(a)(\alpha \text{ Repr}_p x,a \supset p \text{ Under } x,a)$.

But even this principle would not capture the *occasions* of p's taking x under a, nor for that matter the occasions of a painting's representing something for someone. One and the same painting may be taken by

---

8. Strictly this Rule should be written in inscriptional terms. To simplify, however, here and below reference will be to shapes instead.

one and the same person as representing a so and so on one occasion, but not on another, or a so and so on one occasion and a such and such on another. Its representational character is not something a painting possesses necessarily once and for all, but may vary occasion to occasion, or even from culture to culture. To accommodate this variation, which we should be able to do in any adequate theory, event-descriptive predicates may be brought in, so that

(3) $\qquad\qquad$ '$<\alpha,\mathrm{Repr},p,x,a>e$'

and

$$\text{'}<p,\mathrm{Under},x,a>e\text{'}$$

express respectively that e is a state or act of α's being taken by person p to represent x under a, and that e is a state or act of p's taking x under a. In place of **ReprR1'** we would then have that

ReprR1''. $\quad \vdash (e)(p)(\alpha)(x)(a)(<\alpha,\mathrm{Repr},p,x,a>e \supset <p,\mathrm{Under},x,a>e)$.

Or, alternatively, if *parts* of states or acts are recognized in a suitable way, we might require rather that

ReprR1'''. $\quad \vdash (e)(p)(\alpha)(x)(a)(<\alpha,\mathrm{Repr},p,x,a>e \supset (Ee')(e'\ \mathrm{P}\ e \bullet$
$\qquad\qquad <p,\mathrm{Under},x,a>e'))$.

If one or another of these pragmatized forms are adopted, suitable pragmatized forms for **ReprR2** and **ReprR3** must be used also. For **ReprR2**, predicates 'Pntr$_\alpha$' for the painter and 'Vwr$_\alpha$' for the viewer of α are needed, and p is stipulated to be one or the other.

In *Languages of Art*,[9] Goodman distinguishes two senses of 'representation-as'. "To say [p. 27] that a picture represents the Duke of Wellington as an infant, or as an adult, or as the victor at Waterloo is often merely to say that the picture represents the Duke at a given time or period — that it denotes [represents] a certain (long or short, continuous or broken) temporal part or 'time-slice' of him. . . . The second use is illustrated when we say that a given picture represents Winston Churchill as an infant, where the picture does not represent the infant Churchill but rather represents the adult Churchill as an infant" — in infant's clothes, say, with a bottle and rattle.

Both of these uses may readily be handled by means of (1) or (2) by suitably varying the 'a' or otherwise arranging the notation appropriately. Thus if 'DW$_t$' is a proper name for the Duke of Wellington at time t (for constant 't'), the a may be taken merely as

---

9. (Indianapolis: The Bobbs-Merrill Co., 1968).

(4) $\qquad\qquad\qquad\qquad$ '$\{p \ni p = DW_t\}$'.

For the second kind of use the 'a' is taken as giving the content, so to speak, of the representation and is not of the simple form (4). Thus where 'WC' is a proper name for the adult Winston Churchill, the a would be taken for the virtual class of adult persons dressed like infants, with a rattle and bottle, or whatever. The first use is that in which a painting is said to represent a so and so *as such*. The second is genuine *representation-as* in Goodman's sense.

It is important also to distinguish, as Goodman does, between a picture that represents a man (an actual one) and a *man-picture*. "What," he asks (p. 21), "do pictures of Pickwick or of a unicorn represent? They do not represent anything; they are representations with null denotation. Yet how can we say that a picture represents Pickwick, or a unicorn, and also say that it does not represent anything? Since there is no Pickwick and no unicorn, what a picture of Pickwick and a picture represent is the same. Yet surely to be a picture of Pickwick and to be a picture of a unicorn are not at all the same."

There are at least two technically different ways of handling this matter. The first is to regard 'Man-picture', 'Unicorn-picture', and so on, as primitives. So enormous a number of such primitives is required, however, that it would be very difficult to list them all. And concerning each one suitable postulates would be needed laying down its salient characteristics. Also methods would have to be provided for to build up complex predicates of the form 'F-picture' in terms ultimately of the primitives. A simpler method is to admit a *null entity* and to allow it to be represented under as many predicate-descriptions as are desirable. We can then define

'M-picture$_p\ \alpha$' as '(Ex)α Repr$_p x$,'M'',

where 'M' is the predicate 'is a man'. For α to be a man-picture for p is then for α to be taken by p as representing something (perhaps only the null thing) under the predicate 'M'.[10]

Many different kinds of representation are of course to be recognized. Some are merely accidental and some are explicitly intended by the painter. The viewer may regard a painting as representing something not intended by the painter, or fail or refuse to regard it as representing something intended by the painter. Some representational paintings are *veridical,* or genuinely *denotative,* those, namely, in which the predicate-description actually denotes (in the proper lin-

---

10. On the null individual, see especially "Of Time and the Null Individual."

guistic sense) the object represented. Some representational paintings are of objects, but some of course are of events, episodes, happenings, and the like. And most representational paintings are of course representational in more than one part, one part representing such and such, another part such and such else, and so on. The use of the part-whole relation of the calculus of individuals is essential here, as applied to paintings as well as to the objects and/or episodes represented. The various kinds of representation may be handled, it would seem, on the basis of the forms (2) and (3), together of course with a suitable parade of predicate-descriptions.

Another useful aesthetic relation is that of *expressing*. Let

$$\text{`}\alpha \, \text{Expr}_p \, a\text{'}$$

state now that the painting α expresses for person p the "property" or "characteristic" designated by a. This pragmatized, triadic form seems preferable to a semantical, dyadic one. The use of 'a' here, as in the forms above, requires that the form be construed intentionally. Here also the a must be a PredConOne, but any virtual class it designates must be a class of *feelings* or *emotions*, handled here in terms of the event-variables. Feelings may be classified by appropriate predicates and may be said to belong to or to be possessed by, or to bear the *of-relation of possession,* to the person experiencing them. Thus in order to say that person p gains a feeling of grandeur, say, from a painting α, a predicate 'Gr' is needed where 'Gr e' expresses that e is a member of the appropriate class, as well as the two-place predicate 'Of$_{\text{Poss}}$' for the *of-relation of possession*. A general principle concerning feelings is given by the following *Rule of Possession*.

ExprR1. $\vdash (\alpha)(p)(a)(e)(<\alpha,\text{Expr},p,a>e \supset (E e')(a \, \text{Den} \, e' \cdot <e',\text{Of}_{\text{Poss}},p>e))$.

Or, alternatively, a form analogous to **Repr1'''** could perhaps be used here instead. Let 'FPredConOne a' state that a is a one-place predicate for virtual classes of feelings. The *Rule of Limitation* for Expr is then that

ExprR2. $\vdash (\alpha)(p)(a)(\alpha \, \text{Expr}_p \, a \supset ((\text{Pict} \, \alpha \, \text{v} \, (E\beta)(\text{Pict} \, \beta \cdot \alpha \, \text{P} \, \beta)) \cdot (\text{Pntr}_\alpha p \, \text{v} \, \text{Vwr}_\alpha \, p) \cdot \text{FPredConOne} \, a))$.

And the *Rule of Specificity* for Expr is that

ExprR3. $\vdash \ulcorner \alpha \, \text{Expr}_p \, a \urcorner$, where (etc., about '$\alpha$', '$p$', and '$a$').

Again, this schema reports precisely that certain paintings give rise to certain feelings in the appropriate beholders. We cannot complete this list of course, but still the logic of 'Expr' requires that there be such a list if only hypothetically.

Another interesting aesthetic relation is that of *exemplification*, which according to Goodman (*LA*, p. 53) "is possession plus reference," that is, possession of and reference to certain properties. In other words, the relation is to be construed as between the picture and certain properties (or predicates). The general form for handling it can thus be taken as

$$\text{`}\alpha \text{ Exmpl } a\text{'},$$

without a parameter for the painter or viewer, exemplification being independent of such. The kinds of predicates exemplified constitutes a special subclass, for qualities, for properties (WW, p. 65) " that the picture makes manifest, selects, focuses upon, exhibits, heightens in our consciousness — those that it shows forth. . . ." Let 'MQPred-ConOne *a*' express that *a* is a manifested qualitative predicate in this sense. Here again, crucial characteristics should be laid down by suitable rules, first a *Rule of Limitation,* that

ExmplR1. $\vdash (\alpha)(a)(\alpha \text{ Exmpl } a \supset ((\text{Pict } \alpha \text{ v } (\text{E}\beta)(\text{Pict } \beta \cdot \alpha \text{ P } \beta)) \cdot \text{MQPredConOne } a)).$

Let '*a* Des$_{VC}$ *F*' express (as in XIII) that the one-place predicate *a* *designates* the virtual class *F*. The *Rule of Possession* for Exmpl is then that

Exmpl1R2. $\vdash \ulcorner(\alpha)(a)((\alpha \text{ Exmpl } a \cdot a \text{ Des}_{VC} \text{ } F \supset F\alpha)\urcorner$, where in place of '*F*' any one-place predicate-constant is inserted.

This schema is to the effect that any picture is a member of any virtual class designated by any predicate it exemplifies, but not of course conversely. Again, here also a *Rule of Specificity* is needed, that certain pictures do in fact exemplify certain predicates. Thus

ExmplR3. $\vdash \ulcorner\alpha \text{ Exmpl } a\urcorner$, where (etc., about '*α*' and '*a*').

Nothing has been said thus far concerning the referential character of this relation. The various aesthetic relations here are not subsumed under reference or denotation, as with Goodman. (Still, as he points out, a picture exemplifies certain properties much as a tailor's *swatch* is a sample of a certain material.) To handle the referentiality of 'Exmpl' we need to consider another representation-relation, that between pictures and *properties* (or, as here, predicates). This representation-relation is of course very different from that above, which is of objects or events. To handle it we may use

242

(5)   '$\alpha \, \mathrm{Repr}_p \, a$'.

This in turn may perhaps be best handled technically by bringing in the null entity N.[11] If so, we may regard (5) as short for

$$\text{`}(\alpha \, \mathrm{Repr}_p \, \mathrm{N},a \bullet \mathrm{MQPredConOne} \, a)\text{'},$$

expressing that α is taken by p to represent the null entity under the predicate-description a, a itself being an MQPredConOne. Then the following *Rule of Interrelationship* will hold.

ExmplR4. $\vdash (\alpha)(a)(p)((\alpha \, \mathrm{Exmpl} \, a \bullet (\mathrm{Ptr}_\alpha p \, \mathrm{v} \, \mathrm{Vwr}_\alpha p)) \supset \alpha \, \mathrm{Repr}_p \, a)$.

All of these relations are intentional relations, and thus presumably preserved under paraphrase. (Recall XIII above.) Let

$$\text{'}a \, \mathrm{Prphrs}_p \, b\text{'}$$

express that a is taken by p to be paraphrased as b. Then the following *Rules of Paraphrase* should hold, one for each of the aesthetic relations considered.

PrphrsR1. $\vdash (a)(b)(p)(a \, \mathrm{Prphrs}_p \, b \supset (\alpha)(x)(\alpha \, \mathrm{Repr}_p \, x,a \equiv \alpha \, \mathrm{Repr}_p \, x,b))$,

PrphrsR2. $\vdash (a)(b)(p)(a \, \mathrm{Prphrs}_p \, b \supset (\alpha)(\alpha \, \mathrm{Expr}_p \, a \equiv \alpha \, \mathrm{Expr}_p b))$,

PrphrsR3. $\vdash (a)(b)((p)a \, \mathrm{Prphrs}_p \, b \supset (\alpha)(\alpha \, \mathrm{Exmpl} \, a \equiv \alpha \, \mathrm{Exmpl} \, b))$.

A technical word or two now, finally, about *style,* which may be handled as the virtual class of paintings having that style, or having the determinative "characteristics" of that style. The style itself is then just the logical product of those characteristics. Let us regard characteristics (as throughout) merely as one-place predicates, and let $a_1, ..., a_n$ be the predicates determinative of some style. The style itself may then be identified with a special kind of logical product of $a_1, ..., a_n$, as defined as follows. Let '$a \, \mathrm{Den} \, x$' express that the one-place predicate a *denotes* x and perhaps other objects also. Then

(D)   '$\mathrm{prod}(a_1,...,a_n) \, \mathrm{Den} \, x$'   is merely short for   '$(a_1 \, \mathrm{Den} \, x \bullet a_2 \, \mathrm{Den} \, x \bullet ... \bullet a_n \, \mathrm{Den} \, x)$'.

The product of the determinative characteristics of a style thus denotes any painting denoted by all of those characteristics. To determine or select $a_1, ..., a_n$ as providing the full list of characteristics of the style is of course a matter of long and hard empirical or historical

---

11. Or some arbitrarily selected entity such as Carnap's a*. See his *Meaning and Necessity,* pp. 36–37.

investigation on the part of experts, concerning which there may well be dispute and disagreement.

Note that the logical product, as defined in just one kind of context in the definition (**D**), is not the usual logical product of virtual classes. Let the determinative a_1, ..., a_n bear Des_{VC} respectively to F_1, ..., F_n. The usual product is then

$$(F_1 \cap F_2 \cap ... \cap F_n),$$

consisting just of objects common to F_1, ..., F_n. The "style" $\text{prod}(a_1,...,a_n)$ then bears Des_{VC} to $(F_1 \cap ... \cap F_n)$.

Of course any attempt to characterize these aesthetic relations with any exactitude is fraught with difficulties. The attempt above, probably the first of its kind, is thus highly tentative and exploratory, albeit, it is hoped, in the right direction. Also there are many further and more special relations of interest that have not even been mentioned here.

Only painting has been considered in the foregoing, but much that has been said easily may be extended to other arts also, in particular to the *performative* ones. Although we have been speaking here only of objectual works of art, so to speak, performances may also be handled by means of event-variables. Works of art such as physical, spatio-temporal objects (paintings, say) are to be distinguished from performances (of a musical score, say) just as physical objects are distinguished from events, states, acts, and processes.

Although Goodman's work has been used here as a heuristic, the foregoing account of aesthetic relations parts from it in rather crucial ways. In particular there seems to be no need to subsume the various aesthetic relations under denotation, as already suggested. The various rules for Repr, for Expr, and for Exmpl differ radically from the Rules of Denotation[12], both as to the ontologies assumed and as to the inner structure of the principles governing those relations. Goodman relies perhaps too much on a loose, almost metaphorical construal of 'denotes' that is at best misleading. Nothing can take the place of studying each aesthetic relation on its own, so to speak — as as he would no doubt agree — trying to be as clear as we can as to its relata and as to the appropriate postulates or rules needed to govern it, with due attention given to both logico-linguistic matters as well as to matters of historical and analytic fact (as in the Specificity Rules).

Goodman speaks throughout of symbol-*systems*, sometimes as deductive logical systems, sometimes as systems of rules governing a

---

12. Recall *Truth and Denotation*, Chapters IV and V.

natural language, sometimes as something having to do with a specific work of art or with works of art generally. But what *precisely* is a symbol-system of a work of art? All the true specificity statements concerning it perhaps, together with their logical consequences? In any case, the different types of symbol-systems should be clearly demarcated from each other, it would seem, and ultimately clarified in terms of the notion of a logical system with its specified syntax, semantics, and pragmatics. Further, it is not clear that the relations of representing, expressing, and exemplifying are *symbolic* relations in any strict sense. Rather, they are *sui generis*, each having its own structure. They should not be construed as properly symbolic relations, which are always between word or phrase and object or event or virtual class.

Let us contrast a little more deeply properly symbolic relations with aesthetic ones.

The two Rules of Denotation, it will be recalled, are a *Specificity Rule* and a *Rule of Limitation*. The first is, schematically, that

DenR1. $\vdash \ulcorner a \operatorname{Den} x \equiv -x- \urcorner$, where '$-x-$' is a sentential function containing 'x' as its only free variable and in place of 'a' the structural-description name of the virtual-class expression '$\{x \ni -x-\}$' is inserted,

and the second that

DenR2. $\vdash (a)(x)(a \operatorname{Den} x \supset \operatorname{PredConOne} a)$.

This Limitation Rule **DenR2** is of course analogous to those for Repr, Expr, and Exmpl. The Specificity Rule for Den contrasts sharply, however, with those for these aesthetic relations. **DenR1** is *wholly structural*, in the sense that the proviso is concerned only with structural features concerning the interrelation between a and '$-x-$'. Symbolic relations are wholly structural in this sense, their Specificity Rules depending only on structural features of the signs employed, and on nothing else. The specificity rules governing Den, Des$_{VC}$, and Under are of this kind. By contrast those for the aesthetic relations depend for their establishment on experimentation concerning what in fact bears what to what. Also these latter hold only for *certain* choices of values for the schematic letters 'a', and so on, whereas those for properly symbolic relations hold for *all* choices of the appropriate schematic letters or signs when suitably interrelated.

Aesthetic relations are treated here on a par with other non-symbolic relations of the kind studied in the sciences. The relata of the aesthetic relations are concrete entities or performances, objects or qualities represented, feelings expressed, and qualities exemplified, but the work of art does not *stand for* these or "take the place of them" in the classic phrase of St. Augustine. No, it rather bears certain specific relations to them. To symbolize is to take the place of for some purpose or other. A painting does not take the place of whatever it represents, expresses, or exemplifies; its function and purport are totally different.

Another point. Note that in the formulas stipulated by the Specificity Rule for Den, there are no occurrences of whatever is put in in place of 'a' to the right of the '$\equiv$'. This Rule thus provides a kind of ideal statement, a series of real definitions, so to speak, of 'Den' in contexts $\ulcorner a$ Den $x\urcorner$ where a does not occur in the definientia. No analogous real definitions for 'Repr', 'Expr', or 'Exmpl' would appear possible. Ideally we might hope to be able to eliminate or introduce (by real definition) these predicates in favor of simpler or clearer ones, by means of Rules analogous to **DenR1**. To do so would require, however, the use of a name or a description for the relevant painting, person, feeling, or quality. Not to use such a name or an equivalent on the right of the '$\equiv$' would be to fail to achieve the specificity desired. Genuine specificity rules for a symbol, on the other hand, characterize the crucial context in which a symbol is *mentioned* without its being used. There is mention of the symbol on the left of '$\equiv$' without its being used on the right; the mention, so to speak, is explained away structurally. In the case of the aesthetic relations, no such explaining away is likely, one and the same name being — necessarily, it would seem — mentioned on the left and used on the right.[13] Analogous considerations obtain, incidentally, if semantics is developed in the definitional Tarski fashion mentioned above, rather than in terms of a special semantical primitive, as here.

We must all be grateful to Goodman for his valuable clarificatory comments and positive suggestions. At the same time we must lay the foundations for aesthetic analysis more firmly than he has done in preparation for the work ahead.

---

13. Here also, to simplify, we speak in terms of shapes rather than inscriptions. Important as inscriptions are, their use must be paid for by a certain complexity of formulation. Cf. *Truth and Denotation,* Chapters XI and XII, or *Semiotics and Linguistic Structure,* Chapter VI.

CHAPTER XVI

Some Comments on
the Second Antinomy

Ille sinistrorum hic detrorsum abit, unus utrique
Error, sed variis illudit partibus.

In order to have it fresh in our minds, let us recall the second antinomy *verbatim*. The thesis is that "every composite substance in the
world consists of simple parts, and nothing anywhere exists save the
simple or what is composed of it." And the antithesis is then to the
effect that "no composite thing in the world consists of simple parts,
and there nowhere exists in the world anything simple."[1]

According to Kemp Smith, "the substance referred to here, although never itself mentioned by name, is extended matter," and as
Kant himself notes further on, he is speaking of simples (or of the
simplex) in the sense of the Leibnizian system and the thesis itself he
refers to as "the dialectical principle of the *Monadology*,"[2] Crucial in the
statement of the antinomy also is the notion of being a *part of* as between substances as well as its converse relation *consisting of*. Clearly
for x to consist of y (or to contain it) is for y to be part of x.

In his famous comments on this antinomy in *The Principles of
Mathematics*,[3] Russell observes that it "applies to things *in* space and
time, not to space and time themselves. We may extend it to space and
time, and to all collections, whether existent or not. It is indeed obvious that the proposition [the thesis], true or false, is concerned purely
with part and whole, and has no special relation to space and time."

It is no doubt correct to contend that this antinomy is concerned
primarily with the part-whole relation and with simple substances,
and the connection with space and time is secondary. Even so, Russell's comments are troublesome, the extension to space and time
being loaded with difficulties, and the very meaning of an extension

---

1. I. Kant, *Critique of Pure Reason*, A419–B447 ff.
2. *A Commentary on Kant's 'Critique of Pure Reason'* (London: Macmillan, 1918), p.
489.
3. (New York: W. W. Norton Co., 1938, 2d ed.), p. 460.

to "all collections" being in doubt. Collections are presumably classes, whereas the antinomy is concerned with substances and simples — which, whatever they are, are not to be construed as classes. Further, Russell's use of 'purely', when he notes that the thesis is concerned purely with part and whole, suggests that expressions for simples should be definable in terms of the part-whole relation. Otherwise the occurrence of 'purely' here is redundant. This second point will be discussed in a moment.

That Russell is in fact confusing substances with collections emerges with his next remark. "Instead of a complex substance," he continues, "we might consider the numbers between 1 and 2, or any other definable collection. And with this extension, the proof of the proposition [i.e., the thesis] must . . . be admitted; only that *terms* or *concepts* should be substituted for *substances*, and that, instead of the argument that relations between substances are accidental (zufällig), we should content ourselves with saying that relations imply terms, and complexity implies relations."

Let us take the suggested substitutions seriously. We gain two quite distinct theses, that every complex term consists of simple parts, and that no term exists anywhere except the simple, or what is composed of simple parts; and similarly about concepts. In order that the result of the first substitution make sense, we must construe 'part of' as 'is definable in terms of', 'complex' by 'definable', and 'simple' by 'indefinable'. The result is the innocuous statement that every definable term is definable in terms ultimately of the indefinable or primitive ones — all of which has little to do with the second antinomy. The resulting principle concerning concepts is that every concept consists of simple parts, and that no concept exists anywhere except the simple and what is composed of simple parts. This statement, for its defense, would need a very considerable analysis of what it means to say that one concept is a *part of* another, with an attempted characterization of which Frege struggled valiantly.[4] Further, it goes without saying, surely, that in order to have relations, we must have relata, and that complex structures are to be analyzed in terms of the relations determining the structure; but this is an observation quite irrelevant to any purported "proof" of either of the statements resulting from the substitutions Russell suggests.

Terms and concepts are, on Russell's own grounds, very different from *collections*. The thesis for collections would be merely that every

------

4. See especially "Über Sinn and Bedeutung," and "A Reading of Frege on Sense and Designation," in *Pragmatics, Truth, and Language*.

complex collection consists of simple parts, and nothing exists anywhere except the simple, or what is composed of simple parts. Now what is a simple here supposed to be, and what are the parts of a collection? Let us be sure we distinguish class-membership from class-inclusion, a distinction of which Russell himself makes much later in *Principia Mathematica*. 'Consists of' is then ambiguous. It may be construed as 'has as members' or as 'has as a subclass'. What then are the simples? Either the individual members or the ultimate subclasses (presumably the null class and the classes with only one member). The result is then two quite different theses: (1) Every non-null collection has as members members and nothing exists except the members or what has them as members. (2) Every complex collection has as its subclasses the null class and the classes with one member, and nothing exists anywhere except the null class and the classes with one member, or what has such classes as subclasses. The first is presumably true and the second trivially false, under suitable assumptions of existence. But neither of these statements has any special affinity with the thesis of the second antinomy, which somehow seems to have gotten lost in the shuffle.

Russell's comments on the antithesis fare no better upon close examination. He thinks it involves "a covert use of the axiom of finitude, i.e., the axiom that, if a space does consist of points, it must consist of some finite number of points. When once this is denied, we may admit that no finite number of divisions of a space will lead to points, while yet holding every space to be composed of points. A finite space is a whole consisting of simple parts [members] but not of any finite number of simple parts. Exactly the same thing is true of the stretch between 1 and 2." Here too, the membership-relation should be distinguished from class-inclusion, and hence members from subclasses and points from spaces.

In chiding Russell for not adhering to the membership-inclusion distinction, one should not therewith extoll Kant for doing so. The distinction was scarcely known at the time Kant wrote, whereas it is one insisted upon by Russell in the earlier portions of his book.[5] Further, the antinomy is of genuine contemporary interest — so it is contended below anyhow — if viewed in terms of the part-whole relation, but of no interest if viewed in terms of classes or class-inclusion. The reason for this is of course to be found in Russell's own theory of types or Zermelo's set theory or their more recent offspring, in which classes or sets are characterized ultimately in terms of membership.

---

5. See especially pp. 19 ff.

Nothing need be said here concerning Kant's so-called "proofs" of either thesis or antithesis. All proofs, in any strict logical sense, are of course relative to what is assumed by way of axioms, the soundness of any purported theorem then depending on the soundness of the axioms. Proofs for both thesis and antithesis may be given, but questions will remain of course concerning the soundness of the conflicting axioms needed, as Kant in effect pointed out.

Russell's comments on Kant are, on the whole, well-known. Those of C. S. Peirce, on the other hand, are not. They are much more profound than Russell's, and worthy of a full discussion. Only a few items, albeit crucial ones, can be considered here.

Peirce's synechism is one of the keystones of his philosophical and scientific outlook. Synechism is, he wrote in Baldwin's *Dictionary* (1902), "that tendency of philosophical thought which insists upon the idea of continuity as of prime importance in philosophy and, in particular, upon the necessity of hypotheses involving true continuity."[6] Peirce worried long and hard as how best to characterize true continuity. He was of course deeply impressed with the work of Cantor and at first attempted to characterize continuity in terms of sets. By the *Kanticity* of a set of points Peirce meant (6.166) "having a point between any two points," and by its *Aristotelicity* he meant "having every point that is a limit to an infinite series of points belong to the system [or set]." He then (1903) thought that continuity consists in Kanticity and Aristotelicity together. "But further study of the subject," he wrote, "has proved that this definition is wrong. It involves a misunderstanding of Kant's definition which *he himself* likewise fell into. Namely he defines a continuum as that all of whose parts have parts of the same kind [A169, B211]."

Peirce's statement here is not quite accurate, Kant's definition being rather that the "property of quantities, according to which no part is the smallest possible (no part simple [or a *simplex*]), is called their continuity." Kant thinks that it then follows that 'space . . . consists only of spaces, and times of times," and presumably also that any "quantity" then contains only quantities of the same kind. The definition Peirce ascribes to Kant is thus, *prima facie* at least, very different from the one Kant actually gives.

What now is the misunderstanding of his definition that Peirce thinks Kant himself fell into? "He himself," Peirce goes on, "and I after him, understood that to mean infinite divisibility, which plainly is not what constitutes continuity since the series of rational fractional

---

6. *Collected Papers*, Vol. I, §169.

values is infinitely divisible but is not by anybody regarded as continuous. Kant's real definition implies that a continuous line contains no points. . . ." Note here also the failure — Peirce's this time — to distinguish between class-inclusion and membership. It is the *series* or class of rationals that is said to be infinitely divisible, not any one rational "quantity." Kant seems to have the upper hand here, presumably not being aware of the distinction. Further, Kant seems always to use 'consists of' in the sense of the converse of the relation of part-to-whole, and not in the sense of the converse of class-membership or in the sense of the converse of class-inclusion. In any case, *we* must always distinguish these three, and then construe the historical texts in the most charitable way we can. We must not commit the logical sins of our great predecessors. It seems doubtful then that Peirce is correct in thinking that Kant misunderstood his own definition. It is extremely interesting, nonetheless, that Peirce *thought* he did, this throwing more light on Peirce than on Kant, as we shall see in a moment.

On the whole, Peirce contends that Kant's definition, as he misconstrues it (6.168), "correctly defines the common sense idea, although there are great difficulties with it" and that although "the precise definition is still in doubt, . . . Kant's definition, that a continuum is that of which every part has itself parts of the same kind, seems to be correct." We shall see in a moment that Peirce's reading of Kant's definition fails of its mark, not only as a rendition of Kant but as an acceptable way of characterizing continuity howsoever construed, and in particular as construed in the way Peirce wishes.

Kant's actual definition, it will be recalled, is couched wholly in terms of the part-whole relation. The modern theory of this relation is given in Leśniewski's *mereology* or the calculus of individuals, which may now be presupposed. Let '$x \, \mathrm{P} \, y$' express that x is a part of y, x and y being entities or "quantities." It is important to distinguish being a part of from being a *proper* part of. Let

$$\text{'}x \, \mathrm{PP} \, y\text{'} \qquad \text{abbreviate} \qquad \text{'}(x \, \mathrm{P} \, y \cdot \sim y \, \mathrm{P} \, x)\text{'}.$$

Quantity x is then a proper part of y just provided it is a part of y but y is not a part of it. For x to be "smaller than" y is then, presumably, merely for x to be a proper part of y. The essential import of Kant's definition may be provided as follows. We let

$$\text{'}\mathrm{Cont}_K x\text{'} \qquad \text{abbreviate} \qquad \text{'} \sim (\mathrm{E}y)(y \, \mathrm{P} \, x \cdot \sim (\mathrm{E}z)(z \, \mathrm{P} \, x \cdot z \, \mathrm{PP} \, y))\text{'},$$

so that x is continuous in Kant's sense just where x contains no part y not containing a proper part that is also a part of x. An equivalent statement of the definiens here is of course

$$(y)(y \mathrm{P} x \supset (\mathrm{E}z)(z \mathrm{P} x \cdot z \mathrm{PP} y))',$$

to the effect that every part of x has a proper part that is also a part of x.

The calculus of individuals may be formulated in such a way as to condone or admit *atoms,* or *indivisibilia* with respect to the part-whole relation, as entities. An atom, by definition, is any entity that is a part of all its parts. Thus

'Atx'   may abbreviate   '$(y)(y \mathrm{P} x \supset x \mathrm{P} y)$'.

In some formulations of the calculus of individuals with atoms (but of course without the null individual) it obtains as a principle that

$$\vdash (x)(\mathrm{E}y)(y \mathrm{P} x \cdot \mathrm{At} y),$$

that every entity contains an atomic part, and hence that all entities can be decomposed into atomic parts. This principle is the *Principle of Atomicity.* In the theory without atoms all entities are regarded as having Kantian continuity, so that it obtains there that

$$\vdash (x)\mathrm{Cont}_{\mathrm{K}} x.$$

This principle is the *Principle of Kantian Continuity.* In fact it holds as a theorem in either theory that an entity is continuous if and only if it contains no atomic parts, and hence of course that it is non-continuous (or discrete) if and only if it does contain atomic parts.

L1. $\vdash (x)(\mathrm{Cont}_{\mathrm{K}} x \equiv (y)(y \mathrm{P} x \supset \sim \mathrm{At} y))$,
L2. $\vdash (x)(\sim \mathrm{Cont}_{\mathrm{K}} x \equiv (\mathrm{E}y)(y \mathrm{P} x \cdot \mathrm{At} y))$.

Peirce's formulation of Kant's definition involves the additional relation of *sameness of kind.* Let 'SK' designate this relation. Then

'Cont$_{\mathrm{P}} x$'   may abbreviate   '$(y)(y \mathrm{P} x \supset (\mathrm{E}z)(z \mathrm{SK} y \cdot z \mathrm{P} y))$',

so that x is regarded as continuous in the sense of Peirce just where every part y of x has a part z that is of the same kind as y. It is quite evident, then, that Pierce's reconstrual gives a notion *toto coelo* different from that of Kant. The only continuous entities condoned by this definition would be in effect logical sums of atoms, where each atom is regarded as being of the same kind as any sum of such. If each and every individual man is an atom, then any sum of men x is continuous in this sense, just because every part of x has as a part either an individual man or a sum of such. It seems rather bizarre, however, to say that any man is of the same kind as any sum of men. And anyhow this notion seems to have nothing to do with Kant. We must conclude that

Peirce's reading of Kant's definition is wide of the mark, and, as already suggested, it confuses individuals with classes and the part-whole relation with class-inclusion.

How does Peirce's definition fare, then, construed in terms of classes and inclusion? Not very well, it would seem. Allowance must be made for the null class and for proper inclusion. And even then, the resulting notion — with 'PP' in place of 'P' — would be merely of an infinitely large class of entities of the same kind. Anything resembling true continuity would seem to elude its grasp.

What now, precisely, is the interrelation between Kantian continuity, as defined above, and the notion of an atom with the thesis and antithesis of the second antinomy? In the notation here, the thesis would be merely

$$'(x)(\sim \mathrm{At}\,x \supset (\mathrm{E}y)(\mathrm{At}\,y \cdot y\,\mathrm{P}\,x)) \cdot \sim (\mathrm{E}x) \sim (\mathrm{At}\,x \vee (\mathrm{E}y)(\mathrm{At}\,y \cdot y\,\mathrm{P}\,x))'.$$

The second clause, however, is clearly equivalent to the first so that it may be dropped. Also clearly

L3. $\vdash (x)(\mathrm{At}\,x \supset (\mathrm{E}y)(\mathrm{At}\,y \cdot y\,\mathrm{P}\,x)),$

in view of the total reflexivity of the relation P. If this is conjoined with the thesis, the result is equivalent to the Principle of Atomicity. The thesis is thus in effect merely that principle.

The antithesis may be symbolized here as

$$'\sim (\mathrm{E}x)(\sim \mathrm{At}\,x \cdot (\mathrm{E}y)(\mathrm{At}\,y \cdot y\,\mathrm{P}\,x)) \cdot \sim (\mathrm{E}x)\mathrm{At}\,x'.$$

In view of **L2** and **L3** we have

$$'(x)(\mathrm{At}\,x \supset \sim \mathrm{Cont}_K\,x)'$$

and hence

$$'(x)(\mathrm{Cont}_K\,x \supset \sim \mathrm{At}\,x)'.$$

But this and the Principle of Kantian Continuity together entail

$$'\sim (\mathrm{E}x)\mathrm{At}\,x'.$$

Thus the second conjunct of the antithesis, like that of the thesis, may be dropped. The Principle of Kantian Continuity clearly entails

$$'(x)(\sim \mathrm{At}\,x \supset \mathrm{Cont}_K\,x)',$$

and hence, by **L2**, also,

$$'(x)(\sim \mathrm{At}\,x \supset \sim (\mathrm{E}y)(y\,\mathrm{P}\,x \cdot \mathrm{At}\,y))'.$$

And hence

$$‘\sim (Ex)(\sim \text{At}\,x \cdot (Ey)(y\ Px \cdot \text{At}\,y)).$$

The Principle of Kantian Continuity thus logically implies the antithesis. The converse implication also holds, so that the antithesis is logically equivalent to that principle.

It is implicit in this present discussion that "true continuity" — Peirce's phrase — of substances is not to be identified with the mathematical continuity of a class or of a continuous function of a real or complex variable. Peirce himself was not too clear about this distinction, but it is eminently Peircean to be so. In 1906, he wrote (6.174) that "whatever is continuous has *material parts,*" — which of course no class has — hastening on to note that "the *material parts* of a thing or other object, W, that is composed of such parts, are whatever things are, firstly, each and every one of them, other than W; secondly, are all of some one internal nature (for example, are all places, or all times, or all spatial realities, or are all spiritual realities, or are all ideas, or all characters, or are all relations, or are all external representations, etc.);. . . ." This is of course a very generous construal of 'material', but any hope that this passage will lead on to a viable characterization of true continuity is quickly dashed, the subsequent discussion going astray.

Cantor's notion of a continuum as a class whose members can be put into a one-to-one correspondence with the real numbers Peirce regards as a *pseudocontinuum,* for reasons that do not emerge clearly. The reason is, however — or at least so it would seem — that true continuity for Peirce is not to be found in multitudes mathematically regarded, but rather in mental phenomena and the "law of the mind." A paper by that title appeared in *The Monist* in 1892, and William James thought that it was perhaps the best Peirce had ever written. In that paper, Peirce contended (6.104) that "logical analysis applied to mental phenomena shows that there is but one law of mind, namely, that ideas tend to spread continuously and to affect certain others which stand to them in a peculiar relation of affectibility. In this spreading they lose intensity, and especially the power of affecting others, but gain generality and become welded with other ideas."

It is thus in the continuity of ideas that true continuity for Peirce is somehow to be located. And such continuity is closely connected with infinitesimal magnitudes, but it remains yet to be determined precisely how. Peirce's hints on these subjects are obscure and difficult and have not yet been properly studied. Nor have his remarks concerning infinitesimals yet been viewed or assessed in the light of the new interest in the infinitely small that has been taking place recently in the development of non-standard analysis.

It is interesting that the second antinomy, as construed here, reduces then to just the difference between the Principle of Atomicity and the Principle of Continuity in suitable applications of the calculus of individuals. But what an important difference this is! The problem of the antinomy is very much with us in contemporary cosmology and mathematical physics, if the calculus of individuals is used — as no doubt it must be — to help straighten out their foundations.

Very little detailed, responsible work has been done in this direction, so that one can speak here only rather vaguely in terms of general programme or suggestion rather than in terms of actual achievement. Can the ultimate particulars of the cosmos be regarded as atomic in the sense here, or are they rather entities with Kantian continuity? And if the latter, to what extent can such entities be regarded as akin to mind? Adequate answers to such questions must of course await in part the future of physics, to say nothing of psychophysics, neurology, and the like.

Russell, in his misconstrual of the second antinomy, comes out in favor of the thesis. Peirce, in *his* misconstrual of it, comes out in favor of the antithesis. There are valuable philosophical insights underlying each of these misconstruals. Russell's is, in part, that continuity is best to be characterized in definitive mathematical terms along the lines of Cantor, Dedekind, Weierstrass, and Cauchy. Peirce's is, in part, that the cosmos and everything in it is akin to mind and that only such "mind-stuff" and its parts can be said to be truly continuous. Can these two views be combined into a synthesis so as to accommodate basic features of both without too much sacrifice? And if so, in what sense could the result be said to be Kantian? Or, for that matter, Peircean? Or Russellian?

A major difficulty in any attempt to "solve" the second antinomy would be in the handling of mathematical continuity. True continuity, or continuity of mind-stuff, would not be argued for, but would be taken as a metaphysical ultimate, as with Peirce. The Principle of Continuity would be assumed outright. Everything would be assumed continuous in the Kantian sense. How then could we accommodate mathematical continuity and the vast edifice of modern mathematics, including the real and complex numbers, various geometries, topology, the theory of transfinite cardinals and ordinals, and so on, based on it?

One suggestion — there may be others — is the following. Let us embrace modern set theory *sans phrase* and try to provide an appropriate ontology of continuous entities for it. In a previous paper a rendition of the Zermelo-Skolem-Fraenkel set theory was given, in which sets were taken as logical sums of individuals, more particularly, as logical sums of all atomic entities that are parts of some entity satisfying a given condition.[7] Such sums may be symbolized by expressions of the form

(1) $\qquad\qquad\qquad$ '$(x\,1\,(Ey)(x\,Py \cdot -y-))$',

where '$-y-$' is a sentential form containing 'y' as a free variable but not 'x'. In addition to such sums, handled in term of the calculus of individuals with atoms, a new primitive relation for something akin to membership was needed. Let us try to do the same sort of thing here, but *without atoms*.

In place of atomic sums, let us consider *simpliciter* sums of entities satisfying a given condition. Thus we could let

$\qquad\qquad\qquad$ '$(x\,\sigma(Ey)(x\,Py \cdot -y-))$',

with a similar proviso on 'x' and '$-y-$', designate now the logical sum of all entities x that are parts of some y such that $-y-$. Such expressions are of course merely special cases of ones of the form

(2) $\qquad\qquad\qquad\qquad$ '$(x\,\sigma-x-)$'.

Expressions of the form (2) may be taken as primitive terms, and hence as substituends for variables, but this is not strictly needed if suitable contextual definitions of them are given. The 'σ' here is to suggest 'sum' just as '1' in (1) is to suggest 'unit' or 'atom'. Expressions of the form (2) stand for *σ-sums,* just as expressions of the form (1) stand for atomic sums.

As axiom-schemata concerning 'σ' we have the following, where 'F' stands for any virtual-class expression not containing 'x' or 'y' as free variables.

$\qquad\vdash \ulcorner(x)((y\sigma F y)\,Px \equiv (y)\,(Fy \supset y\,Px))\urcorner$,

and

$\qquad\vdash \ulcorner(x)(x\,P\,(y\sigma.F y) \equiv (y)(y\,Px \supset (Ez)(Ew)(z\,Py \cdot z\,Pw \cdot Fw)))\urcorner$.[8]

_____

7. "On Common Natures and Mathematical Scotism," in *Pragmatics, Truth, and Language.*

8. The consequent of the right-hand side here is stated in such a way as to allow that x might have a part in something having F and another part in something having F, without x itself being a part of anything having F.

It is assumed here that the calculus of individuals without atoms is formulated in terms of 'P' taken as a primitive. Further axioms or axiom-schemata are needed to provide for occurrences of expressions of the form '$(y\sigma\text{—}y\text{—})$' in primitive contexts other than on either side of 'P'.

Let us introduce now 'ϵ' as the primitive for the surrogate here of set-membership.

(3) $\qquad\qquad\qquad\qquad$ '$x \in y$'

is thus primitively significant and is to be interpreted as saying that the entity x is a certain kind of part of the entity y. Ultimately both x and y are continuous bits of mind-stuff. (In all interesting cases of formulas of the form (3), the y in turn will explicitly be regarded as a sum of entities satisfying a given condition.) In place of 'ϵ' we might write $\ulcorner P_F \urcorner$ where the given context is determined by F. Thus

$$\ulcorner x\ P_F\ (y\sigma Fy)\urcorner \quad \text{could abbreviate} \quad \ulcorner(x\ P\ (y\sigma Fy) \cdot Fx)\urcorner\ .$$

Thus x is a man-part, so to speak, of the sum of all men, just where x is a part of that sum and is also a man. The utility of any such definition is somewhat limited, however, 'ϵ' being needed as a primitive in contexts '$x \in y$' for *variable* 'x' and *variable* 'y'. Also this definition-schema would not define $\ulcorner x\ P_F\ y\urcorner$ in general but only special cases of it depending on F.

Concerning the new primitive 'ϵ' axioms and axiom-schemata similar to those of the Zermelo-Skolem-Fraenkel theory may be given. As an example, the famous *Aussonderungsaxiom* may be formulated here as follows.

$$\vdash\ \ulcorner(x)(y)(y \in (z\sigma(Fz \cdot z \in x)) \equiv (Fy \cdot y \in x))\urcorner\ ,$$

where (etc., as required). (Actually this statement incorporates also appropriate Principles of Abstraction.) And similarly for the other axioms. It is well known that these axioms suffice for mathematics in the working sense of that term. Still further axioms are needed to interrelate 'ϵ' with 'P' in suitable ways, but nothing difficult in principle here emerges that cannot be accommodated in the theory with σ-sums used in place of atomic ones.

All the usual notion of mathematics are definable now in terms of 'ϵ' as thus construed, in particular notions of (Cantorian) continuity of various orders, that of the set of all real numbers, that of the set of all functions of real numbers, and so on. And this is all done in accord with the thesis of the second antinomy, suitably interpreted so as to allow for the null or empty set and to allow that sets have other sets in turn, these sets still other sets, and so on, until we reach the bedrock of Zermelo's *Urelemente*, taken here as continuous bits of mind-stuff.

The thesis of the antinomy as construed on this basis is then to the effect that every composite (non-null) set consists of other sets, which in turn consist of other sets or of *Urelemente*, which sets in turn consist of either still other sets or *Urelemente*, and so on, and nothing exists other than the *Urelemente* and sets of them, sets of sets, and sets of sets and of *Urelemente*. Here of course the means of "composition" is provided by ϵ, not the part-whole relation P. But the antithesis holds also, the mode of composition being P, not ϵ. No composite thing in the world consists of atoms; in fact there are no atoms. Everything is continuous in the Kantian sense, even sets themselves, the decomposition, remember, now being in terms of P not ϵ.

The theoretical constructs of physics and cosmology can be handled on such a set-theoretic basis by suitable additional primitives, together of course with suitable assumptions. In such a way various theories of time and space may be built up. There are many alternatives here, but all of them would have the feature that time and space regarded as wholes are continuous cosmic elements akin to mind. Some such methods consist of taking a relation B of *before-than* as primitive and then introducing various spatial notions by definition, so that space or space-time becomes a theoretical construct in terms ultimately of B.[9] All such notions as construed here would of course have Kantian continuity.

In A169–170 [B211–212], Kant follows the definition of continuity with some comments concerning space and time. These are to the effect, it will be recalled, that "space and time are continuous quantities because no part of them can be given, save as enclosed between limits (points or moments), and therefore as being itself a space or time. Space therefore consists only of spaces, time only of times. Points and moments are only limits, i.e., mere positions that limit space and time. But positions always presuppose the intuitions which they limit or are intended to limit; and out of mere positions [or moments], viewed as constructions capable of being given prior to space and time, neither space nor time can be constructed. . . ." These comments, as construed in the light of the foregoing, raise the extremely important issue as to how points (or instants) are to be handled. Even if atoms were available, they could not be identified with

---

9. For a valuable recent discussion, see M. Jammer, "Some Historical Problems of Special Relativity in Historical Perspective," presented at the Boston Colloquium for the Philosophy of Science, Nov. 28, 1978.

either. They, rather, would be like the atomic triangles of Plato's *Timaeus* or the actual entities of Whitehead. No, points and instants are to be handled as geometric constructs, all geometries of course finding their place in the vast resources of the set theory available here.

One more comment. All bits of mind-stuff are of the same kind — in one sense anyhow of 'kind'. If we leave aside any considerations concerning infinitude, Peircean continuity can hold, that is, the principle

$$\text{`}(x)(y)(y\;Px \supset (Ez)(z\;SK\,y \bullet z\;Py))\text{'},$$

whether there be an infinity of bits of mind-stuff available or not. If 'PP' is put in here in place of 'P', the result could hold only in an infinite cosmos.

How is it that finitude could hold of the cosmos in view of its containment here of the whole transfinite ontology of set theory? Well, finitude in this sense depends on identity construed mereologically as mutual part to whole. A second kind of identity is ϵ-identity, defined in the usual set-theoretic way, where

$$\text{`}x =_\epsilon y\text{'} \quad \text{is short for} \quad \text{`}(z)(x \in z \supset y \in z)\text{'}.$$

The two identities are very different, one defined in terms of 'P', the other in terms of 'ϵ'. It holds that

$$\vdash (x)(y)(x =_\epsilon y \supset (x\;Py \bullet y\;Px)),$$

but not conversely, so to speak, so that there are fewer mereologically identical objects than ϵ-identical ones. There could thus be only a finite number of the former but with all manner of infinite numbers of the latter.

Mathematical continuity is provided here by set theory. With only slight changes, however, Russell's type theory could be used equally well. The result would be eminently Russellian in a desirable sense.

All critique is of course from the point of view of certain assumptions, usually left tacit. Tacit in the foregoing is the acceptance of set theory and the virtual identification of modern mathematics with it. There are other ways of construing mathematics, e.g., intuitionistic ones, that may be closer in spirit to Kant's views. Brouwer himself apparently read Kant on the nature of mathematics with great interest, and intuitionism is often regarded as a kind of Kantianism in modern dress.

Another tacit assumption in the foregoing is the distinction between the part-whole relation and set- or class-membership, the very distinc-

259

tion itself being due in part to Russell. But Peirce was not very clear about the distinction and it is perhaps a distortion of his views to force it upon him. The problem is related to that of individuation in Peirce.[10] Perhaps the best way to view Peirce's logical work is in terms of mind-stuff and the various relations, objective and other, between or among them.[11] Even so, *we* must provide for the distinction in some form even if Peirce does not, in order to appraise his comments on Kant in modern terms. This we should do in view of the historical importance of the distinction, even if it should turn out not to be ultimately acceptable.

There are no doubt other modes of "solving" the second antinomy than the one suggested here, one of them being in terms of non-standard analysis or the theory of infinitesimals and an appropriate theory of measurement. But that is a story quite different from the set-theoretic one here. Another approach might be in terms of inten-sionality, in which the actual cosmos would be construed in whatever way physics and psychophysics tell us it should be, with set theory then built up intensionally in terms of suitable modes of linguistic descrip-tion (Frege's *Arten des Gegebenseins*). But this also is quite another story.

All such modes of solving the second antinomy are *ontic*, so to speak, and contrast sharply with Kant's own, central to which is the distinction between a *regressus in indefinitum* and a *regressus in infinitum*. This distinction is epistemic, not ontic. Kant observes (A519−520, B547−548) that "however far we may have attained in the series of empirical conditions, we should never assume an absolute limit, but should subordinate every appearance, as conditioned, to another as its condition, and that we must then advance to this condition." The regressūs then concern only the condition of something we do, not of something quite independent of our mental activity. But the very dis-tinction between *in indefinitum* and *in finitum* need not be negelected, from the ontic point of view taken above. Suitable predicates for the required epistemic relations must themselves be introduced, akin to those required in what seems to be the most desirable method for handling intuitionistic mathematics. This method brings in an explicit parameter for the "creative subject" whose mathematical construc-tions are under review.[12] However this may, the details may all be

---

10. Cf. "On Individuality and Quantification in Peirce's Published Logic Papers, 1867−1885," in *Peirce's Logic of Relations Etc.*

11. Cf. "On the Logic of Idealism and Peirce's Neglected Argument," in *Peirce's Logic of Relations Etc.*

12. Cf. *Events, Reference, and Logical Form*, pp. 207 ff.

handled within the classical, non-intuitionistic logic, but only of course with suitable meaning postulates governing (or definitions of) the epistemic predicates introduced. Thus it would seem likely that any adequate contemporary rendition of Kant's own solution would have to rely upon some ontic construction such as the foregoing for its basic logico-linguistic forms.

CHAPTER XVII

Toward a
Constructive Idealism

Qui tegitur, majus creditur esse malum.

The content of a positive faith worth the having should be our highest theoretical construct. Like those of the advanced sciences and mathematics, such content is not given to us just through sense-experience but must be earned with hard labor and much conceptual discipline. It is a matter of delicate adjustment between head and heart, just as the theoretical constructs of science are the result of an almost incredibly subtle weave of logico-mathematical and empirical factors. Positive faith may be founded on all manner of metaphysical schemes, not the least of which is the *philosophia perennis* in one of its forms as absolute idealism. The attempt is made in this paper to formulate an idealist view, in what appears to be the simplest way possible, and intended to be adequate to modern mathematics and the theoretical and empirical sciences, and at the same time to provide rational foundations for positive faith and its ramifications in our human experience. An ambitious task no doubt, requiring a lifetime for completion. Its main features, however, may be sketched summarily here in broad outline.

Technically the material here is somewhat akin to that of V and XVI above, but there will be differences of treatment so fundamental as to justify a reconstruction *de novo*. Objective idealism is so ecumenical a metaphysics as to call for many diverse approaches, each in need of clear formulation in modern terms. Loosely speaking, the material here incorporates that of the two papers above, but goes far beyond them, especially at the metalinguistic level.

Let us assume, as basic *principia logico-metaphysica,* the usual first-order quantification theory with virtual classes and relations, together with the calculus of individuals based on the *part-whole* relation P, a kind of temporal topology based on the *before-than* relation B, and a specifically metaphysical relation Manif for *manifestation.* Six sorts of entities are admitted, *objects, events, inscriptions, sets, logical entities,* and *persons*, by means of sortal predicates 'Obj', 'Ev', 'Inscr', 'Set', 'LEnt', 'Per', respectively. Moreover, a kind of membership relation ϵ is needed to provide a metaphysical framework for mathematics (and theoretical science generally) via a kind of *set theory*. Inscriptional syntax is handled by means of a relation C for *concatenation,* and inscriptional semantics by means of the relations Den for (multiple) *denotation* and Des for (singular) *designation*. Finally, a theory of *primordial valuations* is needed, somewhat in the manner of V above. So much for the mere essentials.[1]

The central notion of the metaphysical idealism here is that of *absolute mind*, designated by a primitive individual constant 'AM'. Immediately it is assumed that AM exists uniquely. The *Principle of Existence* is that

R1. ⊢ E!AM   (or that AM is not the null entity),[2]

that of *Uniqueness,* that

R2. ⊢ $(x)(y)((AM\ P x \cdot AM\ P y) \supset x\ P y)$.

(More will be said about uniqueness in a moment.) The AM is assumed to be *all-inclusive* in the sense of containing everything whatsoever as a part. The *Principle of Unique Inclusiveness* (or of *Fullness*) is that

R3. ⊢ $(x)x\ P\ AM \cdot (y)((x)x\ P y \supset AM\ P y)$.

AM is thus the unique all-inclusive entity, containing everything including itself. Further, it is a part of anything that bears Manif to anything. The *First Principle of Manifestation*, then, is that

R4. ⊢ $(x)(y)(x\ \text{Manif}\ y \supset AM\ P x)$.

Moreover, all of the basic kinds of entities admitted are manifestations of AM, so that a *Second Principle of Manifestation* also holds, that

R5. ⊢ $(x)((\text{Obj}\ x\ \text{v}\ \text{Ev}\ x\ \text{v}\ \text{Inscr}\ x\ \text{v}\ \text{Set}\ x\ \text{v}\ \text{LEnt}\ x\ \text{v}\ \text{Per}\ x) \supset AM\ \text{Manif}\ x)$.

Still, the AM surpasses in plenitude the totality of entities it manifests. The *Principle of Transcendence* is then that

R6. ⊢ $(x)(AM\ \text{Manif}\ x \supset (x\ P\ AM \cdot \sim AM\ P x))$.

---

1. For further details, see *Semiotics and Linguistic Structure,* Part I.
2. On the null entity, see "Of Time and the Null Individual."

Anything manifested by AM is a *proper* part of it only. It follows of course that

$$\vdash \sim AM \text{ Manif } AM,$$

and that Manif is an *asymmetric* relation,

$$\vdash (x)(y)(x \text{ Manif } y \supset \sim y \text{ Manif } x),$$

as well as an *intransitive* one,

$$\vdash (x)(y)(z)((x \text{ Manif } y \cdot y \text{ Manif } z) \supset \sim x \text{ Manif } z),$$

together of course with much else.

The six sorts of fundamental entities are taken as mutually exclusive (but not jointly exhaustive) in the sense that no entity of any one kind is a part of any entity of another. Thus a *Principle of Mutual Exclusiveness* obtains, that

R7. $\vdash \sim (Ex)(\text{Obj} x \cdot (Ey)(x \text{ P} y \cdot (Ev \ y \ v \ \text{Inscr} y \ v \ \text{Set} y \ v \ \text{LEnt} y \ v \ \text{Per}$
$y))) \cdot \sim (Ex)(Ev x \cdot (Ey)(x \text{ P} y \cdot (\text{Obj} y \ v \ \text{Inscr} y \ v \ \text{Set} y \ v \ \text{LEnt} y \ v$
$\text{Per} y))) \cdot ... \cdot \sim (Ex)(\text{Per} x \cdot (Ey)(x \text{ P} y \cdot (\text{Obj} y \ v \ \text{Ev} y \ v \ \text{Inscr} y \ v$
$\text{Set} y \ v \ \text{LEnt} y))).$

By a *pure* or *disembodied spirit* we may mean any part x (of AM) containing no manifested parts (of AM). Thus

D1.   'PSx' may abbreviate '$\sim (Ey)(y \text{ P} x \cdot AM \text{ Manif} y)$'.

The existence of pure spirits is assumed, so that

R8. $\vdash E!PS$ (or $\vdash (Ex)PS x$).

R8 is the *Principle of Transcendence*.

Nothing has been said thus far about *identity*, another most fundamental logico-metaphysical notion (according to Heinrich Scholz[3]). None of the Rules thus far has made use of it. Two different kinds of identity are to be used. Both are to be introduced by definition. The first is the familiar *mereological* identity. Entity x is identical with entity y in the mereological sense just where they are mutually parts of each other. We may thus let

D2.   '$x =_P y$' abbreviates '$(x \text{ P} y \cdot y \text{ P} x)$'.

In terms of '$=_P$', some of the preceding laws may now be strengthened. Thus a uniqueness principle stronger than **R2** is that

$$'(x)(y)((AM \text{ P} x \cdot AM \text{ P} y) \supset x =_P y)',$$

---

3. In his *Metaphysik als strenge Wissenschaft.*

and one stronger than **R3** is that

$$\text{'}(x)x \text{ P AM} \bullet (y)((x)x \text{ P}y \supset y =_\text{P} \text{AM})\text{'}.$$

The second kind of identity will be discussed in a moment.

Let us reflect now upon the *logical entities,* of which only three need be considered, all others being constructs in terms of these. The three are the familiar *negation, disjunction,* and *universal quantification.* These are here regarded as full-fledged entities, and hence as parts of AM. Such entities, unlike virtual classes and relations, are not to be handled just in terms of inscriptions for them. They are here regarded as *real entities* having their locus in the divine mind or AM. For their characterization the semantic notion of truth, the predicate 'Tr', is assumed available, as well as the syntactical 'C' for the triadic relation of concatenation. 'Tr a' expresses that the inscription a is true and 'a C bc' that the inscription a is the concatenate of inscriptions b and c. (Let

$$\text{'}a \text{ C } bcd\text{'} \quad \text{be short for} \quad \text{'}(\text{E}a')(a' \text{ C } bc \bullet a \text{ C } a'd)\text{'},$$
$$\text{'}a \text{ C } bcdd''\text{'} \quad \text{be short for} \quad \text{'}(\text{E}a')(\text{E}b')(a' \text{ C } bc \bullet b' \text{ C } a'd \bullet a \text{ C } b'd')\text{'},$$

and so on.) 'Sent a' is defined to express that a is a sentence. Then

D3. 'Neg x' abbreviates '$(\text{E}a)(a \text{ Des} x \bullet (b)(c)((\text{Sent } b \bullet c \text{ C } ab) \supset (\text{Tr } c \equiv \sim \text{Tr } b)))$'.

Let 'Lp a' express that a is an inscription of the shape of a *left parenthesis*, and 'Rp a' that a is of the shape of a *right parenthesis*. Then

D4. 'Disj x' may abbreviate '$(\text{E}a)(a \text{ Des} x \bullet (b)(c)(d)(a')(b')((\text{Sent } b \bullet \text{Sent } c \bullet \text{Lp } a' \bullet \text{Rp } b' \bullet d \text{ C } a'bacb') \supset (\text{Tr } d \equiv (\text{Tr } b \text{ v Tr } c)))$'.

Let now 'Vbl b' express that b is a *variable,* 'InCon b' that b is a primitive *individual constant,* and 'd' SF$_b^{a'}d$' that d' differs from d only in containing free occurrences of the Vbl or occurrences of the InCon a' wherever there are free occurrences of the Vbl b in d. Also let 'Tilde a' express that a is a *tilde*-inscription (i.e., of the shape '$\sim$'), and 'Vee a' express that a is an inscription of the shape of the *disjunction sign* 'v'. 'a Like b' is to express that a is *like* b in the sense of being of the same length and containing like (typographical) characters in the same left to right order. 'Fmla a' expresses that a is a (well-formed) *formula,* and 'b FrOcc c', that the variable b has a free occurrence in c. 'a Cl b' expresses that a is a *closure* of b, i.e., consists of b preceded by a string of universal quantifiers covering all the free variables of b. These are all familiar notions of inscriptional syntax.

The notion of being a universal quantifier is now definable as follows.

D5.   'UQuant x' abbreviates '$(Ea)(a$ Des x • $(b)(c)(d)(a_1)(b_1)(b_2)(b_2)(b_3)$ $(b_4)(c_1)(d_1)(d_2)(d_3)(d_4)((\text{Vbl } b$ • Lp b_1 • Rp c_1 • a C b_1bc_1 • Fmla d • c C ad • d_1 SF$_b{}^{a'}d$ • (InCon a_1 v Vbl a_1) • Lp b_2 • Tilde b_3 • Vee b_4 • Rp d_3 • d_2 C $b_2b_3cb_4d_1d_3$ • d_4 Cl d_2) ⊃ Tr d_4) • $(b)(c)(d)(a_1)...(a_5)(b_1)...(b_5)$ $(c_1)...(c_3)(\overline{d_1})...(d_8)((\text{Vbl } b$ • Fmla c • ~ b FrOcc c • Fmla d • Lp b_1 • Rp b_2 • Lp b_3 • Vee b_4 • Rp b_5 • a C b_1bb_2 • a_1 C $ab_3cb_4db_5$ • a_2 Like c • Lp c_1 • c_2 Like a • c_3 Like d • a_3 C c_2c_3 • Lp d_1 • Tilde d_2 • Vee d_3 • Tilde d_4 • Vee d_5 • Rp d_6 • Lp d_7 • Rp d_8 • a_4 C $d_1d_2a_1d_3d_7d_4a_2d_5a_3d_6d_8$ • a_5 Cl a_4) ⊃ Tr a_5))'.

Although these definitions, especially **D5**, seem somewhat involved, actually they are quite simple. The definientia of the first two merely spell out the basic truth-conditions for negation and disjunction. In the definiens of the third it is required that all closures of the two basic schemata for quantification theory be true.[4]

It then obtains that

R9. $\vdash (x)(\text{LEnt } x \equiv (\text{Disj } x \text{ v Neg } x \text{ v UQuant } x))$,

Also no LEnt is to be a part of or to have as a part, any other LEnt.

R10. $\vdash (x)(\text{LEnt } x \supset {\sim} (Ey)(\text{LEnt } y \bullet {\sim} y = x \bullet (x \text{ P} y \text{ v} y \text{ P} x)))$.

And each LEnt is to exist uniquely.

R11a. $\vdash (x)(\text{Neg } x \supset \text{E!} x)$,
R11b. $\vdash (x)(y)((\text{Neg } x \bullet \text{Neg } y) \supset x = y)$,
R11c. $\vdash (x)(\text{Disj } x \supset \text{E!} x)$,
R11d. $\vdash (x)(y)((\text{Disj } x \bullet \text{Disj } y) \supset x = y)$,
R11e. $\vdash (x)(\text{UQuant } x \supset \text{E!} x)$,
R11f. $\vdash (x)(y)((\text{UQuant } x \bullet \text{UQuant } y) \supset x = y)$.

These principles concern of course the logical *entities,* not their notations.

The admission of logical entities as parts of AM is a fundamental tenet of idealism as conceived here. The exact role of these entities in the inner structure of the AM must be characterized, a precondition for which is that they be parts of it. The leading idea is that the AM must contain not only all kinds of linguistic expressions, but all that the denotative ones stand for or express as well. The self-containment in AM of all modes of expression and thought is a precondition for its *self-reflective* character, made much of by Aristotle and Hegel among others. Further, to leave out the logical entities, or not to hypostatize

---

4. Cf. *R5* and *R6* , p. 5, of *Semiotics and Linguistic Structure.*

them as parts of the AM, would be to violate the Principle of Inclusiveness. Logical notions and principles, in the exact sense of modern quantificational theory, are then to be parts of the divine inclusiveness along with everything else.

The question arises now as to the status of *virtual classes* and *relations* in the AM. Are they also parts of it, and if so in what sense? Such entities are not values for variables and hence not covered by the Principle of Inclusiveness. Of course *inscriptions* for them are, but this is quite another matter. In particular, the very virtual classes Obj, Ev, and so on, the virtual relations P, Manif, and B, to say nothing of ϵ (to be discussed in a moment), C, Des, and Den (and others) should somehow be included in the AM, for a genuine and not merely specious fullness to obtain. Well, to accommodate this, let us (essentially as in XIII above) speak of virtual-class *concepts* as virtual classes taken under given descriptions. Let 'F Under a' express that the virtual class F is taken under the one-place predicate-description a. And similarly for virtual relations. We can then define

D6a. $\ulcorner(a \; under \; F) \, P x\urcorner$ as $\ulcorner(a \; P x \cdot F \; \text{Under} \; a)\urcorner$

(and (if needed)

D6b. $\ulcorner x \; P \; (a \; under \; F)\urcorner$ as $\ulcorner(x \; P \; a \cdot F \; \text{Under} \; a)\urcorner .^5)$

It can then be postulated that

R12. $\vdash \ulcorner(a \; under \; R) \, P \; \text{AM}\urcorner$, where in place of 'R' a virtual-class or -relation expression is inserted and in place of 'a' its shape-description.

This is the *Principle of Virtual-Class and -Relation Inclusion.* A particular case is that

$\vdash$ (Under *under* 'Under') P AM.

The AM is conceived here as constituted by parts, which in turn are to be regarded as bits of mind-stuff (in the terminology of Peirce), bits of spirit, or whatever. The recognition of some such bits as the entities of the world of our experience, of our science, and so on, seems essential if a suitable *pluralism* for the entities of the world is to be achieved on the basis of the absolute monism of the AM. The recognition of such parts or bits seems a precondition for rational thought and discourse.[6] The question arises as to how "small" the bits are, and as to

---

5. Still their contexts containing '*under*' may be defined appropriately as needed.
6. Cf. Josiah Royce, *op. cit.*

whether any smallest ones need be admitted. One way — but by no means the only one of course — is explicitly to recognize *atomic* bits in accord with the calculus of individuals (or mereology) construed as an atomic Boolean algebra (in the manner of Tarski).[7] The atomic parts would not be further divisible, and would allow of a considerable variety of handling. But whether bits of mind-stuff can be decomposed into atomic parts is at least doubtful. The better procedure perhaps then is that of XVI without the assumption of atoms.

Let us proceed then, essentially as in XVI. The form '$x \in y$' is to express that x is a member of y, and $\in$ is to be characterized axiomatically by means of a suitable adaptation of the work of Zermelo. (Of course there are many alternative versions of set theory that could be used here equally well.) The interesting cases of formulas of the form '$x \in y$' are where y is some sum

(1) $$(z\sigma{-}z{-}),$$

'$-z-$' being a suitable sentential form containing 'z' as a free variable. To say that x bears $\in$ to this sum is to say that x is one of the entities z such that $-z-$, i.e., $-x-$. Of course this holds only for *suitable* '$-x-$', not for all. In the Zermelo set theory the '$-x-$' must be such that it ascribes a *"definite"* property to x, ie., one condoned by the *Aussonderungsaxiom*. But no matter, the purport is clear.

In terms of '$\in$' and expressions of the form (1), suitable axioms may be framed having the full mathematical strength of an axiomatic set theory.[8] Nothing is strange about the ontology of the theory thus regarded, all sets, i.e., entities such as (1), being regarded as parts of AM and thus as bits of mind-stuff or conceptual in nature. We have here a genuinely *conceptualistic* rendering of set theory. Usually conceptualistic interpretations of set theory are such only by proxy — we are told that they are such, but not on the basis of any precise theory as to what concepts are or how they are handled in some general theory. (Further details concerning the theory of membership and its semantics, as construed here, are not needed for present purposes.[9])

The presence of two kinds of identity in the theory is to be remarked upon. First there is mereological identity as defined by **D2**, identity in this sense being merely mutual part to whole. But there is

---

7. Cf. his *Logic, Semantics, Metamathematics*, XI, especially p. 334.
8. Cf. "On Common Natures and Mathematical Scotism," in *Peirce's Logic of Relations Etc.*
9. Its semantics requires special handling, however, as is evident in the "Scotism" paper.

also identity as based on membership or *membership-identity*. This may be defined familiarly as follows.

D7.   '$x =_\epsilon y$' abbreviates '$(z)(x \in z \supset y \in z)$'.

It then obtains that

$$(x)(y)(x =_\epsilon y \supset x =_p y),$$

but not conversely. No difficulty arises in confusing the two notions, one characterized wholly by properties of P, the other by properties of ϵ. These properties in turn determine the way in which the relata of ϵ and P are to be construed in given contexts. The relata of $=_p$ are mereological sums (all entities being merely the sums of the atoms contained in them). The relata of identity as based on membership, $=_\epsilon$, on the other hand, are sums of entities taken as parts of some entity satisfying such and such a suitable condition. To say that $x =_\epsilon y$ thus amounts to saying that y satisfies every condition that x does. Let us speak of the relata of $=_\epsilon$ as ϵ-*sums*. Note that to speak of the identity of a mereological sum with an ϵ-sum is meaningless, even though every ϵ-sum is also a mereological one. In full sentences concerning identity in either sense, however, both relata must be construed in the same sense.

A terminological comment. The words 'property' and 'characteristic' have been used throughout usually uncritically. Properties are sometimes identified outright with virtual classes, but usually they are to be construed as virtual classes in intension, i.e., virtual classes taken under a given predicate-description, or perhaps merely as that predicate-description itself. And similarly for characteristics. When the properties or characteristics of a virtual class or relation are spoken of, these are to be thought of either as virtual classes of those virtual classes or relations, or as second-order predicates for such, or as full sentences containing predicates for those virtual classes or relations which as it were show forth the properties without naming them. Properties in this last sense are also called 'conditions', which the given virtual class or relation is then said to *satisfy*.

It is assumed, as is customary, that the theoretical constructs of mathematical physics may be handled set-theoretically with the addition of suitable primitives. There would seem to be no limits on the expressive power of the theory here, then, as regards mathematics and the sciences. When we move on to the theory of the arts, moral philosophy, and the philosophy of religion, is the situation fundamentally different? one might ask, anxious to get on to forms of value other than truth.

269

In the preceding paper but one, considerable evidence was given that aesthetics is primarily the study of certain specific relations, all of which can easily find their place in the schema here. In particular, relations of representation, expression, and (aesthetic) manifestation may readily be handled. In fact, a considerable enrichment in the variety such relations can be allowed here, along lines as diverse as those of Coomaraswamy and Maritain.

Moral philosophy, it has been suggested, deals with relations expressible in sentential forms such as 'person p has the volition to do e', 'p has pleasure (pain) in doing e', 'p allows e to take place', 'p is obliged to do e (in accord with same code)', 'p is responsible to do e', 'it is good to do e', and so on. Again, all such relations may be accommodated in the framework here. Also social groups may be regarded as logical sums of persons or as suitable virtual classes of such, so that no abrupt transition need occur when we turn to social philosophy. The exact characterization of the relations needed in this domain is a problem of considerable urgency.

Everything said thus far is a mere prelude. The philosophy of religion is fast becoming in our time a subject of much greater complexity than heretofore, involving as it does nearly all the problems with which philosophy has been concerned through the centuries.[10] First there is the whole theory of the *primordial valuations* — as in II and V above — that can now be developed in terms of the AM as the entity or person who bears such and such primordial relations to such and such objects in such and such order. The theory of the "real internal constitution" of the divine will, the subdivisions of it into its constituent parts, and the detailed spelling out of the items in those parts would seem to be the central problem of speculative theology. Alas, how little work along these lines has been done on a secure logical footing. Theologians in our day have turned to problems of a less fundamental nature, skirting the very issues that have concerned the historically greatest of their number beginning with Aristotle. There is an urgent need of a return to the fundamentals in theology that is possible now in view of the developing deeper interest in the manifold relations between the philosophy of religion and the sciences. Note in particular how important in all this the logic of relations is. Until recently only mathematicians and exact philosophers of science have realized its tremendous analytic power. In view of the foregoing, however, it can be seen that its area of applicability is much wider, embracing all fields of philosophic inquiry. This observation is by no

10. Recall I above.

means new, incidentally. Royce himself was perhaps the first to have made it in acceptable contemporary terms.[11]

The relations constituting the primordial valuations are but one side of the coin. They are relations *from* the AM *to* the creatures or sequences of such. Equally important are relations *from* the creatures *to* the AM. One of these is of course P itself, which is a mere logico-metaphysical relation. More important are relations of love, thanksgiving, foregiveness, impetation, and so on, the bearing of which on the part of the creature to the AM constitutes his religious life. These relations are the *specifically religious ones*. Most of them are presumably intentional, a mode of description being needed as one of the relata. Some of these relations might even be regarded as *mystical*. But even mysticism has its rationality, which cries out for being accommodated within a scheme embracing also logic and the sciences — *rational mysticism,* as Richard Hocking would call it.

Much of what has been said here is either mere suggestion or mere programme. On the technical matters, there are always alternatives to consider, and there is inevitably some arbitrariness in the adjustment of detail. To some extent one can pick and choose what he likes here and provide preferred alternatives to the rest. Even so, it should surely be evident that there is no quarrel between the many alternative idealist versions of the *philosophia perennis* and the newer logic. It would also be instructive to explore the basic texts of these alternative versions in the light of suitable adaptations of the foregoing material, in particular some strands of oriental idealism and those of Hegel and post-Hegelian idealism. And of course the idealism of C. S. Peirce is a special case in point, some little progress having been made on that view in the light of material similar in some respects to the above.[12]

More remains to be said concerning the self-reflexivity of the AM. At least three interesting kinds may be distinguished. The AM contains itself (and everything else) as a part. Then there is the sense of self-reflexivity determined by the primordial valuations. The AM bears one or more of the primordial relations to suitable sequences of the manifested entities, *determining* in this way (or *permitting* or *desiring* or whatever) the full character of the cosmos, both as it actually is and as to how it is envisaged ideally. The *acts* or *states* of primordial valuating are not only parts of the AM, they are the very stuff constituting the way in which the AM "broods" upon or "thinks" about the cosmos.

---

11. *Loc. cit.*
12. Cf. "On the Logic of Idealism and Peirce's Neglected Argument," in *Peirce's Logic of Relations Etc.,* and XIX below.

They are in effect the AM's reflections upon a part of himself. Then, thirdly, there is the hierarchy of object-language, metalanguage, metametalanguage, and so on, each of which in turn is (in some sense) a part of the AM. Each such part at any level broods upon or thinks about the parts at lower levels in the very explicit sense in which a metalanguage at any level provides a semantical interpretation of all the languages in that hierarchy below it.

One of the most famous and difficult paragraphs concerning the self-reflexivity of "God" is 1072^{b}14 in Aristotle's *Metaphysica,* which it will be of interest to compare with the foregoing. This paragraph weaves back and forth between divine and human states, life, thinking, enjoyment, goods, and so on — but no matter. Only God's self-reflexivity need concern us here. "On such a principle [of the unmoved or first mover], then, depend the heavens and the world of nature [the Ross translation]. . . . And thought in itself deals with that which is best in itself, and that which is thought in the fullest sense with that which is best in the fullest sense. And thought thinks itself because it shares the nature of the object of thought; for it becomes an object of thought in coming into contact with and thinking its objects, so that thought and object of thought are the same. For that which is *capable* of receiving the object of thought, i.e., the essence, is thought. And it is *active* when it possesses this object. Therefore the latter [possession] rather than the former [receptivity] is the divine element which thought seems to contain, and the act of contemplation is what is most pleasant and best. . . ." The dependence of the heavens and the world of nature or manifest objects upon the first principle or AM is wholly spelled out in the primordial valuations — even though *we* of course can never succeed fully in spelling *them* out. The "best" in thought (or the AM) or "thought in the fullest sense" are no doubt the primordial desires determinative not only of what is best in the cosmos but also of what is best for us. All objects of thought are parts of the AM, this latter thus sharing the nature of the objects of thought. The AM can be an object of its own thinking, so that it and its objects are the "same" in this regard. The AM always thinks actively, so to speak, and it is this activity that constitutes its "divine element." Entities other than the AM are merely passive objects of its thought, even thinking human persons. The divine element in us, however, is also determined by thinking activity. Our thought in the fullest sense has as its object that which is best in the cosmos in the fullest sense, namely, the AM, such thought being contemplation and the life that lives it the contemplative life.

An equally famous, but perhaps more difficult, passage concerned with the self-reflexivity of Absolute Mind consists of paragraphs 553–555 of Hegel's *Phenomenology of Mind*. "The absolute mind [Wallace translation], while it is self-centered *identity*, is also always identity returning and ever returned into itself: if it is the one and universal *substance*, it is so as a spirit discerning itself into a self and a consciousness, for which it is as substance. *Religion*, as this supreme sphere may in general be designated, if it has on the one hand to be studied as issuing from the subject and having its home in the subject, must no less be regarded as objectively issuing from the absolute spirit which as spirit is in its community." The AM is self-centered in having all entities as its parts and in bearing the primordial relations to various sequences of its parts. It is ever returning into itself as being itself a part of itself and as being itself the subject of the valuations, as being the entity that does the valuating. It is ever returned into itself in being self-identical and never a mere proper part of itself. It is a universal or all-inclusive substance or entity, and both discerns itself as object and as subject is the discerner. It is also discerned as object by the creatures as subject. This kind of discernment is presumably to be handled by means of the specifically religious relations spoken of a moment back. Religion in part issues from the creature as bearer or subject of such relations, but in part also from the AM itself, who is the community or logical sum of all persons — and indeed here of all the entities of the embodied cosmos together with all disembodied entities also.

These comments on these two famous passages are by no means intended to capture the full impact or complexity of either in their full *ambiente*. These comments should be sufficient, however, to call attention to some kinship of general attitude and doctrine. Howsoever this may be, the spirit of the foregoing theory is Hegelian in some essentials and is in accord with the basic contention that "*the Absolute is Mind* — this is the supreme definition of the Absolute [§384, *Phenomenology*]. To find this definition and to grasp its meaning and burden is, we may say, the ultimate purpose of all education and all philosophy: it is the point to which the impulse of all religion and science turned: and it is this impulse that must explain the history of the world. . . ." It is difficult to see how so sweeping a contention has much content, however, except in terms of the AM as characterized in the most intimate and logically precise possible way in terms of a full delineation of the theory of primordial valuations. Nothing short of this can succeed in satisfying the impulse of modern philosophers interested in the incredibly complex details and difficulties of science, to say nothing of those of the arts and of society and of the *vita contemplativa*.

The choice of the AM as the fundamental entity rests on the supposition that the detailed development of *all* aspects of the system is possible on such a basis, but more difficult to achieve on a more naturalistic basis. The accommodation of physical objects on such a basis is becoming easier as the notion of the immateriality of "matter" comes to play an increasing role in contemporary physics.[13] The full accommodation of the most delicate aspects of artistic and religious experience on a naturalistic basis, on the other hand, is more difficult and probably impossible to achieve satisfactorily. With the assumption of the AM there is therefore everything to gain and nothing to lose.

Note that the view here is a wholly metaphysico-theological one, and in no way rests upon any specious epistemological claims. Some varieties of idealism rest upon the rather vague view that knower and known are somehow the very same. This may be case, but if so it needs a thorough spelling out. The various relations of believing, knowing, and so on, need exact study on the present kind of basis just as on any other. And similarly for all of the material concerned with the manifested entities. The view here gives us no easy shortcut to knowledge; it affords merely an integrated overview in terms of which all aspects of our experience may be interpreted — the very aim of a speculative philosophy in Whitehead's sense.

"This [then] is what is called Idealism," as Peirce commented (7.564). "As soon, however, as we seek preciser statement [as in the foregoing], difficulties arise, — by no means insuperable ones, yet calling for patient study based upon a thorough understanding of logic."

---

13. For a valuable survey, see W. A. Wallace, "Immateriality and Its Surrogates in Modern Science," a paper presented at the annual meeting of the American Catholic Philosophical Association in Chicago, April 2, 1978.

CHAPTER XVIII

On Peirce's
Analysis of Events

Multi commitunt eadem diverso crimina fato;
Ille crucem sceleris pretium tulit, hic diadema.

A suitable theory of events and of their inner structure, according to Peirce, is a prerequisite for the analysis of time.[1] "The task of the analyst in making out the features of the time-law must begin by formulating precisely what it is which that law explicitly pretends to make subject to time. It is, in the first place, only real events that "take place," or have dates, in real time. . . . What, then, is a real event? It is an existential junction of incompossible facts. A pale yellowish iron solution mixed with a pale yellow solution of ferrocyanide of potassium suddenly turns deep blue. It is requisite that its being of a pale greenish or reddish yellow, and therefore not blue, should be a fact, and that the same thing's being blue should be a fact. Those two facts are contradictory. That is, that both should be true of precisely the same subject is absurd. But that they should be true of a subject existentially identical is not absurd, since they are mere accidents of an individual thing. . . . Still, the two accidents could not be combined with one another. That *would* be absurd. . . . But though the two inherences [accidents] cannot be *combined* they can be *joined*. . . ."

We must straightaway ask: What is the real internal structure of an event? What is the status of its "taking place"? What are its properties? How do we handle 'suddenly' in the statement giving the one crucial example? What are "existentially identical" subjects as differing from "precisely the same subject"? What is the difference between two contradictory accidents as "combined" rather than as "joined"? What are the properties of the operation of joining? What, precisely, are "facts"?

Peirce goes on [1.493] to note that "there are other sorts of events, somewhat more complicated because the characters concerned are

---

1. *Collected Papers,* Vol. 1, §492.

not simple monadic qualities. For example, A may make war upon B, that is, may pass from one sort of relation to B to another sort of relation to B. But they come to much the same thing. There is a re-pugnance between two monad elements. It is hardly for our present purposes worthwhile to undertake a long analysis in order to make the very slight correction of our definition of an event called for on this account. An event always involves a junction of contradictory in-herences in the subjects existentially the same, whether there is a sim-ple monadic quality inhering in a single subject, or whether they be inherences of contradictory monadic elements of dyads or polyads [relations], in single sets of subjects." In accord with this, we may pre-sumably distinguish monadic, dyadic, and in general polyadic events depending on the degree (or "adicity") of the "inherences" involved.

But even this classification of different types of events is not enough, Peirce notes. "In the kind of events so far considered, while it is not necessary that the subjects should be existentially of the nature of subjects — that is, that they should be substantial things — since it may be a mere wave or an optical focus, or something else of like nature which is the subject of change, yet it is necessary that these subjects should be in some measure permanent, that is, should be capable of accidental determinations, and therefore should have dyadic existence. But the event may, on the other hand, consist in the coming into existence of something that did not exist, or the reverse. There is still a contradiction here; but instead of consisting in the material, or purely monadic, repugnance of two qualities, it is an in-compatibility between two forms of triadic relation. . . ." The "sub-jects" of monadic, dyadic, and in general polyadic events must then be "in some measure permanent" or at least capable of "dyadic exis-tence," but need not be "substantial things." We cannot explain 'dyadic existence' here in terms of time-flow, for this would be circu-lar; time-flow itself is to be explained in terms of events. Dyadic exis-tence, we might say, must involve two "atomic" events, but this would not be satisfactory either, for to postulate entities such as these would presumably be to violate Peirce's fondness for continuity. No, dyadic existence is apparently one of the root notions of the theory. Another is that of "coming into existence of something that did not exist," and its "reverse," passing out of existence. Is a notation for this latter de-finable in terms of the former? And what are the two forms of triadic relation, the incompatibility between which is involved in the analysis of coming into being?

"In general," Peirce goes on as though summarizing, "we may say that for an event there is requisite: first, a contradiction; second, existential embodiments of these contradictory states; [third] an immediate existential junction of these two contradictory embodiments or facts, so that the subjects are existentially identical; and fourth, in this existential junction a definite one of the two facts must be existentially first in the order of evolution and existentially second in the order of involution. We say the former is earlier, the latter later in time. That is, the past can in some measure work upon or influence (or flow into) the future, but the future cannot in the least work upon the past. . . ." Actually this passage contains something quite new, the contrast between the order of "evolution" with that of "involution," or, what presumably comes to the same thing, the notion of being existentially "first" or "second." One or the other of these notions seems needed at the very foundation of Peirce's contentions.

This remarkable passage in Peirce has an extraordinarily modern ring. Its contentions are comparable with some suggestions made by contemporary writers so diverse as Reichenbach, Braithwaite, Geach, Richard Montague, Jaegwon Kim, Donald Davidson, and the present author. Because details loom important in any close discussion of the subject, let us examine Peirce's view in the light of the kind of event logic used in the preceding papers.

Let us first contrast the two key examples of events Peirce gives, that of the pale yellowish iron solution mixed with a pale yellow solution of ferrocyanide of potassium turning deep blue — let us postpone discussion of 'suddenly' — and A's making war upon B. Concerning each of these there are four items to observe in Peirce's analysis: a contradiction of states or properties, an "existential embodiment" of them, an "existential junction" of these properties in "existentially identical subjects," with one of these being "existentially first" to the other's being "existentially second." But clearly more is involved than Peirce explicitly notices, although it is implicit in the way in which these two events are differentiated.

In the first example there is the occurrence of the given solution's *turning-deep-blue* and in the second that of A's *making-war-on* B. Now turning-deep-blue is a monadic property and making-war-on is a dyadic relation. What are the contradictory properties involved in the first and the contradictory dyadic relations in the second? In the first, clearly the color properties. A pale yellow solution is not a deep blue one. Yet one and the same solution can turn (suddenly) from having one color to having another, so that two colors can be existentially embodied in existentially identical but successive subjects, one being existentially first, the other existentially second. But no reference need be made here to the contradictory of the monadic property of turning-deep-blue. The contradiction involved is not that of turning-deep-blue and not-turning-deep-blue.

What is this event itself? It is the "existential junction" of the two color properties PY, pale yellow, and DB, deep blue, with the two identical but successive subjects, s_1 and s_2. Let

(1) $\qquad\qquad\qquad$ '[PYs$_1$,DBs$_2$]'

symbolize this, with the comma and the brackets standing for the junction. The moment we symbolize this, following Peirce literally, we see that a crucial item is left out, the *turning* or becoming or merging of something into or with another. Peirce should have made explicit a fifth factor, usually expressed by a gerundive. In place of (1), we need something like

(2) $\qquad\qquad\qquad$ '[PYs$_1$,T,DBs$_2$]',

where T is a relation of turning (in the sense of changing color). Without some such additional factor, the event lacks the necessary specificity. (1) could stand for all manner of events, so long as s_1 is PY and s_2 is DB, the transition being sudden. The solution might be suddenly spatially relocated, or suddenly burst into flames but with the flames immediately extinguished, or suddenly poured into another decanter, and so on. The four factors would be present, but the key factor determining the event to be a turning-into would be missing.

The case of A's making war on B is somewhat more complicated, Peirce tells us, it will be recalled, because the "elements involved" are not simple monadic qualities like PY or DB. It is rather that A passes from one sort of relation with B to another. Peirce thinks that a long analysis is needed here to correct the previous account so that it will apply. Yes, but it must be done, and if we do so, we will see that Peirce has misstated his point. What we need is to correct his account so that it will apply to both kinds of events — and to all others also.

Note that in this second example there is no need to mention existentially identical but successive subjects, although of course one can distinguish A before he makes war on B from A while making war on B. And of course he will have contradictory properties in these two states. And similarly for B. And A in one state will bear to B in one state a relation contradictory to that which he in another state might bear to B in another. But even so, the key item about A's making war on B will not be revealed just by an analysis or "existential junction" of these states or contradictory relations. (To insist upon this would be in effect to reduce the dyadic relation of making-war-on to successive monadic properties, a reduction Peirce would presumably frown upon.) The essential character of this event, so to speak, as contrasted with the previous one, is to be found in the fact that to-make-war-on is a dyadic relation. Let 'W' stand for this relation. Then the triple

(3)   '[A,W,B]'

might be the junction required, although it is not one of "incompossible facts." However, (3) will not do, for it does not distinguish A's making war on B from B's making war on A. Some order is needed here, so let us use an *ordered triple*. Let

(4)   '<A,W,B>'

symbolize the triple of A, the relation W, and B just where in fact A bears W to B. Of course A might make war on B several times, so that even (4) is not adequate without further ado. If, however, we regard it as a monadic *precdicate* and introduce variables for the sorts of entities it is to be allowed to apply to, we gain a more viable notation. Let then expressions such as (4) be regarded *event-descriptive* or *gerundive* predicates, and let

(5)   '<A,W,B>*e*'

express that *e* is an event of A's making war on B.

Let us speak of the relation of turning as the *determinative relation* of the first example and that of making-war-on that of the second. The "inherences" of the first example are PY and DB, and the contradiction resides in these, not in the difference between turning and not-turning. Actually the second example is like the first in depending on a determinative dyadic *relation*, not a monadic property. Peirce does not give us the "inherences" of the second example, but, as already suggested, these could presumably be given in terms of contradictory states pertaining to A before and during his making war on B. If so, then, we must decompose A here into two "existentially identical" subjects, one of them having a property contradictory to one possessed by the other. And similarly for B.

It is interesting that in this discussion Peirce does not go on to give an example of an event with a *triadic* relation as its determinative one. His favorite example of such a relation is that of A's giving B to C. If he were to have given such an analysis, along the lines of his previous examples, it would have to be still more laborious, in terms presumably of contradictory inherences for A, for B, and for C, but without any mention of the triadicity of the determinative relation of giving. Objections similar to those in the dyadic case would also apply.

In the passages in which Peirce does give something like a purported analysis of an event determined by a triadic relation, he sings a rather different tune — but one no less remarkable for its suggestiveness and contemporary relevance. For example, in the *Collected Papers* (1.363), an important passage worth quoting almost in full, Peirce discusses 'A gives C to B' in some detail. "The fact that A presents B with a gift C, is a triple relation, and as such cannot possibly be resolved into any combination of dual relations. . . . [W]e cannot build up the fact that A presents C to B by any aggregate of dual relations between A and B, B and C, and C and A. A may enrich B, B may receive C, and A may part with C, and yet A need not necessarily give C to B. For that, it would be necessary that these three dual relations should not only coexist [with just the relata as given], but be welded into one fact. Thus we see that a triad cannot be analyzed into dyads. But now I will show by an example that a four can be analyzed into threes. Take the quadruple fact that A sells C to B for the price D. This is a compound of two facts: first, that A makes with C a certain transaction, which we may name E; and, second, that this transaction E is a sale of B for the price D. Each of these two facts is a triple fact, and their combination make up [as] genuine [a] quadruple fact as can be found. The explanation of this striking difference is not far to seek. A dual relative term, such as 'lover' or 'servant', is a sort of blank form where there are two places left blank. . . . But a triple relative form such as 'giver' has two correlates, and thus a blank form with three places left blank. Consequently, we can take two of these triple relatives and fill up one blank place in each with the same letter, X, which has only the force of a pronoun or identifying index, and then the two taken together will form a whole having four blank places; and from that we can go on in a similar way to any higher number. But when we attempt to imitate this proceeding with dual relatives, and combine two of them by means of an X, we find we have only two blank places in the combination, just as we had in either of the relatives taken by itself. . . . Thus any number, however large, can be built out of triads; and consequently no idea can be involved in such a number radically different from the idea of three. I do not mean to deny that the higher numbers may present interesting special configurations from which notions may be derived of more or less general applicability; but these cannot rise to the height of philosophical categories so fundamental as those that have been considered."

It is a very striking feature of Peirce's method here, and indeed the crucial one, that in the analysis of the given "quadruple fact" into two triple ones, a notion of a *transaction* is introduced and assigned a name or parameter 'E' on a par with 'A', 'B', 'C', and 'D'. But later in the passage Peirce changes the 'E' to 'X', which "has only the force of a pronoun or identifying index" and thus presumably is to be quantified. The pronoun is to be handled quantificationally rather than referentially, so that

'A sells C to B for the price D'

would come out as

'(EX)(A makes with C a transaction X • X is a sale of B for the price D)'.

This last "forms a whole having four blank places [or names]; . . . ." The transaction here is in essentials what we may regard as an *act* or *event*. The tradition of using names and variables for acts and events is a long one, which in this very passage Peirce may have been the first to initiate in explicit form.

But note the extraordinary gap in Peirce's argument, almost as though a crucial few lines were omitted. From the example concerning "quadruple facts" he goes on to consider one involving "dual relatives," leaving out any involving triadic ones. We cannot imitate the procedure of handling quadruple facts, he says, in the analysis of dual ones because we would end up with "two blank places in the combination, just as we had in either of the relatives [used in the analysis] taken by itself." Very well, dyadicity in some form is here to stay, but there still would be a point in discussing the forms in which it occurs — to be discussed in a moment. But why could we not imitate the procedure of handling "quadruple facts" in the analysis of *triadic* ones?

In another remarkable passage (3.492), Peirce comments that "although the primitive relatives are triadic, yet they may be represented with but little violence by means of dyadic relatives, provided we allow several attachments to one blank. For instance, A gives B to C, may be represented by saying A is the first party in the transaction D, B is subject of D, C is second party of D, D is giving by the first party of the subject to the second party. . . ." This passage can perhaps be taken as an answer to the question at the end of the preceding paragraph. We *can* reduce triadic relations to dyadic ones, by using again variables for transactions, the relation of being-first-party-in-a-transaction, the relation of being-second-party-in-a-transaction, of being subject-of-a-transaction, and a gerundive predicate giving the nature or content of the transaction. These are not to be presumed the only additional notions needed for a general theory, but merely the ones needed for the example concerning giving. However, Peirce made nothing of this

281

suggested way of analyzing triadic relations and apparently persisted unto the end in regarding them as irreducible, in thinking of thirdness as a fundamental category, and in thinking that there is some intimate connection between thirdness and triadic relations.

The relation of being the first-party-in-the-transaction of giving is that of being the *agent* of, and may be handled by the converse of the by-relation-of agency, By_{Agent}. That of being the second-party-of may be handled by the converse of the to-relation of recipiency, $To_{Recipient}$. Peirce's subject-of relation is that of being the direct-object-of, Of_{Object}. Thus we could readily define

'A gives B to C' as '$(EX)(Giving \: X \cdot X \: By_{Agent} \: A \cdot X \: Of_{Object} \: B \cdot X \: To_{Recipient} \: C)$'.

'Giving' here is of course the gerundive or event-descriptive predicate for giving.

Ultimately all prepositional relations may be handled in terms of two fundamental ones, the basic From- and To-relations of event logic.

There are, then, these two, quite distinct methods with which Peirce handles events. In the first two rather complex notions are needed. That of being "existentially identical subjects" of one and the same object, for example, needs a considerable spelling out. Temporal order is handled in terms of the order of "evolution" and "involution," and this too would need a considerable discussion. In the second method, with variables over "transactions" explicitly introduced, a great step forward toward simplicity of expression is taken. All manner of specific predicates upon transactions may be introduced, including ones for such temporal or quasitemporal relations as are needed, for example, one for occurring *wholly before*. However, Peirce never goes on to develop either method.

Let us take a deeper look at Peirce's first example in the light of the method used here for the analysis of his second. Let s be the given mixed solution of iron with ferrocyanide of potassium. Now s's state of being pale yellow, or of its having PY, can in turn be handled gerundively, if we take the logic of '*being*' seriously.

Let

'$<s,PY>e_1$' and '$<s,DB>e_2$'

express respectively that e_1 is a state of s's being PY, and that e_2 is a state of s's being DB. The states e_1 and e_2 are then distinct states ("contradictory" ones) of the same subject s. The turning is *from* the state e_1

to the state e_2. Here the basic Russellian relations From$_{\text{Russellian}}$ and To$_{\text{Russellian}}$ are needed.[2] Peirce's first example thus becomes

'$(Ee)(Ee_1)(Ee_2)($Turning $e \cdot$ <s,PY>$e_1 \cdot$ <s,DB>$e_2 \cdot e$
From$_{\text{Russellian}} e_1 \cdot e$ To$_{\text{Russellian}} e_2)$'.

Here of course 's' is left unanalyzed, being introduced merely as a proper name for the given mixed solution. Alternatively, it could be introduced by means of a definite description. The solution s is a chemical mixture of two solutions s_1 and s_2, these being respectively of such and such a kind and of such and such a color. Let 's_1 M s_2' express that s_1 has been chemically mixed with s_2, and let '$(s_1 \cup s_2)$' be the logical sum of s_1 and s_2 in the sense of the calculus of individuals. Then presumably we could let

's'   be short for   '$(\imath x \cdot (x = (s_1 \cup s_2) \cdot s_1$ M $s_2 \cdot$ PYs$_1 \cdot$ I s$_1 \cdot$ PYs$_2 \cdot$ FPs$_2))$'.

The last four conjuncts could, alternatively, be omitted and merely regarded as boundary conditions or presuppositions of the sentence.

Peirce did not reflect upon his use of 'suddenly' in this example. For its handling, further considerations may be introduced, akin to those needed for the handling of adverbs in general.

All the events considered thus far have been of the kind that have "substantial things" as their "subjects." How now should we handle "a mere wave or an optical focus, or something else of like nature which is the subject of change"? And how are we to handle events consisting of "the coming into existence of something that did not exist, or the reverse"? The event-variables are regarded as taking as values such insubstantial entities as waves, optical foci, occurrences of lightning, and such like, where appropriate predicates are available designating such kinds. All entities are subject to change, which in turn may be handled as a gerundive. Let

'Change e'

express that e is a change or a changing — we can go on to add from what to what as desired.

How now can we handle coming into being and passing out of being? The question is a difficult one, of course, and answers to it should be explored deeply. One method that may be serviceable is in terms of the null individual, N. Let

2. See *Semiotics and Linguistic Structure*, Chapter X.

$$\text{'E!}x\text{'} \quad \text{abbreviate} \quad \text{'} \sim x = N \text{'},$$

so that for x to exist is for it to be distinct from N. But with temporal locutions available, an entity may be said to exist at one time but not at another — but still of course exist timelessly in the logical tense of timelessness. Let

$$\text{'}\langle x, =, N \rangle e\text{'} \quad \text{abbreviate} \quad \text{'(Id } e \cdot e \text{ From}_{\text{Russellian}} x \cdot e \text{ To}_{\text{Russellian}} N)\text{'},$$

where 'Id e' expresses that e is an identity state, i.e., a state of something's being identical with something. Similarly

$$\text{'}\langle x, \neq, N \rangle e\text{'} \quad \text{abbreviates} \quad \text{'}(\langle x, \{yz\ni \sim y = z\}, N \rangle e \cdot e \text{ From}_{\text{Russellian}} x \cdot e \text{ To}_{\text{Russellian}} N)\text{'}.$$

These definienda express respectively that e is a state of x's being identical with N and that e is a state of x's being diverse from N. For x to come into being or to pass out of being is then for x to change from one to the other of these states. Thus

$$\text{'}e \text{ CIB } x\text{'} \quad \text{may abbreviate} \quad \text{'}(Ee_1)(Ee_2)(\langle x, =, N \rangle e_1 \cdot \langle x, \neq, N \rangle e_2 \cdot \text{Change } e \cdot e \text{ From}_{\text{Russellian}} e_1 \cdot e \text{ To}_{\text{Russellian}} e_2)\text{'}$$

and

$$\text{'}e \text{ POB } x\text{'} \quad \text{may abbreviate} \quad \text{'}(Ee_1)(Ee_2)(\langle x, \neq, N \rangle e_1 \cdot \langle x, =, N \rangle e_2 \cdot \text{Change } e \cdot e \text{ From}_{\text{Russellian}} e_1 \cdot e \text{ To}_{\text{Russellian}} e_2)\text{'}.$$

Here the definienda express respectively that e is a coming-into-being of x and a passing-out-of-being of x. Ordinarily, entities come into and pass out of being only once, but this is not required by the notation.

What is the contradiction here upon which Peirce insists? It is not to reside, remember, "in the material, or purely monadic, repugnance of two qualities, it is [rather] an incompatibility between two forms of triadic relation." Well, it does so happen, in the analysis just given, that '$\langle x, =, N \rangle e_1$' and '$\langle x, \neq, N \rangle e_2$' may be written in the form of triadic relations that are incompatible, the first say as '$R(x, N, e_1)$' and the second as '$-R(x, N, e_2)$', for suitable 'R'. Perhaps this is merely coincidental, however, and it is by no means clear just what incompatible triadic relations Peirce intended here to refer to.

Existence, logically speaking, is to entities what occurrence is to events. For an entity to exist is like an event's occurring. Hence occurrence may be handled similarly if a null event NE is available. The null event then has the key property that it does not occur. Thus

$$\text{'Occ } e\text{'} \quad \text{may abbreviate} \quad \text{'} \sim e = NE \text{'}.$$

Then of course

$$`(e)(\sim e = \text{NE} \supset \text{Occ}\, e)'$$

holds as a general principle.

The various comments of this paper are intended only to draw attention to Peirce's remarkable *aperçus* concerning the structure of events, especially concerning items that have come to light in recent analysis. The subject is of course intimately related with that of time, concerning which Peirce has much to say that need not be touched upon here. Time, and indeed space (or rather time-space), requires quite another story, to be told in modern terms only with the help of set theory and some theoretical constructs of mathematical physics.

CHAPTER XIX

The Strange Costume of Peirce's Hegelism: A Dialogue

Urbem lateritiam invenit, marmoriam reliquit.

In the Elysian Fields, late 1979

R.M.M.   Good day, Professor Peirce. Please allow me to address you thus, as your neighbors in Milford were wont to do. It is a delight for me to visit you here and to have the opportunity to ask you a few questions. You are coming to be regarded, as you no doubt realized you would be, as one of the very greatest philosophers in the whole history of the subject, but even now many aspects of your work are not well understood. You are known as a difficult writer, and it is often next to impossible to thread together the various strands you were seeking to unite. "My philosophy," you wrote on one occasion, "resuscitates Hegel, though in a strange costume."[1] You speak of Hegel always in very general terms as the typical idealist metaphysician and theologian, so that 'Hegelism' for you is in effect synonymous with 'idealism'. Your comment has puzzled many of your readers, and I would be grateful if you would be willing to clarify it somewhat.

C.S.P.   Yes, of course. I shall try to recall exactly what I wrote on the subject. The chief difficulty with the "critical [or Hegelian] logicians," it seemed to me (1.40–1.41), was that they know nothing "about the thinking that goes on in the laboratories," and that they "have been [too] much affiliated to the theological seminaries." "Now the seminarists and religionists generally have at all times and places [but particularly perhaps at the end of the nineteenth century] set their faces against the idea of *continuous growth* [italics added]. That disposition of intellect is the most catholic element of religion. Religious truth having once been defined is never to be altered in the most minute particular; and theology having been held as queen of the sciences, the religionists have bitterly fought by fire and tortures all

---

1. *Collected Papers*, Vol. I, §42.

great advances in the true sciences; and if there be no true continuous growth in men's ideas where else in the world should it be looked for? . . . . So shut up are they in this [fixed, static] conception of the world that when the seminarist Hegel discovered that the universe is everywhere permeated with continuous growth (for that, and nothing else, is the "Secret of Hegel") it was supposed to be an entirely new idea, a century and a half after the differential calculus had been in working order. Hegel, while regarding scientific men with disdain, has for his chief topic the importance of continuity, which was the very idea the mathematicians and physicists had been chiefly engaged in following out for three centuries. This made Hegel's work less correct and excellent in itself than it might have been; and at the same time hid its true mode of affinity with . . . scientific thought. . . . It was a misfortune for Hegelism, a misfortune for "philosophy," and a misfortune (in lesser degree) for science."

R.M.M. Perhaps we should add that it is a misfortune for those contemporary Hegelians also who still resolutely disdain the scientific advance, to say nothing of progress in logic and mathematics themselves, as though they have no metaphysical or even theological relevance.

C.S.P. Let me go on. I think we should be careful to distinguish between the "Analytic Method" and the "Historical Method" in philosophy, somewhat as follows (1.63–1.64). "The first problems to suggest themselves to the inquirer into nature are far too complex and difficult for any early solution, even if any satisfactorily secure conclusion can ever be drawn concerning them. What ought to be done, therefore, and what in fact is done, is at first to substitute for those problems other much simpler, much more abstract, of which there is a good prospect of finding probable solutions. Then, the reasonably certain solutions of these last problems will throw a light more or less clear upon more concrete problems which are in certain respects more interesting. This method of procedure is that Analytic Method to which modern physics owes all its triumphs. It has been applied with great success in psychical sciences also. . . . It is reprobated by the whole Hegelian army, who think it ought to be replaced by the "Historic Method," which studies complex problems in all their complexity, but which cannot boast any distinguished successes."

R.M.M. Surely not in mathematics, or in formal logic, anyhow. Carnap, one of your great successors on logical matters, was eloquent also on this point.[2]

---

2. R. Carnap, *The Logical Syntax of Language* (London: Routledge and Kegan Paul, 1936), p. 8.

C.S.P.   Then there is the matter of the *triad*. Of course (1.368) "nobody will suppose that I wish to claim any originality in reckoning the triad important in philosophy. Since Hegel, almost every fanciful thinker has done the same. Originality is the last of recommendations for fundamental conceptions. On the contrary the fact that the minds of men have ever been inclined to threefold divisions is one of the considerations in favor of them. Other numbers have been objects of predilection to this philosopher and that, but three has been prominent at all times and with all schools. My whole method will be found to be in profound contrast with that of Hegel; I reject his philosophy *in toto*. Nevertheless, I have a certain sympathy with it, and fancy that if its author had only noticed a very few circumstances he would himself have been led to revolutionize his system. One of these is ...[that]... he has committed the trifling oversight of forgetting that there is a real world with real actions and reactions [Firstness and Secondness]. Then Hegel had the misfortune to be unusually deficient in mathematics. He shows this in the very elementary character of his reasoning. Worse still, while the whole burden of his song is that philosophers have neglected to take Thirdness into account, . . . he unfortunately did not know, what it would have been of the utmost importance for him to know, that the mathematical analysts had in great measure escaped this great fault, and that the thorough-going pursuit of the ideas and methods of the differential calculus would be sure to cure it altogether. Hegel's dialectical method is only a feeble and rudimentary application of the principles of the calculus to metaphysics. Finally Hegel's plan of evolving everything out of the abstractest conception by a dialectical procedure, though far from being so absurd as the experimentalists think, but on the contrary representing one of the indispensable parts of the course of science, overlooks the weakness of individual man, who wants the strength to wield such a weapon as that." He needs the help of the sciences.

R.M.M.   You are referring of course to the mathematical analysis of continuous series and functions, in the work of Cantor, Weierstrass, and others. It is surely very important to see the connection of this with the metaphysics of continuity, on the one hand, and with the logical foundations of the mathematics involved, on the other. Your conception of logic, incidentally, is more intimately connected with Hegel's "objective logic" than at first appears, is it not?

C.S.P.   Yes. "The term 'logic' [1.444] is unscientifically employed by me in two distinct senses. In its narrower sense, it is the science of the necessary conditions of the attainment of truth. In its broader sense, it is the science of the necessary laws of thought, or, still better (thought always taking place by means of signs), it is general semeiotic, treating not merely of truth, but also of the general conditions of signs being signs (which Duns Scotus called *grammatica speculativa*), also laws of the evolution of thought, which since it coincides with the necessary conditions of the transmission of meaning by signs from mind to mind, and from one state of mind to another, ought, for the sake of taking advantage of an old association of terms, be called *rhetorica speculativa,* but which I content myself with inaccurately calling *objective logic,* because that conveys the correct idea that it is like Hegel's logic. . . ."

R.M.M.   There is also the *architectonic* character of philosophy, of which you made much and which is also very fundamental in Hegel, is it not?

C.S.P.   Yes. "Metaphysics consists [for me] in the result of the absolute acceptance of logical principles not merely as regulatively valid, but as truths of being [1.487]". Indeed (1.625), "unless the metaphysician is a most thorough master of formal logic — and especially of the inductive side of the logic of relatives, immeasurably more important and more difficult than all the rest of formal logic put together — he will inevitably fall into the practice of deciding upon the validity of reasonings in the same manner in which, for example, the practical politician decides as to the weight that ought to be allowed to different considerations, that is to say, by the impression these reasonings make upon the mind, . . . [Hence] the metaphysician who is not prepared to grapple with all the difficulties of modern exact logic had better . . . [close] up his shutters and go out of the trade. Unless he will do one or the other, I tell him to his conscience that he is not the genuine, honest, earnest, resolute, energetic, industrious, and accomplished doubter that it is his duty to be. But [1.625] this is not all, nor half. For after all, metaphysical reasonings, such as they have hitherto been, have been simple enough for the most part. It is the metaphysical *concepts* [italics added] which it is difficult to apprehend. Now the metaphysical conceptions, as I need not waste words to show, are merely adapted from those of formal logic, and therefore can only be apprehended in the light of a minutely accurate and thoroughgoing system of formal logic. . . . To me [2.36], it seems that a metaphysics not founded on the science of logic is of all branches of scientific inquiry the most shaky and insecure. . . ."

R.M.M.   These are strong statements concerning your position. But on the whole metaphysicians have not been taken them seriously.

C.S.P.   As a matter of fact, not many have subscribed to this architectonic view in the whole history of metaphysics. "Some of the most celebrated logics [2.37] . . . are written from the point of view of metaphysical sects." Even the Organon of Aristotle and "about half the scholastic works on logic" base it "on metaphysics to some extent." I could give here an enumeration of considerable length, to substantiate my claim that "a large proportion of all the logics that have ever been written [up to 1902] have more or less pursued this vicious order of thought," of regarding metaphysics as prior to logic. I do not explicitly include Hegel's in this list so much as those of his followers, the Hegelians. It seems to me that (2.166) "the only rational way [of proceeding] would be to settle first the principles of reasoning and, that done, to base one's metaphysics upon those principles. Modern notions of metaphysics are not rationally entitled to any respect, because they have not been determined in that way. . . ." Logic, it seems to me, "is to be used as the [basis and] support of the exactest sciences in their [study of the] deepest and nicest questions."

R.M.M.　It is interesting that, in commenting on "all seven of the mental qualifications of a philosopher" (in 1.522), you place "the ability to discern what is before one's consciousness" at the very top of the list. You mention six others and comment that "Kant possessed in a high degree all seven" of these. Which of them would you attribute to Hegel?

C.S.P.　"Hegel, in some respects the greatest philosopher that ever lived [1.524], had a somewhat juster notion [than Kant did] of . . . [523] the inexhaustible intricacy of the fabric of conceptions, which is such that I do not flatter myself that I have ever analyzed a single idea into its constituent elements. . . . [524] But Hegel was lamentably deficient in . . .[the] requisite of critical severity and sense of fact. He brought out the three elements [Firstness, Secondness, Thirdness] much more clearly [than Kant did]; but the element of Secondness, of hard fact, is not accorded its due place in his system; and in a lesser degree the same is true of Firstness. After Hegel wrote, there came fifty years that were remarkably fruitful in all the means for attaining that fifth requisite, critical severity and the sense of hard fact. Yet Hegel's followers, instead of going to work to reform their master's system, and to render his statement of it obsolete, as every true philosopher must desire that his disciples should do, only proposed, at best, some superficial changes without replacing at all the rotten material with which the system was built up."

My estimate of Hegel depends intimately on my categories of Firstness, Secondness, and Thirdness. "Hegel, [1.532] whose neglect of Secondness was due chiefly to his not recognizing any other mode of being that existence — and what he calls *Existenz* is a special variety of it merely — regarded pure being as pretty much the same as nothing." "Hegel did, after all, [2.157] make it clear that if there is to be any philosophy, everything is to be traced back to one simple elementary principle, and that the only one principle which can explain everything is thought, intellectual thought. But it is obviously an essential factor of . . . [my] doctrine of rationality that there should be [also] a radically irrational element in Fact, an element of brute force. . . ."

My "method [1.544] has a general similarity to Hegel's. It would be historically false to call it a modification of Hegel's. It was brought into being by the study of Kant's categories and not Hegel's. Hegel's method has the defect of not working at all if you think with too great exactitude. . . . [My] method works better the finer and more accurate the thought. . . ."

Indeed, we must be prepared to undertake "reasoning . . . more complicated than one of Hegel's dilemmas. For all reasoning is mathematical and requires effort."

Once all this is said, due credit must be given Hegel for his categories. He [5.38] "was quite right in holding that it was the business of . . . [Phenomenology] to bring out or make clear the *Categories* or fundamental modes. He was also right in holding that these . . . are of two kinds; the Universal Categories all of which apply to everything, and the series of categories consisting of phases of evolution. . . ." In regard to the former, "it appears to me that Hegel is so nearly right that my own doctrine might very well be taken for a variety of Hegelianism, although in point of fact it was determined in my mind by considerations entirely foreign to Hegel, at a time when my attitude toward Hegelianism was one of contempt. There was no influence upon me from Hegel unless it was of so occult a kind as to entirely escape my ken; and if there was such an occult influence, it strikes me as about as good an argument for the essential truth of the doctrine, as is the coincidence that Hegel and I arrived in quite independent ways substantially to the same result." As to the categories concerned with phases of evolution, "I am satisfied that Hegel has not approximated to any correct catalogue of them. It may be that here and there, in the long wanderings of his *Encyclopaedia* he has been a little warmed by the truth. But in all its main features his catalogue is utterly wrong, according to me." But I have scarcely been able to do better, nor have I "been able to draw up any catalogue that satisfies me." The matter is very difficult.

R.M.M.   Yes, indeed. A good deal must depend on the richness of one's underlying logical framework.

C.S.P.   Even so, I do think the science of Phenomenology, in the way in which I conceive it [5.39], "must be taken as the basis on which normative science is to be erected, and accordingly must claim our first attention. . . . Phenomenology is in my view [then] the most primal of all the positive sciences. . . . Logic and the other normative sciences [such as ethics and aesthetics], although they ask, not what *is* but what *ought to be*, nevertheless are positive sciences since it is by asserting positive, categorical truth that they are able to show that what they call good really is so; and the right reason, right effort, and right being, of which they treat, derive that character from positive categorical fact." Although Phenomenology thus "does not depend upon any other *positive science*, nevertheless it must, if it is to be properly grounded, be made to depend upon the Conditional or Hypothetical Science of *Pure Mathematics*, whose only aim is to discover not how things actually are, but how they might be supposed to be. . . . A Phenomenology which does not reckon with pure mathematics, a science hardly come to years of discretion when Hegel wrote, will be the same pitiful club-footed affair that Hegel produced."

R.M.M.   It is very interesting that you include here both ethics and aesthetics among the normative sciences and as dealing with "positive categorical fact." This is a position that seems to need developing in greater detail.

C.S.P.   Yes, probably. Hegel and his followers cast doubt not only upon the *logica utens* that bumps up against hard fact, but also upon the hard fact of mathematical demonstrations. "The effort has been praiseworthy [2.192]; but it has not succeeded. The truth . . . is too evident. Mathematical reasoning holds. Why should it not? It relates only to the creations of the mind, concerning which there is no obstacle to our learning whatever is true of them. The method of . . . [my] book, therefore, is to accept the reasonings of pure mathematics as beyond all doubt. It is fallible, as everything human is fallible. Twice two may perhaps not be four. But there is no more satisfactory way of assuring ourselves of anything than the mathematical way of assuring ourselves of mathematical theorems. No aid from the science of logic is called for in that field. As a fact, I have not the slightest doubt that twice two is four; nor have you. Then let us not pretend to doubt mathematical demonstrations of mathematical propositions so long as they are not open to mathematical criticism and have been submitted to sufficient examination and revision. The only concern that logic has with this sort of reasoning is to describe it."

R.M.M.   You mention somewhere (2.223) also that "one might almost say" that "logic wholly consists . . . in exactitude of thought."

C.S.P.   Yes, especially in philosophy, (also 2.223) which "has a peculiar need of a language distinct and detached from common speech" yet having a positive "need of popular words in popular senses — not as its own language (as it has too usually used those words) but as objects of its study." "Hegel endeavored to destroy . . . [this need]. It is a good economy for philosophy to provide itself with a vocabulary so outlandish that loose thinkers shall not be attempted to borrow its words. . . . The first rule of good taste in writing is to use words whose meanings will not be misunderstood; and if a reader does not know the meaning of the words, it is infinitely better that he should know that he does not know it." It is in exactitude of thought and its expression that I find Hegel most wanting.

R.M.M.   What you are saying could be regarded as an argument for its use of special symbols in philosophy rather than ordinary words. You also object, I believe, to what you regard as Hegel's identification of the syllogism with "the fundamental form of real being" (2.386).

C.S.P.   Yes. He did not "undertake to work over, in the light of this idea, in any fundamental way, what is ordinarily called logic. . . . He simply accepts Kant's table of functions of judgment, which is one of the most ill-considered performances in the whole history of philosophy. Consequently, what Hegel says upon this subject must not be considered as necessarily representing the legitimate outcome of his general position. . . ."

R.M.M.   At one point you even went so far as to say that Hegel, or at least the Hegelians (4.69), condoned reasoning as valid that sets out from falsity and leads to truth.

C.S.P.   Yes, Hegel actually gave several examples of this. As I recall, they are rather obscure and it is difficult to eke them out with any exactitude (5.332). In any case he seems to me to be clearly in error concerning them.

R.M.M.   It is very interesting that, a moment back, you remarked that mathematical reasonings hold — correct ones, of course — because they relate only to the creations of the mind. There is also a close connection, is there not, between this contention and your pragmaticism?

C.S.P.   Yes. "The truth [5.436] is that pragmaticism is closely allied to the Hegelian absolute idealism, from which, however, it is sundered by its vigorous denial that the third category (which Hegel degrades to a mere stage of thinking) suffices to make the world, or is even so much as self-sufficient." We should recall that "the third category — the category of thought, representation, triadic relation, mediation, genuine thirdness, thirdness as such — is an essential ingredient of reality, yet does not by itself constitute reality, since this category can have no concrete being without action [firstness], as a separate object on which to work its government, just as action cannot exist without the immediate being of feeling [secondness] on which to act." "Had Hegel, instead of regarding the first two stages with his smile of contempt, held on to them as independent or distinct elements of the triune Reality, pragmaticists might have looked up to him as the great vindicator of their truth. . . . For pragmaticism belongs essentially to the triadic class of philosophical doctrines, and is much more essentially so than Hegelianism is." And of course pragmaticism, "the one contribution of value" I had "to make to philosophy," involves essentially the establishment of the truth of synechism." Clearly "continuity is an indispensable element of reality, and . . . is simply what generality becomes in the logic of relatives, and thus, like generality, and more than generality, is an affair of thought, and is the essence of thought." Had I time (6.31), "I now ought to show how important for philosophy is the mathematical conception of continuity. Most of what is true in Hegel is a darkling glimmer of a conception which the mathematicians had long before made pretty clear, and which recent researchers have still further illustrated."

R.M.M. Just as the theory of continuity should be firmly based on mathematics, so no doubt the theory of spontaneity, of evolution, and of chance should be firmly based on what you would call inductive and abductive logic.

C.S.P. Yes indeed. Hegel (6.218) "says, if there is any sense in philosophy at all, the whole universe and every feature of it, however minute, is rational, and was contrained to be as it is by the logic of events, so that there is no principle of action in the universe but reason. But I reply, this line of thought, though it begins rightly, is not exact. A logical slip is committed; and the conclusion reached is manifestly at variance with observation. It is true that the whole universe and every feature of it must be regarded as rational, that is, as brought about by the logic of events. But it does not follow that it is *constrained* to be as it is by the logic of events; for the logic of evolution and of life need not be supposed to be of that wooden kind that absolutely constrains a given conclusion. The logic may be of the inductive or hypothetic inference. . . . The effect of this error of Hegel is that he is forced to deny [the] fundamental character of two elements of experience which cannot result from deductive logic." Another way of putting this is to say (6.305) that "the Hegelian philosophy is . . . an

294

anancasticism," that is, a doctrine of evolution by mechanical necessity. "With its revelatory religion, with its synechism (however imperfectly set forth), with its "reflection," the whole idea of the [Hegelian] theory is superb, almost sublime. Yet, after all, living freedom is almost omitted from its method. The whole movement is that of a vast engine, impelled by a *vis a tergo*, with a blind and mysterious fate of arriving at a lofty goal. . . . Grant that it really acts as it professes to act, and there is nothing to do but accept the philosophy. But never was there seen such an example of a long chain of reasoning — shall I say with a flaw in every link? . . . . If we use the one precious thing . . . [the Hegelian philosophy] contains, the idea of it, introducing the tychasm [or chance] which the arbitrariness of its every step suggests, and make that the support of a vital freedom which is the breath of the spirit of love, we may be able to produce that genuine agapasticism [evolution by creative love] at which Hegel was aiming."

R.M.M. What about your "law of the mind," which many have regarded as essentially Hegelian?

C.S.P. Yes, of course it is. "In the absence of external impressions of interest [7.388], thoughts begin to dance through the mind, each leading in another by the hand, like a train of Bacchants on a Grecian vase, as Hegel says. After a while the clear train of thoughts breaks, and for a time ideas are scattered, soon, however, to take places again in another train. There is a *law* in this succession of ideas. We may roughly say it is the law of habit. It is the great "Law of the Association of Ideas" — the one law of all psychical action."

Above all, let us not (7.559–560) make "the real things of this world blind unconscious objects working by mechanical laws together with a consciousness as idle spectator. . . . This makes the universe a muddle. According to it [that view], consciousness is perfectly impotent and is not the original of the material world; nor on the other hand can material forces ever have given birth to feeling, for all they do is to accelerate the motions of particles. . . . Grant [7.562] that that assumption is somehow wrong . . . and the muddle begins to clarify itself. The spectator is no longer on one side of the footlights, and the world on the other. He is, in so far as he sees, at one with the poet of the piece. To act intelligently and to see intelligently become at bottom one. And in the matter of auditing the account of the universe, its wealth and its government, we gain the liberty of drawing on the bank of thought. This method [7.563] promises to render the totality of things thinkable; and it is plain that there is no other way of explaining anything than to show how it traces its lineage to the womb of thought. [7.564] This is what is called Idealism. . . ."

R.M.M.   As a result of which, as you put it on one occasion (1.487), "the universe . . . [may be seen to have] an explanation, the function of which, like that of every logical explanation, is to unify its observed variety. It follows that the root of all being is One; and so far as different subjects have a common character they partake of an identical being. . . ."

C.S.P.   Yes. The crucial difference between Hegel and me [really] is in our methods. "The scientific man [8.118] hangs upon the lips of nature, in order to learn wherein he is ignorant and mistaken: the whole character of the scientific procedure springs from that disposition. The [Hegelian] metaphysician begins with a resolve to make out the truth of a foregone conclusion that he has never really doubted for an instant. Hegel was frank enough to avow that so it was in his case. His "voyage of discovery" was undertaken in order to recover the very fleece that it professed to bring home. The development of the metaphysician's thought is a continual breeding in and in; its destined outcome, sterility. The experiment was fairly tried with Hegelianism through an entire generation. The metaphysician is a worshipper of his own prepossessions. As Royce expresses it, he is intent upon developing his own purpose. The scientific man is eager to submit himself, his ideas, and his purpose, to the Great Power which, no doubt, penetrates his own being, but is yet all but wholly external to him and beyond anything that his poor present notion could ever, of itself, develop unfructified. The Absolute Knowledge of Hegel is nothing but G. W. F. Hegel's idea of himself; and it has not taught him the very first lesson in philosophy, that "whoever shall choose to seek his own purpose and idea shall miss it, and whoever shall abandon his own purpose and idea to adopt the purpose and idea of the Author of nature shall accomplish that, and his own long-abandoned purpose and idea along with it." If the idealist school will add to their superior earnestness the diligence of the mathematician about details, one will be glad to hope that it may be they who shall make metaphysics one of the true sciences. . . . But . . . [this] cannot be brought to accomplishment until Hegel is *aufgehoben*, with his mere rotation on his axis. Inquiry must react against experience in order that the ship may be propelled through the ocean of thought." What needs to be accomplished is precisely what I urged Royce to do, and this must be tied in with the philosophy of religion, which "deeply concerns us all." What we need is "a condensed and severe treatise" in which "*all* the new conceptions of multitude and continuity . . . shall be applied . . . to every subject of metaphysics from top to bottom . . . and so far as it relates to questions of fact be made scientific."

R.M.M.   I am not one to disagree with you on this, but it is very difficult to get one's fellow metaphysicians to lend one their ears. Your comments on Hegel are fascinating. Even if it should turn out that a close Hegel scholar might challenge you on specific points of interpretation, they are of interest in throwing light on what you *took* him to be saying. Often such comments show greater insight than the originals. In any case, it has been a pleasure hearing you out on this subject.

Second Part of the Dialogue — some days later

C.S.P.   Good day, Martin, I am glad to see you here again. I am afraid I was somewhat *eigenbrötlich* in our conversation the other day. There are several questions actually I would like to put to you. Has there been any effort in recent years to put objective idealism on a more secure logical footing than I was able to give it? What has happened since 1914 along these lines?

R.M.M.   Well, as you know, Royce gave the matter some lip service, and so did his follower, William Ernest Hocking. But what you asked for was a deeper and more exact kind of study than either of these writers undertook. In attempting to answer your questions, we ought first to have a look at logic itself, which has made great advances in recent years, along lines you yourself more or less suggested and of which you would on the whole, I think, very much approve. Perhaps you would be interested in hearing, very briefly, my own view of the matter.

C.S.P.   Yes, I would.

R.M.M.   The narrower sense of logic is now taken to include the theory of the truth-functions and quantifiers and perhaps identity. You yourself had these in clear focus but did not unify them in the systematic way that has now become customary. This we now call *first-order logic*. Your "icons of second intention" belong to what we now call *second-order* logic. But there is also a third-order logic, and the logics of higher order are now regarded as a kind of set theory, one way of systematizing the work of Cantor. There are many other ways of doing this also, but none of them is regarded as wholly satisfactory. The details of set theory or *Mengenlehre* belong more to mathematics proper than to philosophy, and no philosopher since 1908 has written anything very basic about it.

In semeiotics, however, the situation is very different. This conveniently breaks into syntax, semantics, and pragmatics, essentially along lines you more or less indicated. What you perhaps did not foresee, however, is that semiotics — we now spell it without the extra 'e' — itself has become highly systematized and subject to very intensive and exact study. Syntax, roughly speaking, is concerned only with signs (regarded either as types or tokens, although it makes a good deal of difference which) and their interrelations. Semantics is concerned with what the signs stand for, their "objects," as you would say, as well as their meanings. The part of semantics dealing only with the interrelations between signs and objects is *extensional* semantics, *intensional* semantics being concerned with meanings or the "interpretants." In pragmatics — the word of course was coined in deference to your use of 'pragmatism' and 'pragmaticism' — the *user* of the language is explicitly brought in together with his various relations with signs (and of course objects too).

What does objective idealism look like from the point of view of the new development of systematic semiotics? No one seems to have worried about this problem quite so much as I have, so perhaps you will allow me to call your attention to some of my own work, which you would, I think, approve of in principle at least if not in full detail.

Our very first task is to be sure that mathematics is provided for. This can be done, somewhat along the lines of Zermelo and other set-theorists, provided all the notions involved be given an idealist setting, the purely logical notions, the sets, and the *Urelemente* or basic individuals. The details here are more troublesome than one might think, and I hit upon some of them by reflecting upon what Duns Scotus might conceivably have meant by a *common nature*. Strangely enough, the idealist setting for set theory is allied with a doctrine that seems akin to that of Scotus.

C.S.P.   This does not seem strange to me, for I was always one to extol the deep insight of Scotus on these matters.

R.M.M.   In what has been said thus far no provision has been made for induction and abduction, to which you have attached so much importance. Would that one could point out definitive recent achievement in these areas, but one cannot. Three different types of probability have been on the market — the relative frequency view, the logical or confirmational view, and the subjective view — and their proponents have been eloquent about their special virtues. It seems to me that we should recognize all three types, each perhaps *sui generis*, and then seek to integrate them in full detail in a general theory and to show their usefulness. But no one seems to have come along to do this, equipped with the necessary mastery of mathematical details. There is also the very fundamental problem as to how initial or *a priori* probabilities, in any of these senses, are assigned in the first place. This seems to remain rather mysterious. Einstein, when once asked why he rejected quantum mechanics, is said to have replied that he could not accept the concept of *a priori* probability. The working scientist assumes that proper *a priori* assignments can be made and then goes ahead as though they already had been. There is no doubt that probability theories are of great help in some sciences but due more to God's grace than to their intrinsic rationality, it is to be feared.

Two additional areas of logic of great utility have not yet been mentioned, the calculus of individuals and event-logic. The calculus of individuals, or mereology, as it is called following Leśniewski, concerns the part-whole relation between individuals and various other relations and notions expressions for which are definable in terms of it. Mereology is an important adjunct to set theory. Event-logic is not too far from what you called 'the logic of events', but is developed in exact terms as an extension of the calculus of individuals. Events, states, acts, processes, and the like, are recognized as objects along with whatever one takes as the individuals or *Urelemente*. Person A's *act* of giving an object B to person C, to use one of your favorite examples, is recognized — as you came very close to doing in several passages — as a respectable entity on a par with any other. It is in terms of variables ranging over events, acts, and so on, that our language can handle such basic ideas as change, growth, coming into being, decay, passing out of being, evolution, change of state, cell fusion, cell division, and so on and on. And of course the theory of time itself, and indeed of space also, is derivative upon certain more fundamental relations between events, as is demanded by relativity theory.

The astonishing fact about modern set theory, with mereological and event-theoretic extensions, is that, with the addition of suitable non-logical constants as primitives, a language-system results in which anything one ever wishes to say in science may be said. Of course, this statement has never really been put to the test, but there is enormous evidence in its favor; and I do not believe it is ever doubted with any seriousness by anyone sufficiently conversant with set theory. So far as concerns science, we have then, in this way of developing set theory and its applications, an idealist foundation as "exact" as ever you could wish.

This extended set-theoretic language is only an object-language, built upon the basis of the first-order kind of logic mentioned above. With a semiotic available for it, a still further extension is available, called 'the *metalogic* of the language'. Whatever reservations one might have about the contention just expressed about the scientific adequacy of the extended set theory would surely evaporate when one takes into account its meta-logic. Especially rich here is the pragmatics of the language, in which the scientist's relations to his linguistic vehicle are explicitly taken into account.

We have been speaking of objective idealism, but we should not fail to recall that the various extensions of set theory mentioned can also be provided on a non-idealist basis, as in fact is usually done. The question arises as to whether we gain anything, so far as concerns the actual practice of science, by adapting the idealist foundation. All the hard work of science must be done quite irrespective of its metaphysical foundation. The latter neither blocks nor paves the road to inquiry, and it should in no way be allowed to hamper the free play of the scientific imagination. At the present stage of research, it is difficult to know what to answer to such a question. Intriguing and deep studies in the interrelations between mind and body are being pursued, in which the hypothesis of the independent reality of the mind in some sense is not ruled out as absurd. The hypothesis that the brain is a "manifestation" of mind is perhaps no more or less otiose than one to the effect that the mind is a "function" of the brain. Is the relation of being a *manifestation-of* here really any more or less mysterious than that of being a *function-of*? The degeneration of "matter" in recent physical theory into quanta of energy and point-events, and the proliferation of elementary particles having almost no properties (if any) in common with traditionally accepted material objects, only accentuates the problem of the tenuous interconnections of so-called "mind" and "matter" and of the very meaning of these hoary terms.

It seems to me there are two attitudes we can take at this point. One is to hew to the scientific *status quo*, if there is one and if we can actually find out what it is at any given time. There are of course many conflicting scientific views, and one can find some eminent authority bolstering up whatever one's favored one might be. If we are real metaphysicians, however, we might wish to be somewhat more daring, and sail forth on a more speculative flying trapeze. Our metaphysical view we will wish to formulate and accept in a hypothetical spirit, as in the sciences themselves, and be ready to abandon it should sufficient evidence or other convincing reasons be forthcoming against it.

The real strength of the idealist position is to be found, one may contend, when we step beyond the sciences to the study of what seem to be distinctively human concerns. Here we must recognize all humane acts and feelings, individual and societal, including those in the moral and aesthetic realms at their highest, to say nothing of religious aspiration. It is in these areas that the idealist metaphysicians throughout history have felt most at home and to which they have made their most distinctive contributions. And if my contentions above are sound, they need have no fear from the sciences, which they can now accommodate in their overall metaphysical view as well as anyone else.

C.S.P. Well, I cannot disagree with you on these points in any fundamental way. Many of the details you have presupposed in your comments I am a bit hazy about, just as I was a bit hazy about Cantor's work, although I never for a moment doubted but that it was of the highest importance, not only for mathematics, but for the very dignity of the mind itself. I hope you are right in thinking that it, Cantor's work, can be given an exact modern formulation within an objective idealism.

R.M.M. In all this, a good many of the details of your philosophic view may have to be abandoned, or at any event may not have the importance you attached to them. The most notable is perhaps your insistence upon trichotomies, and more particularly upon your categories of Firstness, Secondness, and Thirdness. Triadic relations play no more important role now than dyadic ones do. In fact all triadic relations may be explained away in terms of dyadic ones, and all triads construed as dyads. And, even further, all dyads may be construed as monads, that is, as sets of ordered couples. In set theory, where $\{x,y\}$ is the set having just x and y as members, the *ordered* set $<x,y>$ can be identified with $\{x,\{x,y\}\}$, the set whose only members are x and $\{x,y\}$. This set is of course a monad, or a "dyadic monad," as you might say. The triad $<x,y,z>$ can be handled similarly as $\{x,<y,z>\}$ or as $\{<x,y>,z\}$, and this set too is a monad. Of course some dyadic relations — or rather signs for them — must be admitted as primitives, for example, 'ϵ' for the relation of membership. There is thus no special reason, so far as the logic of relations is concerned, for having three categories rather than one or two or four or more. The door is left open here for both a *monism*, of absolute spirit, if you like, and for a *pluralism* of as many types of entities as it serves some useful purpose, scientific or otherwise, to distinguish.

There are many further features of your philosophic position that seem to me to need comment and possible emendation. The other day during our conversation I was itching to interrupt you at almost every point, but it did not seem the occasion to do so. I recall your fascinating comment about Kant, that (2.31) if he "had performed all the work which a thorough, scientific application of his method demanded, he would have had to postpone the publication of his *Critic of Pure Reason* for another century at least, which would have been regrettable. It would be radically contrary to Kant's [own] principles to base logic . . . upon . . . [his] transcendental method. On the contrary, his whole critic of the understanding is deliberately based on a scientific logic supposed to be already established. It is singular that, notwithstanding the gigantic logical strength of the *Critic of Pure Reason*, and notwithstanding Kant's explicit teaching that this hinges upon the scientific perfection of the underlying formal, or ordinary, logic, yet he never touches this last doctrine without betraying unmistakeable marks of hasty, superficial study."

It seems to me that something similar could be said of your own work, *mutatis mutandis*, and in fact of any metaphysical view as architectonically based on the logic of its day. In accord with this, one should simply hold off publication until the underlying logic is in better shape. It is only during the last quarter of the twentieth century that formal logic and semiotics have gained sufficient pliability to handle the kind of philosophy you espoused. But it would surely be regrettable if you had not written the works you did. Perhaps we should allow metaphysics — good metaphysics, that is — always to leap ahead of the logic and science of its time in some respects, but of course to be firmly based on them in others. It is very likely that this is true of all the historically great metaphysical views. Those that fail in this regard would probably fail anyhow. A good metaphysics is always good in its detail, but still, not too much detail should be demanded of it lest it be mistaken for one of the special sciences. Actually it is next to impossible here, it seems to me, to make any clear demarcation. And of course the metaphysical leaping ahead of its time that turns out to be fruitful is that the leads into the logic and science of the future, on the one hand, and to the enhancement of our understanding of value and of humane feeling, on the other.

You leaped ahead of your time in all manner of fascinating ways which now require a closer look. The relation between thought and language, for example, is more difficult than you assumed it to be. The logic of evolution, to give another example, has not even yet gotten off the ground, to say nothing of the special case of the evolution of "mind" and of the laws of nature. The relations between logic and natural language are now being studied in great detail by both linguists and logicians, and a whole new science of logico-linguistics is fast in the making. The subject is turning out to be much more complex and difficult than one might have anticipated. Likewise the mathematical theory of continuity has taken on new wings recently in the study of infinitesimal magnitudes. Your belief in infinitesimals is to some extent being vindicated. Here again, though, the theory was arrived at by very complex metamathematical considerations that far transcend Cantor's methods. Another recent area of development, so-called "epistemic" logic, is concerned with such relations as knowing, believing, and the like, in the light of which your doctrine of the infinitistic character of representation and cognition would have to be reexamined.

It is interesting, isn't it, that we have been conversing only of your interest in Hegel, and yet we have managed to broach in one way or another almost every philosophical topic that concerned you. Your philosophy is a vast edifice, carefully integrated in essentials. It is like a giant mobile or moving sculpture of the kind that if one touches it at any part the whole is instantly put into motion.

One item that we have not mentioned and that comes to mind is your so-called doubt-belief theory of inquiry. Even if correct in essentials, it needs to be given a new twist in at least two directions. On the one hand, a whole *system* may be doubted and then believed in, or conversely, in accord with Tisza's dynamics of logical systems.[3] Or conflicting systems may themselves be respectively doubted or believed in. Or even one and the same system may be both doubted and believed in, but in different senses or for different reasons. The true scientist presumably never regards what he has done as fully satisfactory. "With one hand we believe; with the other, we doubt," as Einstein put it.[4] It seems to me that your doubt-belief theory is really deeper than even you yourself took it to be.

Another point that should be brought up concerns the quantifiers and their connection with generality, infinity, and continuity. It was just a hundred years ago, in 1879, that Frege first hit upon the quantifiers, in his *Begriffsschrift,* and you did so likewise a few years later but by a somewhat different route. It is as though all of a sudden the quantifiers burst forth upon the world, like Venus rising from the sea, in full glory. It was only by a very conscious use of them that the various kinds of transfinite ordinals and cardinals came to be distinguished and characterized in modern set theory. And similarly for the continuity of functions in the theory of real and complex variables. High generality is of course required, namely, quantifiers over very large domains of sets, numbers, and functions. But none of this quite captures "true continuity" according to you, which is related to your

---

3. L. Tisza, "The Logical Structure of Physics," in *Proceedings of the Boston Colloquium for the Philosophy of Science 1961–1962,* ed. by M. Wartofsky (*Boston Studies in the Philosophy of Science,* Dordrecht: D. Reidel Publishing Co., 1963), pp. 55–71.

4. In "Mercer Street and Other Memories" collected by John Archibald Wheeler, in *Albert Einstein, 1879–*1979, ed. by P. C. Eichelburg and R. U. Sexl (Vieweg-Verlag: 1979).

law of the mind. I am afraid this law has never been spelled out in a sufficiently exact way to determine what it says, whether it is true or not (or even probable), or even what evidence there is on its behalf. Until we know what it says there is not much point talking of evidence for or against it. But one thing about it is clear: it needs precise formulation in terms of quantifiers over variables the range of which is explicitly to be determined in a scientific way.

A final point or so. Those of us who are interested in logic and metaphysics — 'logico-metaphysics', may I call it? — should never forget the helpful spade-work that is often done by analytic philosophers. Much analysis is needed about the notion of human action as based on a belief, for example, that (it seems to me) you glide over too readily. You take a stand here that is at best doubtful. Also progress has been made in the "normative" sciences of ethics and aesthetics, as well as in the study of social relations, which seem now ripe for more sophisticated and exact renditions that are currently given. These are areas of philosophy to which you attached the very highest importance. Like Whitehead you came to them late in life and had no time to give them the attention you came to think they deserved.

Also our logical tools have now developed to such an extent as to be able to handle modes of reasoning usually thought to be beyond their purview. The most subtle concepts in ethics and aesthetics may now be handled within the logical framework I have outlined. There is also theology, the queen of the sciences, to which you contributed your notable "Neglected Argument" paper. Your argument now lends itself to a much more exact statement than you were able to give it, and in fact comes out, it seems to me, a much more impressive piece of work than even you probably thought it was.[5] It is interesting, incidentally, that there is no mention of Hegel in this paper, very likely the most Hegelian you ever wrote. Finally, one will come to wish "above all things to shape the whole conduct of one's life and all the springs of action" in conformity with the belief in an *Ens necessarium*. If we ever get to that stage in life, as very few do, I suppose most of our philosophizing will appear rather paltry: *Ut palea mihi vedetur.*

In the course of my remarks, I have done some name-dropping: Carnap, Zermelo, Whitehead, Einstein, Tisza. There are of course many others to add, names of writers in whose work you would be very interested, including of course the many humanists, value-

---

5. Cf. "On the Logic of Idealism and Peirce's Neglected Argument," in *Peirce's Logic of Relations Etc.*

theorists, theologians, and the like, whose work, although not directly leading to logico-metaphysical reconstruction, is nonetheless of the utmost importance in preparing the way and in helping us to keep on the right track.

C.S.P.   Thank you for your comments. The highest compliment you can pay me is that you think my views at least worth considering and updating. When I was alive in the flesh, no one ever paid me any compliment at all. It has been said that one can live for a month on a compliment — one should add that one can languish for years for the want of one. Let me think about the things you have said and I hope we can discuss some of these matters further and in greater detail on another occasion.

R.M.M.   Thank *you*, Professor Peirce, for discussing these matters with me. There is no one in the whole history of philosophy with whom I would rather be in essential agreement. Your "guess at the riddle" seems to me one of the most profound and far-reaching that anyone has yet put forward, and your understanding of and insistence upon logico-mathematical methods, on the one hand, and scientific experimentation, on the other, combined with your uncanny analytic insight into almost everything you ever thought about — to say nothing of your broad humane, ethical, aesthetic, and religious concerns — make you the most "modern" of all the historically great philosophers, one of the very few from whom we all still have much to learn. You yourself noted (8.268) that Hegel "blundered monstrously, as we shall all be seen to do." No one of us is an exception in this regard. We can learn even from your errors, as you would of course wish us to do. Good day.

CHAPTER XX

On Meaning, Protomathematics, and the Philosophy of Nature

Consilia callida et audacia prima specie laeta, tractatu dura, eventu tristia sunt.

"The typically scientific methods assist in the discovery of truth while the effort of philosophy is directed to the elucidation of meaning," Moritz Schlick wrote in a characteristic vein.[1] "The task of a philosophy of nature is thus to interpret the meaning of the propositions of natural science." This is not to be done in an haphazard way, but in terms of an "exact philosophy," a phrase that now, several decades after Schlick wrote, is coming more and more to the fore. Moreover, as Schlick noted (p. 4), "it is the exactitude of natural science that causes it to be, both historically and in actual fact, the most fundamental basis from which to philosophize. Only in the analysis of exact knowledge, is there any hope of achieving true insight. Only here, is there any prospect of attaining definite and final results by means of the elucidation of concepts. The vague, uncertain propositions of the inexact sciences must first be transformed into exact knowledge — that is, they must be translated into the language of the exact sciences — before their meaning can be fully interpreted. And exact knowledge is knowledge that can be fully and clearly expressed in accordance with the tenets of logic. 'Mathematics' is only a name for the method of logically exact formulation. . . . In science, more than in any other domain, the stuff or substance of knowledge is derived from an intellectual activity that enables us to arrive at the greatest heights of abstraction. But the higher the level of abstraction attained by a science, the deeper it penetrates the essence of reality." Let us bring this forceful passage up to date, at first at face value, and then as applied to Schlick's own theory of meaning and other parts of his overall philosophical view.

---

1. In his *Philosophy of Nature* (New York: Philosophical Library, 1949), p. 3.

On an appropriate meaning of 'exact' it may well be that the exact sciences are not so exact, after all. The exactitude of even mathematics, except as formalized in terms of a categorical axiom-system — that is, one all of whose interpretations are isomorphic in an appropriate sense — is in doubt. The Löwenheim-Skolem theorem in fact, if 'exact' is construed in terms of categoricity and mathematics is regarded as formalized in terms of a first-order set theory to which that theorem applies, establishes that it is not. It is doubtful, however, that categoricity has much to do with exactitude, outside of mathematics anyhow. More important would seem to be words and phrases that designate uniquely or denote just such and such objects satisfying some well-defined or -understood condition. Such words and phrases are as "exact" as one could wish, semantically speaking. Many non-semantical features must be brought in for the analysis of 'exactitude' taken epistemically. The word 'exact' of course has a multitude of meanings. One of them no doubt can be tailored to fit mathematics, another perhaps various areas of mathematical physics, still another theoretical biology, and so on. And no doubt these are important family resemblances among these various meanings.

The question arises as to whether the philosophy of language can be made exact in a suitable sense, in terms of which a theory of meaning can be developed. Progress in recent years in structural linguistics, and its offshoot the newer logico-linguistics, suggests an affirmative answer. In fact the progress is so striking and far-reaching that all talk of meaning or of verification except in its terms now seems *retardataire*. A necessary condition for exact knowledge, in whatever domain, is surely that it can be "expressed in accordance with the tenets of logic," whether "fully and clearly" or not being open to question.

By 'logic' we should not understand here the narrow theory of *Principia Mathematica* of 1910–1913, or even of that of its second edition in 1925. It should be construed more widely to embrace (i) the calculus of individuals or mereology, (ii) a metalogic including a syntax, semantics, and even a systematic pragmatics, (iii) a theory of intensionality in one or another formulation, and (iv) a theory of events with event-variables explicitly introduced. To these must be added (v) a theory concerning the exact behavior of all the non-logical predicate- and individual-constants admitted as primitives. It is only in this widened sense that even the statements of the exact sciences can be "expressed in accordance with the tenets of logic." All five of these additional items would seem so necessary that without them the claim that exact knowledge can be so expressed would seem excessive, to say the least. All five of these addenda may be suitably appended to the logic of *PM* but are not explicitly parts of it.

The matter of expressibility "fully and clearly" in accord with the tenets of even the widened logic should be commented on. What is *full* expressibility? Let us attempt to characterize this in the light of a view concerning logical form put forward previously.[2] A given sentence may be said to be fully expressible in a given, interpreted, logical formula provided, roughly, every (natural) word of the sentence has a "representative" in the form with (usually) various symbols of logic interspersed between them, the form capturing all relevant semantical and grammatical features of the original. The form gives the full logical structure of the original, with all non-logical words properly interpreted, and thus may be thought of as providing its "meaning." If the original is ambiguous, it is to be "disambiguated" and forms given for each "reading," the form for the original then being the disjunction of the forms for these readings.

'Clearly' is a pragmatical word, and what is clear to you may not be clear to me. No doubt a social characterization of this word is needed, in which reference to a given group of users of language is made, perhaps to a given group taken as typical, or dominant, or as paradigmatic in some sense.

Already in these few remarks a theory of meaning has been suggested very different from Schlick's own in terms of verification and use. A clear and succinct statement of his view is that "whenever we ask about a sentence, 'What does it mean?' what we expect is instruction as to the circumstances in which the sentence is to be used; we want a description of the conditions under which the sentence will form a true proposition, and of those which will make it false. The meaning of a word, or of a combination of words is, in this way, determined by a set of rules which regulate their use and which, following Wittgenstein, we may call the rules of their grammar, taking this word in its widest sense. . . . Stating the meaning of a sentence amounts to stating the rules according to which the sentence is to be used, and this is the same as stating the way in which it can be verified (or falsified). The meaning of a proposition is the method of its verification."[3]

It is very interesting that grammar, and other grammatical rules, are construed here "in the widest sense," so as to include presumably not only syntactical and semantical matters, but pragmatical ones as

2. See especially *Semiotics and Linguistic Structure*, Chapter XV.
3. *Gesammelte Aufsätze 1926–1936* (Hildesheim: Georg Holms, 1938), pp. 26–36 and p. 340.

well. But just what form do these rules take on when precisely stated? All such rules themselves must, in order to have meaning in the sense of this theory, be "fully and clearly expressed in accordance with the tenets of logic." Syntax and semantics are now rather well-developed areas of logic, but even so there is enormous variation in the current views as to their inner structure. Especially in semantics, and thus in the statement of its rules, the variations are so considerable that there is little if any agreement as to how an acceptable theory of such is to be formulated. When we turn to pragmatical rules, there is even less acceptable formulation to go on. The pragmatical rules required by Schlick's theory concern the "circumstances" and "conditions" in which a word or phrase or sentence is to be used, both linguistic and non-linguistic.

Consider some single word. All the conditions of its use in all manner of situations and linguistic contexts must be given by some set of rules determining its meaning. Has any such set of rules ever been given, even "in principle," for any single word of either a scientific or a natural language? (The notions of logic here are a possible exception to this question, but even here the matter is not beyond all doubt.) Is it *possible* to give such a set of rules? As relativized to all users of the language? Or even to those of some given social group? Or even to some one user? Or even to some one user at some one time? If we bring in other words, to say nothing of combinations of them, especially those constituting sentences, our questions multiply uncomfortably beyond bounds. Nor are they idle or rhetorical questions that may be brushed aside. Rules determinative of the meaning of a given word or phrase or sentence must be fully and clearly expressed or at least expressible, in accordance with the tenets of logic — or logico-linguistics — in order to know that that word or phrase or sentence has meaning at all.

Giving the grammatical rules in the sense required by the theory "is the same as stating the way in which it can be verified (or falsified)." 'The same' here presumably is a surrogate for 'is logically equivalent to' or such like. It would be interesting to have this equivalence, if such it be, fully spelled out in accord with the theory. And even if this were done one might well doubt of the truth of the result. Suppose all the rules governing 'The unicorn has one horn' are spelled out; it is still doubtful as to whether the resulting sentence is true or false. Some theories say 'yes' some 'no'. Again, suppose all the rules governing 'The $1,000,000,000^{1,000,000,000!}$ th place in the decimal expansion of π is occupied by '7'' were available; we still do not know *now* whether the sentence is verifiable or not, even in principle. And even suppose

309

an answer were forthcoming in the future, we do not have to wait for that answer to know *now* that the sentence is meaningful according to the grammatical rules of *present-day* English.

There is a tremendous difference between the "meaning" of a single word and that of a phrase or sentence that contains it. The meaning of a sentence — one supposes, anyhow — is determined in some way by the meaning of its constituent words. An alternative view has it that only in the context of a sentence does a word have a meaning at all. Schlick's theory slights over this difference and in fact is phrased in such a way that only declarative sentences — we need not distinguish them from "propositions" for present purposes — can be true or false, and hence be said to have meaning. Questions, commands, exclamations, and perhaps subjunctives are thus left out, although perhaps they could be squeezed in by suitable technical devices.

Finally, there is the very meaning of 'verifiable' itself that needs spelling out in accord with the exact tenets of a logical analysis. There are two levels of problems here, the one having to do with attempts at analyzing it as criticized by Alonzo Church,[4] the other having to do with the logico-linguistic rules governing the word itself. Further rules are needed governing 'in principle' when verifiability in principle is referred to. These must be formulated with some care, lest some hidden metaphysical reference creep in surreptitiously, contrary to Schlick's intent.

Schlick's use of 'in principle' in fact, is not a happy one. What does it mean? Presumably: in accord with certain principles. What principles? Presumably: those governing 'verifiable'. A theory or set of interrelated principles is then needed to provide for such. One surely cannot contend, then, that such a theory is not needed or that it would not be formulated in a series of "philosophical propositions," and at the same time make such fundamental use as Schlick does of this phrase.

By 'verifiability' Schlick (p. 346) means "possibility of verification," and he calls "a fact or a process 'logically possible' if . . . the sentence which is supposed to describe it obeys the rules of grammar we have stipulated for our language. . . . A fact which could not be described would, of course, not be any fact at all; any fact is logically possible. . . ." But all this, of course, will never do. Schlick's uncritical use of 'fact' has already been lamented. The use of the phrase 'logically possible' is also unfortunate, there being many variant meanings to it, each depending on how 'logic' is precisely construed in a given con-

---

4. See especially Alonzo Church, his review of Ayer, in *The Journal of Symbolic Logic* 14 (1949): 52–53 and elsewhere.

text, whether as a first-order logic, second-order, some set theory, some modal logic, and so on.

The very meaning of the sentences constituting the verifiability-use theory of meaning is thus in doubt, and hence their truth or falsity, on Schlick's own grounds. Even more damaging is its impracticality in requiring rules of a kind that never have, and very likely never can, be given. Further, the theory as actually stated is not a "scientific" theory. It achieved no "true insight," not being based on "exact knowledge" or upon "propositions" that could be "transformed" or "translated" into the language of the exact sciences" of mathematics, physics, and so on — where 'mathematics' is construed in the usual sense and not in the extended sense in which it is construed as "only a name for the method of logically exact formulation." There is no possibility of transforming or translating all the grammatical rules the theory requires into the usual scientific language — without, that is, extension to include the newer logico-linguistics, beyond Schlick's purview.

The conception of language, upon what Schlick's theory was based, is not such as to meet contemporary standards. He frequently referred to "ordinary language" and to the "grammatical rules" of such, as though both, but especially the latter, were not in need of clarification. "Verifiability, which is the sufficient and necessary condition of meaning, is a possibility of the logical order; it is created by constructing the sentence in accordance with the rules by which its terms are defined. . . . Grammatical rules are not found anywhere in nature, but are made by man and are, in principle, arbitrary; . . . ."[5] Many more rules for a given sentence are needed, of course, beyond those "by which its terms are defined." And these further rules are surely not altogether "arbitrary," as any attempt to change in any fundamental way the syntactical and semantical rules of a natural language would show. They are no more arbitrary, nor indeed "made by man," it would seem, than are the laws of some domain of natural science such as physics. An eminent linguist in fact recently contended that grammatical rules are comparable with physical laws as to objectivity, and hence presumably as to their lack of arbitrariness. It seems a pity for Schlick to have based so much of his theory of meaning on notions not satisfying it, on the one hand, and on an inadequate conception of grammatical rule, on the other.

In spite of these criticisms, there is high merit to some of Schlick's observations about language that should not be overlooked. The fullest statement of his views concerning what we now call 'semantics'

---

5. *Gessamelte Aufsätze*, p. 349.

seems to be that in the first of three lectures given at the University of London in 1932.[6] It will be of interest to recall certain key features of that view and to interrelate them with the logical-form theory of meaning put forward here.

Schlick is, it seems, one of the first to have called attention, unwittingly perhaps, to the very central role of *sign-events* or *inscriptions* in the logical study of language. "Is it not astonishing," he asks (p. 157), "that by hearing certain sounds issuing from the mouth of a person, or by looking at a few black marks on a piece of paper I can become aware of the fact that a volcano on a distant island has had an eruption. . . .?" The sounds and black marks on paper are not the shapes or sign-designs that were used in the Tarski-Carnap kind of semantics, or that have been used in some recent model-theoretic approaches to language. No, they are the *inscriptions* or sign-events used in the author's inscriptional semantics of 1958. It never occurred to Schlick to group all inscriptions of the same shape into a class or sign-design, and to regard these latter as the fundamental vehicles of language.

Further, Schlick is remarkably clear as to how the basic semantical relations should be taken. "We say [p. 153] that one fact (the arrangement of little black marks) *expresses* the other (the eruption of the volcano), so the particular relation between them is called Expression. In order to understand language we must investigate the nature of Expression." Both the inscription and what it expresses are referred to here as "facts." However, a "fact" seems always to involve the ascription of a property to something (or of a relation to its relata), and thus should not be confused with that something. On the one hand, there is the inscription, or sign-event, and on the other, what it stands for or "expresses." The eruption of a volcano is not a fact, it is an event or occurrence, although it may be a fact that such and such a volcano occurs.

Ramsey was perhaps the first to distinguish sharply between facts and events; and we cannot do better than to follow him in this. "The connection between the event which was the death of Caesar," he writes, in an admirable passage,[7] "and the fact that Caesar died is, in my opinion, this: 'That Ceasar died' is really an existential proposition, asserting the existence of an event of a certain sort, thus resembling 'Italy has a King', which asserts the existence of a man of a certain sort. The event which is of that sort is called 'the death of Caesar'

6. *Ibid.*, pp. 152–183.
7. F. P. Ramsey, *The Foundations of Mathematics* (London: Routledge and Kegan Paul, 1931), p. 144.

[quotes added], and should no more be confused with the fact that Caesar died than the King of Italy should be confused with the fact that Italy . . . [had, in 1927, when this passage was written] a King."

In similar fashion, an event should not be confused with what we regard as a physical object. A physical object has certain kinds of properties, mass, temperature, size, and so on. But no event can be said to weigh so many grams, or to be 68° Fahrenheit, or to be 4 feet in height. Likewise, an event may be said to take place quickly, but, ordinarily anyhow, no physical object is quick, or loud, or joyous, or kind, or merciful, or the like. It seems best then to distinguish physical predicates of objects from the *event-descriptive predicates* applicable to events, including states, acts, and processes.[8]

We can easily arrange Schlick's comments on expression to accommodate both physical objects and events, leaving then to further research the delicate matter as to how the two are interrelated. The justification for this postponement is that ordinary language contains both kinds of terms and both kinds of predicates, and leaves upon the question as to how they are interrelated, whether either is to be "reduced" to the other, precisely how if so, and so on.

Schlick's relation of expression is taken to relate names of objects or events with the corresponding objects or events. A good word for this kind of relation is Frege's 'Bedeutung' or 'designation', which has become more or less standard in recent years. How does Schlick propose to handle whatever it is that *predicates* express? The answer to this is not too clear. He tells us (p. 157) that the "signification [or expression] of a simple name has to be explained separately, [whereas] the meaning of . . . a proposition explains itself, if only the vocabulary and the grammar of the language are known." But the vocabulary of course must include more than mere names. Some semantical relation is needed to interrelate predicates and whatever they "express," perhaps something like virtual-class designation (as discussed in XIII above), or perhaps *denotation* in the sense that a predicate denotes each and every object (or event) to which it correctly applies. Given the vocabulary, with suitable rules of designation and/or denotation, the "meaning" of each properly constructed sentence is forthcoming, as Schlick observes — provided of course that suitable rules of transformation are at hand to lead us to (or to generate) the meaning.

The theory suggested above as an alternative to Schlick's verifiability-use theory — we might call it 'the meaning-as-logical-form theory' — is not subject to these criticisms. This is not to suggest

---

8. As in *Semiotics and Linguistic Structure* and *Events, Reference, and Logical Form*.

that it does not have sufficient difficulties of its own. Sufficient unto each theory of meaning, however, are the difficulties thereof.

It is interesting to observe that the theory here construes meaning in what Peirce called "its primary acceptation, the translation of a sign into another system of signs, and which . . . is a second sentence from which all that follows from the first assertion equally follows, and *vice versa*."[9] And again, "the meaning of a representation can be nothing but a representation. In fact, it is nothing but the representation itself conceived as stripped of irrelevant clothing. But this clothing never can be completely stripped off; it is only changed for something more diaphanous."[10] Peirce goes on to say that "there is an infinite regression here" — but not so in the theory above, in which *primitive* terms or predicates are admitted. (Peirce seems nowhere to have discussed the need for primitives.) The way is left open of course for the further explanation of the primitives in terms of ostension, the psycho-physiology of the learning process, and such other considerations as might be needed in a full account. Also, ultimately, exact *rules of translation* are to be given in terms of linguistic transformations. And, finally, the "something more diaphanous" is nothing more or less than interpolated logical material between the "representations" in the logical form of the words of the parent sentence.

In general Schlick advocated a conception of philosophy (p. 132) akin to that described by Wittgenstein in his famous comments that "the object of philosophy is the logical clarification of thoughts. Philosophy is not a theory but an activity. The result of philosophy is not a number of 'philosophical propositions,' but to make propositions clear." To do this latter, however, we have to do one of two things, either to "make propositions" that serve to make other propositions clear or to perform certain non-linguistic actions. The propositions that serve to clarify other propositions (even paraphrases of themselves) will be formulated in accord with the tenets of logic. Some of these might be "philosophical" if the original ones are. The other way of making propositions clear is to perform certain actions related to the given proposition in a certain way, for example, by ostention. The theory concerning how such actions are related to propositions, like the notion of *acting on a belief*, remains largely undeveloped. A considerable amount of analysis is needed to clarify it, and no doubt, once given, the results of such analysis will be expressed in a number of "philosophic propositions." Wittgenstein's comments thus seem

9. *Collected Papers*, Vol. IV, §127.
10. Vol. I, §339.

314

much too glib and based on an oversimplified conception of language and how it is related to human action. Again, it is a pity that Schlick followed suit so literally.

The problem of the meaning of the sentences of mathematics is laid aside in Schlick's general view. The justification for this is presumably that mathematical sentences are regarded merely as sentences of logic in a suitable disguise, with defined numerals and the like appearing in place of, ultimately, only undefined or primitive expressions of logic (plus variables). But this contention is subject to considerable ambiguity, depending on just how widely 'logic' itself is construed. If it is construed so as to include type or set theory in some form or other — as it must be for the contention to have cogency — the sheer multiplicity in the number and varieties of set theory developed within the last decades could seem embarrassing. And even more disheartening in the apparent unsatisfactoriness of them all, both as regards suitability for founding mathematics axiomatically and as regards ontic commitment. Before a sentence of mathematics can be regarded as having meaning, it has to be translated into one or the other of these various alternatives. And of course it takes on a different meaning in each theory. Thus even '$(1 + 1) = 2$', for the positive real numbers 1 and 2, has as many meanings as there are distinct (in a suitable sense) set theories in which it may be accommodated. The problem of the meaning of the sentences of mathematics must be faced along with that of those of the natural sciences.

Schlick seems to think that all this is easy sailing, the sentences of mathematics and the natural sciences having meaning in some sense beyond reproach. Again, during recent decades numerous attempts to construct suitable systems for given areas of natural science have been made. The success of most of these is at best dubious, and problems have arisen that could not easily have been foreseen in advance. And even if satisfactory systems should be forthcoming for certain domains of science, the problem of their unification arises. In any attempt at unification unexpected problems may arise, even if attention be confined to just one science. Even in physics, it is not clear that a unified system is possible on the basis of what is now commonly accepted.

In an important paper, "The Logical Structure of Physics," the eminent physicist Laszlo Tisza[11] addressed himself to what he calls '*dynamic logical analysis*' or '*the dynamics of logical systems*'. The widening gap between the various specialized domains of physics makes a uni-

---

11. *Loc. cit.*, p. 56.

fied view increasingly difficult to achieve. Some narrow area of physics may be adequately stated in terms of a hypothetico-deductive system. The cure for such narrowness, Tisza suggests, is to be found in "the simultaneous use of many deductive systems. Whereas traditionally a deductive system was usually the entire universe of discourse, according to the present point of view deductive systems are themselves conceptual elements and their interrelations, particularly the conditions of mutual consistency, become the main objects of study."

This is a fascinating suggestion, and no doubt well accords with some aspects of the actual practice of physicists. It does presuppose, however, that adequate hypothetico-deductive systems are available for the separate parts. For *adequacy* here, it should presumably be required that all the linguistic elements be axiomatized, not merely the mathematical and specifically physical ones. *Every non-logical predicate used in any sentence in a given area of physics must be either taken as a primitive and suitably axiomatized, or else unambiguously defined in terms of such.* Likewise variables are to be presumed available for all the kinds of entities considered. Just as there should be no "hidden variables," so to speak, there should be *no hidden predicates*. The whole structure of the system should be characterized, if needed, with "maximum logical candor," no linguistic or logical factor being left unspecified, if full adequacy is to be achieved. And in all this, as already suggested, difficulties may arise that are not anticipated.

An interesting case in point is the language of quantum mechanics in its various formulations. This is not the occasion to adjudicate amongst these formulations, even if this could be done on the basis of present knowledge. Some think that the difficulties in "interpreting" quantum mechanics are due to a gap in our physical knowledge — more physics is needed.[12] Some think the difficulties are due to our inability to provide a semantics for the equations in a satisfactory way. Others think the difficulty is in the "logic" presupposed, some deviant logic being needed in place of the classical one.

The notion of a "hidden predicate," casually mentioned above, may be more important than appears at first. The claim that classical logic must be given up in quantum mechanics, for example, may rest upon the refusal to incorporate into the language certain predicates concerning *observation* or *measurement*. Thus Hilary Putnam claims[13] that "the only laws of classical logic that must be given up in quantum logic

---

12. The author is indebted to Professor Abner Shimony for essentially this point.

13. In his *Mathematics, Matter, and Method* (Cambridge: Cambridge University Press, 1975), p. 184.

are distributive laws, e.g., $p \cdot (q \vee r) \equiv p \cdot q \vee p \cdot r$; and every single anomaly vanishes once we give these up." (It is on this contention that Putnam bases his view that logic is "as empirical as geometry" and is, "in a certain sense, a natural science.") But surely this cannot be the case. It is not the classical distributive law that is at fault here, but rather the failure to spell out fully the internal structure of all of the sentences needed in the context.

Consider some epistemic predicate, say 'Blv' for believes. One can *believe* a sentence without believing all its logically equivalent sentences; one can observe what a given sentence says obtains without observing what all of its logical equivalents say obtains; and so on. Let 'p Obs a,t' express that person p observes at time t that what sentence a states does in fact hold or take place. Clearly, it might then obtain that

$$p \text{ Obs } \ulcorner(a \cdot (b \vee c))\urcorner ,t$$

without its obtaining that

$$p \text{ Obs } \ulcorner((a \cdot b) \vee (a \cdot c))\urcorner ,t.$$

It is not at all remarkable that this might be the case. The experimental condition or circumstances needed for the one might be very different from those needed for the other. We should not conclude therewith that the distributive law is at fault; rather we should reflect upon the properties of Obs, and explain the inner structure of a, b, and c, and how they are interrelated in the circumstances at hand. If Putnam were to do this, *for all the sentences required both in the theory and application* of quantum mechanics in a suitable formulation, he would see that there is no need to abrogate the laws of classical logic, and that his arguments to the effect that logic is "empirical" are ill-founded.

It is a remarkable fact how much conceptual clarity is gained with proper symbolization of all the non-logical words and phrases occurring in a given scientific or other context. Oskar Morgenstern, the eminent economist, used to say that there was often great conceptual gain in saying 'The man M crossed the street S' rather than merely 'The man crossed the street', and that the insistence upon such explicitness was one of the high merits of the work of the Viennese positivists. Indeed, the gain is often way out of proportion. The mere addition of variables or names calls attention to the ontology needed, as well as to the predicates and/or functors being employed. It calls our attention to lurking ambiguities or inadequacies of statement we might easily let pass otherwise. Especially is this the case in areas of science where we get into conceptual difficulties not easy to see our way out of. The situation in quantum mechanics has some similarity to that in the foundations of mathematics at the turn of the century, before ways were forthcoming for avoiding the set-theoretic and semantic paradoxes. Recall how important a suitable symbolization was for handling both kinds of paradoxes, without which ways of avoiding them could not have been formulated so readily.

On the logical-form theory of meaning, the problem of what we mean is as keen in the sciences, even in mathematics, as anywhere else. The problems and difficulties become even more acute if we take seriously Tisza's dynamics of logical systems. According to this view we let a hundred schools contend until science itself achieves some modicum of harmonization. If the task of the philosophy of nature is conceived to be just "to interpret the meaning of the propositions of natural science," the logical-form view might conceivably help in the harmonization. But with the incredible advances in recent science, and the extreme degree of specialization now needed even to understand them, let alone to contribute to them in any substantive way, little help is to be expected from the philosopher of nature. The best he can do as a contributor to the development of science is to sit on the sidelines and make an occasional suggestion, especially as regards logical form.

There is a wider sense in which the philosophy of nature has often been taken, however, as comprising a more speculative, perhaps even metaphysical, view as to the nature and structure of the cosmos. Peirce and Whitehead are outstanding philosophers of nature in this sense, both of whom were willing to extrapolate beyond what is scientifically known. Tisza's attitude is more restrained. "It is an important aspect of the present method," he noted (p. 73), "that, in contrast to the traditions of speculative philosophy, we [scientists] do not have to, in fact we should not commit ourselves regarding such deep problems [of a metaphysical sort]. The important matter is the method that allows us to improve in a systematic fashion the logical structure of the existing [scientific] theories. I believe that this method of analysis, in conjunction with new experiments, will lead to a reasonably unified logical structure. Strong beliefs concerning the specific features of this structure might interfere with the free functioning of the method." Thus for Tisza a scientifically based speculative metaphysics might be possible. "Maybe," he writes, "but I do not know."

Of course no one else knows either, and perhaps never will. With the scientific advance, difficulties increase geometrically, as Harlow Shapley used to observe, and new problems emerge with new methods needed to try to solve them. And surely no philosophical bias of any kind should be allowed to interfere with the free functioning of

318

the scientific method. This latter, however, is always subject to some underlying logic — perhaps the standard form of logic we now have, perhaps some improved form or extension of it that will be forthcoming in the future. Also there is the very important role that mathematics — quantitative mathematics in particular — plays in science. And it is terribly important to be as clear as we can about mathematics and its foundations and their relation to logic howsoever conceived. And, contrary to a widespread opinion, we know much less about this than is ordinarily supposed. So important is mathematics in the logical structure of science and therewith in the structure of the nature that science purportedly describes, that it is no exaggeration to say: as goes our understanding of mathematics, so goes our understanding of the cosmos.

A fundamental matter in understanding any scientific discipline is to understand its *ontology*. Nothing perhaps is more important than this. Of course understanding an ontology, within a given context, is nothing more or less than understanding the sentences put forward — the purported truths — governing that ontology. And to understand the truths is to understand the predicates occurring in them. The possibility of a "reasonably unified logical structure" for science thus would seem to hinge fundamentally upon the possibility of a reasonably unified ontology. And of course one must include here the ontology required for mathematics. Indeed, so fundamental is this latter, that, again, it would be no exaggeration to say: as goes the ontology of mathematics, so goes that of natural science.

The philosophy of nature, or "speculative philosophy" in Whitehead's sense, should, then, according to the foregoing, follow the lead of the most satisfactory formulation of mathematics that we can find or think up, whichever. Of course the hundred schools will contend here as to how 'most satisfactory' is to be construed. According to the above, one of the requirements will be that the ontology it demands should be such as to lead us directly into that demanded in natural science. And conversely also, if any clear conception of the latter were forthcoming. The hope would be that the two would eventually harmonize. The most desirable harmonization no doubt would be that of *unity of kind*. The objects of nature should be of the *same kind* as those of mathematics, it might be thought. If they should turn out to differ in kind, there would remain then an awkward dichotomy to be explained. However, unity of kind should not be imposed in advance but rather should await patient scientific research.

Let us construe mathematics set-theoretically, as is customary (although perhaps not altogether satisfactory), and seek a formulation of it somewhat along the lines suggested in two previous papers (XVI and XVII above). We will then be in a position to see to what extent the resulting ontology can be harmonized with that of physical science.

What is the fundamental difference between the part-whole relation P of mereology and the membership relation ϵ of set theory? Nelson Goodman has put the matter well in suggesting that there should be no "distinction of entities without a distinction of content;" in other words, it is desired that "two different entities can be made up of the same entities."[14] In set theory this does not obtain; in mereology it does. It might appear in the rendition of set theory to follow that Goodman's stipulation is not satisfied; however, we shall see that it is, although in a somewhat new way.

The key difference between the mereological sum of individuals satisfying a given condition and the set of such individuals is then that the individuals retain their individuality as members of the set, to speak loosely, but lose it as parts of the sum. The sum of any two of the individuals, for example, is a part of the sum, yet the two individuals become "lost" in the sum of them, so to speak, all their parts being also parts of the sum. Given the set, we can "read off" the members, but given the sum we cannot read off the individuals of which it is composed in the same way. What we need is a method for "reading off" the various parts of the sum *in the same way* that one reads off the subsets of the given set. The question arises then as to whether mereology can be extended to allow the individuals to retain their individuality as parts of a sum.

Let us use 'partition' to help provide a way of doing this. The partition of an *integer*, roughly speaking, is a way of writing it as a sum of integers. The number of partitions of a positive integer m is then the number of ways of writing a name for m as a sum of positive integers $a_1 + a_2 + ... + a_k$ where $a_1 \geqq a_2 \geqq ... \geqq a_k$ for $k \geqq 1$. Similarly the partition of a *set* is usually said to be any finite set of disjoint sets whose union or sum is the given set. Alternatively the partition of a (finite) set might be taken as a "way of writing" a name for the set as a finite sum of subsets, perhaps disjoint, perhaps not, whose sum is the given set. There would then be as many partitions of the set as there are ways of writing names for sums of its subsets.

Similarly the partition of an *individual* might be taken as any finite sum of non-overlapping individuals whose sum is the given individual. This would be too narrow a notion, for we might wish to rec-

---

14. In his *Problems and Projects*, p. 158.

ognize overlapping individuals as distinct objects in the partition. What we wish is a notion of being a partition of an individual that will correspond with the intuitive notion of being the set of those individuals. Let x_1, x_2, and x_3 be disjoint individuals, for example, and consider the set (or virtual set)

$$\{(x_1 \cup x_2),(x_2 \cup x_3)\},$$

where '$\cup$' is the sign for mereological summation. The two members of this set are not disjoint, yet the sum

$$((x_1 \cup x_2) \cup (x_2 \cup x_3))$$

we wish to recognize as one of the ways of partitioning the individual

$$(x_1 \cup x_2 \cup x_3).$$

Another way of partitioning it results in

$$(x_1 \cup (x_1 \cup x_2) \cup x_3),$$

corresponding with the set

$$\{x_1,(x_1 \cup x_2),x_3\},$$

and still another way

$$((x_1 \cup x_2) \cup (x_2 \cup x_3) \cup (x_1 \cup x_3)),$$

corresponding with the set

$$\{(x_1 \cup x_2),(x_2 \cup x_3),(x_1 \cup x_3)\}.$$

And so on. In such manner distinct ways of partitioning one and the same mereological sum will correspond with distinct sets. All of this will be made more precise in a moment.

The key idea is that partitioning is to be regarded as a mental *act* the set-theorist performs, and the resulting set can then be identified for all mathematical purposes with that act. To see this more clearly, we let 'Prtn' be a primitive predicate and let

(1)   'p Prtn y,x'

. . . p[person] p partitions the sum-individual y with x retained as one of the summands. Then, in familiar fashion

(2)   '$<p,\text{Prtn},y,x>e$',

with '$<p,\text{Prtn},y,x>$' as an event-descriptive predicate, expresses that e is an act of p's partitioning y with x retained as a summand. Of course there may be many such acts, some of them partitioning y in the same way, others of them not. For the present, those acts that partition them in the same way may be identified, as will be postulated in **P4** below.

As principles governing this new primitive 'Prtn' we have immediately a *Principle of Limitation,* that

P1. $\vdash (x)(y)(p)(e)(<p,\text{Prtn},y,x>e \supset x \text{ P} y)$.

Only if x is a part of y is there a partitioning of y with x retained as a summand.

Also there is the *Principle of the Null Partition,* that

P2. $\vdash (p)(x)(e) \sim <p,\text{Prtn},\text{N},x>e$,

where N is the null individual.

We can now let

$$\text{'}x \ \epsilon_e \ y\text{'} \quad \text{abbreviate} \quad \text{'}(Ep)<p,\text{Prtn},y,x>e\text{'},$$

and

$$\text{'}x =_\epsilon y\text{'} \quad \text{abbreviate} \quad \text{'}(e)(z)((Ep)(Ew)(Ew')<p,\text{Prtn},w,w'>e \supset$$
$$(x \ \epsilon_e \ z \supset y \ \epsilon_e z))\text{'},$$

gaining therewith in effect the familiar membership and identity relations of set theory.

We have then an *Identity Principle,* that

P3. $\vdash (e)(y)(z)((x)(x \ \epsilon_e \ y \equiv x \ \epsilon_e z) \supset y =_\epsilon z)$.

This principle establishes that it is the act e that determines the "membership" in a mereological sum, not just the sum itself. A second *Identity Principle* is that

P4. $\vdash (e_1)(e_2)((x)(y)(x \ \epsilon_{e_1} y \equiv x \ \epsilon_{e_2} y) \supset e_1 = e_2)$.

Acts of partitioning that partition mereologically identical sums into the same individuals are identified (in the sense of act-identity, which will be commented on in a moment).

Let $(x \, \sigma \, Fx)$ be the sum of all individuals such that Fx, where F is a virtual class or virtual-class function, essentially as in XVI and XVII. Expressions such as '$(x \ \sigma \ Fx)$' are expressions for σ-sums and may be taken as primitive terms. The *Principle of σ-Summation* is then that

P5. $\vdash \ulcorner (Ee)(Ex)(y)(y \ \epsilon_e x \equiv Fy) \supset (Ee)(y)(y \ \epsilon_e (x \sigma Fx) \equiv Fy) \urcorner$.

The notation for σ-sums gives in effect a notation for the familiar set-abstraction. **P5** may then be recognized as a kind of *Principle of Abstraction* on a suitable existence hypothesis.

These five principles are put forward somewhat tentatively and perhaps may be improved upon in some respects.

Let us, by way of example, take the axioms as those of the Skolem-Fraenkel reading of Zermelo. The *Paarungsaxiom,* the Axiom of the Existence of Pairs, becomes a statement to the effect that

$$\vdash (x)(y)(Ez)(E e)(w)(w \ \epsilon_e z \ \equiv \ (w =_\epsilon x \ \vee \ w =_\epsilon z)),$$

and the *Aussonderungsaxiom,* the Axiom of Subset Formation, that

$$\vdash \ulcorner(x)(e')(Ey)(E e)(z)(z \ \epsilon_e y \ \equiv \ (z \ \epsilon_{e'} \ x \cdot Fz))\urcorner \ .$$

The Axiom of the Existence of the Null Set is that

$$\vdash (Ex)(E e) \sim (Ey)y \ \epsilon_e x.$$

And so on for the other axioms needed, including the Axiom of Extensionality, the Power Axiom, Axioms of Infinity and Choice, and so on.

How now do we move on from these bare assumptions of existence to the corresponding statements concerning the appropriate σ-sums? Simply by using **P5**. Thus we can show that

$$\vdash (x)(E e)x \ \epsilon_e (z\sigma z =_\epsilon x),$$

for example, by noting that

$$\vdash (x)(Ez)(E e)(y)(y \ \epsilon_e z \ \equiv y =_\epsilon x)$$

by the *Paarungsaxiom.* Thence by **P5**, that

$$\vdash (E e)(y)(y \ \epsilon_e (z\sigma z =_\epsilon x) \equiv y =_\epsilon x),$$

and thence to the theorem desired.

Three notions of identity have been used thus far, mereological identity (as in '$x =_P y$'), ϵ-identity (as in '$x =_\epsilon y$'), and event or act identity (as in '$e = e''$'). How is this last to be construed? The general theory of events may be formulated with '=' taken as a primitive subject to the usual rules. In effect then "two" events are identical just where every event-descriptive predicate applicable to one is applicable to the other also. Of course this cannot be said within the language, but merely provides a metalinguistic criterion in accord with which the rules are framed. If a part-whole relation between events is admitted, event-identity becomes mutual part-to-whole. Because there is no need to recognize parts of acts of partitioning here, '=' is taken as a primitive.

It is easy to see how, from this rough sketch, the full peroration of set theory can be carried out. There are of course many alternative ways of arranging the axioms. (The problem of which if any formulation is the "best" in some suitable sense need not be considered here.) The situation is not dissimilar to that in relativity theory, with its many competing formulations.[15]

The most interesting feature of this rendering of set theory is in its recognition of mental acts of partitioning or "ways or writing" σ-sums, so to speak. Such acts are conceptual, and set theory here is thus explicitly *conceptualistic,* not just by proxy but in the very direct sense that such acts are taken as values for variables and the real content of mathematics is spelled out partly in terms of them. There are also the mereological variables, which can be taken to range over *whatever is required by natural science*. Mathematics, as conceived of here, is thus seen to involve a complex ontology, *part* of which is conceptualistic in structure. Any philosophy of nature incorporating mathematics, as indeed it must in some form or other, may then recognize a conceptualistic realm at its very foundation if so desired. The admission of a realm of mental acts is needed for many other philosophic and perhaps scientific purposes anyhow, not least in the logical-form theory of meaning discussed above. Thus no new ontology is introduced in their use here, merely their further exploitation.

Competing ways of rendering a set theory, e.g., those discussed by Quine,[16] are such as to require a new ontology of sets over and above whatever ontology is required in physical science *sans* mathematics. However, the nature of this new ontology remains somewhat obscure, a realm of platonic universals *sui genuis* of some kind, over and above whatever is taken to constitute the cosmos. If these universals are to be regarded as conceptualistic in some sense, then this should be explicitly spelled out in terms of some theory. If not, their ontic status remains in doubt.

The sophisticated set theorist will find no new mathematics in the foregoing remarks. The interest is rather in *protomathematics,* which can be regarded as consisting of **P1–P5**, mereology, and the theory of acts and events. The number and variety of acts admitted in the theory are of course staggering — but so is mathematics likewise with regard to its sets. Modern mathematics is a creation — or discovery — of incredible conceptual complexity and depth, and the proliferation of acts of partitioning admitted here explicitly recognizes this

---

15. For an informative recent discussion, see Max Jammer, *op. cit.*

16. In his *Set Theory and Its Logic* (Cambridge: The Belknap Press of Harvard University Press, 1969).

fact. Other versions of set theory would recognize this in other ways. But no matter how this is done, the proliferation must be such as to provide for whatever it is that classical mathematics is taken to include. There may be some interest in keeping the proliferation at a minimum. Quine has noted (p. 328) that "for a constructivistic set theory, with its economy of means, there is both philosophical and aesthetic motivation. And there is a methodological motivation as well, knowing as we do the threat of paradox. There are all these counsels for keeping things down as best we can without quite stifling classical mathematics. And on the other hand there are motives for stepping things up. That there is again an aesthetic one can scarcely be doubted. Also a practical motive for generosity in the ontology of set theory is coming to be felt from the side of abstract algebra and topology, as MacLane has stressed." Indeed, once the dykes of proliferation have been opened in the first place, there would seem to be no reason for stopping them at any point so compelling as those required by the inner workings of mathematics itself. Philosophical, aesthetic, and even methodological motives should surely be assigned a secondary status, lest the road to mathematical inquiry be blocked or "strong [extra-mathematical] beliefs" be allowed to "interfere with the free functioning" of the mathematical imagination.

The acts of partitioning recognized here may be presumed to occur simultaneously, or virtually so. In any case, no role is assigned to differences of time. It might be of interest to explore such differences, however, and to take them seriously. Intuitionistic mathematics is sometimes construed in terms of the "constructions" actually performed by the "creative subject" at a given time. We can let 'e B e''' express that the partitioning act e occur temporally wholly before e'. In terms of this a kind of diachronic theory of partitioning could be developed, taking account of just the portions of mathematics developed on the basis of the partitioning made up to a certain time. It is always left open that further partitionings may be made later. It might be of interest to explore a diachronic, temporally constructivistic set theory of this kind.[17]

In terms of 'B', it is of interest to reflect again for a moment on Tisza's dynamics of logical system. The formulation of any one system for some area of physics is a way of "worldmaking" (in Goodman's phrase) and itself the result of certain complex conceptual acts on the part of the physicist. The system in fact may in effect be identified

---

17. Cf., for example, William Powell, "Extending Gödel's Negative Interpretation to ZF," *The Journal of Symbolic Logic* 40 (1975): 221–229.

with this complex act. Let us assume that the system is finitely axiomatizable, and let 'Ax$_i$ a' express that a is the conjunction of the axioms of the system i. Then a relation of *formulating* is needed, something like *asserting*, no doubt, involving simultaneous utterance (or writing down) and acceptance in the sense of tentatively putting forward for the purposes of further exploration. Let 'p Fmlt a' express that p formulates a in this sense. Then

$$\text{`(E}a)(\text{Ax}_i a \bullet <p,\text{Fmlt},a>e)\text{'}$$

expresses that e is the act of physicist p's formulating the system i in this sense. Some acts of formulating, by p and his fellow physicists, may be simultaneous, some successive. The use of this notation opens the door to the exact study of how these systems are interrelated, of how and why one may be reformulated to "change" into another, of how one is "stronger" than another, even perhaps of how one may be "closer to the truth" or "truer" than another. If the dynamics of systems is of any importance for the philosophy of physics, and indeed of science generally, then we ought at least to be able to study it in exact terms of acts of formulating.

It might seem that Goodman's stipulation, spoken of earlier, that there be no two different entities made up of the same entities, is violated here. But acts of partitioning are *sui generis* and are not "made up" of the summands of the sum partitioned. The fact is that a mereological sum can be partitioned in different ways, just as the integer 4 can be partitioned into $(1 + 1 + 1 + 1), (2 + 1 + 1), (3 + 1), (1 + 3), (1 + 2 + 1)$, and so on. The difference lies in the "way" the partitioning is carried out. The novelty in the treatment here is in explicitly providing for these ways in terms of human acts.

The idea of mereological or Boolean sums satisfying a given condition, used here, is by no means new. Tarski is perhaps the first to have used it, in his famous paper on Boolean algebra, in which one expression is taken to stand for the (Boolean) sum of all members of the set X, and another for "the sum of all elements y of the form $y = f(x)$, which correspond to elements satisfying the condition $\phi(x)$."[18] Tarski presupposes in these notations the notion of set and of membership as already given. His interest is in algebraic properties of these sums rather than in their role in mereology. Further, Tarski has no interest in the logic of partitioning such sums in ways that would lead to other sets. Such partitioning of course transcends the bounds of Boolean algebra, even in the extended sense in which Tarski considers it.

---

18. *Op. cit.,* p. 322.

It has been suggested above that as goes mathematics, so goes physical science. The presence of conceptual elements, acts of partitioning, at the very heart of mathematics, suggests that there should be no hesitation in admitting such entities in physics also if needed. The role in quantum theory and the theory of relativity of the observer, of instruments, and of specific acts of measurement and the like are cases in point. And *a fortiori* for the sciences concerned with biological and mental phenomena, and hence for the philosophy of mind itself.

These various reflections are in accord with Schlick's contention that the task of the philosophy of nature is just "to interpret the meaning of the propositions of natural science." This has been seen to be a task of enormous difficulty, and of even greater difficulty if we construe the philosophy of nature in the broader Whiteheadian sense and insist upon including mathematics in our purview, to say nothing of cosmology, cosmogony, and the like.

Index